Imperial Visions of Late Byzantium

Edinburgh Byzantine Studies

Innovative approaches to the medieval Eastern Roman empire and its neighbours

Edinburgh Byzantine Studies promotes new, theory-driven approaches to the empire commonly called Byzantium. The series looks at the literary, historical, material and visual remains of this long-living political order and its neighbours, often from a multi-disciplinary and/or cross-cultural vantage point. Its innovative readings highlight the connectivity of Byzantine culture as well as of Byzantine Studies.

Series Editors
Niels Gaul, University of Edinburgh
the late Ruth Macrides, University of Birmingham
Alexander Riehle, Harvard University
Yannis Stouraitis, University of Edinburgh

Books available in the series
Imperial Visions of Late Byzantium: Manuel II Palaiologos and Rhetoric in Purple
Florin Leonte

Books forthcoming
The Earthly Order: Social Stratification in Late Byzantium
Christos Malatras

The Monotheisation of Pontic-Caspian Eurasia: Eighth to Thirteenth Centuries
Alex Mesibov Feldman

Visit the Edinburgh Byzantine Studies website at edinburghuniversitypress.com/series-edinburgh-byzantine-studies.html

Imperial Visions of Late Byzantium

Manuel II Palaiologos and Rhetoric in Purple

Florin Leonte

EDINBURGH
University Press

Edinburgh University Press is one of the leading university presses in the UK. We publish academic books and journals in our selected subject areas across the humanities and social sciences, combining cutting-edge scholarship with high editorial and production values to produce academic works of lasting importance. For more information visit our website: edinburghuniversitypress.com

© Florin Leonte, 2020, 2022

First published in hardback by Edinburgh University Press 2020

Edinburgh University Press Ltd
The Tun – Holyrood Road, 12(2f) Jackson's Entry, Edinburgh EH8 8PJ

Typeset in 10.5/13 Goudy Old Style by
IDSUK (DataConnection) Ltd,

A CIP record for this book is available from the British Library

ISBN 978 1 4744 4103 2 (hardback)
ISBN 978 1 4744 4104 9 (paperback)
ISBN 978 1 4744 4105 6 (webready PDF)
ISBN 978 1 4744 4106 3 (epub)

The right of Florin Leonte to be identified as the author of this work has been asserted in accordance with the Copyright, Designs and Patents Act 1988, and the Copyright and Related Rights Regulations 2003 (SI No. 2498).

Contents

Acknowledgements	viii
Abbreviations	ix
Introduction	1
Manuel II Palaiologos: A Short Biography and an Overview of the Historical Context	1
Aims of the Present Study	5
Structure	7
Sources	8
Theoretical Framework	9
Previous Scholarship	11

Part I Dissent and Consent

1 Voices of Dissent: Preaching and Negotiating Authority — 19
    Organisation of the Ecclesiastics' Group — 21
    Major Political and Social Themes in the Ecclesiastics' Writings — 31
    Conclusion — 54

2 Voices of Consent: Imperial Rhetoricians, *Theatra* and Patronage — 58
    Theatra and Imperial Involvement — 59
    Profile and Organisation of the Rhetoricians — 64
    Connections among the Members of the Literary Court — 68
    The Rhetorical Landscape in the Late Palaiologan Period — 75
    Main Themes in the Rhetoricians' Writings — 79
    Conclusion — 100

Part II Other Voices, Other Approaches: Manuel II's Political Writings

Introduction to Part II	105
Further Methodological Considerations	105
An Overview of the Emperor's Rhetorical œuvre	108
The Emperor's Political Texts	111
3 The Deliberative Voice: The *Dialogue with the Empress-Mother on Marriage*	113
Contents and Structure	115
Genre	116
Constructing Dialogic Authority	117
Conclusion	123
4 The Didactic Voice: The *Foundations of an Imperial Education*	124
Context of Production	126
Contents and Structure	128
Genre	135
Authorial Voice	149
Conclusion	159
5 The Didactic Voice: The *Orations* (*Seven Ethico-Political Orations*)	161
The Dramatic Setting	163
The Contents of the *Orations*	165
Major Themes in the *Orations*	165
The *Orations*: Summary and Form	172
Between Teaching and Preaching: Constructing the Genre of the *Orations*	183
Authorial Voice: Teaching the Son and Admonishing the Emperor	189
Conclusion	196
6 The Narrative Voice: The *Funeral Oration on His Brother Theodore, Despot of Morea*	199
Contexts of Production	200
The Rhetorical Template and the Compositional Structure of the *Funeral Oration*	203
The Narrator and the Narrative	209
Authorial Voice	233
Conclusion	234
7 Towards a Renewed Vision of Imperial Authority	237
Society and Social 'Classes'	240
Enemies and Allies	241

Markers of Byzantine Identity	244
Renewal of Imperial Ideology in Manuel's Texts	246
Manuel II's Imperial Vision and Style of Government	264

Conclusions 270

Appendices
    Appendix 1   Members of Manuel II's Literary Circle   281
    Appendix 2   The Contents and Structure of Manuel II's
      Foundations   284
    Appendix 3   Translation of Gemistos Plethon's Preface to
      Manuel II's *Funeral Oration*   288
    Appendix 4   Network of Ecclesiastics and Rhetoricians during
      Manuel II's Reign   290

Bibliography
    Manuscripts Consulted   293
    Primary Sources   293
    Secondary Literature   300

Index   323

Acknowledgements

It is my pleasant duty to acknowledge the support I have received from others in completing this volume.

I am much indebted to Niels Gaul, who provided help and inspiration from the earliest stages of the project and through the publication process of this volume. I am grateful to a number of other people from whom I received great help at various moments: Margaret Mullett, Erich Trapp, Ida Toth, Charalambos Dendrinos, Stephanos Efthymiadis, Dimiter Angelov, Markéta Kulhánková, Alexander Riehle and the late Ruth Macrides.

I am also thankful to the institutions which offered me the possibility of working on this book: the Department of Medieval Studies at Central European University, the Dumbarton Oaks Research Library and Collection, the Department of the Classics at Harvard University, the Institute for Byzantine and Modern Greek Studies at the University of Vienna and the Department of Classical Philology at Palacký University of Olomouc.

Finally, I am grateful to my family, David and Madalina, for their support and patience. This book is dedicated to them.

Abbreviations

BF	*Byzantinische Forschungen*
BMGS	*Byzantine and Modern Greek Studies*
BNJ	*Byzantinisch-Neugriechische Jahrbücher*
BZ	*Byzantinische Zeitschrift*
Dialogue	Manuel Palaiologos, *Dialogue with the Empress-Mother on Marriage*, ed. and trans. A. Angelou (Vienna: Verlag der Österreichischen Akademie der Wissenschaften, 1991)
DOP	*Dumbarton Oaks Papers*
ΕΕΒΣ	Ἐπετηρὶς Ἑταιρείας Βυζαντινῶν Σπουδῶν
EO	*Echos d'Orient*
Foundations	Manuel Palaiologos, *Foundations of an Imperial Education*, PG 156, 313–84
Funeral Oration	Manuel Palaiologos, *Funeral Oration on His Brother Theodore, Despot of Morea*, ed. and trans. J. Chrysostomides (Thessalonike: Association for Byzantine Research, 1985)
GRBS	*Greek, Roman and Byzantine Studies*
JÖB	*Jahrbuch der Österrreichischen Byzantinistik*
JÖBG	*Jahrbuch der Österreichischen Byzantinischen Gesellschaft*
MM	F. Miklosich and W. Müller (eds), *Acta et Diplomata Graeca Medii Aevii Sacra et Profana*, 6 vols (Vienna: Carolus Gerold, 1860–90)
OCP	*Orientalia Christiana Periodica*
ODB	*The Oxford Dictionary of Byzantium*, 3 vols, ed. A. Kazhdan (Oxford: Oxford University Press, 1991)
Orations	Manuel Palaiologos, *Seven Ethico-Political Orations*, PG 156, 385–562
PG	J. P. Migne (ed.), *Patrologiae Cursus Completus, Series Graeca*, 161 vols (Paris, 1857–66)

PLP	E. Trapp (ed.), *Prosopographisches Lexikon der Palaiologenzeit*, 12 vols (Vienna: Verlag der Österreichischen Akademie der Wissenschaften, 1976–96)
PP	S. Lampros (ed.), *Παλαιολόγεια καὶ Πελοποννησιακά*, 3 vols (Athens: Gregoriades, 1926)
REB	*Revue des Études Byzantines*
RESEE	*Revue des Études Sud-Est Européennes*
TLG	*Thesaurus Linguae Graecae*
TM	*Travaux et Mémoires*
ZRVI	*Zbornik radova vizantološkog instituta*

Introduction

This book is equally about people and their texts. It seeks to explore how a Byzantine emperor negotiated his authority in the troubled waters of late Byzantium where churchmen and court-based interest groups vied for the attention of wider audiences. And it is about the construction of discursive strategies by adapting the rules of rhetorical genres to historical circumstances. The focus of the book is Manuel II Palaiologos, both emperor of Byzantium (r. 1391–1425) and prolific author of a range of oratorical and theological texts. The argument is that the emperor maintained his position of authority not only by direct political agency but also by rhetorically advertising his ideas about the imperial office. Throughout his reign, Manuel II created a parallel literary court where he presided over a group of peer literati who supported his position and did not contest his imperial prerogatives. It was within this group that his texts were copied and subsequently disseminated in order to promote a renewed version of the idea of imperial authority. His ideological commitments valued education and the use of rhetorical skills as instruments of social and political change. His vision evolved and changed according to the opportunities and conditions of his reign. In order to understand it one needs to attend not only to his texts but to other contemporary written sources. This will allow us to further scrutinise the late Byzantine understanding(s) of the imperial office as well as the extent to which Manuel II's writings mirrored or obliterated contemporary concerns.

Manuel II Palaiologos: A Short Biography and an Overview of the Historical Context

The life of Manuel II Palaiologos coincided with a period of upheavals occurring in the last century of Byzantine history. He was born in 1350 as the second son of Emperor John V Palaiologos (r. 1354–91) and of Helena Kantakouzene, the daughter of another ruler, John VI Kantakouzenos (r. 1347–54). As the emperor's second son, in the beginning Manuel did not attract the same attention as his elder brother Andronikos IV (1348–85), considered to be destined to become John V's legitimate successor.[1] Even so, Manuel soon came to play a key role in his father's diplomatic plans. The first information on Manuel dates from 1355 when his father sent him to Pope Innocent IV as hostage to be educated in the spirit of Latin Christianity, in a move meant to obtain Western support.[2] At the age of sixteen, in 1366, Manuel travelled to Buda together with his father, who was visiting King Louis I (1342–82), the Angevin ruler of Hungary, in another attempt to attract the Christian rulers into a joint venture against the Ottomans. In Buda Manuel stayed for almost a year. His father promised Louis that his son would convert to Catholicism, as he himself had already been contemplating this idea.[3] The plan did not materialise and after several years Manuel was offered his first administrative position as despot of Thessalonike (1369–73).[4] The very fact that Manuel was appointed despot indicates his secondary position in his father's plans, since the late Byzantine practice was to attach the title of despot to imperial sons who were not destined to become emperors. Yet, soon, Manuel emerged as the main heir to the throne, following his brother Andronikos's failed coup d'état in 1373. Eventually, in that same year, Manuel was formally proclaimed co-emperor.[5]

Nevertheless, the problem of John V's succession had not been solved. With Ottoman help, in 1376, Andronikos imprisoned most members of the ruling family.[6] Manuel was captive several years until his father escaped and resumed rule of the empire.[7] Despite the dynastic troubles, the ensuing truce between Andronikos and John stipulated that the former and his line were recognised as legitimate successors to the throne.[8] This caused Manuel dissatisfaction as he saw himself deprived of the right of succession, despite the many proofs of loyalty to his father, the emperor.[9] In 1382, Manuel returned to his previous appanage, Thessalonike, where, disregarding his father's appeals to return to Constantinople, he took the title

---

[1] See Barker, *Manuel II*, 5–6.
[2] The chrysobull recounting this information was dated to 1355; Dölger, *Regesten*, 5. no. 3052. See also Halecki, *Empereur de Byzance*, 24–31.
[3] See Wirth, 'Haltung Kaiser Johannes' V.', 271–2.
[4] Ryder, *Career and Writings*, 47, on Kydones' *prooimion* which mentions John V's conferral on his son Manuel of territories in Macedonia and Thessaly.
[5] Schreiner, *Chronica Byzantina Breviora*, 1. no. 47.
[6] Ibid. nos. 9, 24–6. On Andronikos's rule see Katsone, *Ἀνδρόνικος Δ' Παλαιολόγος*.
[7] Schreiner, *Chronica Byzantina Breviora*, 1. nos. 9, 17.
[8] Dölger, *Regesten*, 5. no. 3177. On the settlement see also Dölger, 'Johannes VII.', 26.
[9] Barker assumes that Manuel intended to resume his position in Thessalonike as despot: *Manuel II*, 43.

of *basileus*.¹⁰ His main achievement in this position was the restoration of Byzantine authority in Thessaly and Macedonia.¹¹ Yet, shortly afterwards, the Ottomans retaliated and blockaded Thessalonike in a siege that was to last until 1387.¹²

After the Thessalonike episode, Manuel went to Brusa to show submission to the Ottomans. He also accepted his father's, John V's, policy of appeasement with the Ottomans and defended his authority. In 1389, he supported John V in resisting the pressure coming from Andronikos's son, John VII,¹³ who in April 1390, after his father's death, deposed John V for a short time.¹⁴ In the same year, in obedience to the request of the new sultan, Bayezid, he travelled to Asia Minor to join the Ottoman forces with a military contingent. Nevertheless, in 1391 at the news of his father's death, he escaped from the Ottoman camp. He reached Constantinople and swiftly assumed power.

He was crowned emperor a year later in 1392 at a ceremony which coincided with his marriage with Helena Dragaš, the daughter of the Serbian lord of Serres.¹⁵ After this event, he no longer answered Bayezid's appeals for submission, a refusal which led to a blockade of Constantinople. Manuel continued to live in the beleaguered city for several years, but in 1399, following the advice of the French marshal Boucicaut who was in charge of the defence of Constantinople, he embarked on a journey to Western Europe in search of financial and military aid. The journey lasted four years during which Manuel resided in Paris at the court of Charles VI and in London at the court of Henry IV.¹⁶ The strong impression Manuel produced upon the Western rulers and courts is reflected by the lavish reception of the Byzantine emperor in France and England.¹⁷ A sign of the importance of the diplomatic relations with the West was that the Byzantine emperor offered a decorated manuscript of Dionysius the Areopagite to the French king.¹⁸

---

¹⁰ Dölger, *Regesten*, 5. nos. 3173a, 3175a, 3175b, 3180a, 3181c, 68–70.
¹¹ Demetrios Kydones, *Letters*, nos. 243, 244, 247, 249, 250, ed. Loenertz. In several of these letter, Kydones remarks an increased influx of people into the city of Thessalonike during the siege. See Dennis, *Reign of Manuel II*, 61–4.
¹² During the blockade, Manuel established an alliance with Theodore Palaiologos, Nerio Acciaioli and Pope Urban VI; Barker, *Manuel II*, 54.
¹³ Andronikos died in 1385 in another attempt to overthrow his father.
¹⁴ Manuel's reply was quick; in August he secured the Hospitallers' support and pushed John VII out of the capital.
¹⁵ Manuel married quite late according to Byzantine standards, at the age of 42; Dąbrowska, 'Ought one to marry?'
¹⁶ Andreeva, 'Reise Manuels II.'; Jugie, 'Voyage de l'empereur Manuel Paléologue'.
¹⁷ Nicol, *'Byzantine Emperor in England'*, 220.
¹⁸ His travel to the West was celebrated by many panegyrists; for instance, Isidore of Kiev, *Encomium for John VIII*, 219, ll. 26–8.

Upon his return to Constantinople in 1403, Manuel found the empire in a better political situation generated by the military disaster the Ottomans had suffered from Tamerlane's advances in Asia.[19] Manuel ensured his succession by appointing his first-born son, John, as co-emperor and strengthened his control over the remote provinces of the empire, the Morea and Thessalonike. There, after the death of his younger brother, Theodore, he installed his underage son Theodore II Palaiologos as despot of the region, thus strengthening his control of the province. Later on, in 1415, he returned to the region and rebuilt the Hexamilion wall, in order to keep the Ottomans from descending into the Peloponnese.[20] Due to illness, Manuel retired from the imperial position in 1422 when his eldest son, John VIII, stepped in. He died in 1425.[21]

Manuel's biography suggests that he rose to power from a weak political position in a period of deep social, economic and political transformations. To a certain extent, his three-decade-long reign mirrored political processes originating in his father's rule, like the efforts to obtain substantial Western aid or to maintain peaceful relations with the Ottoman conquerors. To an even larger extent, Manuel's career was also influenced by other processes as well: Byzantium's territorial fragmentation reflected in the autonomy of provinces and cities from the central government; the drop in the numbers of the population after 1348 owing to the combined impact of factors like plagues, invasions, wars and civil strife;[22] the gradual replacement of the land-owning aristocracy with a new class of entrepreneurs and tradesmen;[23] and the passing of various territories under foreign jurisdictions both Ottoman and Latin.[24]

Not only was the Byzantine state significantly diminished as a result of these processes, but, after the battle of the river Maritsa (1371), it became a tributary vassal to its powerful eastern neighbours, the Ottoman Empire. Although the battle of Ankara, in which the Tatars annihilated the Ottoman army, temporarily restored Byzantine prestige in the Eastern Mediterranean, Manuel's position remained fragile. Throughout his reign, he controlled only a few territories: Constantinople and its hinterland; parts of the Peloponnese, including

---

[19] Sphrantzes, *Memoirs*, II.1.
[20] Barker, 'Chronology'.
[21] He was buried in the Pantokrator monastery.
[22] Laiou and Morrisson, *Byzantine Economy*, 169–70; see also Laiou, *Constantinople and the Latins*, 85–126.
[23] The phenomenon has been extensively documented. For overviews see Barker, *Manuel II*, 1–200, or Nicol, *Last Centuries of Byzantium*, 251–394. On the concept of liberty as an ideal pertaining to the rights of cities, reflected in rhetoric, see Angelov, 'Three kinds of liberty'.
[24] Laiou, 'Byzantium and the neighboring powers'.

the capital, Mystras; and Thessalonike (1408–23), the second-largest city in the empire.

Moreover, he had to cope with internal challenges. In the Peloponnese up to the early 1380s, the powerful family of the Kantakouzenoi exerted a strong influence. This influence was felt even during the Palaiologan rule of the Morea in the 1390s when local lords supported a certain Matthew Kantakouzenos as potential despot.[25] Another serious threat to Manuel's authority came from the protracted dynastic strife with his nephew, John VII. As the son of Andronikos IV, John V's oldest and rebellious son, John VII inherited the right to rule in Constantinople and enjoyed the support of many ecclesiastics and a part of the population in both Constantinople and Thessalonike. When in 1391 Manuel secured imperial authority in the city, John VII also inherited his father's, Andronikos IV's, appanage of Selymbria, close to Constantinople. Despite persistent accusations of having sided with the Ottomans in the siege of 1394–1402, Manuel entrusted him with the administration of Constantinople during his sojourn in the West (1399–1403). Yet, upon Manuel's return to Byzantium, John resumed his claims to the Byzantine throne. The result was an agreement between the two, following which in 1403 John VII moved to Thessalonike, where he exerted full imperial authority and enjoyed enthusiastic local support.[26]

Aims of the Present Study

Doubtless, all these processes and challenges played a crucial part in shaping Manuel's reign. As a result, more often than not, his biography has been analysed primarily against the backdrop of the political and economic upheavals of the late fourteenth century. In doing so, historians of late Byzantium have largely overlooked the functions rhetoric fulfilled in the critical decades of the end of the fourteenth century and the beginning of the fifteenth century. Yet arguably the hitherto unstudied or little-studied rhetorical texts written in late Byzantium can shed further light on various aspects of political history and especially on the conceptualisation of imperial authority.

With a focus on Manuel Palaiologos's prolific textual production and on his involvement in the intellectual circles of the period, the principal aim of this book is, therefore, to interpret and explain the emperor's rhetorical

---

[25] Loenertz, 'Pour l'histoire du Péloponnèse'.
[26] Mešanović, *Jovan VII Paleolog*.

action in the late Byzantine context. This study shifts the focus away from political history and investigates the rhetorical and ideological facets of his political messages. My analysis proceeds from two observations: that these texts do not represent isolated artefacts but are part of larger historical and cultural matrices; and that rhetorical texts, such as orations, dialogues or panegyrics, actively mirrored and mediated the negotiation of political power. In Byzantium a close relationship was established between politics and highbrow literacy, a relationship reflected in the activities of the Constantinopolitan courtiers.[27] Furthermore, with the changes taking place in late Byzantine society and institutional order, there were also shifts in the indicators of social status, in ideas about power, and in what constituted the suitable system of virtues.

I conduct this analysis on two levels: first, the rhetoric of Manuel's writings that included references to political events, with special emphasis on the reasons behind the author's adherence to, or departure from, the literary tradition in which he was working; second, the ideological statements which Manuel inserted in these highly rhetorical texts, which can help us identify the nuances of his political visions or actions. Within this framework the goal of the present research here is threefold: first, to contextualise the emperor's political texts written during his reign by looking into the changes that led to the specific political and social conditions at the turn of the fifteenth century. Arguably, the emperor, confronted with multiple challenges to his authority, created a parallel court of peer literati which constituted a platform from which to disseminate his political messages. The second goal of the book is to identify and scrutinise the literary structures underlying Manuel's political texts: the narrative structures of the *Funeral Oration on His Brother Theodore*, the dialogic construction of political messages in the *Dialogue with the Empress-Mother on Marriage*, as well as the compositional features specific to a fully fledged didactic programme addressed to his son and co-emperor John VIII Palaiologos. It will be argued that Manuel approached the rhetorical traditions of composing texts for court performance in a creative fashion so as to accommodate his theoretical and practical ideas of governance.

Finally, this book seeks to map the political attitudes and perspectives of the power agents in Constantinople towards the end of the fourteenth century: the Orthodox clergymen, the rhetoricians and the emperor. By indicating how various aspects of political power were negotiated across separate interest groups, ultimately I will try to pinpoint the new features of

---

[27] Holmes, 'Political literacy'.

kingship whereby Manuel II advertised the imperial position in Byzantium. On the one hand, this renewed representation of the imperial function was the manifestation of a constant need to maintain popularity. On the other hand, it was also the expression of a coherent political programme connected with the idea that rhetorical education, ethical values and political power were correlated, a notion that largely drew on conceptions outlined by Hellenistic and late antique rhetoricians.[28] Accordingly, unlike most court rhetoricians, whose understanding of political rhetoric was rather centred on the betterment of personal affairs which continued to depend on the emperor's person, Manuel claimed a different role for rhetoric in the political sphere that had to do with civic engagement for the community's benefit.

By this account, this study strives to integrate Manuel's distinct imperial vision, based on the use of rhetoric, into a broader picture of Byzantine theories and practices of power. In particular, it will illustrate the role of the late Byzantine emperors as mediators between an aristocracy composed of courtiers and a church whose dominant attitude was to reject any attempts to unite with the Latin church, other than on its own terms.

Structure

The study is divided into two parts. The first part discusses the profile and the ideological stance of the ecclesiastics and the rhetoricians. The connections with the emperor and the challenges or the support they provided to Manuel II will cover a significant section in these preliminary chapters. The second part, which is also the most substantial part of the book, provides close readings of the emperor's texts and focuses on his particular stance regarding the imperial office. In this part, in order to assess the emperor's strategies of generating political messages, I document the features of presentation typical of Manuel's persuasive speech. In particular, I note the shifts in the construction of multiple authorial voices. The focus of my inquiry here will be the practice of rhetoric, and more specifically the techniques through which Manuel turned his rhetorical writings into ideologically effective tools to disseminate political messages. Based on the discussion of the underlying socio-political developments and the authorial rhetorical strategies, in the last chapter, the focus of my investigation widens to encompass the whole spectrum of political texts produced at the end of the fourteenth and the beginning of the fifteenth centuries. Here, I look into the political aspects of Manuel's discourse as

---

[28] Morgan, *Literate Education*, 190–240.

mirroring themes of other contemporary political discourses and putting forward an alternative political vision.

Sources

Much depends on the sources used, their advantages, their limitations, or the subjectivity of their authors. By and large, unlike in the case of other studies of Manuel's reign which primarily used official documents as source material, the texts which I explore here fall between oratory and literature. Certain compositions were meant for performance in the court, but often they were only circulated within circles of acquaintances and supported subsequent re-elaboration in order to be enjoyed as pieces of written literature. I have chosen to focus only on four major texts by Emperor Manuel II Palaiologos: the *Dialogue with the Empress-Mother on Marriage*, the *Foundations of an Imperial Education*, the so-called *Seven Ethico-Political Orations*, and the *Funeral Oration on His Brother Theodore, Despot of Morea*.[29] The reasons why I have limited my research to these four texts pertain to the fact that they were composed during his reign and, unlike in the case of other texts of his, they reflected in a systematic way the problems and issues specific to Byzantine rule of that period. These writings reveal the extent to which the emperor regarded his literary activities as intertwined with, and reflected in, the administration of the Byzantine state. Moreover, the intended similarities of content between the four works are indicated by their inclusion in a single manuscript, the Vindobonensis phil. gr. 98, part of a series of four manuscripts which were dedicated to his son and successor, John VIII Palaiologos.

Moreover, these four texts stand for particular ways of writing about the empire which emerge from the use of different authorial voices: the *Dialogue* reflects a deliberative voice; the *Funeral Oration* a narrative voice; the *Foundations* and the *Orations* a didactic voice. Taken together, the strategies originating in the modulations of the author's voice constitute a kind of full repertoire for imperial discourse, on a wide range of topics and concepts. Since they were not confined to Manuel's texts, I will also have occasion to cite their occurrence in other contemporary writings that deal with political aspects of rulership. In doing so, I wish to suggest that Manuel's multiple texts were also adapted to particular events so that they could appeal to multiple audiences.

---

[29] These texts are henceforth referred to as *Dialogue*, *Foundations*, *Orations* and *Funeral Oration* respectively. The Abbreviations list and the Bibliography give details of the editions used.

Apart from these four main texts, this study will make use of the emperor's other texts as well. His collection of letters is particularly important for this research as it provides additional information not only about his political vision but also about his connections with various courtiers. The political texts written before his accession to the throne (the *Admonitory Oration to the Thessalonians* and the *Panegyric on the Recovery of His Father from an Illness*), the theological treatises (the *Dialogues with a Muslim* [*Dialoge mit einem Muslim*] and *On the Procession of the Holy Spirit*) and the rhetorical exercises play a key role in acquiring a thorough picture of his literary activity. Although I will not deal *in extenso* with this part of his work, particular attention will be paid to his liturgical texts and homilies, which reveal his approach to the church.

In treating an emperor's rhetorical-ideological self-representation, much depends on other comparative sources which offer background material. It is, therefore, necessary to proceed with a brief review of the main categories of sources used in the present volume. As historical narrative was a popular genre in Byzantium, one would expect a sizeable number of these narratives. However, as has been noted, the period of Manuel's reign represented a puzzling gap in the production of historiographical accounts or chronicles. Thus, for more extensive and detailed narratives we have to turn to the later historians who wrote after the Fall of Constantinople: George Sphrantzes' *Memoirs*, Doukas's *History*, or Laonikos Chalkokondyles' *Histories*. Among these authors, only the first, Sphrantzes, was acquainted with the emperor; he even held a position at Manuel's court which allowed him to record some of the emperor's sayings.

On the other hand, since the focus is on court rhetoric, I will draw extensively on texts produced in this milieu. In particular, several orations addressed to the emperor included multiple themes and notions which will be used as a backdrop against which the emperor's self-representation will be traced. Several texts stand out: Demetrios Chrysoloras's *Comparison between the Emperor of Today and the Ancient Rulers*, John Chortasmenos's *Address upon the Emperor's Return from Thessalonike*, Makarios Makres' *Funeral Oration for Emperor Manuel Palaiologos*, or Gemistos Plethon's *Address (Memorandum) to Emperor Manuel II on the Situation in the Peloponnese*. Other important categories of texts comprise letters addressed to the emperor, ecclesiastical treatises and chancellery documents.

Theoretical Framework

In comparison with previous studies of imperial visions in Byzantium, the present one is both narrower and larger in its scope. It is narrower because it focuses mainly on the texts of a single author, yet broader because these compositions are treated not only as objects of political propaganda but also as writings belonging to the rhetorical tradition. I proceed from the assumption that the Manuel II's authority was not absolute and he had to act in order to secure it.[30] In addition, I underline the close relationship between rhetorical texts and their political and cultural contexts. As such, instances of rhetorical discourse become instances of social action. This perspective allows us to throw light on specific power relations established among different groups (institutionalised or not) and to historicise the development of discursive themes. Along these lines, I look at the texts, on the one hand, as vehicles for political ideas and, on the other hand, as statements embedded in a network of political processes and social practices.

Therefore, in terms of my approach, the investigation will involve several steps. In a first stage, I will try to establish the main features of the political and intellectual context, which in turn will support our understanding of the scope of Manuel's texts. I touch on issues of social divisions as well as on questions of Byzantine identity, a concept that arguably needs to be regarded as fluctuating according to various political or cultural contexts.[31] As a way of organising information about self, identity has been analysed as a multifaceted theoretical construct. Given the historical-rhetorical nature of the sources used in the present study, here I will use this concept in a broad manner and focus on its religious and ethnic aspects. Furthermore, understanding the audiences of the political messages requires a look into the messages' performance and circulation. We are fortunate to have evidence about the oral presentation in the court milieu of several texts, such as Manuel's *Orations* and *Dialogue*. Concomitantly, the study of manuscripts and the information included in epistolary exchanges reveals that his texts were circulated and received feedback from peer scholars. To this extent, given their attested dissemination, I regard these texts as having a public character. The analysis will also be supported by several concepts of social network analysis, such as degrees of acquaintance with the emperor and the instrumentality of the network. Connected to this preliminary contextualisation is the discussion of Manuel's 'literary court', which can be defined as a group of readers and writers acquainted with one another. Second, as I explore notions of political thought in rhetorical

---

[30] See Beck, 'Reichsidee und nationale Politik'.

[31] See especially Stouraitis, 'Roman identity in Byzantium', who argues that ideas of collective identity need to be disconnected from essentialist and reifying views on perennial ethnicity. On Roman and Hellenic traits of identity see also Stouraitis, 'Reinventing Roman ethnicity'.

writings, I will try to answer the following questions: how does the Byzantine ruler construct his representation in writing and what are the cultural or ideological presuppositions upon which such a representation is based? Despite their conventions and the audience's expectations of conformism, the texts depend heavily on the use of metaphors, with elaborated imagery often drawn from poetry, myths or other literary accounts. Thus, with the caveat that an exclusive rhetorical approach can lead to accepting a text's own premises, this kind of analysis will draw extensively on concepts central to rhetorical and literary theory, such as genre understood as an aspect which combines the form (e.g. collections of chapters, moral essays, dialogues, speeches) and the function of a text shaped by its performance; and authorial voice seen as a changing aspect across the texts of the same author.

Furthermore, in order to map the competing political discourses during Manuel II's reign, I will use an approach inspired by critical discourse analysis which relies on the investigation of the form of the writings as well as of the 'structural relationships of power and control as they are expressed in language use'.[32] As discourse engages three aspects – language, context and group interaction – I will focus on the connections between texts and social and political action. This perspective can provide useful analytical tools for assessing the dynamics of enunciations of a political and social nature. Lastly, this mapping of political discourses will be accompanied by an attempt to provide a discourse genealogy in which various discursive themes will be seen to operate across a range of late Byzantine contexts.

Previous Scholarship

As one of the last Byzantine emperors whose reign spanned a period of more than thirty years, Manuel II Palaiologos has received much scholarly attention. In recent decades several critical editions of his texts have been published, thereby drawing attention to his personality.[33] Most often, these have included the emperor's activities in broader accounts of social and political history. This is the case of the recent volume by Antonia Kioussopoulou, who used evidence drawn from Manuel II's biography for her argument regarding the political and institutional transformations in late Byzantium under the influence of similar processes in the Italian city-states.[34] While

---

[32] See Wodak and Meyer, *Methods*, 2–3.
[33] One of the latest editions of one of Manuel's texts is by Kakkoura, *Annotated Critical Edition of . . . 'Seven Ethico-Political Orations'*.
[34] Kioussopoulou, *Emperor or Manager*, 94–5, 105–6.

Kioussopoulou saw the emperor as an agent of these transformations, Nevra Necipoğlu's account of late Byzantine history emphasises the role of other social groups in the configuration of the political landscape: aristocrats, businessmen, ecclesiastics and local *archontes*.[35] Remarkably, both these accounts take as a point of departure the same statement preserved in Sphrantzes' *Memoirs*, according to which an emperor should act as a manager rather than as a ruler in the common sense of the word.[36] Still, because of their focus on late Byzantine social and political changes, neither volume engages with Manuel's political ideas and rhetorical œuvre in a comprehensive manner.

As far as the investigation of political ideology and its expression in rhetoric in late Byzantium are concerned, important comparative material is provided by two studies. One is Dimiter Angelov's *Imperial Ideology and Political Thought in Byzantium (1204–1330)*, which deals with innovative political ideas on society, economy and imperial authority circulating in the early Palaiologan period. Angelov argued that the most important development in early Palaiologan political thought was the growing gap between official ideology on the one hand and the political ideas of lay and ecclesiastic thinkers on the other. He noted that, in this period, some political debates were aimed against the emperor's autocratic attributes, and that the emerging theories of governance as a reciprocal relationship between ruler and subjects paralleled Western theories.[37] The other study, Ida Toth's unpublished doctoral dissertation titled *Imperial Orations in Late Byzantium (1261–1453)*, provides an analysis of the rhetorical and performative aspects of the speeches addressed to late Byzantine emperors. Toth described a specific Byzantine rhetorical form over the last centuries of its use. To these two studies can be added Anthony Kaldellis's recent problematisation of Byzantium as a rigid imperial theocracy.[38] These recent volumes indicate that late Byzantine ideological enunciations surface in a variety of texts and are often hidden behind common rhetorical *topoi*.

Apart from these accounts of late Byzantine cultural and political history, three books deal specifically with the emperor's personality and activity. The earliest one, Jules Berger de Xivrey's *Mémoire sur la vie et les ouvrages de l'empereur Manuel Paléologue* (1853), was a biography which, however, remained incomplete. The second in chronological order, George Dennis's *The Reign of Manuel II in Thessalonica: 1382–1387* (1960), deals

---

[35] Necipoğlu, *Byzantium*, 41–55, 119–48.
[36] Sphrantzes, *Memoirs*, XXIII.7.
[37] Angelov, *Imperial Ideology*, 417–23. See also Angelov, *Church and Society*, 1–10.
[38] Kaldellis, *Byzantine Republic*, 165–98.

with the short episode of Manuel's rebellious rule in the second city of the empire between 1382 and 1387, but focuses exclusively on political events. Likewise John Barker's monograph *Manuel II Palaeologus (1391–1425): A Study in Late Byzantine Statesmanship* (1969) treats extensively the internal and external affairs of Manuel's reign and uses most of the sources available to that date, without, however, looking into the emperor's ideological tenets. Finally, a recent doctoral dissertation by Siren Çelik aims at reconstructing Manuel's biography both as a literatus and as a power broker.[39] To these can be added substantial chapters such as the study by Klaus-Peter Matschke dealing with political, social and economic aspects of the history of late Byzantium.[40] More recently, Cecily Hilsdale has discussed the role of Manuel's diplomatic gifts of religious representations and relics.[41] All these scholarly treatments have touched upon crucial topics such as the dynastic conflicts, the wars with the Ottomans, or the negotiations with the Latins for military aid. However, even if these authors do not completely overlook the emperor's literary output, they never appear to consider it as a corpus of sources worth investigating for its picture of late Byzantine society. For instance, Barker's statements on the prolixity and the lack of historical value of the emperor's letters suggest the persistence of a predominant attitude among some Byzantinists of the past in search of different types of evidence.[42] On the other hand, more often than not, Manuel was described as an active ruler concerned with military and political developments, who acted according to a political vision that encompassed the entire region of the Eastern Mediterranean, with its powerful players. If his military efforts to pacify or recapture Byzantine territories were generally acknowledged, secondary literature also puts forward the image of a diplomat balancing between regional players. He is presented as a ruler who made the best of the resources at his disposal, including fostering commercial relations with different trading groups.[43] For that reason, scholars have described Manuel as an administrator rather than an emperor in the traditional sense of the term.[44]

---

[39] Çelik, *Historical Biography*.
[40] Nicol, *Last Centuries of Byzantium*, 296–317; Matschke, *Schlacht bei Ankara*; Matschke and Tinnefeld, *Gesellschaft im späten Byzanz*; Dendrinos, *Annotated Edition of 'On the Procession of the Holy Spirit'*, i–xvii.
[41] Hilsdale, *Byzantine Art and Diplomacy*.
[42] Barker, *Manuel II*, 393. A similar opinion was expressed by Dennis in Manuel II, *Letters*, IX.
[43] Matschke, *Schlacht bei Ankara*, 220–35.
[44] Ibid.

Building on previous scholarship, my intention is to provide an alternative perspective on the emperor's activity and personality, taking as a starting point his intense rhetorical activity. This perspective has been only tentatively explored in previous scholarship. The few studies dealing explicitly with the oratorical discussion of empire in Manuel's texts are generally attached to larger scholarly enterprises concerning Manuel's imperial power. While they touch upon his rhetorical output, a study that would take the imperial texts into serious consideration is still lacking.[45] Notably, when dealing with the emperor's literary output, many scholars have turned to his theological texts, as these could be more easily integrated into the intense doctrinal debates of the late Palaiologan period. Thus, albeit in sarcastic terms, as early as the seventeenth century Leo Allatius (1586–1669), the keeper of Greek manuscripts in the Vatican Library, remarked on the emperor's penchant for learned argumentation in his treatise *On the Procession of the Holy Spirit*:

> To a brief public statement by a certain Latin, <Manuel> replied in a long treatise comprising many arguments, for he believed that by making use of a verbose speech (*prolixiore sermone*) he could break the power of reason, and by the multitude and excessive size of chapters, as if by dissipating darkness, he could bring forth the light of truthfulness.[46]

Fortunately, the more recent scholars of Manuel's œuvre were more sympathetic than Allatius. With the publication of several important critical editions, judgements concerning the form and function of individual texts have become more nuanced. For instance, in the introduction to the *Dialogue*, Athanasios Angelou discussed in detail the text's prose rhythm.[47] In their critical editions of Manuel's texts, Erich Trapp, Julian Chrysostomides, Christina Kakkoura and Charalambos Dendrinos provided important hints as to the historical, doctrinal and literary contexts of the writings they edited: the *Dialogues with a Muslim*, the *Funeral Oration*, the *Orations* and the treatise *On the Procession of the Holy Spirit* respectively.[48] All these historians and philologists noted the emperor's literary preoccupations, without, however, proceeding to a more comprehensive discussion.

---

[45] This absence had already been noticed by Dennis, *Reign of Manuel II*, 16.
[46] Allatius, *De ecclesiae*, 2. ch. XVII, 854. Here and throughout this book, translations are mine unless otherwise stated.
[47] Angelou in Manuel II, *Dialogue*, 31–8.
[48] Trapp, 'Sprachgebrauch', 189–97; *Funeral Oration*, 10–12; Dendrinos, *Annotated Edition of 'On the Procession of the Holy Spirit'*.

In contrast, the ensuing study will proceed differently, although it will refrain from offering a global interpretation of the emperor's œuvre. It will strive nevertheless to spell out the major rhetorical features and ideological implications of this late Byzantine emperor's political writings.

Part I

Dissent and Consent

1
Voices of Dissent: Preaching and Negotiating Authority

As the bulk of rhetorical production remained religious in nature and the church continued to provide a solid framework of action, it is fair to begin by looking into this area for clues about dominant discursive themes and voices in late Byzantium. As in other periods of Byzantine history, most ecclesiastical writers belonged to high church echelons or to the monastic circles of Mount Athos where high-profile learned individuals lived for certain periods of time. The group's cohesiveness was reflected by their adherence to common intellectual and theological Orthodox traditions that spanned the fourteenth and the fifteenth centuries. Concomitantly, the differences between existing subgroups indicate that even if their members' approaches and views were often similar, this group was far from monolithic. Its members were often active in communities outside Constantinople and their contacts with the emperor involved a wide range of interactions, from close ties to open conflict.

The issues which they approached were not new in the history of the Byzantine church. Confrontation with the emperor, internal factionalism, social care and claims of theological doctrinal purity found frequent expression in Byzantium. Understanding these authors' actions, organisational means, arguments or textual choices will in turn enable us to see in a better light the emperor's own uses of rhetoric or discursive themes for representing his variant of imperial authority. Therefore, in an attempt to paint a key element of the broader picture in which Manuel's rhetorical œuvre appeared, this chapter will look into the ideas that guided ecclesiastics at the turn of the fourteenth century.

Several phenomena impacted on the ecclesiastics' views of worldly affairs in the late fourteenth century. First, political decisions like those concerning temporary alliances with Ottomans or Latins and the internal strife affected the integrity of the Byzantine church.[1] In particular, the growing pressure of the Ottoman Sultan Bayezid put the Byzantine state into a condition of subservience which limited the scope of imperial action.[2] The limitations of authority were further exacerbated by the dynastic conflicts that eventually generated an unstable situation of dual rule, in which power was shared by emperors with a similar range of authority: John VII and Manuel II. Conversely, the church assumed a more prominent role in Byzantine society at large. Second, the ecclesiastical authors increasingly assumed a group identity, reflected in their remarks about the differences between the imperial and the church sphere.[3] One of the key factors that contributed to the consolidation of a church writers' group identity was the rise of hesychasm, a religious movement that valued the contemplation of God through incessant prayer. Hesychasts promoted an inward-looking attitude and rejected the idea of a religious or political rapprochement with the Latins.[4] Notably, after 1351, the year when hesychasm was integrated into the official doctrine of the Byzantine church, most patriarchs came from hesychast circles and held anti-Latin positions: Philotheos Kokkinos (1353–4, 1364–76), Neilos Kerameus (1380–8), Anthony IV (1389–97), Kallistos II Xanthopoulos (1397), Matthew I (1397–1410) and Euthymios II (1410–16).[5] Third, the church became more assertive in the interactions with other power brokers. For instance, in 1396 Patriarch Anthony IV summoned a synod intended to reinforce the hesychast doctrine, at a time when the number of Byzantine supporters of the Latin church increased. The synod revealed the influence which the church exerted at that time as a number of scholars and ecclesiastics were forced to leave Constantinople or declare their Orthodoxy. Another example involved the influence of churchmen in blocking and delaying the negotiations with the church of Rome after the accession of Martin V as pope.[6]

Often, the texts penned by the late Byzantine ecclesiastics had multifaceted audiences. This is suggested both by the stylistic registers employed (from lowbrow to highbrow) and by their topics (religious but also social and political). Homilies generally addressed wider audiences since authors used a less sophisticated language to comment on aspects that affected the daily life of

---

[1] Negotiations for union especially influenced the church's attitude; Nicol, *Church and Society*, 98–128.
[2] Necipoğlu, 'Aristocracy', 136.
[3] Authors such as Mark Eugenikos, George Gennadios Scholarios, Sylvester Syropoulos.
[4] Krausmüller, 'Rise of hesychasm', 126.
[5] On the Byzantine Palamite patriarchs see ibid. 125.
[6] See Patacsi, 'Joseph Bryennios', 73–96.

Byzantine communities. Other texts like theological treatises had a predominantly clerical audience, which occasionally included the emperor or other lay scholars present in the emperor's court. The address to multiple audiences suggests that the messages of the ecclesiastic authors could also exert social or political influence and that their writings enjoyed high popularity.

Organisation of the Ecclesiastics' Group

First, let us look at the composition of this group in which several prominent figures stand out. In addition to the patriarchs, among its members we find theologians like Nicholas Kabasilas Chamaetos, known for his theological writings inspired by hesychasm; the three metropolitans of Thessalonike of this period, Isidore Glabas, Gabriel and Symeon, who expressed their position vis-à-vis the Ottoman presence in Byzantium and proposed various solutions; court preachers with a prolific homiletic and liturgical œuvre, like Joseph Bryennios and Makarios Makres; or canonists like Makarios, the metropolitan of Ankara, with expertise in ecclesiastical law. In this group, we can also include later writers like John Eugenikos, Mark Eugenikos and George Scholarios, who had biographical and authorial trajectories closely connected with the previous ecclesiastics.

The preserved evidence indicates that these ecclesiastics entertained mostly symmetric relations of cooperation and friendship. The letters of Isidore Glabas or Joseph Bryennios indicate connections of respect and affection. Their close ties find further reflection in the fact that several of them, like Gabriel of Thessalonike, Patriarch Euthymios, Makarios Makres and Joseph Bryennios, collaborated in writing religious texts.[7] Teachers and students also established close bonds indicating group cohesion. Joseph Bryennios mentored Makarios Makres, George Scholarios, and Mark and John Eugenikos, while Gabriel was Isidore Glabas's disciple. Information about teacher–student relations does not come only from passing references; it appears that the reputation of the spiritual teacher (διδάσκαλος) remained high among these authors who often evoked influential figures like the monks David and Damian on Mount Athos.[8]

---

[7] Loenertz, 'Écrits de Macaire Macres et de Manuel Paleologue', 185–92; Dendrinos, 'Co-operation', 12.

[8] E.g. Makarios Makres on the role of teachers, Λόγος εἰς τοὺς ἐν Ἁγίοις Θεοφόρους, in Μακαρίου τοῦ Μακρῆ συγγράμματα, 83, ll. 624–8, ed. Argyriou. See also Makres' Monody for Hieromonk David and his Life of Andrew of Crete, in Μακαρίου τοῦ Μακρῆ συγγράμματα, 227–34, ed. Argyriou.

Not only were they closely connected but, as synodal documents reveal, they enjoyed authority in both administrative and theological matters. Their preaching at the Constantinopolitan court or in local communities and the elaboration of theological treatises defending Orthodox principles offered them a high degree of visibility.[9] The prevalence of hesychasm in the doctrinal debates of the mid-fourteenth century led to a strengthening of the coherence of the higher ecclesiastical echelons. Within monastic circles, cases of Byzantine monks (like Manuel Kalekas) advocating a renewed dialogue with the Latins became scarce. The participation of these influential ecclesiastics and authors in synodal meetings suggests that they often had to decide upon sensitive matters that affected the society at large. If metropolitans engaged in the debates on the emperors' intervention in the church, court preachers like Joseph Bryennios and Makarios Makres, who never held high-ranking positions, participated in embassies to the Latin courts with a twofold purpose: theological and political.

Collaboration with the emperor

During the last two centuries of Byzantine history and beginning with the Arsenite schism, relations between emperor and church were often marked by tensions. The Arsenites, who from 1265 refused to recognise the legitimacy of the Constantinopolitan patriarchs, provoked a deep split in the church that was to last until 1310. Despite its ecclesiastical implications, the Arsenite schism is generally viewed as part of the political opposition to the Palaiologan dynasty by the supporters of the Laskarids.[10] Such tensions and oppositions continued throughout the fourteenth century, as the Byzantine emperors actively asserted their role as defenders of Orthodoxy in both ecclesiastical and political affairs.[11] Further evidence shows that emperor Manuel II, like his grandfather John VI Kantakouzenos, maintained a keen interest in religious affairs and held a favourable attitude towards the Athonite

---

[9] Patacsi, 'Joseph Bryennios'.
[10] Laurent, *Grandes crises religieuses*, 225–313.
[11] In undertaking the role of *defensor fidei*, Manuel echoed previous imperial confessions of faith that go back to Anastasios. In the early fourteenth century, Pseudo-Kodinos (*Treatise on Offices*, 253.22–254.3, ed. Verpeaux) mentions that the emperor had to write with his own hand a confession of Orthodox faith, which he signed and deposited with the patriarch and the synod. Pseudo-Kodinos offers the text of the confession, which was a copy of a previous confession. See Angelov, *Imperial Ideology*, 411. Furthermore, after 1403, Manuel's role of protector emerges from a *typikon* for an Athonite monastery. See Constantinides Hero, *Byzantine Monastic Foundation Documents*, 1613–15.

community.¹² His theological preoccupations central to the construction of his political and literary persona facilitated attempts to establish closer relations with the church.¹³ In addition, in contrast to his father, John V, a ruler rather indifferent to the matters of the church, Manuel made clear his interests in theology by authoring numerous apologetic texts as well as by his close association with theologians.

Several leading late Byzantine ecclesiastics, like Joseph Bryennios and Makarios Makres, had close ties with the emperor. If the relationship between Joseph Bryennios and Manuel is not well attested by the surviving epistolary evidence, this situation may be explained by the fact that they probably had daily contact at court. Bryennios's only letter to Manuel, dated to 1407, reveals a rather conventional attitude of respect towards the emperor.[14] Yet later he spent many years at the imperial court as preacher, a position which allowed him to stay in the emperor's proximity for longer periods. Bryennios's relation to Manuel seems to have become closer, for, by 1420, Sphrantzes counted Bryennios among the three individuals to whom the emperor entrusted his will.[15] In addition, Bryennios's close connections with the emperor are also indicated by his relations with other members of the emperor's close circle of friends.[16] Many of his letters addressed several of Manuel's own correspondents or people with court positions, like Demetrios Kydones, the emperor's mentor, or Patriarch Euthymios.

Another ecclesiastical writer, Makarios Makres, also enjoyed close ties with the emperor, as indicated by two texts he dedicated to Manuel in which he praised the ruler's intellectual achievements: a funeral oration and a verse *ekphrasis* of a tapestry representing the emperor.[17] As codicological evidence indicates, he collaborated with Isidore, later metropolitan of Kiev, in revising some of the emperor's texts.[18] Both their hands have been detected in manuscripts Vat. Barb. gr. 219 and Vat. gr. 1107, containing the texts of Manuel.[19] Makres and Manuel shared the spiritual guidance of the hieromonk David,

---

[12] His spiritual fathers David and Damian were from Mount Athos and the Athonite community supported him during his reign in Thessalonike. For Manuel's land grants to Athonite monasteries, see 'Patriarch Matthew I's Testament' in Constantinides Hero, *Byzantine Monastic Foundation Documents*, 1662.
[13] For instance, the discussion on Manuel as a literary personality in Barker, *Manuel II*, 395–440; Beck, *Kirche und theologische Literatur*, 712–84.
[14] Joseph Bryennios, *Letters*, no. 12, ed. Thomadakes.
[15] Treu, 'Demetrius Chrysoloras', 106–28.
[16] Loenertz, 'Pour la chronologie des œuvres de Joseph Bryennios', 12–14.
[17] Makarios Makres, *Life*, ed. Kapetanaki.
[18] Dendrinos, 'Co-operation', 10–16.
[19] See Dendrinos, 'Palaiologan scholars', 25–51.

and because of their friendship, Manuel insisted that Makres undertake the task of renovating the Pantokrator monastery. Makarios seems to have acted as an intermediary between the emperor and Mount Athos at the time when the emperor sought the support of the Athonite monastic community.

Action against the emperor

The emperor's interest in theology and his close ties with several churchmen did not prevent institutional conflicts with the church.[20] Neither did the role of protector traditionally assigned to the emperor[21] mitigate the ecclesiastics' confrontational attitude. Such disputes were certainly not unique to the later years of Byzantium, and, as Averil Cameron has argued, friction and discord were, in fact, widespread in Byzantine society.[22] Partly, this situation was rooted in the church's steady rise as an institution whose influence grew during decades of political instability.[23] As scholars have long argued, from the time of the installation of the first Palaiologan emperor, Michael VIII, the church underwent several changes which affected its relationship with the emperor and increased its influence in extra-ecclesiastical matters.[24] The Byzantine church's opposition to the union with Rome agreed by Michael VIII, movements like the Arsenite schism, Patriarch Athanasios's reforms or the clerics' pressures on Emperor John V had deep implications for the political and the intellectual landscape. Arguably, one of the effects of this consolidation was the strengthening of the patriarch's position at the political level. Several late Byzantine clerics began to claim that the patriarch's office was superior to the emperor's; the best-known instance is to be found in Patriarch Antony IV's letter from 1396 to the Russian Prince Basil in which he extolled the patriarch's central position and reserved to the emperor the role of defender of the church.[25]

---

[20] Manuel's theological preoccupations were linked to his political activities. It has been noticed that the treatise *On the Procession of the Holy Spirit* was written in view of a possible future church union: see ibid. ed. Dendrinos, VII.
[21] Meyendorff, *Byzantine Theology*, 82–4.
[22] Cameron, *Byzantine Matters*, 12.
[23] Angelov, *Church and Society*, 1–2. See the synodal decision confirming the agreement between John V and Andronikos IV in 1381.
[24] On the relations between the emperor and the church in general in Byzantium see Dvornik, *Early Christian and Byzantine Political Philosophy*; Magdalino, 'Basileia'; Angelov, *Church and Society in Late Byzantium*, 1–10.
[25] On the patriarch's office see Kydones' letter from 1386 in which he alerted Manuel to the hesychasts' arrows 'that do not spare even an emperor' (Demetrios Kydones, *Letters*, no. 327, ed. Loenertz). See Hussey, *Orthodox Church*, 267. For a translation of Antony's letter, see Barker, *Social and Political Thought*, 194.

Throughout his reign, Manuel resisted such claims and asserted the authority traditionally assigned to his office.[26] However, like other Byzantine emperors of the later period, he realised that due to the shortage of resources, the church remained one of the few institutions in possession of valuable assets which could furnish support to the state. Already in the fourteenth century, John V resorted to confiscations of land properties belonging to the monasteries which he then distributed as *pronoia*.[27] Manuel pursued a similar policy, as can be seen from documents which attest to the emperor's intervention in the economic life of monasteries.[28] These actions indicate that not only did he defend the Orthodox position, but he also intervened in ecclesiastical life, thereby challenging episcopal authority. This happened on several occasions and each time the church reacted.[29]

The earliest instance of a conflict between the church and the emperor dates from 1397, when the latter issued a *prostagma* whereby he demanded that the bishops celebrate a liturgy in commemoration of his mother, Helena.[30] The *prostagma* caused dissatisfaction among the high-ranking clergy, who responded that the emperor had no right to formulate such demands in ecclesiastical issues. Although we lack detailed information on the development of the matter, it is likely that, by this move, Manuel intended to demonstrate his authority in ecclesiastical affairs rather than to simply commemorate his mother. Since at the time of the request, in 1397, the patriarch's position was vacant after the death of Patriarch Kallistos II, one can interpret this move as an intention to act during a vacuum of power in the church.

The second and best-documented instance of Manuel's engagement in church affairs concerned his involvement in the controversy over the deposition and restoration of Patriarch Matthew I (1397–1402, 1403–10).[31] Upon assuming his office, Matthew was accused by a group of metropolitans of holding the position uncanonically, primarily because he was guilty of being τρισεπίσκοπος (three-times bishop). This was a rare charge in the history of the Byzantine church, which incriminated clerics who served as metropolitans three times.[32] Since Matthew had already been ordained metropolitan

---

[26] On the emperor's role in appointing the bishops see Laurent, 'Trisépiscopat', 89–93.
[27] See Bartusis, *Land and Privilege*, 336.
[28] Smyrlis, 'State, the land and private property', 66–7.
[29] At the Council of Basel and the negotiations of 1422–3.
[30] Darrouzès, *Regestes*, no. 319; Dennis, 'Official documents', 41.
[31] Matthew I was a Palamite and, according to Kalekas, the leader of this group: Demetrios Kydones, *Letters*, ed. Loenertz, 315–44. On Matthew I see Dennis, 'Four unknown letters'; Laurent, 'Trisépiscopat', 52–3, 93–6, 132, 169–73; Dennis, 'Deposition and restoration'.
[32] For a detailed discussion of this charge, see Laurent, 'Trisépiscopat', 64–87.

of Kyzikos and was appointed (*hypopsēphios*) metropolitan of Chalcedon, in 1397, when he became patriarch, certain metropolitans opposed this third appointment.[33] On this occasion, Matthew's opponents launched charges against the emperor's involvement in ecclesiastical matters.[34]

This conflict, which plagued Matthew's thirteen-year-long patriarchate, involved the participation of numerous clerics and court officials as well as several church councils.[35] In 1397, a hieromonk, Makarios, claimed that the appointment of Matthew I was illegal because during the election process Matthew's name was fraudulently introduced among the candidates by the *megas chartophylax*, John Holobolos.[36] Yet the consequence of the accusation was that the leader of the accusers, Makarios, was denied the right to vote in the synod following pressure from the emperor. For a while, although metropolitans continued to make accusations of imperial interference, the whole issue seemed settled: in 1399 Makarios left Constantinople together with the emperor on his long journey through Europe. It appears that the reason for Manuel taking the turbulent hieromonk with him was that he wished to keep ecclesiastical affairs in the capital free of any troubles.

However, during the emperor's absence from Constantinople, the conflict between a part of the clergy and the patriarch resurfaced. In 1402, added to the previous accusations,[37] rumours were spread that Matthew I had been negotiating the surrender of the city to the Ottomans.[38] Consequently, the four metropolitans residing in Constantinople still under siege summoned a

---

[33] For a complete list of the synods in this case see Dennis, 'Deposition and restoration', 102–4.

[34] Makarios devoted several treatises to this issue. In his Καθολικὴ Πραγματεία (in Laurent, 'Trisépiscopat', 20–2) as well as in several polemical treatises against Patriarch Matthew I (Πίναξ σὺν Θεῷ τῆς παρούσης πραγματείας, τοῦτ' ἔστι τίνες καὶ πόσαι αἰτίαι κανονικαὶ δι' ἃς κανονικῶς ἡμεῖς τε ἀποστρεφόμεθα τὸν νῦν πατριαρχεύοντα, Paris. gr. 1379, f. 15r) he exposed the arguments on the deposition of Patriarch Matthew, among which he also counted Patriarch Matthew's immoral behaviour and alleged simony and organised prostitution (πορνοβοσκεῖν) in the monastery of Charsianites (Paris. gr. 1379, f. 11r; see Laurent, 'Trisépiscopat', 37).

[35] See the list of participating individuals in the Synodal Tome of 1409; Necipoğlu, *Byzantium*, 304.

[36] See Laurent, 'Trisépiscopat', 153.

[37] Matthew was accused of allowing the monastery of Charsianites to degenerate into a place of ill fame.

[38] In his testament, Patriarch Matthew mentioned the episode of his deposition (1403). He praised Manuel for his support of the church and for his gifts to the Charsianites monastery. See Konidares, 'Ἐπιτελεύτιος βούλησις'. Papademetriou, 'Turkish conquests', 195, argues that Patriarch Matthew's collaboration with the Ottomans is plausible.

synod which deposed Matthew.³⁹ John VII, the ruler of the city at that time, validated the synodal decision as he was happy to remove a patriarch so close to his rival and uncle, Manuel. Several months later, immediately after the end of the siege, in order to confirm the previous decision, a new synod was summoned in which more metropolitans confirmed the verdict.⁴⁰

Once he returned from Europe in 1403 and replaced John VII, Manuel tried to restore Matthew I to his position and to reconcile his favourite patriarch with the rebellious metropolitans. Manuel issued a decree summoning another synod larger than the previous ones in order to discuss Matthew I's deposition.⁴¹ Yet the synod had an unexpected result: not only was Matthew's deposition confirmed but also the former patriarch was anathematised. The emperor did not accept the result and forced the members of the synod to accept the appointment of Matthew as patriarch.⁴² Manuel also organised a synod because he feared possible future rebellions.⁴³ Significantly, this time the synod took place in the imperial palace.⁴⁴ At the synod, Manuel forgave the rebellious metropolitans and reinforced all the decisions already taken in a chrysobull.⁴⁵

Still, Manuel's involvement in this debate further provoked Makarios and Matthew of Medeia, who refused reconciliation and circulated more pamphlets against the patriarch in which they criticised the emperor. A contemporary document echoes the fierce debates between the metropolitans and the emperor:

> Since our most divine emperor and lord considered that the zeal for making those accusations came from their envious disposition, he disregarded their reproaches and the insolent accusations which the metropolitan of Medeia uttered against him in the Patriarchate in the very monastery of Stoudios in which he contended that the emperor had acted like a tyrant against him for twelve years [...] It was, therefore, necessary to

---

³⁹ The synod included Matthew of Medeia and the metropolitans of Kyzikos, Gothia and Severin. According to the church canons, at least four metropolitans were needed to summon a synod. Due to the siege it was impossible for other metropolitans to enter the capital; Dennis, 'Deposition and restoration', 101.
⁴⁰ Makarios, *Apology*, Paris. gr. 1378, f. 11v: πατριάρχην ὑπὸ δύο συνόδων ἐκβληθέντα τοῦ τε θρόνου καὶ τῆς τιμῆς.
⁴¹ See Dennis, 'Deposition and restoration', 103.
⁴² For the translation of the emperor's answer see ibid. 105.
⁴³ Laurent, 'Trisépiscopat', 41.
⁴⁴ In a text in Paris. gr. 1379, f. 49v.
⁴⁵ For the text of the chrysobull see Laurent, 'Trisépiscopat', 124, 56–9.

bring those to a trial so that they would defend themselves and justify their actions. Nevertheless, the emperor rather wished to reconcile (πρὸς εἰρήνην ἐπραγματεύετο) with them and he did not even make public the abusive letter so that they would not be covered in shame, and addressed them in a humane and gentle way [. . .]. Yet they rather asked for the trial to be made so that they might point out the innovations which generated a heresy (αἵρεσις) in the church, arguing that we introduced an innovation by saying that the candidate (ὑποψήφιος) is not a bishop [. . .]. Whence our most divine lord and emperor laid down the definitions.[46]

In circulating these pamphlets, Makarios expected an official reaction, which nevertheless the emperor delayed. Only much later, in 1409, in response to the attacks, did Manuel summon another synod which discussed the charge of Matthew's three successive appointments as metropolitan. At the synod, apart from members of the clergy an important number of the emperor's supporters and *oikeioi* were present.[47] The two metropolitans, Makarios of Ankara and Matthew, sent a report detailing their two chief accusations: that the current patriarch was guilty of having been appointed a bishop for the third time and that he had been restored with the emperor's and not the church's support.[48] The synod, which by now included mostly supporters of the emperor, definitively condemned Makarios and Matthew. Despite this heated argument with the bishops, it appeared nevertheless that Manuel continued to believe in reconciliation for, after Patriarch Matthew's death in 1410, he appointed Euthymios II as patriarch. Previously, Euthymios had been Makarios's teacher in the monastery of Stoudios, and during his trial, he had agreed with the arguments against Matthew I.

The metropolitans opposed to the deposition of Makarios and Matthew of Medeia formulated arguments primarily against the emperor's involvement in ecclesiastical affairs. In one of his treatises, Makarios specifically addressed the emperor's right to intervene in ecclesiastical affairs.[49] Makarios disparagingly labelled Matthew I with the term ἀρχοντοεπίσκοπος, that is, a bishop appointed by a secular lord. Yet Makarios's attacks on the emperor's interventions in the church were rather indirect, since he was surely aware that Byzantine emperors often appointed patriarchs and bishops. He must also have been aware that

---

[46] Ibid. 131, 167–85.
[47] For a list of the participants in the synod see Necipoğlu, *Byzantium*, 304.
[48] Laurent, 'Trisépiscopat', 60.
[49] This was by far the longest treatise in the series of Makarios's polemical texts (Paris.gr. 1379, f. 98r–148r). Titled *A Partial Selection* (ἐκλογὴ μερική), it makes several important statements with regard to the emperor's office (chs. 1–10), e.g. emperors have to obey the canons of the church; clerics who ask for the help of, and plot with, the secular power should be deposed; sacerdotal power is superior to imperial power; etc.

senators and *oikeioi* (i.e. lay people) had participated in recent synods concerned with the election of patriarchs.[50] The main problem was the fact that an imperial *prostagma* for the nomination or transfer of a bishop equalled the validity of a synodal vote. Hence Makarios's problem: the *cheirotonia* could not be offered by the emperor himself, who, despite being anointed by the patriarch, had no ecclesiastical attributes. Second, according to Makarios, who cited the authority of other canonists, the clergy were not supposed to have recourse to imperial power in ecclesiastic matters, particularly in cases of promotions.[51] Thus, the *basileus* could preside over the synod and senators could participate in church affairs only if the bishops had previously agreed. Makarios argued that Manuel II acted against the bishops' quasi-unanimous opinion and reinstalled Matthew I on the ecumenical throne in 1403. This was also the case in 1397 when Matthew I, with the emperor's support, became patriarch against the vote of the majority of the synod. In both cases, according to Makarios, the emperor altered the election process.

Makarios's allegations from 1405 incriminated Matthew I and Emperor Manuel II. By accusing the emperor, Makarios positioned himself in a long series of ecclesiastics who contested the traditional view that the ruler was *isapostolos*, the supreme authority both civil and religious, placed above the ecclesiastical law.[52] Earlier in the fourteenth century Philotheos Kokkinos had taken advantage of civil discord and tried to escape imperial tutelage, especially due to John V's rapprochement with Rome.[53] The latent conflict between the emperor and the church re-emerged under Patriarch Neilos Kerameus (1380–8). During his patriarchate, in order to find a definitive solution to the situation, the emperor summoned a synod which eventually produced an agreement about his rights in the church.[54]

---

[50] During the trial of John Bekkos, before his ascension to the patriarchate, the synod was supplemented with senators representing the emperor. See Kyritses, *Byzantine Aristocracy*, 58–63.

[51] Theodore Balsamon argued that the patriarch of Constantinople represented the supreme instance. All the appeals formulated in the Orthodox realm could have final recourse to his authority. Lauchert, *Kanones*, 46.

[52] This view contrasted with the statements in the treatise against the Latins where Makarios admitted that the emperor had the right to summon a synod.

[53] Halecki, *Empereur de Byzance*, 70–92.

[54] The agreement of 1380/1382 regulated two issues: the choice of new metropolitans and the transfer of a bishop from one see to another. On the second point the emperor obtained extended power: all the movement of nominations, promotions and changes within the church was subordinated to his goodwill. The synodal decree noted that this was an old imperial privilege. Regarding the first point, it seems that the emperor arrived at a compromise, necessary according to both the canons and the circumstances. The synod of 1380 allowed the emperor only the right to the supervision of the synodal transactions and to veto. See Laurent, 'Droits de l'empereur'.

The debate over Matthew's patriarchate was not the only case of conflict between emperor and church. Other instances indicate that a large number of clerics wanted to reduce the imperial authority in the church. These intentions became clear as early as 1397 when two metropolitans, of Nicomedia and of Corinth, were asked by the emperor to provide explanations for their support of Makarios of Ankara in the latter's argument with Patriarch Matthew. In response, they demanded a written canon for the emperor's right to delegate representatives in the synod to judge ecclesiastical matters. In a document dating from those years, the two metropolitans suggested that the emperor acted unlawfully because he did not have the church's approval.[55]

The tensions between the emperor and the church erupted again in 1416 upon the direct appointment of the metropolitan of Moldavia without the prior approval of the synod.[56] This case was to some extent similar to other instances of Manuel's involvement in ecclesiastical affairs. As in previous cases, important clergymen perceived the ruler's intervention as an abuse. Upon his arrival from the Peloponnese, Manuel found in Poliaina, Macedonia, a bishop whom he considered fit for the vacant metropolitan see of Moldavia. Yet when Manuel sent his proposal to Constantinople, Patriarch Euthymios refused to make the appointment and contested the emperor's right to appoint metropolitans. Moreover, he threatened to quit his position unless the emperor admitted his abusive intervention in church affairs and a synod was summoned to discuss the appointment.[57] Although with the death of Euthymios in the same year, 1416, the conflict ceased, eventually Manuel requested a synod to define more precisely his rights over the church.[58] He also sought to ease the tensions that emerged once he imposed Joseph, his favourite for the patriarchal throne, a move that, according to Sylvester Syropoulos, enraged most metropolitans.[59] In doing so, Manuel echoed a tendency observable in his father's, John V's, approach to relations with the church. As mentioned above, John had also requested the elaboration of a document which would accurately state his rights within the church.[60]

---

[55] MM 2, 271–2, which discusses the imperial right to decide in church matters: ὅταν ζητήσῃ αὐτὰ ὁ βασιλεὺς ὁ ἅγιος μετὰ ἐξετάσεως, ἐὰν ἀποδειχθῇ, ὅτι ἔχει δίκαιον ὁ βασιλεὺς εἰς τοῦτο, μέλλομεν καὶ ἡμεῖς ἀκολουθεῖν τῇ ἱερᾷ συνόδῳ καὶ τοῖς εὑρεθεῖσιν· ἐὰν δὲ οὐδὲν εὑρεθῇ, στέργομεν καὶ ἡμεῖς τοῦτο κατὰ πᾶσαν ἀνάγκην.

[56] Darrouzès, *Regestes*, nos. 3025, 3027, 3031; Laurent, 'Trisépiscopat', 9–11, 96; Runciman, 'Manuel II and the see of Moldavia'; and Laurent, 'Droits de l'empereur'.

[57] The conflict between Manuel and Euthymios is presented by Barker, *Manuel II*, 323.

[58] Sylvester Syropoulos, *Memoirs*, 49–55, ed. Laurent.

[59] Gill, *Personalities*, 23.

[60] Laurent, 'Droits de l'empereur', 1–8. The synod awarded the emperor several rights, such as those to veto the election of a metropolitan whom he did not like, or to reformulate the patriarch's charter by creating, promoting or downgrading episcopal sees, combining sees as a reward or transferring bishops.

Arguably, John V's and Manuel's attempts to define their relations with the church remain singular in Byzantine history. In addition, scholars have long noted that Manuel's attempt to regulate the relations between the emperor and the church constituted the foundation for his son, John, to successfully negotiate church union in 1439.[61]

These instances of ecclesiastical opposition to the emperor's interventions in church affairs allow us to draw two conclusions. First, by the end of the fourteenth century, Byzantine bishops claimed more independence in electing patriarchs. Alongside Makarios's opposition, Symeon of Thessalonike also emphasised that the emperor could participate in church synods only as an observer but never as an elector. According to this view conveyed by Byzantine liturgists and canonists, the emperor was rather the patriarch's agent and not his superior. Certainly, Makarios's and Symeon's claims were not new or singular and they have to be understood in the context of developments taking place earlier in the Palaiologan period, especially the new confidence of churchmen after Michael VIII Palaiologos's bitter disputes with the church in the late thirteenth century. Yet it seems that Manuel II, just like his father John V and his son John VIII, successfully opposed this view and eventually imposed his authority on church affairs. Second, it appears that the high-ranking Constantinopolitan clergy developed a strong group consciousness, which surfaces in several texts. Perhaps the most emphatic expression of this consciousness can be found in Sylvester Syropoulos's chronicle of the Council of Ferrara-Florence (1438–9): he referred to a so-called 'our order' (ἡμετέρα τάξις) which he considered should hold exclusive rights on ecclesiastical issues. In the same way, Syropoulos considered that the *archontes* represented a separate group defending the emperor's interests.[62]

Major Political and Social Themes in the Ecclesiastics' Writings

Arguably, these actions and attitudes reflective of a group consciousness were underpinned by a set of connected principles about Byzantine society which church authors put forward on various occasions. An examination of early fifteenth-century ecclesiastic writings makes apparent that they included abundant references to ongoing political and social processes. Doubtless, the themes fleshed out in the writings of the ecclesiastics were not entirely new, as many of them had been debated during previous centuries as well. Yet there

---

[61] Sylvester Syropoulos, *Memoirs*, 52, ed. Laurent.
[62] Ibid. 104. See John Eugenikos, who distinguished the position of his fellows from those of other potentates (πάντας μὲν ἤδη σχεδὸν τοὺς ἄρχοντας), PP 1, 127, ed. Lampros.

was one important difference, which concerned the context of the late fourteenth century: the political pressures under which these extra-ecclesiastical matters came to be scrutinised called for immediate action, and hence the sense of urgency that dominates these texts. To this extent, these themes became instrumental in the ecclesiastics' discursive strategies of claiming authority in state affairs.

From the extant texts, it appears that the ecclesiastics followed several courses of action: they sought to defend the autonomy of the church, rejected most forms of unionism with the Roman church, and reacted to the Ottoman regime under whose authority they claimed responsibility for the local communities. In addition, their pastoral obligations allowed them to remain in close touch with large communities and to exert their influence at the level of the lower social strata. All these issues were interconnected and they revealed the efforts of the church to remodel Byzantine society according to a religious frame. Such attempts of thorough reform went back to Patriarch Athanasios (1230–1310), who did not separate the moral reform of the church from an overhauling of the entire state.[63] From this perspective, the late Palaiologan ecclesiastics did not bring new perspectives but rather continued the efforts of ecclesiastics from the previous decades.

The ecclesiastics' response to the transformations taking place in late Byzantium was articulated in numerous moralising homilies, prayers, hagiographies, orations and treatises on theological topics. While they produced many kinds of rhetorical compositions (orations, educational treatises and others), the pastoral and the theological genres predominated. Given their contexts of production, they all reflected a hitherto unparalleled awareness of the threats against the empire. Furthermore, like many of their predecessors, the late Byzantine ecclesiastical authors did not place a particular value on highbrow rhetoric, since they often addressed audiences outside the circles of the Constantinopolitan elites. Only rarely do we find references to classical rhetoric as a major instrument of persuasion, as in Joseph Bryennios's *Oration on the Reconstruction of the Walls of Constantinopole*, where the author highlighted the role of *rhetoreia* and pointed to two features of rhetorical speech which he deemed important: clarity and brevity.[64]

More often than not the ecclesiastics' texts addressed non-elite large communities. Homilies continued to hold a central place in the religious rhetorical landscape: homilists celebrated saints, comforted local communities attacked by enemies, or chastised their flocks for allegedly wrong opinions or behaviour.

---

[63] Boojamra, *Church and Social Reform*, 170.
[64] Joseph Bryennios, *Oration on the Reconstruction*, 23, ed. Thomadakes.

Significantly, many homilies of this period were written not in Constantinople but in other territories, especially Crete (Joseph Bryennios) or Thessalonike (Isidore Glabas, Gabriel and Symeon). Church leaders used homilies as a means to explain principles of Orthodox faith or to establish closer interactions with their communities. However, as noted, they also addressed the concrete concerns of Byzantine communities and provided concrete information about attitudes or ideas for action intended for social and political change.[65] Even homilies on saints' feasts offered ethical and political advice based on descriptions of outstanding saintly figures. St Demetrios, the fourth-century warrior martyr and patron of Thessalonike, was a particularly honoured saint. Following other fourteenth-century Thessalonican authors, Symeon of Thessalonike dedicated several homilies to Demetrios. One of them stands as more than a homily, for Symeon writes a narrative report of the Byzantine conflict with the Ottomans that led to the fall of Thessalonike.[66] As he addressed the community of Thessalonike with its concerns for the threats of the Latins and the Turks, he also touched on serious issues of governance and ethics. His detailed report, framed by praise of St Demetrios and titled *Historical Oration* (Ἰστορικός λόγος), was also an indictment of the dissensions among Byzantines. Likewise, Bryennios addressed in many of his texts the concerns of the communities in Crete where he resided for a while. During the last decades of his life, he moved to Constantinople, where he participated in the court life.

Along with homilies, one finds a plethora of dogmatic and apologetic treatises written in the form of lectures or dialogues that were intended to clarify current religious debates.[67] In contrast to the homilies, such texts were produced mostly in Constantinopolitan circles. Many argued against tenets of Latin faith and Islam (Makarios of Ankara, Makres, Bryennios). They rejected the introduction of doctrinal innovations and preached a return to the theological principles of the Church Fathers. Heavily influenced by Palamism and hesychasm, the theological texts of this period maintained apologetic and polemical overtones. Perhaps the most extensive treatise of late Byzantine theology was Symeon's *Against all Heresies*, a text written in the form of a dialogue that deals not only with the presentation of heresies like polytheism, Judaism, Islam or Catholicism, but also with the Christian sacraments and

---

[65] On Isidore Glabas's and Gabriel's homilies see Beck, *Kirche und theologische Literatur*, 777–8. Beck notices Isidore's social views and mentions Isidore's influence on Gabriel. See Necipoğlu, *Byzantium*, 43.
[66] Symeon of Thessalonike, *Historical Oration on St Demetrios*, in *Politico-Historical Works*, 39–69, ed. Balfour.
[67] Such as Makarios's *Dialogue with the Pope*.

ecclesiology. Symeon relied on the traditional teachings of the Fathers and showed a polemical attitude towards deviations from Orthodox teachings and practices.[68]

This look at late Palaiologan ecclesiastical texts allows us to make two observations before proceeding to the analysis of the messages of the texts: first, all these texts with their embedded messages were generated in different contexts. Second, despite these differences, arguably, the authors' reliance on common themes, the predominance of homilies and treatises, and the adherence to conventions of spiritual guidance were underpinned by their similar concerns and by the use of a *pedagogical voice*, which sought to provide the local communities and the elites with a reminder of the common principles of Christian conduct. In the following, I will deal not only with how they intervened to address issues of appropriate conduct, of enemies and allies and of Byzantine identity, but also with how they expressed dissent on questions of imperial authority.

Moralisation and the social divide

The most manifest aspect of the ecclesiastics' texts was, unsurprisingly, their highly moralising character. While the number of moralising texts in this period is high, several examples of the ecclesiastics' values and attitude will suffice here. Often we see the ecclesiastics acting as teachers or *didaskaloi* of their communities. Joseph Bryennios, who undertook intense pastoral activity in Crete, for instance, addressed a didactic farewell letter to his flock in which he explained Orthodox teachings on the afterlife. In the same period, in Thessalonike, Isidore Glabas also chastised his flock for marrying impious spouses.[69] The causal relation between sin and political decline as well as social and political crises also accounted for frequent appeals for the amelioration of the people's mores and for the cultivation of doctrinal purity.[70] As a result, many late Byzantine homilies blamed individual sins, such as drunkenness (μέθη) or desperation (ἀπόγνωσις) generated by economic and social hardships.[71]

---

[68] PG 155: 140c; see Gospel of St John 10.1. Symeon is critical of philosophy in general. He thinks, for instance, that false Platonic doctrines are behind the heretical teachings of Origen (PG 155: 84d) and he criticises Epicurus's 'atheist doctrine', according to which everything came into being automatically (PG 155: 88a; see also ibid. 149b). Symeon also associated Platonic ideas with the heretical teachings of Barlaam (PG 155: 149a).

[69] On Bryennios's many works written during his sojourn in Crete see Bazini, 'Première édition des œuvres de Joseph Bryennios'.

[70] Krausmüller, 'Rise of hesychasm', 126.

[71] E.g. Gabriel, Metropolitan of Thessalonike, *Homilies*, nos. 1, 7, ed. Laourdas.

Authors increasingly made clear that they considered the low ethics and the manifold sins of their contemporaries as the main causes of the state's catastrophic situation.[72] In his sermon on the defeat of the Turks, Gabriel of Thessalonike stated that the problems of the Byzantines represented, in fact, divine trials for the people's sins:

> Whenever you see an archon of this world or a bishop, unworthy or knavish, do not be surprised and do not blame divine providence, but notice and believe that we have been deserted because of our lawlessness, and the man-loving righteous God left us sinners to our enemies not in order to be destroyed but in order to be disciplined (οὐκ εἰς ἀπώλειαν, ἀλλ' εἰς παιδείαν).[73]

The connection between contemporaries' wrongdoings and the reality of economic and social decline had a particular thrust in Joseph Bryennios's texts composed during his stay in Crete.[74] One of the most emphatic expressions of this view can be found in a chapter titled *On the Causes of Our Pains* (Τίνες αἰτίαι τῶν καθ' ἡμᾶς λυπηρῶν) and included in his more extensive hortatory composition, *Forty-Nine Chapters*, where he sets forth his views on religious and social causation.[75] Like so many other previous moralists, Bryennios complained that the morals of his times were far below those of the 'good old days', and for this reason, God had punished the Christians through the Turks.[76]

Within the same moralising framework, Bryennios deplored a series of novel irregularities in religious life on the island of Crete. He highlighted

---

[72] See Necipoğlu, *Byzantium*, 221.
[73] Gabriel, metropolitan of Thessalonike, *Homilies*, no. 6, ed. Laourdas, 82–92. See ibid. 119–20, where Gabriel reasons that sin is the cause of the Byzantines' troubles: διὰ ταῦτα, ἀδελφοί μου ἀγαπητοί, κἂν ἄρτι κατανοήσωμεν ἡμᾶς αὐτούς. γνῶμεν ὅτι διὰ τὰς ἁμαρτίας ἡμῶν παρεδόθημεν.
[74] On Bryennios's moralising discourse see Congourdeau, 'Procès d'avortement'; on the influence of Marcus Aurelius's Stoic ethics on Bryennios, see Rees, 'Joseph Bryennios and the text of Marcus Aurelius' *Meditations*'. See also Vryonnis, *Decline of Medieval Hellenism*, 419.
[75] This section of Bryennios's *Forty-Nine Moral Chapters* has been edited by Oeconomus, 'État intellectuel et moral'.
[76] Joseph Bryennios, *Forty-Nine Chapters*, in Παραλειπόμενα, 65, ed. Voulgares: 'If one who views the chastisements inflicted upon us by God is astonished and perplexed, let him consider not only these but our wickedness as well and then he will be amazed that we have not been struck by thunderbolts. For there is no form of evil which we do not anxiously pursue through all our life.' See also Symeon's *Historical Oration on St Demetrios*, where he reproves the Thessalonicans for their ungratefulness and moral corruption (in *Politico-Historical Works*, 47.1–38, ed. Balfour).

examples of sacrilege when church rituals were disregarded: some were baptised by single immersion, others by triple immersion; many Christians refused to make the sign of the Cross or simply did not know it.[77] For their part, priests were asking for cash payments in order to remit sins, perform ordinations and administer communion. Bryennios bitterly noted that there was no blasphemy which Christians did not employ.[78] Although his observations were circumscribed by his pastoral activity in Crete, they echo broader assessments about Byzantine society. Thus, in the same text, he noted that the general morality of the laity is not superior to that of the clergy:

> Not only men but the race of women also are not ashamed (οὐκ ἐπαισχύνονται) to sleep as naked as when they were born; to give over their immature daughters to corruption; to dress their wives in men's clothing; they are not ashamed to celebrate the holy days of the feasts with flutes, dances, all satanic songs, carousel, drunkenness, and other shameful customs.[79]

Yet, despite his general social criticism, Bryennios clearly allotted far more negative traits to the higher social echelons, both lay and clerical, which he considered responsible for the fact that the Byzantine state was disintegrating:

> Our rulers are unjust (ἄδικοι), those who oversee our affairs are rapacious, the judges accept gifts, the mediators are liars, the city dwellers are deceivers, the peasants are unintelligible, and all are useless. Our virgins are more shameless than prostitutes, the widows more curious than they ought to be, the married women disdain and keep no faith, the young men are licentious and the aged drunkards. The nuns have insulted their calling, the priests have forgotten God, the monks have strayed from the straight road. Many of us live in gluttony, drunkenness, fornication, adultery, foulness, licentiousness, hatred, rivalry, jealousy, envy, and theft. We have become arrogant, braggart, avaricious, selfish, ungrateful, disobedient, irreconcilable.[80]

In another homily, Isidore Glabas urged the elites of Thessalonike to show more solicitude for the common affairs of the city and, especially, to contribute

---

[77] Joseph Bryennios, *Forty-Nine Chapters*, in Παραλειπόμενα, 65, ed. Voulgares.
[78] Ibid. 120.
[79] Ibid.
[80] Ibid. (trans. in Vryonis, 'Byzantine attitudes').

to the city's defence.⁸¹ Another author, Symeon of Thessalonike, expressed similar views, particularly in his prayers.⁸² His liturgical texts are replete with references not only to the situation of the city, and indeed of the whole Byzantine world, but also to the need for moral reform. For instance, in a prayer, Symeon describes the judicial malpractices of judges, abuses committed by the *archontes* and money-lenders, and the social atmosphere of hatred and strife, which eventually lead him to conclude that the Byzantines have become 'the slaves of impious and cursed peoples'.⁸³

This moralising approach, which went back to the early fourteenth century⁸⁴ and mainly targeted the *archontes*, gave way to further reflection over an issue that affected Byzantine society before the Fall of Constantinople, namely the social divide between the poor and the rich, a phenomenon which threatened the already fragile stability of Byzantium.⁸⁵ Many church writers highlighted the accelerated impoverishment of a large part of the population. Frequently, within this moralising framework, the clergymen adopted a position against the richer families who showed off their possessions. Already by the middle of the fourteenth century, Gregory Palamas urged those 'who love money and injustice' to practise equity and temperance.⁸⁶ Palamas's successors in Thessalonike, Isidore Glabas and Symeon of Thessalonike, continued to complain about the injustices and offences which the more well-off individuals committed, such as the breaking of laws. At the same time, these ecclesiastics pointed to the conflicts between the powerful rulers and their

---

⁸¹ See Isidore Glabas's requests to the *archontes* to take care of the common good of the communities; *Homilies for St Demetrius*, 5.65, ed. Laourdas: διὰ ταῦτα λοιπόν, ἀδελφοί, ὅσοι τῶν τῆς πολιτείας προΐστασθε πραγμάτων, δέος ἅπαν τῆς ψυχῆς ἐκβαλόντες καὶ ὅ, τι ἄλλο τῶν ἀηδῶν, προθύμως ἀντέχεσθε τῶν κοινῶν, ἀκίβδηλον ποιούμενοι τὴν τῆς φροντίδος ταύτης διακονίαν.
⁸² Phountoules, *Λειτουργικὸν ἔργον*, 23.
⁸³ Symeon of Thessalonike, *Liturgical Writings*, 54, ed. Phountoules. See ibid. 39, 19–26, on the horrors of Turkish slavery. In particular Symeon seems harsher with the *archontes*, whom he accuses of accumulating richness in excess: καὶ ἄρχοντες μὲν καταπαταλῶσι, θησαυρίζουσί τε καὶ ὑπεραίρονται κατὰ τῶν ὑπὸ χεῖρα, πᾶν ἀδικίας ἔργον ἀνέδην διαπραττόμενοι (in *Politico-Historical Works*, 47.9–11, ed. Balfour). Then he addresses the issue of the attitude of the poor people of the city: πτωχοὶ δὲ πάλιν τὸ ἄρχον μιμούμενοι κατ' ἀλλήλων ὁπλίζονται (47.13–17).
⁸⁴ Philippidis-Braat, 'Captivité de Palamas', 164.
⁸⁵ Earlier in the fourteenth century, John Charsianites, the founder of the eponymous monastery, expressed his rather negative opinion of the wealthy. He was said to have believed that 'wealth is a cause for spiritual destruction for those who do not divert it to needful purposes'; see Talbot, 'Charsianites', in Constantinides-Hero (ed.) *Byzantine Monastic Foundation Documents*, 1625.
⁸⁶ Necipoğlu, *Byzantium*, 42.

powerless subjects.⁸⁷ The frequency of such assertions in the early fifteenth century, despite their typical exaggerations, can be correlated with the intensified Ottoman attacks which, during this period, produced trade opportunities for certain groups of people who took advantage of the circumstances. Therefore ecclesiastics like Isidore Glabas and Symeon of Thessalonike reacted to the new socio-political conditions that characterised the internal divisions of Thessalonican society; these conditions were considered the major cause for the city's failure to defend itself against the enemy.

A connected theme – the antagonism between the need to ensure the proper defence of the city and the private interests of a small group of individuals with commercial relations with the Latins – emerged in Joseph Bryennios's deliberative *Oration on the Reconstruction of the Walls of Constantinople*, written during his residence at the Byzantine court.⁸⁸ Bryennios reminded his audience that unless they gave priority to the common good and contributed financially to the restoration of the defensive walls, their personal prosperity, reflected in the lavish mansions of the richn would cause the city's collapse.⁸⁹ The divide between rich and poor also came to be noted by Symeon of Thessalonike in several homilies addressed to the Thessalonians. In a long passage, after blaming the wrongdoings and ingratitude of the citizens towards God, Symeon concluded:

> The archontes live wantonly, hoard their wealth, and exalt themselves above the ones under their authority, freely performing injustices, not only offering nothing to God but also stealing away from God. They believe this to be their power (ἀρχή), and they consider the poor citizens and their subordinates as scarcely human. But the poor, too, imitating those in authority arm themselves against each other and live rapaciously and greedily, and they are ungrateful to God and disdain the divine churches, the hymns, and the prayers.⁹⁰

Defending Byzantium: enemies and allies

Fifteenth-century Byzantine ecclesiastics were preoccupied not only with the ethical standards and social welfare of their flocks but also with the ways in which the state could maintain its autonomy while threatened by the growing

---

⁸⁷ See Isidore Glabas, *Homilies*, nos. 19, 21, 22, ed. Christophorides, 299–300, 329–30, 344–7; Isidore Glabas, *Two Unedited Homilies*, nos. 31, 85–95, ed. Tsirpanlis; Symeon of Thessalonike, *Liturgical Writings*, 16, 22, ed. Phountoules.
⁸⁸ Joseph Bryennios, *Oration on the Reconstruction*, 11, ed. Thomadakes.
⁸⁹ Ibid. 12.
⁹⁰ Symeon of Thessalonike, *Historical Oration on St Demetrios*, in *Politico-Historical Works*, 47, 9–20, ed. Balfour (trans. in Necipoğlu, *Byzantium*).

influence of the Ottomans and the Latins' economic interests. In one of his homilies, Bryennios bitterly noted the Byzantines' hopeless circumstances in both state and ecclesiastical affairs:

> We have been scattered (διεσκορπίσθημεν) through all the kingdoms on the face of the earth, other peoples rule us, we do not rule, and the foreigners devour our country before our eyes, and the country was deserted and subdued, and there is no one to help. [. . .] The Muslims are chasing us, the Tatars inflict indignities upon us, the Ishmaelites gather from the West, and the Turks spread out from the East. We ran away from the dragon and found the Basilisk.[91]

Authors often understood the threats against the state as threats against the church itself.[92] On many occasions, the clergymen voiced their concerns vis-à-vis the attempts of the political authority to forge alliances with its neighbours. Despite the virulence of the attacks against the Ottomans, often dubbed 'the impious people' (οἱ ἀσεβεῖς καὶ οἱ ἄθεοι), Necipoğlu has recently unveiled a whole range of nuances in the positions the ecclesiastics adopted with regard to the foreigners: anti-Latin, anti-Ottoman, pro-Latin and pro-Ottoman.[93] Sometimes the ecclesiastics changed their position to a stricter or a more lenient one. Isidore Glabas, once an opponent of Ottoman and Latin interests, witnessed the subjection of Thessalonike to Ottoman domination and, in the end, advocated a more flexible attitude towards the Turks. Likewise, Symeon of Thessalonike, a fierce opponent of both the Ottomans and the Latins, eventually came to accept the city's transfer to Venetian rule as an act that prevented its betrayal to the Ottomans.[94]

More frequently the ecclesiastics formulated plain opinions vis-à-vis the Latins or the Ottomans. To a certain extent, the oft-quoted statement falsely attributed to Lukas Notaras, that 'the turban of the Turk was better than the kalyptra (head cover) of the Latin', echoed early fifteenth-century opinions among the group of stricter Orthodox who regarded the renunciation of their doctrinal foundations as unacceptable.[95] Yet in many cases, the predominant attitude towards the Ottomans remained deeply negative. Prayers for the delivery of Constantinople from the enemy abounded. Symeon wrote a

---

[91] Joseph Bryennios, Third Oration on the Crucifixion, in Εὑρεθέντα, 2.247–8, ed. Voulgares.
[92] For a detailed investigation of the difficulties encountered by clerics in the provinces occupied by the Ottomans in Asia Minor and in Europe, see Papademetriou, 'Turkish conquests'. Cf. Vryonis, Decline of Medieval Hellenism, 302.
[93] Necipoğlu, Byzantium, 4.
[94] Dennis, 'Late Byzantine metropolitans'.
[95] Reinsch, 'Lieber den Turban als was?'

series of four model prayers to be used not only in situations of extreme necessity such as drought but also during the enemies' destructive raids (ἐπὶ ἐθνῶν ἐπιδρομῇ).⁹⁶ Apart from prayers, other ecclesiastical authors wrote about the Ottoman incursions. In a series of four *Orations* addressed to those offended by the success of the 'impious ones' (i.e. the Ottomans), Makarios Makres argued vehemently against Islamic customs:

> What else can be said about their unlawful and barbaric law and about the multiple sacrileges and nonsense and rumours? What else about their wonderful and kind prophet, and legislator and saviour, as they say?⁹⁷

In their attacks against the Ottomans, these authors focused on religious differences and on the Ottomans' customs, which they presented as savage and discussed in several polemical texts and dialogues on Islam.⁹⁸ Sometimes, these polemics also touched on political aspects like the forced conversions of Christian youth. Already in the fourteenth century the Latin translation of the Qu'ran, the *Improbatio Alcorani* by the Dominican friar Ricaldo da Monte Croce (d. 1320), provided Byzantine polemicists with a fresh arsenal of doctrinal details and arguments. By the mid-fourteenth century, Emperor John VI Kantakouzenos produced a text of religious polemics against Islam. Later on, towards the end of the fourteenth century, just like the emperor Manuel II, Joseph Bryennios, Isidore Glabas and Makarios Makres composed fictitious doctrinal dialogues with Muslims.⁹⁹ The polemics with Islam were concerned with the veracity of the revelations in the Qu'ran and in the Bible. At the same time, these polemics included arguments concerning the doctrine, ethical commands and ritual practices of both religions, thereby indicating an

---

[96] Symeon of Thessalonike, no. 9, *On Earthquakes and Invasions* (Εὐχὴ ἐξομολογήσεως καὶ αἰτήσεως λεγομένη ἐπὶ σεισμῷ καὶ αὐχμῷ καὶ ἐθνῶν ἐπιδρομῇ, 23–5); no. 10, *On Attacks of the Enemies* (Εὐχὴ εἰς ἐπιδρομὴν ἐθνῶν καὶ εἰς πᾶσαν αἴτησιν, 38–41); no. 24, *Against Foreign Warriors* (Εὐχὴ κατὰ ἐθνικῶν πολεμίων, 58–61); all in *Liturgical Writings*, ed. Phountoules.

[97] Makarios Makres, *Four Orations for Those Offended by the Success of the Infidels*, in *Macaire Makrès et la polemique*, I.5, ed. Argyriou.

[98] The polemic between Christian priests and Muslims appears especially from the synodal documents of the fifteenth century. Matthew, metropolitan of Ephesus, complained that his religious debates with the Muslims of Ephesus provoked the hostility of the Turks. Matthew of Epheseus, *Letters*, no. 54, ed. Treu: 'We freely declare that all their religious beliefs are of use only to the eternal fire and worm. Seeing these things, the accursed ones always cry out, giving way to their desire to taste flesh and blood, and they would not have abstained if they had not seen that their chieftain was not at all permissive to their madness, not easily joining the assault (trans. Vryonis, *Decline of Medieval Hellenism*, 425).

[99] For example, Joseph Bryennios, *Conversation with an Ishmaelite*, 158–95, ed. Argyriou.

attempt to establish intellectual contact and a way of communication with the Muslims.[100]

Unsurprisingly, the gradual Ottoman conquest of Byzantine territories also occupied a significant place. Isidore Glabas, who had been involved in the political negotiations with the Ottomans in Thessalonike, wrote several homilies describing the kidnapping of Christian children by the Ottomans, in which he incorporated a great many statements slandering Islam on political grounds. In an oration addressed to those 'offended by the success of the infidels', Makarios Makres spoke about the wrongdoings of the Muslims and about their prophet's falsity.[101] Still, other texts which focused on doctrinal issues indicate that, beyond the standard arguments and slanders repeated on other occasions, in the opinion of the supporters of Orthodoxy, the Ottomans deserved admiration and respect on account of their religion. As a matter of fact, the same Isidore Glabas, despite his opposition to Ottoman authority in Thessalonike, eventually admitted the benefits of the peaceful Turkish rule of the city. Even Bryennios in his *Conversation with an Ishmaelite* showed awareness of the Byzantines' decline and questioned their capacity to defend themselves, thereby acknowledging Ottoman military superiority.[102]

If it was easier to reject an alliance with the Ottomans, on the basis of the differences of religion, the approach to the presence of the Latins at the gates of Constantinople posed further difficulties. Due to religious similarities and to the fact that the Latins were the only force which could provide defensive means against the Ottomans, Byzantine clerics were forced to restrain their attacks and put forward a discourse based on religious differences. Although a group of pro-union and pro-Latin clerics seems to have been promoted by Emperor Manuel II once the moderate Patriarch Joseph II was installed in a position previously occupied by strict Orthodox ecclesiastics, this group did not succeed in influencing decisions during Manuel's reign.[103] Thus, the pro-unionists failed to convince the other, stricter ecclesiastics of the necessity to intensify the negotiations for church union. This failure was even more notable because it happened at a time when the newly installed Pope Martin V, after the end of the Western Schism, showed himself more favourable to a solution of the schism than his predecessors.[104]

---

[100] Trapp, 'Quelques textes'.
[101] Makarios Makres, *Four Orations for Those Offended by the Success of the Infidels*, in *Macaire Makrès et la polemique*, I.6–7, ed. Argyriou.
[102] Joseph Bryennios, *Conversation with an Ishmaelite*, ed. Argyriou, 159.
[103] In his *Dialogue with the Pope* Makarios alluded to Manuel's treatise *On the Procession of the Holy Spirit* when commenting that the negotiations with the Latins failed. Makarios Makres, *Dialogue with the Pope*, in Μακαρίου τοῦ Μακρῆ συγγράμματα, 237, ed. Argyriou.
[104] Patacsi, 'Joseph Bryennios', 73–94.

On the contrary, after 1415, and particularly around 1422 when these negotiations intensified, authors like Joseph Bryennios or Symeon of Thessalonike became increasingly defensive with regard to the Orthodox doctrine. In his *Historical Oration on St Demetrios*, Symeon of Thessalonike underscored the connection between the Byzantines' misfortunes during the siege of 1422 and the previous alliance with the Latins effected through the marriage of the emperor's successor, John VIII, to an Italian woman (Sophia of Montferrat).[105] In addition to these allegations, Symeon criticised the Latins' religious art and accused them of representing the saints in an irreverent manner.[106] Likewise, Joseph Bryennios's political-religious position against union with the Latins was seemingly very influential. Eventually, his arguments prevailed as the negotiations with Rome were discontinued before Manuel's death. Bryennios composed several lengthy orations in which he combined political and doctrinal issues such as the use of leavened bread in the liturgy or the procession of the Holy Spirit. One of them, an *Admonitory Oration on the Union of the Churches*, was delivered in 1422 at the debut of the negotiations for a church union after another Ottoman siege of the city.[107] Bryennios, a leading court polemicist, made it clear that a union could not ensure sufficient military support from the Latins.[108] While he admitted the importance of the connections between Byzantines and Latins, his main criticism of the project of church union concerned the planned submission of the Byzantine Orthodox church to the pope.[109]

It appears, therefore, that the doctrinal question of the *filioque*, debated among theologians in polemical works and at the Council of Ferrara-Florence (1438–9), partially masked the underlying hostility between Greeks and Latins. Bryennios's inflexibility about the union nevertheless became predominant among the Byzantine theologians of the last decades of Byzantium. Several decades later, John Eugenikos, an adversary of the union, wrote a

---

[105] Symeon of Thessalonike, *Historical Oration on St Demetrios*, in *Politico-Historical Works*, 53, ed. Balfour.

[106] Symeon of Thessalonike, *Against Heresies*, PG 155, 112 a–b: 'What other innovations have they [the Latins] introduced contrary to the tradition of the church?' (τί δὲ καὶ ἄλλο αὐτοῖς παρὰ τὴν ἐκκλησιαστικὴν ἐκαινοτομήθη παράδοσιν).

[107] Joseph Bryennios, *Admonitory Oration on the Union of the Churches*, in Εὑρεθέντα, 2. 469–99, ed. Voulgares. The alliance with the Latins was discussed especially in the first part of the discourse (472–8) while doctrinal issues are addressed in the second part (479–99).

[108] Kalogeras, *Μάρκος ὁ Εὐγενικὸς καὶ Βησσαρίων ὁ Καρδινάλις*, 70.

[109] Bryennios speaks about a refusal to address the pope as holy (ἅγιος) during the liturgy. See Joseph Bryennios, *Admonitory Oration on the Union of the Churches*, in Εὑρεθέντα, 2. 473, ed. Voulgares.

treatise in which he specifically addressed Emperor Constantine XI as if from the Orthodox community.[110]

Markers of Byzantine identity

The ecclesiastics' concern for the growing influence of the Ottomans and Latins in the Byzantine realm further shaped the claims of Byzantine individuality.[111] Faced with the danger of state dissolution and with visible territorial losses, Byzantine authors began to emphasise the distinguishing features of Byzantine identity, like cultural heritage and faith. By and large, in their definitions, late Byzantine ecclesiastics introduced a limited set of themes and older beliefs which crystallised into a new combination expressing the churchmen's political outlook. On the one hand, they continued to use the term 'Rhomaioi' when referring to themselves. The texts of Joseph Bryennios, Makarios Makres and Sylvester Syropoulos include occasional references to the Byzantines' Romanness.[112] On the other hand, in opposition to the Ottomans and to the Latins, Italians or Franks, whom they often regarded as barbaric, the same authors identified themselves as Hellenes.[113] For Bryennios, as for other Palaiologan authors, all Hellenes, despite severe decline and defeats, remained Orthodox in faith, 'the most pious race of all and the most devoted to God' (τὸ εὐσεβέστατον γένος πάντων καὶ τῷ Θεῷ τὰ μάλιστα προσανέχον.)[114] For Mark Eugenikos, the Byzantines were the 'sacred race' (ἅγιον ἔθνος) and the 'chosen people' (λαὸν ἐκλεκτόν).[115]

These writers stressed the continuity between the problematic present and the Hellenic past and often identified themselves as Hellenes. Yet, unlike the previous authors, the early fifteenth-century ecclesiastics appear more interested in emphasising Hellenic features not just for their cultural value but, most of all, for the underlying ideological belief in the church's mission to

---

[110] John Eugenikos, *Against the Union*, PP 4, 151–3, ed Lampros: ὡς ἀπὸ τῆς κοινότητος τῶν ὀρθοδόξων.

[111] Bryennios recognised the existence of a multitude of nations and races (ἔθνος, γένος); Joseph Bryennios, *Admonitory Oration on the Union of the Churches*, in Εὑρεθέντα, 2.477, ed. Voulgares.

[112] Bryennios also emphasised Roman ancestry, ὑμεῖς ἐστε μόνοι τῶν Ῥωμαίων τὸ ἄνθος, οἱ τῆς πρεσβυτέρας Ῥώμης ἀπόγονοι, καὶ τῆς νέας ταύτης [Κωνσταντινουπόλεως] υἱοί, *Hortatory Oration*, in Εὑρεθέντα, 2, 604–6, ed. Voulgares.

[113] According to Bryennios, the Ἰταλοί are Franks living in Italy. The Λατῖνοι are the ancient Romans. Ibid.

[114] Joseph Bryennios, *Homilies*, in Παραλειπόμενα, 18, ed. Voulgares.

[115] Mark Eugenikos, *Prayer for the Emperor*, PP 4, 31, ed. Lampros.

maintain the unity of Orthodoxy as well as of the Byzantines. Often, Bryennios contended that, in such times of distress, the church remained the only institution with the appropriate means to maintain the unity of the Hellenes against the attempts of the political elites to push for church union. Moreover, Orthodoxy was conceived as the common denominator of the many different surrounding peoples which other lay authors perceived as barbaric. In his *Admonitory Oration* Bryennios enumerates the list of all the Orthodox peoples who, unlike the Latins, used leavened bread in their church services:

> Even to this day, the Romans, the Melchians, the Syrians, the Ethiopians, the Alans, the Abasgians and Iberians, Colchidians, Russians, Goths, Dacians, Paeonians, Mysians, Triballians and very many other peoples (γένη), which live in various places and differ in customs and language, offer to the God of all the sacrifice by leavened bread, not because they previously used unleavened bread and afterward changed to leavened bread, but because the leavened bread has been introduced to them in the divine service.[116]

On the contrary, according to Bryennios, the negotiations for a church union with the Latins could not provide actual union of the churches but could only generate division of the Byzantines into separate factions and the 'Latinisation' of the Greeks.[117] In another oration he added that the differences of faith and ethnicity between the Latins and the Byzantines would bring further damage.[118] It thus appears that Bryennios envisaged the Byzantine church as a core aspect of Byzantine unity. Eventually, proceeding from his discussion of ethnicity, he preached the unity of the church by a return to the old teachings:

> How shall we bear the change of faith (μετάθεσις πίστεως)? And these [troubles] after we escaped so many dangers and suffered such terrible things? We have been stripped of all goods in this world for our true faith: cities, provinces, lands, vineyards, honours, and we have been blamed by all other peoples, and now shall we stand aloof? In no way, Lord, will you allow this to happen. But take to yourself from here all those who live in Orthodoxy, those who are the sons of true-believing fathers.[119]

---

[116] Joseph Bryennios, *Admonitory Oration on the Union of the Churches*, in Εὑρεθέντα, 2.486, ed. Voulgares.

[117] Joseph Bryennios, *On the Union of the Cypriots*, in Εὑρεθέντα, 2.13–14, ed. Voulgares: ἢ λατινίσαι τοὺς πάντας, ἢ εἰς μυρία σχίσματα μερισθῆναι τὸ ἡμέτερον γένος.

[118] Ibid. 2.14: καὶ ἁπλῶς οὐδὲν ἔσται τὰ τῆς ἑνώσεως, εἰ μὴ ἀπάτη πρότερον ἡμετέρα, καὶ ὕστερον τῶν Κυπρίων πρὸς ἡμᾶς ἐπικαύχησις, καὶ τοῦ κοινοῦ γένους ὄνειδος. See τὸ ἡμέτερον γένος ἀφανισμῷ παραδίδοται, *On the Joint Contribution*, in Παραλειπόμενα, 244, ed. Voulgares.

[119] See Thomadakes, Σύλλαβος Βυζαντινῶν μελετῶν, 609.

When evoking such claims in favour of the church's increased role in shaping Byzantine identity, Bryennios certainly spoke from the experience he gained during the period he spent in Crete and Cyprus, two territories under Latin jurisdiction.[120] There as well as in other Latin-held territories, like the Aegean islands, Byzantine Orthodoxy was constantly challenged. For this reason, in the eyes of many ecclesiastics, Orthodoxy increasingly became a core element that was assimilated into their self-identification as Byzantines. Finally, it should also be noted that, in stressing the centrality of Orthodoxy, late Byzantine ecclesiastics continued a process that started after 1204, for, with the Fall of Constantinople, the struggle against the Latins gave the church renewed popular approval and support.[121]

Imperial authority

One of the most important elements in the ecclesiastics' discourse was the approach to imperial authority. As noted above, if some ecclesiastics appreciated the emperor's intellectual profile, others contested his involvement in the ecclesiastical realm. In the first category can be included several of his closest collaborators: the theologian Nicholas Kabasilas Chamaetos, Patriarch Matthew I, Makarios Makres and Joseph Bryennios.[122] In his testament, Matthew showed his high regard for the support Emperor Manuel awarded to the monastery of Charsianites.[123] Makres, much appreciated by Emperor Manuel for his ascetic profile, wrote an *epitaphios* at the emperor's death and dedicated to him another short poem in which he praised the emperor's intellectual and diplomatic skills.[124] In the funeral oration, Makarios included both conventional and personal elements of praise. He compared Manuel with an 'Aphrodite of

---

[120] On Bryennios's activities in Crete and in Cyprus see ibid. 509–17.

[121] Angelov, *Church and Society in Late Byzantium*, 1.

[122] On their collaboration with the emperor in literary matters, see above.

[123] 'I also petitioned on their behalf the holy emperor, who with great kindness granted this concession, referring the favour to my Virgin, that the imperial treasury would collect only three hyperpera annually on every hundred-measure of wine produced at the dependency, and, of the two zeugaria of land which we own, that one zeugarion should be maintained in perpetuity completely exempt and not liable for the customary tithe of the crops harvested, and that absolutely all our land should be free of tax, just as we had it previously' (trans. in Constanides-Hero, *Byzantine Monastic Foundation Documents*, 1659).

[124] Makarios Makres, *Funeral Oration for Emperor Manuel*, ed. Sideras, 38, praises the emperor's qualities and nobility: ἀγωνοθέτης καὶ βραβευτὴς οὐχ ἧττον δὲ καὶ πατὴρ καὶ μήτηρ καὶ ἀδελφός, εἰ βούλει, καὶ παῖς καὶ τῶν ἐξ αἵματος πάντων ὁ γνησιώτατός τε καὶ οἰκειότατος, ὑπὲρ ὧν ἀφαιρεθέντων ἀθρόον δέον πενθεῖν. The *epitaphios* further praises the emperor for his leadership and intellectual virtues. On the poem see Makarios Makres, *Life*, 254, ed. Kapetanaki.

rhetoricians and writers' and noted the emperor's intellectual merits in cultivating the Attic language, philosophy, knowledge, reason and literature.[125]

For his part, Joseph Bryennios addressed the emperor in a letter from Crete and in a funeral oration in the standard encomiastic terms of the panegyrists,[126] while Isidore Glabas stated the importance of submitting to the emperor in a letter addressed to the Thessalonicans.[127] Apart from the texts of these two writers we find appreciation of the emperor even in some of the texts of ecclesiastics who later voiced their discontent with his actions. In an early treatise titled *Against the Latins*, probably written during Manuel's visit to Paris in 1400, Makarios of Ankara made a convincing exposition of traditional ideas of imperial priesthood.[128] At that moment, Makarios took a stand in favour of the idea that the emperor was entitled to preside over a unionist church council which would bring the schism to an end.[129] He attributed to the emperor the titles of both *dephensōr ekklēsias* and *epistēmonarchēs*, titles which denoted the power of the emperor to summon and participate in church councils.[130] The epithet *epistēmonarchēs* had particular connotations. If initially this title referred to a disciplinarian officer in monasteries and was conferred by the church on the emperor,[131] during the reign of Manuel Komnenos it came to signify the imperial sanctity which derived from unction.[132] Thus, already in the Komnenian period, the title of *epistēmonarchēs* reflected the emperor's way of showing his superiority over the church.[133] Later, Michael VIII Palaiologos also made use of this title in his disputes with the church.[134]

Another author, Symeon of Thessalonike, who later contested imperial authority, did not deny the fact that the emperor's anointment entitled him to be designated as 'holy' (ἅγιος).[135] Nevertheless, Symeon maintained that this kind of holiness conferred on the emperor only the special right to enter

---

[125] Makarios Makres, *Funeral Oration for Emperor Manuel*, ed. Sideras, 38.
[126] Joseph Bryennios, *Letters*, no. 12, ed. Thomadakes, addressed to the emperor, indicates a longer exchange of letters and praises his wisdom and defence of church doctrine.
[127] Isidore Glabas, *Letters*, no. 7, ed. Lampros.
[128] This appears to have been inspired by the pro-imperial texts of the previous famous Byzantine canonists Theodore Balsamon and Demetrios Chomatenos; see Demetrios Chomatenos, Πονήματα διάφορα, 106.271–2, ed. Prinzing.
[129] Makarios of Ankara, *Against the Latins*, 1–205, ed. Dositheos.
[130] Ibid. 194–5.
[131] See Darrouzès, *Recherches*, 323.
[132] Dagron, *Emperor and Priest*, 254.
[133] Magdalino, *Empire of Manuel I Komnenos*, 286–7.
[134] Dagron, *Emperor and Priest*, 254.
[135] Symeon of Thessalonike, *Explanation on the Divine Temple*, PG 155, 353.

the sanctuary of the church on the day of his coronation.[136] Such examples indicate that good relations with the emperor did not always represent a precondition for a favourable attitude towards the emperor's rights in the church. Even Patriarch Euthymios II, who shared the ruler's literary preoccupations,[137] opposed him vigorously in the affair of the nomination of the metropolitan of Moldavia. To this list of positive attitudes towards the emperor should be added that some ecclesiastics had a positive attitude towards Manuel's nephew, John VII, during his rule in Thessalonike. The positive references in the *Synodikon of Orthodoxy*, Symeon of Thessalonike's homily on St Demetrios, or John Eugenikos's advice to Constantine XI to follow his father's model of action in ecclesiastical matters point to Manuel's administrative skills and devotion to the cause of the church.[138]

Despite the favourable attitude of a part of the clergy towards the emperor, as expressed at various moments during his reign, the main tendency of ecclesiastical writers was to emphasise their hierocratic claims and to minimise the significance of imperial authority. Already in the early fourteenth century Theoleptos, the metropolitan of Philadelphia, defied Emperor Andronikos II's orders, stating that it was not an emperor's prerogative to discipline a priest.[139] As for the later periods, I have already noted that the ecclesiastics' attitude towards the lifestyle of the *archontes*, especially after the end of the Ottoman siege in 1402, was far from favourable. Joseph Bryennios expressed this general criticism of the lay political authority when he noted that 'the rulers (*archontes*) are unjust, those who oversee our affairs are rapacious, and the judges accept gifts'.[140] Many ecclesiastics during Manuel's reign thus opted for a different position on the issue of the pre-eminence of the church over the emperor.[141]

---

[136] Ibid. 155, 352c–d. See *On Ordinations*, ibid. 432a–b.
[137] See above.
[138] John Eugenikos, 'Oration to Constantine', PP 3, 130.21, ed. Lampros: καὶ ἐξ' ἐκείνου μέχρι πρώην τοῦ σοῦ ἁγίου πατρός, τοῦ μακαριωτάτου καὶ ἀοιδίμου βασιλέως ἡμῶν, κατὰ διαδοχὴν ὥσπερ τις πατρῷος κλῆρος ὁ πρὸς τὴν εὐσέβειαν ζῆλος καὶ τὸ τῆς πίστεως ἀκραιφνὲς παρεπέμφθη.
[139] See *Life and Letters of Theoleptos of Philadelphia* ed. Constantinides Hero, 17.
[140] Joseph Bryennios, *Forty-Nine Chapters*, in Παραλειπόμενα, 122, ed. Voulgares.
[141] In the fourteenth century, Patriarch Athanasios took a more temperate position. He refused the extreme view according to which the patriarch was the emperor's superior and did not question the emperor's sacerdotal charisma. For Patriarch Athanasios the ruler continued to exercise a divine ministry. Yet Athanasios constantly reminded the emperor of the idea of the liberty of the church. See Angelov, *Imperial Ideology*, 393–410.

Hierocratic views of imperial power

If already in 1393, Patriarch Anthony IV suggested that the spiritual power of Byzantium had become more significant than the secular one,[142] the first document disputing Manuel's authority is a notice about the position of the metropolitans of Nikomedeia and Corinth. In a letter from 1396, they demanded from the emperor further explanations and an official response for his actions when he intervened in a synod in order to impose his decision in a certain matter.[143] Although it represented only a short notice, this document echoed the church's claims to autonomy of decision and freedom from secular power, as well as its claims to universalism. In the early decades of the fifteenth century, such claims came to be expressed especially in treatises that dealt with the appointment of bishops and with the political theology of imperial unction. Building on previous insights into late Byzantine hierocratic political thought,[144] I will look more closely at texts by two authors. The first is Makarios of Ankara's polemical treatise occasioned by the debate over the canonicity of Patriarch Matthew I's appointment, provocatively titled *A Partial Exposition that the Emperor Should Abide By and Observe the Canonical Ordinances and Should Respect and Defend the Canons* (Ἐκλογὴ μερικὴ περὶ τοῦ ὅτι ὀφείλει ὁ βασιλεὺς στοιχεῖν καὶ ἐμμένειν τοῖς κανονικῶς ὁρισθεῖσι, στέργειν τε καὶ δεφενδεύειν τοὺς κανόνας).[145] The treatise was included in his collection of polemical texts occasioned by the controversy over the installation and deposition of Matthew I as patriarch, a move in which Manuel II had a direct part.[146] Symeon of Thessalonike's orations, letters and liturgical treatises will also serve my purpose here. He was the author of a 'handbook' of Orthodox faith and practice, titled *The Dialogue in Christ*, dealing with a range of subjects such as church rites, heresies and the theology of prayer.[147] Of particular interest here are the sections *On the Sacred Church* (Περὶ τοῦ θείου ναοῦ)[148] and *On Ordinations* (Περὶ τῶν ἱερῶν χειροτονιῶν),[149] where Symeon gave a comprehensive account of Byzantine ecclesiastical usage. In these two texts, he not only described church ritual but also explained its meanings and frequently criticised other, rival interpretations. Apart from the

---

[142] Darrouzès, *Regestes*, no. 2931, 6.210–11.
[143] Miklosich and Müller, *Acta et Diplomata*, 2.271–2.
[144] Dagron, *Emperor and Priest*; Angold, *Church and Society in Byzantium*; Angelov, *Imperial Ideology*.
[145] Paris. gr. 1379 (f. 98v–148r).
[146] Laurent, 'Trisépiscopat', 25–7. On imperial power and the appointment of bishops in Makarios of Ankara's view see also ibid. 89–93.
[147] On Symeon see Phountoules, Λειτουργικὸν ἔργον.
[148] PG 155, 305–61.
[149] Ibid. 361–469.

liturgical treatises, the letters he addressed to Andronikos, despot of Thessalonike, also constitute important documents of the ecclesiastics' view on imperial power.[150]

Both authors, Makarios and Symeon, were very popular in their day. Makarios played the role of a champion of church interests in the face of imperial power, as his views were supported by a large number of bishops and necessitated no fewer than five synods in order to be completely refuted.[151] In particular, Symeon's texts enjoyed a very wide readership. The editor of Symeon's liturgical works, Ioannes Phountoules, lists more than a hundred manuscripts of the two texts dealing with the rituals which involved the emperor and the patriarch, *On the Sacred Church* and *On Ordinations*.[152] Furthermore, the popularity of his ideas is illustrated by a sixteenth-century Greek vernacular text describing the emperor's coronation, which bears traces of the influence of Symeon's account.[153]

Doubtless, Makarios's and Symeon's ideas were not new, since both authors grounded their claims in previous allegations recorded in texts dating from the thirteenth and fourteenth centuries. The anonymous *Life of Patriarch Arsenios*, written by an Arsenite monk at the end of the fourteenth century, stated that the patriarch did not depend on the emperor for his election and that, in fact, the patriarch was higher in rank than the emperor.[154] Arsenios's biographer highlighted the idea of the grace of God granted by the patriarch to the emperor. According to him, Emperor Theodore II Laskaris was obedient to the church and this was so because:

> The head of the church is Christ, of whom the patriarch bears the imprint, and, since he anoints with imperial oil the emperors, he would reasonably have them [the emperors] as his subordinates who yield to his will. For he who anoints is greater (μεῖζόν ἐστι) than the anointed, in the same way that the one who sanctifies is greater than the sanctified. It is by all means necessary that the emperor who is sanctified and anointed by the patriarch, because he [the emperor] lacks this grace, should obey like a servant the church, and its leader.[155]

---

[150] Symeon of Thessalonike, *Hortatory Letter for Despot Andronikos*, in *Politico-Historical Works*, 77–82, ed. Balfour.

[151] Dennis, 'Deposition and restoration'.

[152] Phountoules, Λειτουργικὸν ἔργον, 17–19. Most of the manuscripts dating from the fifteenth century have been preserved in the monastic libraries of Mount Athos.

[153] See Schreiner, 'Volkssprachlicher Text', 55.

[154] Anonymous, *Life of Arsenios*, 460.331–461.343, ed. Nikolopoulos. See Angelov, *Imperial Ideology*, 386.

[155] Ibid. See also Macrides, 'Saints and sainthood', 78.

This attitude to imperial authority persisted in the following decades for, around 1430s, Theodore Agallianos (1400–74) wrote another encomium for Arsenios where he listed the arguments on the superiority of the patriarchal position and of the church in general over the imperial office.[156] Drawing on a similar idea, other contemporary strong-minded ecclesiastics used the document known as the Donation of Constantine, a forged Roman imperial decree in which the emperor Constantine I supposedly transferred authority over Rome and parts of the Western Empire to the pope. Among other things, the Donation supported the ideological status of the patriarch of Constantinople. This document served the claims to authority of fourteenth- and fifteenth-century Byzantine ecclesiastics, such as Patriarch Athanasios (1289–93, 1303–9), who considered Pope Sylvester as a model to imitate and regarded the alleged submission of Constantine to the pope as a political matrix for the relationship between the emperor and the patriarch.[157] Following this tendency, in the early fifteenth century, Symeon of Thessalonike used the Donation in his description of the ecclesiastical ritual of the election of the patriarch when he gave an account of an electoral practice similar to the traditional one.[158] At the same time, he reinforced the idea of the emperor's submission to the patriarch's power by adding new elements to the ceremony of imperial coronation. The emperor chose the patriarch from among three nominees proposed by the synod. However, as noted,[159] in Symeon's account, the ensuing festive procession presents several differences from the one related by the roughly contemporary *Treatise on Offices* by Pseudo-Kodinos.[160] In Pseudo-Kodinos's account, the patriarch led the imperial officials and the dignitaries towards the church of St Sophia after he had mounted his horse outside the courtyard. On the other hand, in Symeon's text, following his investiture, the patriarch mounted his horse inside the imperial courtyard;[161] in addition, the emperor's

---

[156] These arguments concerned Arsenios's reinstatement in Hagia Sophia, the office celebrating him as a champion of the truth, and his perfectly preserved body as a source of healing compared to the 'bloated' body of Michael VIII lying in a church in Selymbria. See Magdalino, 'Byzantine churches of Selymbria', 316.

[157] Angelov discussed the several late Byzantine versions of the Donation attributed to both Orthodox apologists and Latin converts: those of Balsamon, of Matthew Blastares, of Demetrios Kydones and of Andrew Chrysoberges. Angelov also offered an account of the different competing interpretations (legalistic and politic) of this text in the last centuries of Byzantine history. See Angelov, 'Donation of Constantine', 91–158.

[158] Symeon of Thessalonike, *On Ordinations*, PG 155, 429d–433a and 437c–440a. See Angelov, 'Donation of Constantine', 112.

[159] Angelov, *Imperial Ideology*, 384–91.

[160] See Macrides, Munitiz and Angelov, *Pseudo-Kodinos and the Constantinopolitan Court*.

[161] Symeon of Thessalonike, *On Ordinations*, PG 155, 437–44.

son and a special servant who held the so-called *officium stratoris* leads the patriarch's horse from the imperial palace to the building of the patriarchate near St Sophia. According to Symeon, this servant stood for the emperor and did to the patriarch the homage that Constantine had once done to Pope Sylvester.[162] Pseudo-Kodinos also pointed to another aspect that revealed the increase of the ecclesiastical power over imperial authority. Thus, prior to the ceremony of his coronation the emperor was supposed to sign a confession of Orthodox faith, which he gave to the patriarch and the synod. The emperor took an oath to respect the doctrine of the church, and promised to be a 'faithful and a genuine son and servant of the holy church, and, in addition, to be its dephensōr and vindicator'.[163]

Both Makarios and Symeon treated in detail the process of electing the patriarch, which, according to their interpretation, clearly showed his pre-eminence over the emperor. For Makarios, the emperor, as he handed over the staff of the patriarch, was a 'servant of the church of a low order', mirroring the clerical rank of *depoutatos*. Even if the emperor invested the patriarch, this act did not automatically mean that the former had any spiritual power over the latter. In fact, Makarios argued, when handing the staff to the patriarch, the emperor showed his secular power, for the patriarch already possessed spiritual power before this act.[164] Symeon of Thessalonike approached the issue of the patriarch's investiture in a similar way. He argued that the emperor simply acted as the synod's servant in handing over the staff to the patriarch, for only the synod conferred active power (ἐνεργεῖ) on the patriarch. The emperor was anointed by the church not in order to be its master but to be one of its associates and faithful servants.[165]

---

[162] Symeon of Thessalonike, *On Ordinations*, PG 155, 441d: καὶ ὑπὸ πεζοῦ κόμητος τὸν χαλινὸν τοῦ ἵππου κατέχοντος ἄντι τοῦ βασιλέως αὐτοῦ, ὡς ὁ μέγας ἐν βασιλεῦσι Κωνσταντῖνος τῷ ἱερῷ πεποίηκε Σιλβέστρῳ. Nevertheless, it remains unknown whether Symeon's addition reflects real practices or whether the ecclesiastic made up the entire story of the groom in accordance with his hierocratic agenda. See Pseudo-Kodinos, *Treatise on Offices*, 281–2, ed. Verpeaux.

[163] Pseudo-Kodinos, *Treatise on Offices*, ed. Verpeaux, 253.22–254.3. In his *Histories* John Kantakouzenos (I.196–203) gave a similar account of the protocol of Andronikos III's coronation as co-emperor in 1325, omitting nevertheless the confession of faith. John Eugenikos also mentioned the emperor's confession (ὁμολογία) in his imperial 'oration' addressed to Constantine XI: τὴν σὴν εὐεργεσίαν καὶ ὁμολογίαν, PP 4, 124.35, ed. Lampros.

[164] Paris. gr. 1379, f. 46v. See Laurent, 'Rituel de l'investiture', 232.

[165] Symeon of Thessalonike, *On Ordinations*, PG, 155, 440c–d.

Following in the steps of Arsenios's representation, Makarios of Ankara asserted that since God anointed the head of the emperor through the hands of a priest, the priest held a higher rank:

> The authority of priesthood (ἡ τῆς ἱερωσύνης ἀρχὴ) is higher than the emperor's, because the emperor is in charge of the individuals' bodies, whereas the priest is of the souls. For this reason, in olden times the priests anointed the emperors; and now God sets the emperor's head under the priest's hands, and thus he teaches us that <the priest> has more authority than the emperor.[166]

Symeon of Thessalonike expanded this argument. In his treatise *On Ordinations*, he compared the two types of anointing: the material unction of the emperor and the spiritual unction of bishops. If the emperors were 'anointed by the church thus receiving from the church their position of potentates (*archontes*)', by contrast 'the bishops were anointed by the grace of the Holy Spirit' and were the true holders of spiritual power.[167] Later, in the commentary on the meaning of the emperor's coronation in his treatise *Explanation on the Divine Temple*, Symeon repeated the common notion that the unction of the emperor echoed the model of Christ's anointment and represented an act of the Holy Spirit. Yet, significantly, he added that it was the priest performing the ritual of anointing who conferred on the emperor a special 'grace of imparting' (μεταδοτικὴ χάρις) which gave the latter the power 'to appoint secular officials and generals'.[168] His account was slightly different from the one included in the *Life of Arsenios*, as the latter did not describe the grace bestowed by the priest, but refrained from investigating the further consequences of the patriarch's transmission of grace to the emperor.[169] From this perspective, Symeon envisaged the emperor's anointment by the priest as an essential act of legitimisation which marked the moment of inauguration of the emperor's rule.

---

[166] Makarios of Ankara, Paris. gr. 1379, f. 102r. See Angelov, *Imperial Ideology*, 392. Even later, in an oration addressed to Emperor Constantine XI, John Eugenikos offered a forceful representation of the emperor as servant and defender of the church, and as subordinate of the patriarch: 'Your majesty is the vindicator and defender of the Church, <while> the patriarch is the Church's shepherd and the one who crowns you and anoints you with the divine myrrh', PP 4, 125.5–10, ed. Lampros.

[167] Symeon of Thessalonike, *On Ordinations*, PG 155, 416c.

[168] Symeon of Thessalonike, *Explanation on the Divine Temple*, PG 155, 353b–c: καὶ μεταδοτικὴν διὰ τῆς εὐωδίας τοῦ μύρου χαριζόμενος αὐτῷ χάριν, εἰς τὸ ἄρχοντας κατὰ κόσμον καὶ στρατηγοὺς καθιστᾶν.

[169] Angelov, *Imperial Ideology*, 392.

Symeon rejected the idea that the emperor could hold the same kind of spiritual power as the patriarch.[170] In the treatise *On the Sacred Church* he stressed the separation between the imperial and the priestly offices by bringing into play a strict interpretation of Christological symbolism. At the ceremony of coronation, which usually took place in the church, after receiving the signed confession of Orthodox faith from the ruler, the patriarch gave him the symbols of power and proceeded to anoint him. In this way, the patriarch made clear that the Spirit was bestowed upon the emperor by Christ through the patriarch's power. In another treatise, *On Ordinations*, Symeon further attacked the idea of imperial sanctity: while the patriarch possessed the sanctity bestowed by his consecration in the Holy Spirit, the term 'holy' for the emperor was used only because of the unction with myrrh.[171] Therefore, Symeon concluded, the emperor could not be said to possess the sacerdotal gifts (χαρίσματα).

Symeon used an extensive set of arguments to minimise the significance of the coronation ceremonial and to prove that the patriarch alone could provide the emperor with the symbols of power and with a limited holiness. According to the ecclesiastical writer, the unction of the emperor by the patriarch pointed to the former's inferior position: through anointment the emperor was bestowed with the ecclesiastical rank of *depoutatos*, who, according to the church hierarchy, was directly answerable to the patriarch.[172] As they lacked priestly power, emperors could not have administrative rights in the church such as the right to transfer bishops.[173] Similarly, in his *Partial Exposition* Makarios of Ankara used the same argument when he quoted the clause of the emperor's promise to be the church's servant and argued that this promise compelled the emperor to abide by the canons of the church.[174] The claim survived even after the end of Manuel's reign, for several decades later, John Eugenikos argued that an emperor who broke the oaths taken during the coronation ceremony lost his legitimacy.[175]

The hierocratic claims supported by a large part of the clergy were not limited to the argumentation included in liturgical treatises or works of canonical treatment. In the section dedicated to the sanctity of priesthood (περὶ ἱερωσύνης) of

---

[170] In the *Explanation on the Divine Temple*, PG 155, 353, he asked: 'Why is the emperor anointed with myrrh and consecrated with prayers?'
[171] Symeon compares the use of 'holy' in this context with the way in which St Paul called all baptised Christians 'holy brothers'.
[172] Symeon of Thessalonike, *Liturgical Commentaries*, 133, ed. Hawkes-Teeples.
[173] This was a practice which much earlier canonists had supported, among them Demetrios Chomatenos in his canonical writings, *Πονήματα διάφορα*, 86.55, ed. Prinzing.
[174] Paris. gr. 1379, f. 98r, f 142r.
[175] PP 1, 124–5, ed. Lampros.

his collection titled *Two Hundred Theological and Ethical Chapters*, Joseph Bryennios states that the priestly authority was higher than the emperor's:

> If you want to know the difference between a priest and emperor, look closely at each one's given share of authority (δεδομένη ἐξουσία): the priest is situated on a much higher level than the emperor.[176]

Furthermore, in two hortatory letters addressed to Despot Andronikos of Thessalonike, Symeon reiterated the idea that the ruler should be obedient to the church:

> Priesthood establishes your authority as sacred and accomplishes it by prayers. Therefore the emperors are anointed and are proclaimed by the hierarchs' voices and ordained by divine laws so that the divine designs be fulfilled.[177]

The downplaying of Manuel's authority in the ecclesiastics' texts was supplemented by attacks on the emperor himself. Makarios circulated a series of denigratory pamphlets against the emperor which seem to have acquired relative popularity, since the emperor himself considered it necessary to answer them in a series of letters. In Makarios's legal battle against Matthew I it is clear that many clerics created a group opposed to the emperor. Probably the clearest expression of hostility to the Emperor Manuel's actions concerning the church came from a later author, Sylvester Syropoulos. His words from the beginning of his *Memoirs* prove the enduring legacy of Manuel's tendency to act in accordance with the old views that gave the emperor pre-eminence in the church:

> I have always admired the deeds of this wonderful emperor, and I never considered myself capable enough of praising him. Nevertheless, in one respect I cannot praise him: for it is unworthy (ἀνάξιος) of his virtue and the wisdom of his much-tried soul to bring Christ's church into slavery.[178]

Conclusion

Several decades ago, in an article that drew on texts authored by churchmen, Ihor Ševčenko suggested that Byzantine authors had an ingrained awareness of the decline of their state.[179] If multiple references of a religious character

---

[176] Joseph Bryennios, in *Garden*, Vindob. theol. gr. 235, f. 47v.
[177] Symeon of Thessalonike, *Hortatory Letter to Despot Andronikos*, in *Politico-Historical Works*, 77.2–7, ed. Balfour.
[178] Sylvester Syropoulos, *Memoirs*, 2.4, ed. Laurent.
[179] Ševčenko, 'Decline', 186.

illustrate this attitude, it is no less true that Byzantine ecclesiastics seriously engaged in the process of identifying the means of survival at a time of crisis. The above analysis has shown that the concerns of early fifteenth-century high-ranking ecclesiastics did not pertain only to hotly debated doctrinal matters, such as the *filioque* or the truth of Christianity versus Islam, but also included ideas about society and politics. In their concerted efforts to construct a coherent programme of action, the churchmen saw themselves both as defenders of social fairness and as promoters of an Orthodox spirituality which they deemed to be core connected aspects in defining Byzantine identity. The evidence presented here also suggests that they avoided showing allegiance to imperial policies. Instead, what they valued in the imperial persona was rather the cultural and spiritual aspects. While, naturally, the church continued to claim authority in the spiritual sphere, it also increasingly asserted the links between religious reform and social changes. The church made these claims by means of a rhetorical voice modulated by the idea of spiritual authority.

Arguably, the process we see at work here involved the crystallisation of a stance vis-à-vis the theory and practice of power in the Palaiologan period. This process was neither continuous nor without obstacles and gaps. Even if the authors who documented this process had a variety of goals and wrote under different circumstances (some in the provinces and some in Constantinople), the evidence presented above suggests that many ecclesiastics had similar ideas about Byzantine authority. Often, Emperor Manuel attempted to attract to his court churchmen whom he involved in his literary endeavours. Yet his close allies, Bryennios, Makres and the Athonite hieromonk David, did not hold high-ranking positions and could offer only partial ecclesiastical support for his actions. What Manuel could not claim was the backing of the majority of high-ranking ecclesiastics. The latter used and inspired discursive strategies ranging from constructing ideas of community protection (in homilies) to promoting ecclesiastical-political authority (in theological treatises). One can note a tendency to desire changes as well as to dissent from other actors and institutions of the *politeia*, particularly the emperor. This stance emerged with the Arsenite schism and the reforms of Patriarch Athanasios, whose ideas about moral amelioration were tied to a plan of general state reform.[180] The process of articulating it continued with the recognition of the Orthodoxy of hesychasm, the ensuing vigorous involvement of hesychasts and Athonite monks in higher church politics, and the renewed claims about the centrality of Orthodoxy in Byzantine identity. Furthermore, it added a layer of social protection for local communities against the abuses of both the

---

[180] Boojamra, *Church and Social Reform*.

Ottomans and the *archontes*. Eventually, in the very last decades of the empire, the churchmen increasingly acted as a separate group with a sphere of action parallel to and often conflicting with the imperial one, as in the appointment of Patriarch Joseph. Sylvester Syropoulos referred to 'our order' (ἡμετέρα τάξις) while Mark Eugenikos distinguished between state, churches and the monastic order (πολιτεία, ἐκκλησίαι, and the μοναχικὸν τάγμα).[181] It was in the decades preceding the Fall of Constantinople that all these ideas came to be articulated more clearly and placed in a larger theoretical framework of religious inspiration. In an anti-unionist dialogue on the procession of the Holy Spirit, George Scholarios concluded that individuals have no control over the course of history, which remains in God's hands,[182] and that Christ had already told his apostles to expect misfortunes and conflicts.[183] Thereby Scholarios implied that a deterioration of the situation was not unexpected and that the church remained the only institution to provide a path to salvation.

Within this process of formulating a global political and social stance, the themes circulating during Manuel's reign represented a key aspect of agency. Even if relations with the emperor were often cordial, several leading ecclesiastical authors overwhelmingly pursued a hierocratic agenda. Remarkably, the description of the patriarch's nomination indicates that in the early fifteenth century the political theology previously embraced by Pseudo-Kodinos and the anonymous author of the *Life of Arsenios* was expanded into a form of hierocratic reasoning which claimed that the emperor received authority from the church whereas the patriarch was his anointer.[184] Primarily, the shift of discourse to a less flexible position was the result of the fact that the church gained not only in prestige vis-à-vis the imperial office but also in concrete prerogatives, like substantial rights as judges in civil matters. This process started in the early Palaiologan period and became more prominent during the reign of Manuel II, who tried to regulate the activity of these judges, who included both lay people and ecclesiastics. He formulated the principles of their activities, according to which all subjects and all cases came under their jurisdiction. This move considerably strengthened their social influence.[185]

---

[181] Mark Eugenikos, *Prayer for the Emperor*, PP 4, 30, ed. Lampros: ταῖς ἐκκλησίαις σου δι' αὐτοῦ τὴν εἰρήνην χορήγησον, τῇ πολιτείᾳ τὸ ἀσφαλές, τῷ ἱερατικῷ καὶ μοναχικῷ τάγματι τὴν ἀταραξίαν· ἐργάτην αὐτὸν ἀνάδειξον καὶ ἐκδικητὴν τῶν σεβασμίων σου ἐντολῶν καὶ τῶν ἀποστολικῶν καὶ πατρικῶν παραδόσεων.

[182] Turner, 'Pages', 366.

[183] George Scholarios, *Dialogues*, 43, ed. Jugie, Petit and Siderides.

[184] Angelov, *Imperial Ideology*, 391.

[185] See Schilbach, 'Hypotyposis'; Lemerle, 'Juge général'.

Furthermore, the change of discourse took place on the fertile ground of Byzantium's internal crises, which prompted writers to dig deeper for the causes of political decline. Admittedly, their awareness of the economic differences and the general criticism of archontic power had a strong bearing on their predominant attitude towards imperial power. Several ecclesiastics went so far as to liken imperial power to archontic power, which in turn was regarded as responsible for the misfortunes of the many local communities unable to provide the resources for defence and survival. Illustrative of the extent to which the imperial authority was deemed incapable of providing the Byzantines with the proper means of defence was Symeon's consideration of Emperor Manuel's policies of alliance with the Ottomans and the Venetians as destructive in the Thessalonians' attempts to defend the city's autonomy.

The articulation of the ecclesiastics' discourse of authority continued after the end of Manuel's reign when it was fuelled by the negotiations of union taking place in the reigns of the last two Byzantine emperors, John and Constantine. Several decades after Manuel's death, Mark Eugenikos emphatically asserted his liberty of faith: 'Nobody has authority over our faith (κυριεύει τῆς ἡμῶν πίστεως): neither the emperor, nor any false synod.'[186] He also noted that emperors could save their people only if they remained pious.[187] Thus, in the political scheme conceived by the late Byzantine ecclesiastics, the emperor would have continued to be active but with the diminished role of a serviceman providing protection to his people and the church.[188] Even if the clergymen did not entirely discard the imperial institution, they maintained silence about the imperial legislative rights which previously had been exercised by other emperors. From this perspective it must come as no surprise that in 1393, in a letter addressed to Basil, grand duke of Russia, Patriarch Anthony IV remarked that the emperor and the church could not exist separately.[189] In this way, the churchmen redefined the fundamentals of Byzantine identity, not only in opposition to the Latins and Islam, but also by revisiting and questioning central tenets of political authority. Ultimately, having dissociated the figure of the emperor from their idea of Byzantine identity and having placed it in a secondary position, Byzantine ecclesiastics provided for Orthodoxy the central place which they reclaimed from the emperor. Nevertheless, as we will see in the following chapters, this position did not remain unchallenged.

---

[186] Mark Eugenikos, *Letters*, PP 4, 2.20–32.
[187] Mark Eugenikos, *Prayer for the Emperor*, PP 4, 31, ed. Lampros.
[188] See Symeon's advisory texts addressed to Despot Andronikos, in *Politico-Historical Works*, 77–82, ed. Balfour.
[189] Darrouzès, *Regestes*, no. 2931, 6.210–11.

2

Voices of Consent: Imperial Rhetoricians, *Theatra* and Patronage

However strong the position of the church in late Byzantium and however intensely it sought political primacy, the ecclesiastics were not the only group who articulated a set of political and social solutions. Other individuals belonging to the non-ecclesiastical elites often promoted ideas and representations that went against the political tenets held by the church.[1] Significantly, these elites cultivated the image of an omnipotent ruler, much more in tune with Byzantine theories of kingship reflected especially in court rhetoric. Many members of the latter group were educated authors and, even if lacking any institutional organisation, they formed smaller influential clusters of individuals sometimes acting on the emperor's behalf. Emperor Manuel himself had close connections with this group, played a key role therein, and sought to develop relations with its members. They also constituted the main audience of his writings. Because the members of this group followed different career paths, for the sake of simplicity I will refer to them as imperial rhetoricians. By and large, they were skilled lay writers associated with the imperial court who, at different moments of their careers, addressed the emperor in letters or orations: epideictic ones that sought to praise the ruler and his deeds or deliberative ones that provided counsel for the emperor on specific decisions. They were also able to exert political influence as they interacted with other members of Manuel's court: officials, *oikeioi* or family members (a category that designated both real and symbolic kinship with the emperor), members of aristocratic families (e.g. the Palaiologoi, the Kantakouzenoi, the Asanes, etc.), or imperial servants like physicians or scribes.[2]

---

[1] On their social status in the Palaiologan period see Toth, *Imperial Orations*, 190–2. On the opposition between the ecclesiastics and the entrepreneurial aristocracy see Kioussopoulou, *Emperor or Manager*, 52–128; Kioussopoulou, 'Hommes d'affaires byzantins', 15–21.

[2] For a complete list of the scholars and rhetoricians in the emperor's service, see Appendix 1.

As in the previous chapter, the aim here will be threefold: to analyse the activities of the scholars in the imperial service, to explore the emperor's interactions with them, and to understand their views on the main socio-political challenges in late Byzantium. While several recent studies have looked at the political attitudes and intellectual careers of the late Byzantine intelligentsia, there still remain several unanswered questions. How important was imperial patronage? What was the nature of the relations established among Byzantine authors and with other centres of power and knowledge dissemination? What was the nature of their rapport with political authority? What was the cultural and social role of the performative frameworks in the late Palaiologan period? To answer these questions I focus also on the values of the *pepaideumenoi* who gravitated towards the emperor. After a discussion of the major practice of late Byzantine public rhetorical performance, the *theatron*, and a survey of the authors and of the main sources used,[3] I deal with the organisation of the rhetoricians and their interactions with the emperor. In the second part of the chapter, I treat the four main themes which were also central in the ecclesiastics' contemporary texts: social divisions, attitudes towards Byzantium's enemies and allies, the formulation of Byzantine ethnic particularities and, finally, the conceptualisation of imperial authority. This analysis allows us to get further insights into several key aspects of Manuel's imperial authority: the late Byzantine rhetorical practices and milieu in which the emperor lived and wrote; the channels which the emperor used for disseminating his political messages; and finally, the views to which Emperor Manuel responded in his texts.

Theatra and Imperial Involvement

The late Byzantine letter collections suggest that, even in this period of scarce resources, a continuous exchange of ideas and texts between the members of a group of active lay intellectuals took place.[4] These individuals formed a group which can be described as a literary circle.[5] Among the members of this group, one finds mostly lay rhetoricians of various religious or political persuasions mirroring the transformations that Byzantium underwent in this period:

---

[3] For a discussion of their biographies and texts see Toth, *Imperial Orations*, 120–68.
[4] See Tinnefeld, 'Intellectuals'; Ševčenko, *Society and Intellectual Life*, 65–92; Mergiali, *Enseignement*, 165–92.
[5] The idea of the group of literati in terms of a cohesive literary circle has been discussed by several scholars: Manuel II, *Letters*, ix, ed. Dennis; Ševčenko, *Society and Intellectual Life*, 3; Matschke and Tinnefeld, *Gesellschaft im späten Byzanz*, 307.

anti-unionists or supporters of the union, members of the old aristocracy or people of lower social status. Emperor Manuel himself had been a member of this circle ever since his youth in Constantinople and, over time, his connections and uses of the network multiplied. Furthermore, owing to his position of political authority, he patronised scholars and played a decisive part in maintaining connections between the members of this group and often in promoting them to administrative positions.

The pursuits of this group of individuals are documented by their substantial extant correspondence and by meetings in the framework of the so-called *theatra*. Most activities of these rhetoricians involved the performance of texts and providing adequate feedback to peer writers in these informal *theatra*. These were organised gatherings patronised by aristocrats and had a long tradition in Byzantium, traceable in late antiquity and in the Komnenian and Palaiologan periods. As places of both literary and social performance[6] they find a parallel in other instances of ritualised social practice in Constantinople, such as court ceremonies or imperial triumphs.[7] Often *theatra* were designed for authors to read aloud their texts and, following such performances, to receive comments from their peers. Evidence from the Palaiologan period indicates that such meetings enjoyed popularity among authors and patrons.[8] Specifically, during Manuel's reign, the evidence concerning *theatra* is enough to allow us to conjecture that, at least during the first decades of his reign, *theatra* represented regular occasions of meeting and performing literary texts. Although not so varied and numerous as for the earlier Palaiologan period, the extant sources dating from the late fourteenth century suggest that most instances of *theatra* were sponsored and chaired by the emperor himself.[9] Already during his initial stay in Thessalonike (1382–7) Manuel had organised *theatra* where scholars met regularly.[10] In a letter addressed to Triboles, one of his supporters,[11] the young Manuel offered a vivid image of the enthusiasm of the audience who listened to the performance of Triboles' text:

> We made a serious effort to have your letter read before as many people as you would wish, and you surely wished a large number to hear it, confident in your literary skill and expecting to be praised for it. And this is just what

---

[6] On *theatra* in late antiquity, see Libanius, *Opera*, 10.1259, ed. Förster. For the same phenomenon in the twelfth century, see Magdalino, *Empire of Manuel I Komnenos*, 429–32. On *theatra* in the Palaiologan period, see Gaul, *Thomas Magistros*, 17–61.

[7] Late Byzantine imperial orations were also delivered in a *theatron*-like setting. See Toth, 'Rhetorical *theatron*'.

[8] For earlier periods we have evidence about *theatra* from scholars like Demetrios Kydones, John Kantakouzenos and Nikephoros Gregoras.

[9] For the early period see Gaul, *Thomas Magistros*, 18–38.

[10] See Tinnefeld, 'Intellectuals'.

[11] Manuel II, *Letters*, liii, ed. Dennis.

happened. For the entire audience applauded and was full of admiration as the letter was read by its grandfather. [...] But while others were expressing their wonderment, I seemed to be the only one who was not doing so. Someone asked me how it could be possible that among the entire group I alone appeared unaffected, that is, uninspired and lacking in admiration. 'I too am greatly impressed', I replied, 'for I cannot help being thoroughly amazed, not because a noble father brings forth noble children', referring to you and your writings, 'but because the rest of you marvel at this as though you had unexpectedly come across something new.'[12]

Although couched in elaborate encomiastic terms, this passage provides vivid details about the atmosphere and the activities taking place in a *theatron*: the audience was comprised of listeners who were able to understand and appreciate the intricacies of a sophisticated rhetorical text; the emperor seems to have played a leading role in the gathering; sometimes the audience responded loudly and the speaker had to initiate a dialogue; public recitations could increase or decrease an author's social reputation (τιμή). Manuel's letter, which was sent from Thessalonike during his residence there, indicates that *theatra* took place not exclusively in Constantinople, but in other towns as well.[13]

When mentioning the court *theatra*, the emperor stresses that they represented occasions for discussing the literary achievements of certain authors, especially those close to the ruling family. This was the case with some of his addressees: Demetrios Kydones, the emperor's mentor; Theodore Kaukadenos, the instructor of Manuel's sons; Demetrios Chrysoloras; and Constantine Asanes.[14] The echoes of such literary debates indicate that the *theatra* were occasions not only of praise but also of criticism: a letter addressed by the emperor to 'a certain foolish person' shows that *theatra* also involved debates over values or actions.[15]

Manuel was not the only Palaiologan author who described *theatra* in the imperial palace. In a letter addressed to Eustathios, a καθολικὸς κριτής (general judge), John Chortasmenos, praised the emperor for the fact that, during his reign, rhetoric became again highly valued in the imperial palace.[16]

---

[12] Manuel II, *Letters*, no. 9, 3–17, ed. Dennis. The ensuing translations of the letters are from Dennis's edition. See Gaul, *Thomas Magistros*, 27–8.
[13] John Chortasmenos, *Letters*, in *Briefe*, nos. 44, 47, ed. Hunger. On the circle of literati in Thessalonike see Dendrinos, *Annotated Edition of 'On the Procession of the Holy Spirit'*, IV; Matschke and Tinnefeld, *Gesellschaft im späten Byzanz*, 323.
[14] Manuel II, *Letters*, nos. 23, 27, 30, 61, ed. Dennis.
[15] Ibid. no. 28.16–20.
[16] John Chortasmenos, *Letters*, no. 10, ed. Hunger.

In the same letter Chortasmenos also recounts how the latter's oration was received by the emperor in a public reading:

> Your oration was read with much earnestness, in the emperor's presence who listened with eagerness. The crowd of important men praised the oration and said that the text needed no further addition, [...]. I thought that your words have a certain charm, and the emperor later agreed with this. For this emperor is filled with wisdom, he is the home of all virtues and of the Charites (Graces), and if he wanted to accomplish something with them he would easily succeed.[17]

Such remarks testify not only to the late Palaiologan revival of court rhetoric but also to Manuel's chief role as convener of *theatra*. This situation contrasted sharply with the reign of his father, John V, who does not appear to have shown any particular interest in court rhetoric.[18] Most plausibly, John V's disposition towards the practical matters of 'Realpolitik' and lack of interest in cultivating rhetorical performances at court reflected an important element of his style of government that rather pursued practical objectives.[19] From his five decades of rule there is little evidence about any sustained rhetorical activities at court.[20] Tellingly, it was John's wife and Manuel's mother, Helena Kantakouzene, who encouraged literary activities at court by supporting authors and organising *theatra*.[21] By contrast, based on the extensive references to such meetings in his epistolary collection, it appears that Manuel rather wished his contemporaries to consider the *theatra* organised in the imperial palace as elements of his particular style of government. This idea emerges even more vigorously when we compare Manuel's *theatra* with those of the earlier Palaiologan era. If the imperial *theatron* of the early fourteenth century increased the social clout of the participating scholars, Manuel leveraged this opportunity to increase not only the prestige of his scholar friends but his own as well.[22]

Viewed within the framework of court ceremonial, it can be argued that Manuel's *theatra* constituted attempts not only to turn attention on himself as *arbiter elegantiae* but also to reinvigorate ancient court practices, which

---

[17] Ibid.
[18] Demetrios Kydones, *Letters*, no. 340, ed. Loenertz. See Matschke and Tinnefeld, *Gesellschaft im späten Byzanz*, 307.
[19] Ryder argues that John V consciously emphasised actions rather than rhetoric: *Career and Writings*, 111.
[20] The panegyrics addressed by Demetrios Kydones are concerned primarily with the emperor's military efforts against the Ottomans.
[21] Demetrios Kydones, *Letters*, no. 222, ed. Loenertz.
[22] See Magistros's case; Gaul, *Thomas Magistros*, chs. 2 and 3.

included the periodical delivery of panegyrics or the presence of an officially appointed orator, a μαΐστωρ (ῥήτωρ) τῶν ῥητόρων, a court position which disappeared at the beginning of the fourteenth century. Clearly, under Manuel II's rule, the situation changed and the emperor became again interested in promoting literary debates. Thus, it can be suggested that under the difficult circumstances of the late fourteenth and early fifteenth centuries, Manuel aimed at befriending other rhetoricians as he attempted to fulfil the role of court orator himself.

With regard to the nature of rhetorical court activities during Manuel's reign, one can distinguish two major periods: in the first period, from the 1390s until c. 1415, there are a very few public addresses, like Manuel's own orations. In a second phase, particularly during the years 1415–17, several panegyrics were addressed to the emperor: a panegyric for the emperor's return from Thessalonike by John Chortasmenos, another panegyric acclamation by John Chortasmenos in the name of Manuel Asanopoulos, a panegyric by Gemistos Plethon, a panegyric in the form of a comparison between the present and the ancient rulers by Demetrios Chrysoloras, and an anonymous panegyric.[23] Several causes may have triggered this situation: during the first half of his reign, the Byzantine state faced the real danger of dissolution, both internal and external, and, as a result, the occasions for celebration by public encomia were very few. It is hard to imagine that during the eight-year blockade of Constantinople, there could have been celebratory meetings at court. Moreover, for half of this period, the emperor was away from the capital. Therefore, arguably, during the first decade of Manuel's reign when we have strong evidence for literary meetings, the *theatron* may have fulfilled the role of public meetings where the emperor could receive his due praise. At the same time, as will be pointed out later in this volume, the emperor portrayed himself as a public orator by delivering several orations. After 1415 the extant written sources reveal a different picture. After several military and diplomatic successes, such as the rebuilding of the Hexamilion wall in the Morea and the peace with the Ottomans under Mehmed I, public rhetorical performances in the imperial palace became much more frequent. Many of Joseph Bryennios's texts, including his sermons, were performed in the palace (ἐν τῷ παλατίῳ), often in the emperor's presence.[24] Evidence for intense literary activity around

---

[23] Vat. gr. 914. To these can be added Gemistos Plethon's *Address on the Situation in the Peloponnese* (1416), and the three later funeral orations for the emperor by Makarios Makres and two further anonymous authors (all 1425).

[24] Likewise, during John VIII Palaiologos's reign, George Scholarios would perform several homilies in the imperial chamber: Petit, Siderides and Jugie, *œuvres complètes de Georges Scholarios*, II.2.1, VI.178, 1.30.

the year 1415 at Manuel's court comes from other sources as well, for the official texts of court rhetoric were not the only texts performed. The satirical dialogue *Mazaris' Journey to Hades: Or, Interviews with Dead Men about Certain Officials of the Imperial Court* (c. 1415), despite its distortions, suggests that the court included a great many individuals who could appreciate such a text.[25]

The imperial patronage and the activity in the *theatra*, though certainly less frequent than in the early decades of the Palaiologan period, suggest that the audience for late Byzantine public oratory included not only the connoisseurs of sophisticated rhetoric but also other individuals holding official positions. The court therefore included not a single type of audience but many. As a matter of fact, Manuel himself testified to this situation when he noted the differences of rhetorical taste: that some people preferred the order of the composition, others elegant wording, others brevity or measure.[26] Thus, when considering the audience of the emperor's texts, we should keep in the back of our minds its social and cultural diversity rather than its uniformity or conformity.

Profile and Organisation of the Rhetoricians

In the following section I will look at the configuration of the circle of rhetoricians as well as its functions and uses. A conspicuous feature of the rhetoricians' biographies was that they had close connections with the emperor and the imperial families of the Palaiologoi and the Kantakouzenoi. These ties, strengthened by, participation in *theatra*, were grounded in common interests in rhetoric and ancient authors on the one hand, and the pursuit of patronage, mentorship or service on the other hand. By the end of the fourteenth century, the court rhetoricians were not constrained any more by the obligation to hold official oratorical court performances delivered on religious feasts like that of Epiphany.[27] This relative flexibility and independence allowed them to pursue more openly both their individual careers[28] and a political agenda which included, but was not limited to, the emperor's glorification. Often we find such rhetoricians in the service of other members of the political and

---

[25] See Garland, '*Mazaris' Journey to Hades*: Further reflections'; Trapp, 'Zur Identifizierung'.

[26] Manuel II, *Letters*, no. 24, ed. Dennis, addressed to Phrangopoulos.

[27] See Toth, *Imperial Orations*; Angelov, 'Byzantine imperial panegyric', 55. This situation was largely due to the context of post-1204 rhetorical performance. In contrast, many imperial panegyrics have survived from the reign of Manuel I Komnenos and the Angeloi emperors (1185–1204). See Magdalino, *Empire of Manuel I Komnenos*, 248.

[28] Instances of requests addressed to the emperor can be identified in the letters of John Chortasmenos and Demetrios Chrysoloras. Throughout the late Palaiologan period, panegyrics continued to constitute platforms used for requesting benefits. E.g. see Michael Apostolios's speech addressed to Constantine XI, *Prosphōnēma*, PP 2, 87.5–10, ed. Lampros.

social elites.[29] Variations in terms of religious orientation and social status also shaped the profile of this group. If most of them were laymen, several held strong religious convictions, either in favour of the Latin church or defending an Orthodox position; some belonged to the aristocracy while others came from not so well-off families and had to teach grammar and rhetoric to earn their living.[30] Such differences of status make it difficult to reconstruct a uniform portrait of Byzantine scholars at the turn of the fourteenth century or to fully track the contours of the network they formed. The element that certainly connects them is dependence on the ruler's benevolence, as numerous letters or orations indicate the still strong reliance on imperial generosity.[31]

Several individuals of this group stand out. By far its most prominent and influential member was Demetrios Kydones (1324–96), a prolific scholar and Manuel's mentor, whose political role in the second half of the fourteenth century can hardly be overestimated.[32] His family connections with the Kantakouzenoi and later with the Palaiologoi helped him acquire the position of *mesazōn* as well as the possibility of exerting considerable influence on John V. Kydones' disciples, Manuel Kalekas (1360–1410) and Manuel Chrysoloras (1370–1415), followed closely in the steps of their mentor. The first, a teacher of grammar and rhetoric in the 1380s, converted to Catholicism and became increasingly involved in defending and promoting the Catholic faith in Constantinople.[33] The activity of Manuel Chrysoloras, a leading late Byzantine scholar and diplomat in Manuel's service, was tied to the early fifteenth-century emigration of Byzantine scholars to the West.[34] In 1396 he moved to Florence, where a teaching position in Greek language had been set up by Coluccio Salutati, one of the Italian founding fathers of the *studia humanitatis* and a friend of Demetrios Kydones.[35]

---

[29] For instance, Demetrios Chrysoloras was *mesazōn*, a kind of prime minister, of John VII for several years, while Demetrios Kydones acted as a representative of John Laskaris Kalopheros, whose economic and financial interests he represented in Italy. See Eszer, *Leben des Johannes Laskaris Kalopheros*.

[30] See Appendix 1. Partial lists of Palaiologan literati were compiled by Ševčenko, *Society and Intellectual Life*, and Matschke and Tinnefeld, *Gesellschaft im späten Byzanz*, 371–86.

[31] Ševčenko, *Society and Intellectual Life*, 4.

[32] For much of his political career he held the position of *mesazōn* of emperors John VI and John V (1354–70). See Demetrios Kydones, *First Oration to John Kantakouzenos*, 6–7, ed. Loenertz.

[33] In 1396, after the synod organised by Patriarch Matthew I intended to reaffirm Orthodox principles, Kalekas fled to Pera; Manuel Kalekas, *Letters*, no. 21, ed. Loenertz.

[34] Chrysoloras's career has been treated in several monographs and extensive studies: Cammelli, *Dotti bizantini*; Maisano, *Manuele Crisolora*; and the recent monograph by Thorn-Wickert, *Manuel Chrysoloras*.

[35] It was Kydones who recommended him to Coluccio for this position, which attracted the attention of numerous young Florentine students such as Leonardo Bruni.

Several elements increased the cohesion of this cluster of Latinophrones. As their correspondence shows, they all regarded Kydones as their mentor, *didaskalos* and protector, who did not hesitate to make use of his connections in the political and scholarly spheres.[36] In his turn, Kydones asserted his role in the many letters he sent to his disciples and protégés.[37] At the end of the fourteenth century, they participated in common diplomatic actions, like the attempt to recover the Venetian assets of John Laskaris Kalopheros, a friend of Kydones.[38] As a distinctive group in Constantinople they also enjoyed the protection of a high-ranking courtier, Constantine Asanes, a skilled rhetorician himself and also a *theios* (uncle) of the emperor.[39] At the same time, they all worked together on a long-term project: the translation of the Dominican liturgy into Greek. The letters exchanged between Chrysoloras, Kalekas, Kydones and Chrysoberges indicate that each of them undertook the responsibility of translating a section of the text.[40] Finally, they all had close ties with the humanists in Italy. Among Manuel Chrysoloras's students one can identify some of the most distinguished humanists of early quattrocento Florence: Guarino of Verona, Leonardo Bruni, Palla Strozzi, Roberto Rossi, Jacopo Angelli da Scarperia, Uberto Decembrio and Paolo Vergerio.[41] Manuel Chrysoloras's name appears frequently in the epistolary collections of Coluccio Salutati,[42] Guarino of Verona and Ambrogio Traversari, with whom he often corresponded.[43] For these scholars Chrysoloras was the *eruditissimus et suavissimus litterarum Graecarum praeceptor*,[44] or a *vir doctissimus atque optimus*, according to Leonardo Bruni.[45] Some of them also appear among Manuel Kalekas's correspondents or friends.[46]

---

[36] Manuel Kalekas, *Letters*, no. 4.14–15, ed. Loenertz.
[37] E.g. the letters to Maximos Chrysoberges (nos. 333, 385, 387, 394, 402, 428, 443) or to Manuel Kalekas (no. 437), ed. Loenertz.
[38] On their friendship see Demetrios Kydones, *Letters*, nos. 37, 73, ed. Loenertz; Jacoby, 'Jean Lascaris Calopheros'.
[39] Asanes' rhetorical output remains unknown. However, *Mazaris' Journey to Hades* (56.20) ridiculed his rhetorical skills. See Kydones' letters addressed to Constantine Asanes, and Kalekas; Demetrios Kydones, *Letters*, nos. 73–7, ed. Loenertz.
[40] Violante, *Provincia Domenicana di Grecia*, 202–5; Mercati, *Notizie*, 77–85.
[41] Thomson, 'Manuel Chrysoloras', 63–6.
[42] Coluccio Salutati, *Letters*, 3. no. 14, 119–25, ed. Novati.
[43] Thomson, 'Manuel Chrysoloras', 70–82.
[44] See Cammelli, *Dotti bizantini*, 180.
[45] Leonardo Bruni, *Epistularum Libri*, 1.52.
[46] Demetrios Skaranos enjoyed the friendship of many Italians, who offered him a shelter in Florence; Cammelli, *Dotti bizantini*, 66.

Since all these Greek scholars lived for long periods of time in Italy, it is highly plausible that such connections with the humanist movement influenced not only the rise of Greek studies in Italy but also the circulation of new ideas or practices in the Eastern Mediterranean. Byzantium and Italy became entangled in many aspects so that by the end of his reign, Manuel recruited Giovanni Aurispa (1376–1459), a humanist living in Constantinople and manuscript collector, as his secretary and ambassador.

Alongside the members of this distinct party, the late Palaiologan rhetorical landscape included other literati with no Latinophile attitudes who held high positions at the imperial court. One of them was Demetrios Chrysoloras, who served both Manuel II and John VII.[47] His rhetorical skills and theological knowledge were also highly praised by contemporary literati,[48] for he composed several homilies, theological dialogues, a panegyric for emperor Manuel II titled *Comparison between the Emperor of Today and the Ancient Rulers*, letters and several rhetorical exercises. John Chortasmenos (1370–1439), another member of this literary circle, was a teacher, writer and patriarchal notary in Constantinople for several decades. In addition to being connected to influential circles like the Asanes family, he was also an active scholar and collector of manuscripts.[49] Yet, unlike other scholars of his time, Chortasmenos never travelled outside Constantinople, in search of a better life or for the company of humanists.[50] Several of his pupils, like Mark Eugenikos and Bessarion, later received important positions at court. Isidore, who became cardinal of Kiev (1390–1463), was also very close to the emperor as he copied many of his texts. His œuvre consisted mainly of theological treatises on the union of the churches, letters, and panegyrics addressed to Manuel's son, John VIII.[51] Gemistos Plethon, the Platonising philosopher, spent several years in Constantinople before leaving for the Peloponnese, where he had connections with the Palaiologos family. He benefited from his connections with the despots of the Morea and retained a special profile among the late Byzantine scholars for his expertise in ancient philosophy, especially Plato. In several of his texts written during Manuel's reign, he outlined a set of social and political reforms focused on the Peloponnese but which could also be applied to the entire Byzantine

---

[47] Not much is known about his office in Thessalonike. In 1407 we find him in a delegation sent by John VII; Dölger, *Regesten*, 5. no. 3207, 77.
[48] Manuel II, *Letters*, no. 45, ed. Dennis; John Chortasmenos, *Briefe*, 90–4, ed. Hunger.
[49] John Chortasmenos, *Briefe*, 20–9, ed. Hunger. On Chortasmenos's scribal activity see Schreiner, 'Johannes Chortasmenos', 193–9.
[50] John Chortasmenos, *Briefe*, 13–20, ed. Hunger.
[51] Mercati, *Scritti d'Isidoro*, 130.

state. The motivation behind these three works dating to the period between 1407 and 1418 probably originated in the events surrounding the visits of Manuel II to the Peloponnese.[52]

Since all these scholars were connected among themselves often by very strong bonds of friendship or of the teacher–student type, it is fair to assume that they also held several ideas in common. However, tensions and conflicts often arose, sometimes with serious consequences. The most critical event leading to a separation of individual groups within the Byzantine intelligentsia occurred in 1396, when intellectuals suspected of a pro-Catholic stance were asked to sign a profession of faith in favour of Orthodoxy. Within this framework of action, in a letter addressed to Manuel Chrysoloras, John Chortasmenos asks him to clarify his position. Although we do not know Chrysoloras's answer, we know that immediately after this event (1397) he left for Florence to teach Greek, from where he returned to Constantinople only to leave again on a long diplomatic voyage throughout Europe. We also know much about the tribulations of Manuel Kalekas, who was forced into exile when he refused to sign this profession of faith and consequently moved to Pera and then to Italy. Later echoes of the adversity towards the pro-Latin scholars can be found in Demetrios Chrysoloras's *Dialogue on Demetrios Kydones' Antirrhetic against Neilos Kabasilas*. Written in 1429, several years after the death of Emperor Manuel, the text presents Kydones, the symbol of the pro-Latin movement in Byzantium, in a highly negative light, as an enemy of Byzantine identity.[53]

Connections among the Members of the Literary Court

The identification of these members of the scholarly network[54] allows us to turn to other parameters which define its extension: connectivity understood as the ability to maintain relations between the members of the same group,[55] ties with the emperor, and use of the network for various purposes.

---

[52] For a discussion of the dates of composition of these works, see Woodhouse, *George Gemistos Plethon*, 92; Mamalakes, *Georgios Gemistos Plethon*, 73; Masai, *Pléthon et le platonisme*, 205; Zakythenos and Maltezou, *Despotat grec de Morée*, 1. 176; Peritore, 'Political Thought', 171. For Manuel's visits in the Peloponnese see Barker, *Manuel II*, 273–80, 301–18.

[53] See Demetrios Chrysoloras, *Dialogue on Demetrios Kydones' Antirrhetic*, 189–397, ed. Pasiourtides.

[54] For a network chart of the connections between scholars, ecclesiastics and the emperor, see Appendix 4. See also Appendix 1 for a list of scholars in the emperor's service.

[55] On the connectivity of scholarly groups in late Byzantium see Ševčenko, *Society and Intellectual Life*; Gaul, 'Twitching shroud'; Cavallo, 'Sodalizi eruditi'. On broader issues of connectivity among literati see Preiser-Kapeller, 'Letters and network analysis'.

Unlike in the ecclesiastics' case, where the church provided an institutional foundation for their connectivity, most evidence regarding the level of connectivity within Manuel's network emerges from the letters exchanged between the members of the circle gathered around Manuel. In addition to relations of friendship, letters suggest that frequently, rhetoricians were connected by teacher–student relations. In the Peloponnese, Plethon founded and led an intellectual circle within which he disseminated his teachings, which often pertained to the revival of an ancient form of Hellenism.[56] Kydones was also regarded as a mentor by his disciples: Manuel Kalekas, Manuel Chrysoloras, Maximos Chrysoberges.[57] Kydones instructed Kalekas on gathering his own letters, while Kalekas and Manuel Chrysoloras also exchanged several letters.[58] Similar connections of the teacher–student type were established between the latter and several Italian humanists.

Furthermore, epistolography allows us to acquire an insight into the ties between these scholars and the emperor and to assess the emperor's centrality in this literary circle. Again, Demetrios Kydones' case stands out due to the extent of his letter collection, which suggests a privileged relationship with Emperor Manuel.[59] Almost eighty letters in the *mesazōn*'s collection were addressed to Manuel II, attesting a strong connection spanning a period of several decades. This close relationship indicates Kydones' influence on both the emperor's literary choices and his approach to foreign relations.[60] Several earlier letters indicate that during the emperor's youth, Kydones guided the emperor's studies in the study of rhetoric.[61] Almost twenty letters were sent while Manuel lived in Thessalonike from 1382 to 1387, highlighting Kydones' concern for the empire's unity and the ruling dynasty.[62] Conversely, Manuel addressed more than ten letters to Kydones, whom he portrayed as a respected teacher.[63]

---

[56] Akışık, *Self and Other*, 34–58.
[57] Manuel Kalekas, *Letters*, no. 25, ed. Loenertz. See also Kianka, *Demetrius Cydones*, 213–14.
[58] Loenertz, *Recueils*, 10–48. Kalekas sent seven letters to Chrysoloras (Manuel Kalekas, *Letters*, nos. 24, 48, 59, 62, 86, 89, ed. Loenertz).
[59] On the letter exchange between Kydones and Manuel see Loenertz, 'Manuel Paleologue et Demetrius Cydones'.
[60] Manuel often acknowledged Kydones' influence, e.g. Manuel II, *Letters*, nos. 5, 10–12, ed. Dennis.
[61] E.g. Demetrios Kydones, *Letters*, no. 80, ed. Loenertz.
[62] E.g. ibid. no. 348.
[63] The book exchange between the two as well as the exchange of their own texts is attested in their correspondence. In a letter Manuel speaks about his refusal to return one of Kydones' texts; Demetrios Kydones, *Letters*, no. 5, ed. Loenertz.

Owing to his influential position, Kydones maintained wide-ranging connections at court, including with the emperors John VI Kantakouzenos and John V, the empress Helena Palaiologina, Manuel's mother, and Theodore Kantakouzenos, the despot of the Morea.[64] Moreover, Kydones' connections with the imperial court opened the doors for his close disciples, Manuel Chrysoloras and Manuel Kalekas. The latter's relations with Manuel II are attested by four letters he addressed to the emperor, who had asked Kalekas about a manuscript.[65] The exchanges of letters and texts as well as diplomatic services testify to a close relationship between Manuel Chrysoloras and the emperor.[66] Part of these efforts concerned the advertising of the emperor's rhetorical skills in the humanist intellectual circles, as indicated by Manuel's letter asking Chrysoloras to read, and comment on, the *Funeral Oration*. In return, Chrysoloras wrote an epistolary discourse praising the emperor's achievements and addressed to him another text which compared the old and the new Rome.[67] Notably, as the emperor's agent in the West, Chrysoloras must have been in constant contact with the emperor.[68] As for Demetrios Chrysoloras, eight letters in Manuel's collection suggest that the emperor held him in high esteem, especially for his rhetorical skills.[69] The strength of their connection might have also been determined by Demetrios's role of *mesazōn* at the court of John VII. For his part, John Chortasmenos wrote encomia for the emperor and addressed to him several letters which point to his own influence at the court. Albeit brief in comparison with other contemporary epistolary collections, his letters reveal connections with other members of the Palaiologos family or Manuel's circle of close acquaintances.[70] Finally, Isidore of Kiev's connection with Manuel is reflected in his activity as imperial copyist. As a matter of fact, the four de luxe manuscripts of the emperor's texts (Vat. gr. 1619, Vat. Barb. gr. 219, Vindob. phil. gr. 98 and Crypten. Z δ 1) that were dedicated to his son,

---

[64] Kydones' connections with the imperial family were due to the relationship between his father and John VI Kantakouzenos; Demetrios Kydones, *Letters*, ed. Loenertz, 1. 4–6.

[65] Manuel Kalekas, *Letters*, nos. 14, 26, 47, 71, ed. Loenertz. Letters 34 and 39, also addressed to the emperor and dated to 1397–1401, were written in the name of other individuals who were asking favours of the emperor.

[66] In the *Epistolary Oration on Manuel Palaiologos's 'Funeral Oration'*, Manuel Chrysoloras recalls the intense correspondence with the emperor: *Epistolary Oration*, 98, ed. Patrineles and Sophianos.

[67] Manuel Chrysoloras, *Comparison of the Old and the New Rome*, ed. Billò.

[68] Manuel Chrysoloras, *Epistolary Oration*, 130.8–14, ed. Patrineles and Sophianos: δέδωκας γὰρ ἡμῖν ταῦτα πρὸς σε τολμᾶν φθέγγεσθαι, οὐ δεσπότης μόνον ἀλλὰ καὶ πατὴρ ἡμῖν γινόμενος.

[69] Manuel II, *Letters*, nos. 33, 41, 43, 44, 46, 48, 50, 61, ed. Dennis.

[70] See Chortasmenos's letters and the *Monody on Theodore Antiochites*, in John Chortasmenos, *Briefe*, 139–43, ed. Hunger.

John VIII, were copied by Isidore.[71] He also delivered Manuel's oration for his deceased brother, Theodore, in Mystras (1409) and praised him extensively in an encomium again dedicated to John VIII (1429).

The network in action: the rhetoricians and the emperor

This literary network attested by numerous letters served a variety of purposes for both the emperor and its members. At the most basic level, it had a practical function, since Manuel often played the role of a patron of scholars who subsequently used their acquaintance with the emperor to acquire material benefits. In their letters addressed to the emperor, Kydones, Manuel Chrysoloras and Demetrios Chrysoloras show gratitude to the emperor for the gifts and probably salaries they received, for most of the participants in the *theatra* still depended on the emperor's largesse.[72] Reflecting the same kind of network usage, Manuel Kalekas, Kydones and Chortasmenos also wrote in the name of other individuals who were looking for administrative positions or other benefits.[73]

Second, another function of this network was to provide a platform for cooperation among scholars in the process of writing. The emperor not only delivered several of his texts in public but also circulated them among fellow authors. Often, Manuel sent versions of his texts together with cover letters in which he requested opinions regarding their quality. Among the addressees were Demetrios Kydones,[74] Manuel Chrysoloras[75] and Demetrios Chrysoloras.[76] The process was mutual, for Manuel himself read and commented on his friends' compositions.[77]

---

[71] Ibid. The more official character of these manuscripts is underlined by the presence of the original binding with the monogram of the Palaiologos family on the cover of Crypten. Z δ 1. See Irigoin, 'Reliure de l'Athos'.

[72] John Chortasmenos, *Letters*, in *Briefe*, no. 35, ed. Hunger: πένης μὲν εἶναι ὁμολογῶ καὶ λέγων οὐ ψεύδομαι. Chortasmenos repeated his request for financial help in a poem addressed to John VIII Palaiologos, *Hortatory Poem to Emperor John the Younger*, in ibid. 5–9. Another scholar, Manuel Chrysoloras, acknowledged having received gifts from the emperor (*Epistolary Oration*, 54, ed. Patrineles and Sophianos).

[73] E.g. Demetrios Kydones, *Letters*, no. 210, ed. Loenertz.

[74] Manuel II, *Letters*, no. 62, ed. Dennis, to Demetrios Kydones, asking for feedback on the *Dialogue*. Kydones answered in another letter (*Letters*, no. 398 ed. Loenertz). Manuel's letter 11 addressed to Kydones is a cover letter for his *Admonitory Oration*. Again, the *mesazōn* answered in another letter (*Letters*, no. 262 ed. Loenertz).

[75] Manuel II, *Letters*, no. 56, ed. Dennis, addressed to Manuel Chrysoloras on the *Funeral Oration*.

[76] Manuel II, *Letters*, no. 61, ed. Dennis. In response to Chrysoloras's *One Hundred Letters* Manuel sent him a *Homily on the Dormition of the Theotokos*, for revision.

[77] E.g. Manuel II, *Letters*, no. 15, ed. Dennis, to Kabasilas: 'First of all then, I can give no higher opinion about your most recent letter to us than that which you know we have already given about your previous ones.'

Often the feedback addressed to the emperor took the form of lengthy and detailed interpretations. An example of the echo which the emperor's texts found among contemporary authors is the *Funeral Oration*, commented on extensively by Manuel Chrysoloras and Gemistos Plethon.[78] Feedback was often backed up with collaboration. Gabriel, metropolitan of Thessalonike, helped Manuel in writing the *Homily on Sin and Penance* and the *Homily on St Mary of Egypt*.[79] Further evidence from late Palaiologan manuscripts analysed in the past few decades indicates that the scholars gathered around Manuel worked together on copying and improving the emperor's texts. Manuscript Vat. gr. 1619 provides evidence for contacts between the members of Manuel's learned circle in the late fourteenth century.[80] The same type of collaboration is detectable in other manuscripts as well: in Vat. Barb. gr. 219 and Vat. gr. 1107, containing the texts of Manuel, the hands of both Makarios Makres and Isidore of Kiev have been identified.[81]

Third, Manuel actively sought to engage his literary friends in his political endeavours. Despite the predominant literary topics, the emperor's letters addressed to his friends often allude to the political situation. He maintained contact with Manuel Chrysoloras, his ambassador, to whom he transmitted his plans on the progress of negotiations with the Western leaders. At other times, in letters addressed to friends, he alluded to his daily activities or the problems he encountered in establishing order in the empire.[82] In a letter sent to Kydones, Manuel summoned his mentor to take a more active part in state affairs.[83] The same request to Kydones was made in another lengthy letter sent while he resided in Venice. The literary circle also provided the emperor with intellectual and political contacts beyond the Byzantine realm, in the Latin world, particularly Italy.[84] In addition to Manuel Chrysoloras, the cases of John Chrysoloras, his nephew,[85] and of

---

[78] Shorter comments on the same text were written by Manuel Chrysokephalos and Joasaph the monk: *Funeral Oration*, 70–1.

[79] This collaboration is recorded in Manuel II, *Letters*, no. 52. 35–7, ed. Dennis: 'From then, an offering from the fruit of our labors comes to you. And if something worthwhile should be found in it [i.e. *Homily on St Mary of Egypt*], you may show it to the right people and not keep it for yourself.'

[80] Dendrinos, 'Co-operation', 8.

[81] See also Dendrinos, 'Palaiologan scholars'.

[82] Manuel II, *Letters*, no. 44, ed. Dennis, addressed to Demetrios Chrysoloras.

[83] Manuel II, *Letters*, nos. 3, 4, ed. Dennis.

[84] Plethon, for instance, was aware of the philosophical debates in Italy: τοὺς δὲ νῦν Πλάτωνος ἡττωμένους ἐν Ἰταλίᾳ, οἷς φησὶ χαριζόμενος τὴν τοιαύτην πραγματείαν λαβεῖν ἐπὶ νοῦν, ἴσμεν τίνες εἰσί; Gemistos Plethon, *Against Scholarios*, 2.14–17, ed. Maltese.

[85] Manuel's letter 56 (ed. Dennis) indicates that John Chrysoloras was the bearer of the emperor's *Funeral Oration* and of the letter whereby he asked for a Latin translation.

Demetrios Skaranos[86] indicate that the emperor used his literary friends as agents in the West.[87]

This evidence for the rhetoricians' functions can further suggest the absence of established rhetorical services such as the regular performance of imperial orations on designated dates by designated people. We can therefore conclude that Emperor Manuel used this scholarly circle as a platform to advertise an image of authority at both the rhetorical and the political level. As indicated above, if in the early decades of the fourteenth century, for many scholars like Thomas Magistros, the *theatron* was a means of social upward mobility, now *theatra* came to serve the emperor's purposes rather than the scholars'.

Ihor Ševčenko's statement that in the Palaiologan period everybody knew everybody accurately reflects the situation of Manuel's circle of intellectuals.[88] One can even draw a parallel with the contemporary humanist intellectual groups, since both the learned Italian and Byzantine circles seem to have promoted mentoring and friendly connections.[89] Furthermore, the evidence presented here indicates a revival of court rhetoric during Manuel's reign in comparison with the previous reign of John V Palaiologos. Based on the evidence of Manuel's epistolary collection, we may assume that the emperor wished to portray himself as an expert in rhetoric and encouraged his friends to consider him as a kind of first among equals rather than an emperor. In doing so, it is possible that he wished to follow the model of his mentor, Demetrios Kydones, who also gathered around him a circle of friends with literary preoccupations.

The profile of this group which constituted the primary audience for Manuel's texts allows us to make two further observations about its composition and development. First, most of the group were divided with regard to their religious or political opinions. These differences between the members of the same literary circle might have encouraged the emperor to tune his discourse according to the views characteristic of each of these different subgroups and to approach a multitude of genres. And second, in chronological terms, this

---

[86] Manuel's letter 49 (ed. Dennis) addressed to Manuel Chrysoloras suggests that Demetrios Skaranos promoted the emperor's interests in Italy.
[87] Relations with the Latin West are attested by the significant number of Latin letters issued from Manuel's chancery and often conveyed by his ambassador, Manuel Chrysoloras. We also know of four letters addressed by Manuel to Martin V and Ferdinand I of Aragon. See Barker, *Manuel II*, Appendices.
[88] 'The criss-crossing of the lines of correspondence shows that everybody was in touch with everybody at some time'; Ševčenko, *Society and Intellectual Life*, 70.
[89] In his letters, Guarino often reminded his fellow scholars of their debt to Manuel Chrysoloras. See Thomson, 'Manuel Chrysoloras', 70.

literary circle underwent several transformations throughout Manuel's reign. The group to which he belonged was also active before his reign, as testified by the many letters dating from the period before 1391.[90] In the beginning, following his mentor, Demetrios Kydones, Manuel maintained closer relations with several Byzantines who upheld pro-Western views. Later, the number of people with strict Orthodox views, especially members of the clergy, like Makarios Makres, Joseph Bryennios and the hieromonk David, increased. This change in the group configuration can be explained by the fact that many members of the pro-Latin group gradually left Constantinople for Italy while the influence of Orthodox ecclesiastics increased.

Manuel's influence as convener of literary circles becomes clearer when compared with similar contemporary activities. We know of few contemporary patrons of literature like Constantine Asanes, who offered limited protection to the pro-Latin group in Constantinople. In contrast, Manuel not only managed to offer shelter to the literati, but also organised assemblies in the imperial palace in a sizeable library like the one described by Pero Tafur, a visitor to Constantinople around 1430.[91] In addition a recent study has suggested that the emperor sponsored a workshop of manuscript production in Constantinople where Isidore of Kiev and Demetrios Pepagomenos, two copyists connected to the imperial family, were active. This workshop functioned in the first decades of the fifteenth century.[92] Based on this evidence, it is plausible that Manuel tried to establish the imperial court's role as a pre-eminent centre of literary patronage, given the fact that previously during the Palaiologan period other local centres of patronage had multiplied: Thessalonike, Mystras and especially Italy.

As it seems, this substantial group of rhetoricians played an important role within both the political and the intellectual spheres of late Byzantium. While it reflected the late Byzantine authors' common preoccupations, it also served the emperor's needs. From this perspective, the rhetoricians' support became a valued currency in the political negotiations of the period, as they were frequently complicit in the emperor's efforts to disseminate a message of political stability. Besides, arguably, by attaching himself to a scholarly circle and by constantly seeking recognition for his literary achievements, Manuel

---

[90] See the letters addressed by Manuel to Kydones, Kabasilas and Triboles; Manuel II, *Letters*, nos. 3–12, ed. Dennis.

[91] 'At the entrance to the Palace, beneath certain chambers, is an open loggia of marble with stone benches around it. Here are many books and ancient writings and histories, and on one side are gaming boards so that the Emperor's house may be well supplied'; Pero Tafur, *Travels and Adventures*, 145, ed. and trans. Letts.

[92] Grosdidier and Förstel, 'Quelques manuscrits grecs'.

attempted to legitimise himself as a different kind of ruler. The scholarly network he gathered around himself appears to have played the role of a parallel court endorsing the emperor especially during the times when he lacked full support for his political actions. Manuel needed this protection, as a variety of interest groups which comprised mostly members of aristocratic families vied for influence over the imperial decisions. In order to gain the support of this parallel court of literati he became one of its most active members, by composing and presenting his literary productions to an educated audience. Yet, before looking at how the emperor's texts and ideas circulated within this literary circle, we need to first understand the strategies and the values the rhetoricians privileged in their text. The ensuing sections in this chapter will explore in depth these aspects that pertain to the profile of the literary and ideological milieu the emperor inhabited.

The Rhetorical Landscape in the Late Palaiologan Period

As pointed out previously, despite a setback in the last decade of the fourteenth century, intellectual life in Constantinople continued to flourish during Manuel's reign.[93] The high number of court rhetorical texts attests the high value of rhetorical education as a social currency. The scholars' effort to produce well-rounded compositions indicate that rhetoric had a different meaning for them and for the ecclesiastics. While the latter used rhetoric primarily for urgent calls to action and addressed large audiences, for the rhetoricians, rhetoric rather constituted an instrument of praise and advice. According to Demetrios Chrysoloras, speeches addressed to the emperor were a way to respond to imperial omnipotence.[94] The vivid debates or simply letter exchanges between traditionalists like Chortasmenos and West-oriented scholars like Chrysoloras attest to this role of rhetoric. After the end of the Ottoman siege in 1402, the number of orations, homilies and verse compositions increased, possibly also because of the new, positive political conditions that saw a significant decrease of Ottoman pressure.[95] As a result, references to particular political conditions such as the conflicts in the Peloponnese or

---

[93] On the situation before 1402 see Manuel II, *Letters*, no. 34, ed. Dennis, addressed to Balsamon.
[94] Demetrios Chrysoloras, *Comparison*, 222.1, ed. Lampros.
[95] At the same time the number of encomia or *psogoi* increased, while the admonitory orations popular in the later decades of John V's reign are noticeably fewer during Manuel's reign. Many historians have looked at the encomia and *epitaphioi* for their historical information (Kioussopoulou, *Emperor or Manager*, 163–81).

church union proliferated in the admonitory rhetoric of this time.[96] While in Thessalonike and in Mystras, learned circles met occasionally, the centre of this intense rhetorical activity remained Constantinople, which continued to attract most of the educated elites from the provinces.

Because rhetoric continued to play a key role in court life, the rhetoricians approached a variety of topics and displayed a close familiarity with rhetorical rules.[97] For instance, in the preamble to his *prosphōnētikos logos* for emperor Manuel II, Chortasmenos sharply defined his oration in a threefold classification, according to the genre, type and species (κατὰ γένος ἰδέας, κατὰ τύπον, κατ' εἶδος).[98] In a similar vein, Manuel Chrysoloras praised the emperor for having applied these rules correctly in his texts.[99] Slightly later, Isidore of Kiev also highlighted his acquaintance with the rules of speech composition when he described the differences between rhetorical praises and when he set out his views on how an oratorical piece should look.[100]

As part of their acquaintance with the rhetorical rules, authors of Manuel's reign also developed a set of rhetorical standards that privileged selected rhetorical virtues drawn from the handbooks of rhetorical theory, especially Hermogenes': clarity, vigour, intensity, adequate composition and density of arguments (τὸ σαφές, δύναμις, δεινότης τῶν λόγων, ὀνομάτων συνθήκη, καὶ ἡ τῶν ἐνθυμημάτων πυκνότης).[101] We see these standards at work when Manuel Kalekas praised clarity above all else,[102] while, later, Manuel Chrysoloras also praised the δύναμις καὶ δεινότης τῶν λόγων (force and intersity of a speech).[103]

---

[96] Gemistos Plethon, *Address ... on the Situation in the Peloponnese*; Joseph Bryennios, *Admonitory Oration on the Union of the Churches*, in Εὑρεθέντα, 2, ed. Voulgares.

[97] On the literary interests of Palaiologan authors see Schreiner, 'Literarische Interessen', 205–11.

[98] John Chortasmenos, *Prooimion*, in *Briefe*, 217, ed. Hunger.

[99] Manuel Chrysoloras, *Epistolary Oration*, 75.28–30, ed. Patrineles and Sophianos. In addition, in the same passage, he praised the emperor for not mixing monodies and *epitaphioi*.

[100] Isidore introduces his encomium for John VIII with a discussion on the three parts of such a speech, namely deeds, family and fatherland: τριχῇ τοίνυν τοῦ τῶν ἐγκωμίων θεσμοῦ τοῖς ᾑρημένοις καθόλου λέγειν προαναφωνοῦντος, ἔργα, γένος, καὶ πατρίδα ταύτην κρηπῖδα τῶν ὅλων ἐκεῖνος ὑποθεῖναι; *Encomium for John VIII*, 135. 25, ed. Lampros.

[101] The idea of density of arguments (πυκνότης τῶν νοημάτων) was a literary feature which Manuel often mentions, e.g. in his letters 24 (to Frangopoulos, ed. Dennis) and 27 (to Theodore Kaukadenos, ed. Dennis); see also Manuel Chrysoloras, *Epistolary Oration*, 75.5, ed. Patrineles and Sophianos. On the resilience of this Hermogenian series of literary virtues in Byzantium see Kustas, *Studies in Byzantine Rhetoric*, 13.

[102] Manuel Kalekas, *Letters*, no. 10.31–2, ed. Loenertz, which stresses the need for clarity: ἐπεὶ καὶ ὁ μικρός σοι λόγος ἐκεῖνος, τὸ σαφὲς ἐν οἷς γράφω τιμᾶν παραγγείλας.

[103] Manuel Chrysoloras, *Epistolary Oration*, 74.17–18, ed. Patrineles and Sophianos.

However, awareness of the rules of rhetorical composition did not prevent the court authors of the Palaiologan period from taking the freedom to introduce several innovations within the Byzantine rhetorical tradition to which they belonged.[104] The increased literary activity of the post-1402 period reveals a tendency to experiment with different literary forms, a phenomenon also observable in the Komnenian and early Palaiologan periods. Within this tendency towards experimentation, one can count several texts like John Chortasmenos's *Funeral Lament* for a member of the Asanes family, Andreas, or Demetrios Chrysoloras's *One Hundred Letters Addressed to Emperor Manuel II*.[105] In the first-mentioned text, Chortasmenos skilfully combined verse, prose and dialogue to produce a hybrid text. The choice of a *thrēnos* instead of a monody or an *epitaphios* is also surprising since, in Byzantium, *thrēnoi* were used to relate unfortunate historical events.[106] Demetrios Chrysoloras's text also has a unique form resulting from the learned combination of advisory texts for rulers with epistolography.[107] They were not intended as letters per se but as an exercise to prove that the author was able to write in a concise form after the emperor accused him of excessive wordiness.[108] As Treu pointed out,[109] the *One Hundred Letters* may have constituted an attempt to emulate Manuel II's *Foundations* and it is akin to another text by Chrysoloras, the *Comparison between the Emperor of Today and the Ancient Rulers*, written in the manner of a panegyric for the emperor Manuel II.[110]

Following a similar trend to experiment with literary forms, many late Palaiologan authors introduced extensive narratives into their epideictic compositions. As a matter of fact, given the glaring absence of grand historical narratives,[111] it is noticeable that the epideictic oratory of this period

---

[104] Toth, *Imperial Orations*, 183, argues that Menander's rhetorical rules were constantly overlooked in late Byzantine rhetoric.
[105] To these texts can be added further contemporary writings such as Manuel Chrysoloras's *Epistolary Oration*, a panegyric disguised as a letter.
[106] Hunger, *Hochsprachliche profane Literatur*, 161–9.
[107] Hunger designated this strategy as 'Raffinement der variatio' because it combined arguments of political thought, theology and private life: ibid. 163.
[108] Manuel II, *Letters*, nos. 46, 48, ed. Dennis.
[109] Treu, 'Demetrius Chrysoloras', 106.
[110] The form of the text (one hundred brief letters) echoed to a large extent Manuel's hundred paragraphs in his *Foundations*, a text which treated the same range of topics in a similar fragmentary manner. In letter 75 (ed. Conti Bizzarro), Demetrios Chrysoloras alluded to the emperor's text. The text has a paraenetic character and it is possible that it was connected with the beginnings of John VIII's effective rule.
[111] Dennis designated it as 'the great gap' of Byzantine historiography, which lasted for about a hundred years: *Reign of Manuel II*, 18.

underwent a process of narrativisation whereby rhetoricians transformed disparate images into coherent stories. Many late Palaiologan authors of oratorical texts were often preoccupied by ways to depict the rulers' deeds instead of simply providing strings of conventional virtues.[112] Symeon of Thessalonike's *Historical Oration on St Demetrios*, despite fitting into a tradition of religious encomia of which the author was certainly aware,[113] replaced the account of the saint's miracles with a lengthy account of the regional relations of Thessalonike in the early fifteenth century. Likewise, John Chortasmenos's *Oration on the Miracles of the Theotokos* featuring a description of the Battle of Ankara in 1402, Demetrios Chrysoloras's *Comparison between the Emperor of Today and the Ancient Rulers* and Isidore of Kiev's *Panegyric Addressed to Emperor John VIII* used detailed narratives of events; in fact, micro-histories of Manuel II's reign.[114] The intellectual preoccupations of the scholars in the emperor's proximity concerned not only the display of rhetorical skill but also the pursuit of other areas of study, such as philosophy, theology and political reflection. The theological debates of the earlier decades continued to dominate the religious spectrum and a certain tension between the defenders of Orthodoxy and the pro-Latin scholars continued to mark the intellectual positions of the scholars contemporary with Manuel. Theologians often cast this tension in terms of an opposition between Byzantine theology and the scholastic syllogistic methods drawn from the works of Thomas Aquinas, who found adherents among the Byzantines. Demetrios Chrysoloras's *Dialogue on Demetrios Kydones' Antirrhetic* reflects this ongoing debate that also took on nationalistic overtones: Chrysoloras claimed that the Orthodox faith represented a core feature of Byzantine identity and that Kydones' Byzantine Catholicism was an attack on the freedom of the community.[115]

The traits of the rhetoricians' intellectual profile were further determined by other areas of expertise. Doubtless, a strong pedagogical focus influenced their texts and connections established within or beyond Byzantium. Most of them, like Chortasmenos, Kalekas, Manuel Chrysoloras and Plethon, taught extensively and their pedagogical skills were greatly appreciated by students

---

[112] E.g. Isidore of Kiev, *Panegyric*, 133, ed. Lampros.
[113] Symeon of Thessalonike, *Politico-Historical Works*, 104, ed. Balfour.
[114] For a discussion of these texts and their historical narratives see Schmitt, 'Kaiserrede und Zeitgeschichte'; Toth, *Imperial Orations*, 197; Leonte, 'Visions of empire'. It is also plausible that this kind of narrative functioned as a sort of newspaper for the populace. This seems to have started in Eustathios of Thessalonike's homilies and was taken to an extreme in Nikolaos Mesarites' Lenten homily. See Nikolaos Mesarites, *His Life and Works*, trans. Angold, 7–12.
[115] Demetrios Chrysolaras, *Dialogue on Demetrios Kydones' Antirrhetic*, 12–58, ed. Pasiourtides.

of different ages, geographical location and social status. The rhetoricians dominated the intellectual landscape not only because of a chronic shortage of resources, but also because of the high demand for teachers of Greek, especially in Italy. The trend inaugurated by Manuel Chrysoloras, the first Byzantine teacher in Florence, continued during the early fifteenth century. Sometimes, these teachers taught basic disciplines like grammar and rhetoric, as appears from a letter which Kalekas addressed to the father of a certain Matthew.[116] Later, the same Kalekas urged Jacopo Angeli to continue the study of Greek grammar in Florence.[117] At other times, they provided their disciples with a far deeper intellectual understanding, in a move which ensured the survival and influence of their ideas in various intellectual circles. A telling example was Plethon's school of Mystras, whose members disseminated their mentor's radical ideas of Hellenic identity. Among his most celebrated students one finds Mark Eugenikos, Bessarion and Isidore, future metropolitan of Kiev.[118] Some of his disciples, like a certain Iouvenalios, were even persecuted for continuing to endorse their mentor's ideas.[119]

Main Themes in the Rhetoricians' Writings

As in the ecclesiastics' case, the analysis of the rhetoricians' texts reveals the same key topics dominating their discourse: education and the social and economic divide; enemies and allies; markers of Byzantine identity; and the political sphere and imperial authority. In the following I will deal with each of these.

Education and the social and economic divide

Although Byzantine political thinkers rarely advocated reforms of political institutions, they nevertheless tended to prize education. Their criticism of contemporary dominant cultural values and social realities largely shaped their political attitudes. Just like the ecclesiastics, the imperial rhetoricians became well aware of the empire's difficult social and economic situation, particularly during the long Ottoman siege of 1394–1402. An anonymous account of the siege of Constantinople explained Byzantine weakness during the Ottoman siege by reminding the audience of the inhabitants' immoral excesses (ὕβρις):

---

[116] Manuel Kalekas, *Letters*, no. 2, ed. Loenertz. Cf. letters nos. 6, 7.
[117] Ibid. no. 64.
[118] Akışık, *Self and Other*, 34–58.
[119] Ibid.

This virtuous emperor was forced to submit (εἴκειν ἠναγκάζετο) to a most impious barbarian and the Roman Empire became so weak during those times that the affairs of the Romans were left with no other resources but the City of Constantinople. Under these circumstances, as the situation constantly worsened, the Romans suffered all kinds of misfortunes due to their excesses.[120]

But if the ecclesiastics disapproved of the Byzantines' low ethics and improvisations in matters of Orthodox faith, in addition to the moral decline of the state the imperial rhetoricians bemoaned the deterioration in the levels of knowledge and education. In the section dedicated to *paideia* from his *Epistolary Oration* Manuel Chrysoloras urged the emperor to support education in Constantinople, at a time when many Byzantine teachers preferred to move to Italy and undertake teaching positions there:

> It is paradoxical that in Italy as well as in other places certain people study our literature and have become knowledgeable in this, but in Greece and in Constantinople it is neglected. This must not happen, for the love of God: but despite this situation, help the common people, support the men of old who wrote something so that their texts and their good and honorable efforts would not disappear.[121]

In his letters, Kydones expressed bitterness about the impossibility of finding individuals knowledgeable about ancient rhetoric in Constantinople. This attitude persisted until the last decades of Byzantium, for Bessarion, another high-profile Byzantine scholar, remarked that the Byzantines, once considered highly educated individuals by their Western peers, were now frowned upon as ignorant. In a deliberative address to the emperor Constantine XI, Bessarion noted that the technical knowledge and the wisdom of the Byzantines had almost completely vanished or had been entirely transferred to the Latins. The level of education, he concluded, could be raised only by inviting Latin specialists to Constantinople or by sending Byzantine students to Italy.[122]

---

[120] Anonymous, *Oration on the Siege of Constantinople*, 104.28–106.1, ed. Gautier.

[121] Manuel Chrysoloras, *Epistolary Oration*, 119, ed. Patrineles and Sophianos. See the entire section dedicated to education, titled *paideia*, 117–23.

[122] According to Bessarion, these half-dozen students should not be too young, nor should they be too old, for otherwise it would be difficult for them to learn a foreign language. Their programme of study should include technological training. See Ševčenko, 'Decline', 177–80.

More often than not, remarks on the state of learning and education in Byzantium were connected with proposals to introduce social reforms meant to improve the economic situation of large, impoverished parts of the population. Ever since the early fourteenth century, rhetoricians had noted the increasing social gap between the rich and the poor. In an address to the Thessalonicans, Thomas Magistros (c. 1275–c. 1348) advocated the idea of harmony and concord of interests among the members of social and political elites, the rest of the population (οἱ προὔχειν λαχόντες) and the less well off (οἱ πολλοί). Magistros thus urged the citizens to maintain their cohesion and called for a humane attitude towards the city's disadvantaged population.[123] Magistros's contemporary Alexios Makrembolites (d. 1353) also warned that exploitation of the poor by the rich might lead to the decline of the state.[124] Like their ecclesiastic contemporaries, John Anagnostes and Demetrios Kydones presented the economic divisions in Thessalonian society as one of the major reasons for the empire's failure to defend itself properly. Both authors noted that the difficult political situation was largely due to internal social gaps, especially within Thessalonian society.[125]

Hints of the intellectuals' awareness of the social divisions emerge in other authors as well. In his *Oration for the Theotokos*,[126] which celebrated the delivery of the city from the Ottoman siege (1403), Demetrios Chrysoloras observed that in order to continue to enjoy divine protection it was necessary for the Byzantines to establish a certain level of social and economic fairness. He demanded that those who possessed wealth should share their possessions with those in need.[127] Accordingly, Demetrios urged his fellow citizens to adopt an austere way of life and not to indulge themselves in luxuriousness:

> Let us not eat excessively. Let us not become like southern Libya, an arid and infertile land. When we blame depravity, drunkenness, and love of money, let us not practice these. When we exhort others to tell the truth, let us not turn our tongue and tell lies. Let us not allow pleasure to be an enemy in our words and let us not strive to defeat Epicurus in pleasure, but let us bring gifts as sacrifices to the Virgin, the one who gave us gifts, for she will rejoice upon seeing our gifts. What does this mean? Faith and humility in love.[128]

---

[123] Gaul, *Thomas Magistros*, 144–59.
[124] Alexios Makrembolites, 'Dialogue between the Rich and the Poor', ed. Ševčenko.
[125] Demetrios Kydones, *Letters*, no. 273 (addressed to Rhadenos in 1384), and no. 299. 8–17 (addressed to Emperor Manuel in 1384), ed. Loenertz. See also John Anagnostes, *Account of the Siege*, 12.
[126] Demetrios Chrysoloras, *Oration for the Theotokos*, 348–56, ed. Gautier.
[127] Ibid. 356.142–8.
[128] Ibid. 356.149–56.

Regardless of its moral undertones, Chrysoloras's text pointed to the deep economic and social differentiation among the residents of the capital. The solution he envisaged regarded mainly the redistribution of wealth from which the majority of poverty-stricken inhabitants would benefit. According to Chrysoloras, in addition to divine action, wealth redistribution represented a solution for stopping less well-off Constantinopolitans from fleeing from the city into the enemies' territories.[129]

Kydones' and Chrysoloras's remarks on the necessity for social reform based on the idea of redistribution of wealth found elaboration in a completely new political and social system imagined by Plethon and presented to the emperor and his son, Theodore Palaiologos, in several advisory texts.[130] Plethon envisaged a political system inspired by Plato's *Republic* that put forward the idea of an ideal society where every citizen belonged to a particular class with a specific social function: those willing to work their own land (τὸ αὐτουργικόν), the servants (τὸ διακονικὸν) and the leaders (τὸ ἀρχικὸν φύλον).[131] Within his system, Plethon emphasised the idea of social justice, arguing for the belief in a deity whose main feature was the disposal of justice.[132] The social division which he envisaged would have ensured a righteous distribution of wealth according to each individual's role. More exactly, Plethon's texts proposed radical agrarian reforms according to which the land would belong to all its inhabitants, and no one would have the right to claim any part of it as private property. Instead, land resources were supposed to be redistributed to those who could best make use of them, with each individual, according to his abilities, putting an area under cultivation and making it productive.[133] Taxes should not take the form of ill treatment similar to enslavement, but be such as would seem light and appropriate, as well as of a nature sufficient to provide appropriate means for the affairs of the state.[134] Instead of extraordinary taxes, whose level could change significantly, Plethon proposed that there should be one tax calculated according to a single, set formula.[135]

---

[129] Ibid. 354.105–10.

[130] On Plethon's social and political reforms see Nikolaou, Περὶ πολιτείας. It is likely Gemistos was also aware of earlier developments regarding social and political reforms. See Masai, *Pléthon et le platonisme*, 62; Mamalakes, *Georgios Gemistos Plethon*, 18; Woodhouse, *George Gemistos Plethon*, 22.

[131] On Plethon's social-political and religious utopia and its possible connections with the fifteenth-century Muslim world see Siniossoglou, 'Sect and utopia'.

[132] Gemistos Plethon, *Admonitory Oration*, 119–20. See also Peritore, 'Political thought', 160–72; Baloglou, 'Institutions'.

[133] Gemistos Plethon, *Address . . . on the Situation in the Peloponnese*, 260–1, ed. Lampros.

[134] Gemistos Plethon, *Admonitory Oration*, 123, ed. Lampros.

[135] Gemistos Plethon, *Address . . . on the Situation in the Peloponnese*, 255–6, ed. Lampros.

In a similar vein, Plethon also rejected consumerism as another phenomenon that plagued Byzantium. All desire for luxury items must be restricted, he claimed, for 'the way of life of citizens, and notably of those who govern, should not be luxurious but measured'.[136] He argued against the purchase of foreign clothing, declaring that it is much more appropriate for people to dress in clothes made locally, out of native fabrics, rather than in woollen stuff brought 'from the Atlantic Ocean'.[137] The Peloponnese, according to him, was capable of producing goods sufficient to cover the needs of its inhabitants provided that export was avoided; for this reason, whatever was produced should remain in the country and not reach the hands of foreigners.[138] Such a policy could be easily achieved through a prohibitive tax upon foreigners, who would then be heavily disadvantaged and unable to compete when seeking to acquire goods.[139] All in all, despite their singularity it appears nevertheless that Gemistos's detailed measures of reform reflected the general concerns expressed by contemporary late Byzantine authors.

Enemies and allies

Such texts, which provided solutions and explanations for the sudden changes occurring in Byzantium, indicate that the imperial rhetoricians did not regard political decline as an irreversible process.[140] Although many authors, like Manuel Kalekas, deplored Constantinople's situation under a long-lasting military blockade,[141] Bayezid's unexpected defeat in 1402 brought the hope that the end of Byzantium was still far away.[142] Attempts to formulate solutions consisted not only in preaching moral and economic reforms but also in pointing out forces hostile to Byzantium or identifying reliable military allies.[143] A topic that repeatedly occurred in their texts was Bayezid's military pressure culminating in his siege of Constantinople in the late fourteenth and early fifteenth centuries.[144]

---

[136] Gemistos Plethon, *Admonitory Oration*, 124, ed. Lampros.
[137] Ibid.
[138] Gemistos Plethon, *Address . . . on the Situation in the Peloponnese*, 263, ed. Lampros.
[139] Gemistos Plethon, *Admonitory Oration*, 128, 157, ed. Lampros; *Address . . . on the Situation in the Peloponnese*, 264, ed. Lampros.
[140] See also Keller, 'Byzantine admirer'. See Kydones' exhortation to the Byzantines to halt the Turkish advance by a greater display of vigour.
[141] Manuel Kalekas, *Letters*, no. 73, ed. Loenertz.
[142] See Demetrios Chrysoloras, *Oration for the Theotokos*, 47.21–34, ed. Gautier: ὡς θαυμαστὰ τὰ ἔργα σου, δέσποινα. Ἐταπείνωσας ἡμᾶς, ἀλλ' οὐκ ἐξέτριψας· ἠσθενήσαμεν, ἀλλ' οὐκ ἀπεθάνομεν· ἐφθάρημεν, ἀλλ' οὐ κατεφθάρημεν.
[143] For earlier rhetorical treatments of enemies see Gaul, *Thomas Magistros*, 136–44.
[144] E.g. in Isidore of Kiev, *Panegyric*, 161.26–163.9, ed. Lampros.

Unlike the ecclesiastics who dismissed any form of Latin foreign support, many imperial rhetoricians supported the idea of an alliance with the more powerful Christian neighbour, despite the differences of doctrine. The main supporter of an alliance with the Latins against the Ottomans was Demetrios Kydones.[145] This idea, which fuelled Kydones' diplomatic efforts, was the major theme of most of his texts, including the admonitory speeches, the *Pro subsidio Latinorum* (*On the Support of the Latins*) and the *Oratio de non reddenda Gallipoli* (*On Not Abandoning Gallipoli*).[146] In the former composition, as in other texts,[147] Kydones used the term βάρβαροι (barbarians), assuming that the Ottomans represented an uncivilised, impious and cruel people. He provided a long list of their crimes and immoral acts, concluding that their aggressiveness provoked the Byzantines' present situation.[148] Furthermore, in condemning the Ottoman action Kydones insisted on the opposition between freedom and slavery. In the other oration, the *Oratio de non reddenda Gallipoli*, he treated similar themes, identifying the Ottomans as the major threat to the Byzantine state and defending the idea that Gallipoli was a strategic place for the Byzantines.[149] Demetrios's treatment of the Turkish menace combines aspects of ideological opposition, an assessment of the military and strategic situation, and disapproval of pro-Ottoman views among the Byzantines. As for the allies which the Byzantines could engage with, Kydones discarded the help of Bulgarians and Serbs, who, he said, had proved to be unreliable allies in the past.[150] In contrast, the Latins, apart from numerous cultural ties, possessed the necessary military experience required.[151] Unlike the Bulgarians and the Serbs, Kydones claimed, the Latins had no record of deceit, and they always acted in good faith as liberators.[152]

Kydones was not the only author advocating an alliance with the Latins. In his *Comparison of the Old and the New Rome*, by praising the Latins and their connections with the Byzantines, Manuel Chrysoloras similarly suggested that a political and military alliance between Latins and Byzantines was legitimate

---

[145] Demetrios Kydones, *Oratio de non reddenda Gallipoli*, PG 154, 977d. Kydones praised the Latins and likened them to the Byzantines.

[146] Ibid. 1010–36; Demetrios Kydones, *Oratio pro subsidio Latinorum*, PG 154, 961–1008. See also Ryder, *Career and Writings*, 57–82.

[147] On the *Apologiae*, see Ryder, *Career and Writings*, 42–9.

[148] PG 154, 964b: οὗτοι γὰρ μόνοι σχεδὸν τῶν ἡμετέρων κακῶν εἰσὶν αἰτιώτατοι, καὶ οἷς τὰ τῆς ἡμετέρας συμφορᾶς δικαίως ἄν τις λογίσαιτο.

[149] Ibid.

[150] Ryder, *Career and Writings*, 63–9.

[151] Ibid. 71–3.

[152] Demetrios Kydones, *Pro subsidio Latinorum*, PG 154, 968.

based on the common history of the two peoples. Doubtless, the assumptions and suggestions included in this text testifying to his admiration for Italy mirrored his apprenticeship with Kydones and his activity as a teacher of the Italian humanists in Florence or as ambassador in the West.[153]

The court rhetoricians did not deal exclusively with external threats and the possibilities for alliances, but equally treated the growing internal opposition to the central authority, a topic not entirely new for Byzantine panegyrists. Plethon's preface to Manuel's *Funeral Oration* and, most of all, the panegyrics addressed to Manuel, by Demetrios Chrysoloras, John Chortasmenos and Isidore, allude to the emperor's conflicts with those who posed a threat to the imperial authority.[154] They called attention to the increased disobedience, in various territories of the empire, of the local landowners who preferred foreign tutelage to Byzantine overlordship. In his *Comparison*, Demetrios Chrysoloras related that some of those who resisted the reconstruction of the Hexamilion attacked and occupied several fortresses, hence testifying to the efforts of Peloponnesian magnates to extend their control over new regions.[155] In his *Panegyric*, Isidore of Kiev stated that during his stay in the Morea Manuel II re-established order and 'relieved certain people who had been seized by tyrannical power'.[156]

While many attacked the actions of the landowners in the remote Morea, in Constantinople orators adopted a favourable position towards the members of the ruling family and other aristocrats. It is known that Demetrios Chrysoloras, an intimate of John VII Palaiologos, supported many members of the aristocracy with business connections in the Latin world. For his part, John Chortasmenos had numerous connections with Byzantine aristocrats and many of his texts, such as poems or ekphrastic epigrams, were addressed to members of the Palaiologos family.[157] Arguably, therefore, while reflecting the previous concerns of identifying solutions to the ongoing military crises by calling on Latin help, the late Palaiologan panegyrists also supported and lobbied the Byzantine aristocracy based in Constantinople.

---

[153] Manuel Chrysoloras's *Comparison* identifies many common points among them. For a discussion of Chrysoloras's approach to the description of Rome and Constantinople, see Kioussopoulou, 'Ville chez Manuel Chrysoloras'.

[154] See Gemistos Plethon, *Protheoria*, in *Funeral Oration*, 1–3.

[155] Demetrios Chrysoloras, *Comparison*, 243, ed. Lampros.

[156] Isidore of Kiev, *Panegyric*, 166, 2–3, ed. Lampros. On the Moreote magnates' opposition to Manuel's control see Necipoğlu, *Byzantium*, 261–2.

[157] See John Chortasmenos's poems-*ekphraseis* on the palaces of Theodore Kantakouzenos, in *Briefe*, 190–5, ed. Hunger.

Markers of Byzantine identity

The approach to Byzantine identity in the texts of the imperial rhetoricians falls into two broad categories: on the one hand there are multiple references to Byzantium's Hellenic roots, and on the other hand there emerges a tendency to stress the connections between Latins and Greeks. At the extreme end of these variations of the idea of a Byzantine individuality, one finds the national ideal of Gemistos Plethon reflecting a potential plan to create a Greek nation (τὸ τῶν Ἑλλήνων γένος) with a well-defined history and mythology.[158] In his three texts written during Manuel's reign Plethon outlined a kind of political utopianism and openly supported the idea of Hellenism. While he rejected Romanness, his focus was on the Peloponnese, which he saw as the cradle of a reborn Greek nation. Plethon sharply identified Sparta as the model for his ideal polity and took the legendary Lacedaemonian legislator Lykourgos as his example.[159] On many occasions, Plethon also praised the ancient Greek way of life, while in the *Admonitory Oration* addressed to Manuel on the situation in the Peloponnese he detailed his programme of returning to the values of ancient Sparta.[160]

In contrast to Plethon's Hellenism, for other contemporary Palaiologan authors the empire remained essentially Roman. For instance, in his *Panegyric*, Isidore of Kiev associated the idea of fatherland with Roman identity (τὴν πάτριον καὶ ῥωμαϊκὴν ἐλευθερίαν).[161] The occurrences of the terms 'Roman' and 'Hellene/Hellenic' in the panegyrics and encomiastic texts of the rhetoricians illustrate this situation. The five texts in Table 1, which focus on Manuel's personality, were written during his life or shortly after his death and circulated widely at the Constantinopolitan court.

A powerful statement of Byzantium's brilliant past centred on Roman ideals emerges in forging the literary image of Constantinople as a unique city and capital of the *oikoumenē*. Two lengthy *laudes Constantinopolitanae* date from the time of Manuel's reign: Manuel Chrysoloras's *Comparison of the Old and the New Rome*, in the form of a letter addressed to Emperor Manuel, and Isidore of Kiev's detailed description of the urban settlement of Constantinople, included in his first panegyric for John VIII (1429).[162] Owing to their concern for eulogy both texts seem to have followed in the steps of the early

---

[158] Gemistos Plethon, *Admonitory Oration*, 117.4, ed. Lampros. See also Beck, 'Reichsidee und nationale Politik'; Siniossoglou, *Radical Platonism*, 327–94.
[159] See Shawcross, 'New Lycourgos'.
[160] Gemistos Plethon, *Admonitory Oration*, 248–9, ed. Lampros.
[161] Isidore of Kiev, *Panegyric*, 176. 11, ed. Lampros.
[162] Isidore of Kiev, *Panegyric*. On Constantinople see also Isidore's *Encomium for John VIII*, 202–3, ed. Lampros.

Table 1 Occurrences of 'Roman' and 'Hellene/Hellenic' in the panegyrics

Author and text	'Roman'	'Hellene/Hellenic'
Anonymous, *Funeral Oration on Manuel II*, ed. Dendrinos	443.47, 444.85	446.23
Anonymous, *Panegyric*, in *Two Panegyrics*, ed. Polemes	–	–
Demetrios Chrysoloras, *Comparison*, ed. Lampros	224.23, 226.8, 229.5, 234.20, 237.5, 245.14	222.2, 239.28
John Chortasmenos, *Panegyric*, in *Briefe*, ed. Hunger	ll. 26, 73, 94, 98, 108, 115, 169, 170, 173	l. 4
Isidore of Kiev, *Panegyric*, ed. Lampros	145.31, 152.3, 157.15, 159.9, 151.8, 151.30, 152.9, 152.12, 155.17, 156.12, 160.12, 160.20, 162.18, 162.23, 163.24, 165.29, 172.29, 176.11, 176.27, 176.28, 179.27, 198.23	158.3, 174.28

Palaiologan rhetors who put forth a series of ideological claims pertaining to Constantinople as the centre of the *oikoumenē*.[163] As his title indicates, Chrysoloras discussed the parallels between the new and the old Rome and dedicated a lengthier praise to Rome's architectural wonders.[164] He insisted on the representation of Constantinople, founded by both Greeks and Romans, as a reflection of the old Rome.[165] In Chrysoloras's view, the Byzantines descended from the Romans and, for this reason, he underlined the political model which the Latins provided. He highlighted the advantages of the political organisation of ancient Rome which made possible the accomplishments of the early Roman emperors.[166]

Isidore takes a step further in the exploration of Byzantine Romanness. In his encomium he emphasises that the Roman Empire was the predecessor of

---

[163] Angelov, *Imperial Ideology*, 114.
[164] Kioussopoulou, 'Ville chez Manuel Chrysoloras', 79.
[165] Demetrios Chrysoloras, *Comparison*, PG 156, 45: 'Had I wished to enumerate the memorials, the tombs, the monuments and statues that are or have been in our city [Constantinople], I would not have been at a loss to do so. I might have to acknowledge that there are fewer of them than there are in here [in Rome].'
[166] Ibid.

the Byzantines, and he draws the contours of a consistent picture of the glorious Roman past when both Asia and Europe were under its authority. Eventually, in order to express the ties between Byzantines and Romans, Isidore introduces a compound term, *Rhomhellenes* (Ῥωμέλληνες), to define the Byzantine ethnos which underlines the Latin element:

> For there is nothing as highly esteemed as the Hellenes and the Romans living under the sun, nor another more significant race (οὐδὲν ἄλλο γε ἴσον, οὐχ ὅτι μεῖζον τῷ γένει). [. . .] Thus, two similar elements were adapted and combined in a good and appropriate way, and from both these prominent nations one single genos emerged, at the same time splendid and excellent, and which could be rightly designated as the race of the Romhellenes.[167]

Such approaches to the Byzantines' Romanness were not new for Byzantine authors. Manuel Kalekas's letter to the humanist Jacopo Angeli dating from 1395 argues in favour of a common Graeco-Latin ethnic community (κοινωνοῦμεν πατρίδος), since Constantinople was a Roman colony.[168] Finally, a similar double Graeco-Roman national and cultural identity whose cornerstone was education emerges later in Manuel Chrysoloras's *Epistolary Oration*:

> Let us remember that we were born from such men like the ancient Greeks and from those who came after the Greeks, our forefathers (γενομένων ἡμῖν προγόνων), the Romans, whose name we now have. Rather both these races coexist in us, and whether one wishes to call us Greeks or Latins, we are both Romans and the inheritors of Alexander's race.[169]

Political sphere and imperial authority

In the previous chapter, I indicated how the ecclesiastics' political contestation of imperial power went hand in hand with their attempts to offer a response to the political events which triggered the questioning of the emperor's position within the Byzantine political system. This section will try to find out how the rhetoricians defined the emperor's role in the late Byzantine political realm.

---

[167] Isidore of Kiev, *Panegyric*, 152, ed. Lampros.
[168] Manuel Kalekas, *Letters*, no. 5, ed. Loenertz (to Jacopo Angelli): τήν τε ἡμετέραν πολλοῖς ὕστερον χρόνοις τῶν αὐτῶν ἄποικον ἴσμεν ('we know that our land was afterwards their [i.e. the Romans'] colony').
[169] Manuel Chrysoloras, *Epistolary Oration*, 117.4–13, ed. Patrineles and Sophianos.

As in the case of the ecclesiastics, the rhetoricians approached the theme of imperial authority within the framework of a *political sphere* shaped by specific rules and practices. If John Chortasmenos defined this separate sphere in terms of court conflicts between ambitious and 'vainglorious' officials,[170] Isidore of Kiev set it rather in terms of a fully fledged science ranking among the highest human preoccupations:

> The study of all good things, the education and knowledge of everything, the experience of philosophy, both theoretical and practical, this is the political sphere (τὸ πολιτικόν), on which legislation and justice depend in addition to theology, learning, and natural sciences.[171]

Traces of a political consciousness correlated with actions aiming for the benefit of the community of citizens (τὸ κοινόν, πολῖται) appear frequently in other authors as well. Demetrios Chrysoloras speaks about the emperors' political authority (πολιτικὴ ἡγεμονία) in contrast to other types of authority.[172] In the *Epistolary Oration on Manuel Palaiologos' 'Funeral Oration'*, Manuel Chrysoloras highlights the key role of political expertise (πολιτικὴ ἐπιστήμη). Among the emperor's main features, Chrysoloras includes thoughtfulness and acquaintance with πολιτικὴ ἐπιστήμη, which the emperor used in times of distress.[173] At the same time, Chrysoloras also operates a distinction between the imperial (τὸ βασιλικόν) and the political (τὸ πολιτικόν) aspects of Manuel's activity. Thus he states that the emperor had both an imperial and a civic education which encapsulated the values and the aspirations of the rhetoricians.[174]

From the outset, it is notable that the emperor's rhetoricians supported the absolutist and the universalist claims, despite an acute sense of the declining authority of the imperial office.[175] Moreover, the rhetoricians vowed their attachment to the dynasty of the Palaiologoi and stressed the importance of the connection between fathers and sons. In his panegyric, Isidore praised

---

[170] John Chortasmenos, *Moral Counsels* (Ἠθικὰ παραγγέλματα), in *Briefe*, 238–42, ed. Hunger. See also John Chortamenos, *Letters*, in ibid. no. 51, 22–6, on the πολιτικὸς ἀνήρ.

[171] Isidore of Kiev, *Panegyric*, 182.27–30, ed. Lampros.

[172] Demetrios Chrysoloras, *One Hundred Letters*, no. 15, ed. Conti Bizzarro.

[173] Manuel Chrysoloras, *Epistolary Oration*, 114.13, ed. Patrineles and Sophianos.

[174] Ibid. 64.26: βασιλικῆς τε καὶ πολιτικῆς παιδείας τύπον ἔφηνας. Chrysoloras describes the oration as being both an imperial and a civic oration: σὺ τὸν λόγον τοῦτον καὶ πενθῶν ἅμα ἐξήνεγκας βασιλικὸν ἄντικρυς καὶ πολιτικόν (ibid. 64.16).

[175] See Demetrios Kydones, *Letters*, no. 397. 31–2, ed. Loenertz: ἴσμεν γὰρ καὶ αὐτοὶ ὡς νῦν ἡ τύχη καὶ τοῖς βασιλεῦσι πάντα συνέστειλεν. For a discussion of the Byzantine intellectuals' perception of the decline see Ševčenko, 'Decline', 172–5.

extensively not only John but also his entire family, dominated by the figure of Manuel. Earlier, Kydones, even if he had a difficult relation with Emperor John V, advised Manuel not to disobey his father.[176] In putting forward such ideas, the rhetoricians reflected longstanding ideas and notions of official ideology.[177]

Yet the court political rhetoric of the last decades of the fourteenth century was not as systematic and coherent as before. No panegyric from this period is known. On the contrary, after the end of the siege in 1402, and especially after 1410, the texts performed at the court or addressed to the emperor multiplied. More significantly, counsels set forth in hortatory language pertaining to specific policies also found a place in the panegyrics.[178] Owing partly to these irregularities in the performance of imperial propaganda and partly to the rhetoricians' interests, several particularities of their discourse can be traced vis-à-vis Manuel's imperial authority.

A key feature of the panegyrists' approach to imperial authority was their attempt to provide political solutions by means of advice. Notably, unlike in the early decades of Manuel's reign, the court oratory of this period lacks any trace of *Kaiserkritik*.[179] On the contrary, counsel in particular matters of state administration abounds. It is in this frame that we should understand Gemistos Plethon's political reforms encapsulated in an advisory speech. Demetrios Chrysoloras also reflects this hortatory attitude when he praises the participation in debates where courtiers, including the rhetoricians, could express personal political views:

> The emperor is gentle (ἤπιος) in his anger and mild (πρᾶος) when chastising others. He accomplishes everything in a rightful manner and it is now possible for the Romans to speak in opposition, to pass judgments, and to make use of any argument one considers appropriate, if only the words and the deeds are right. Thus, he restored the private and the public affairs of the cities which often were in decay.[180]

Advice for the emperor emerged especially in exhortations to acquire various military and intellectual virtues. In the *Epistolary Oration*, Manuel Chrysoloras offered elaborate definitions of virtues and urged the emperor

---

[176] Kydones sent this letter to Manuel while in Thessalonike and on the run to Lesbos.
[177] Hunger, *Prooimion*, 49–158.
[178] E.g. Gemistos Plethon's *Address . . . on the Situation in the Peloponnese*. The use of court oratory as instances of edification and advice for emperors had important precedents in the period of late antiquity.
[179] Zgoll, *Heiligkeit*, 23–122.
[180] Demetrios Chrysoloras, *Comparison*, 229.3–11, ed. Lampros.

to follow them.¹⁸¹ Here, Chrysoloras identified justice (δικαιοσύνη) as the most important virtue. For his part, in the *Comparison*, Demetrios Chrysoloras places humbleness (ταπεινοφροσύνη) at the top of the list of the most important virtues, thus paralleling the emperor's view on virtues as analysed below. Echoing the social and economic conditions of the state, Chrysoloras advises the emperor to remain poor but, at the same time, just and helpful to his subjects.¹⁸²

Most virtues attributed to Manuel in panegyrics were drawn from a common reservoir of imperial features used on various occasions by Byzantine rhetoricians.¹⁸³ Panegyrists presented him in various ways: as a saviour, a doctor, a helmsman, shepherd of the people, philosopher or legislator.¹⁸⁴ The four cardinal virtues of prudence, bravery, justice and wisdom were also central in these praises. Yet, notably within this set of standard imperial virtues, several values ascribed to Manuel received more attention than others. They reflect the particularities of the rhetoricians' conceptualisation of imperial office. First, most panegyrics emphasised the emperor's political and military prowess displayed in quelling revolts or in repelling enemy attacks.¹⁸⁵ Owing to the rules of the encomiastic genre,¹⁸⁶ the panegyrists adopted a triumphalist attitude vis-à-vis the emperor's actions, which gains visibility only after 1403 (the year of Manuel's return from the West after Bayezid's defeat). This event was celebrated in the panegyrists' texts as a triumph which entailed Manuel's march from the Peloponnese through continental Greece in the guise of a liberator.¹⁸⁷

The panegyrists recounted in detail the emperor's military achievements, especially in pacifying Thessaly (1411–16) and the Peloponnese (1415) after the return from his European journey.¹⁸⁸ Isidore's panegyric describes

---

[181] Manuel Chrysoloras, *Epistolary Oration*, 86.8–91.3, ed. Patrineles and Sophianos. See 91.25: ἡ ἀρετὴ τῆς τιμῆς βελτίων.
[182] Demetrios Chrysoloras, *Comparison*, 229, ed. Lampros: ἔνεστι καὶ τῷ βασιλεῖ πλοῦτος ὀλίγος μέν, ἀλλὰ δίκαιος.
[183] Kioussopoulou, *Emperor or Manager*, 131–49; Angelov, *Imperial Ideology*, 78–115.
[184] Angelov, *Imperial Ideology*, 78–115.
[185] See Makarios Makres' *Funeral Oration*, praising Manuel for the ability to foresee political developments, in Sideras, *Byzantinische Grabreden*, 306.1–2.
[186] Not only Menander's handbook (Menander Rhetor, *Treatises*, ed. Russell and Wilson, 181) but also the fourteenth-century *Synopsis Rhetorike* of Joseph the Philosopher advised panegyrists to praise the emperor's military virtues (Walz, *Rhetores Graeci*, 3. 524).
[187] Isidore of Kiev, *Panegyric*, 164.3–6, ed. Lampros: καὶ πόλεις εὐθὺς ἀπολαμβάνει πολλάς, τὰς μὲν Θρακικάς, τὰς δὲ Θετταλικάς, καὶ φόρου ὑποτελεῖς βαρβάρων οὐκ ὀλίγοι γίγνονται.
[188] Demetrios Chrysoloras, *Comparison*, 239, ed. Lampros: ὅταν ἐκ Βρεττανῶν ἐπὶ τὴν οἰκείαν ἐπαλινδρόμει.

Manuel's deeds and especially his activity in the Morea.[189] The same kind of depiction can be encountered in Demetrios Chrysoloras's *Comparison*, which also emphasised the emperor's ability to ward off the attacks of the Moreote landlords against the central imperial authority, and praised it as an act that made the emperor look more capable than the heroes of the past.[190] Accounts similar to Chrysoloras's *Comparison* and Isidore's *Panegyric* can be found in the Anonymous's *Funeral Oration* and John Chortasmenos's *Panegyric Delivered upon the Return of Manuel*.[191]

These encomiastic accounts of military campaigns can be explained through both an appeal to the history of court oratory and the political context. On the one hand, the late Palaiologan panegyrists continued the tendency to replace the miracles and divine omens of the previous panegyrics with detailed accounts of military campaigns and achievements, particularly those of the liberation of Byzantine territories in Thessaly or the Peloponnese.[192] From this viewpoint and to a certain extent, the panegyrics addressed to Manuel marked a return to the militaristic images cultivated in the court rhetoric of the Nicaean period. On the other hand, the long descriptions of military campaigns had an ideological function: to create the compensatory image of an emperor successful in wars, particularly after the defeat of the Ottomans in 1402.

Another topic common to imperial propaganda, namely the imperial dynastic succession, received a rather ambiguous treatment during Manuel's reign. Unlike those of the first decades of the fourteenth century, the rhetoricians of Manuel's reign did not develop theories of succession.[193] Many rhetoricians in charge of praising the emperor overlooked the ties with his father and previous ruler, John V, most probably on account of their disputes over the succession. Perhaps it was for this reason that Demetrios Chrysoloras produced an encomium where he compared Manuel more to past heroes and less with the members of the Palaiologan family (*Comparison between the Emperor of Today and the Ancient Rulers*, c. 1415). In the preface to his panegyric, John Chortasmenos also dismissed the treatment of fatherland (πατρίς) and family (γένος) as irrelevant,[194] while Manuel Chrysoloras considered that these two rubrics were

---

[189] Isidore of Kiev, *Panegyric*, 162.1–13, ed. Lampros.
[190] Demetrios Chrysoloras, *Comparison*, 242.4–24, ed. Lampros.
[191] Anonymous, *Funeral Oration on Manuel II*, 423–51, ed. Dendrinos; John Chortasmenos, *Panegyric Delivered upon the Return of Manuel*, in *Briefe*, 217–24.
[192] See Angelov, *Imperial Ideology*, 51–64; Toth, *Imperial Orations*, 108.
[193] See Angelov, *Imperial Ideology*, 116–33.
[194] John Chortasmenos, *Preface*, in *Briefe*, 225–6, ed. Hunger.

not important in a panegyric.¹⁹⁵ These passages, combined with the evidence about the emperor's support for these rhetoricians, suggest that Manuel himself could have encouraged them to introduce such changes. The only author who reminded Manuel of his obligations to his father, John V, was Demetrios Kydones, who, in a letter addressed to Manuel, rebuked him for disregarding the emperor-father.¹⁹⁶ This contrast in eulogising the emperor's immediate ancestors between Manuel's panegyrists and Demetrios Kydones, whose career flourished during the reign of John V, reveals a shift in the understanding of imperial authority that occurred in the early fifteenth century. Now, Manuel enjoyed the support of a new group of orators no longer connected with the rule of John V.

On the other hand, while overlooking John V, most rhetoricians stressed the connection between Manuel and his firstborn son, John VIII. Although attempts to rehabilitate John VII were made, in order to present the image of dynastic harmony, it was Manuel's son who received constant attention as the legitimate successor.¹⁹⁷ Many orations, like Isidore's *Panegyric*, recorded Manuel's decision to leave behind his son John as co-emperor and ruler in Constantinople while he went to the island of Thassos.¹⁹⁸ Even a later panegyrist, John Dokeianos, in a *prosphōnēmation* addressed to Despot Theodore II, accentuated the connection between the ruler (John VIII) and his immediate ancestors, reflected in their common virtues.¹⁹⁹

Another issue approached by the rhetoricians, sacral rulership, was fundamental to Byzantine imperial ideology.²⁰⁰ If relations with the church and the clergy remained tense for most of Manuel's reign, the panegyrists consistently described the emperor's office as possessing more authority than the church. The emperor, Demetrios Chrysoloras claimed, receives his power directly from God's hands.²⁰¹ Likewise, Isidore's encomium for John VIII alludes to the honours which the church offered to the emperor upon his return from a

---

¹⁹⁵ Manuel Chrysoloras, *Epistolary Oration*, 58, ed. Patrineles and Sophianos.
¹⁹⁶ In his panegyrics addressed to John V and John VI, Demetrios Kydones underlined the rulers' relations with their parents; Demetrios Kydones, *Letters*, nos. 1–23, ed. Loenertz.
¹⁹⁷ John Chortasmenos, *Panegyric Delivered upon the Return of Manuel*, in *Briefe*, 205.46, ed. Hunger. As a matter of fact the last section of Chortasmenos's panegyric dealt with the co-rule of Manuel II and John VIII.
¹⁹⁸ Isidore of Kiev, *Panegyric*, PP 3, 165.24, ed. Lampros.
¹⁹⁹ John Dokeianos, Προσφωνημάτιον τῷ δεσπότῃ Θεοδώρῳ πορφυρογεννήτῳ, PP 4, 237.15–17, ed. Lampros: τῆς γὰρ πατρῴας κληρονομεῖς ἀρετῆς, ὥσπερ καὶ τῆς ἐξουσίας αὐτῆς.
²⁰⁰ Dvornik, *Early Christian and Byzantine Political Philosophy*, 2. 320–44.
²⁰¹ See Demetrios Chrysoloras, *One Hundred Letters*, no. 32, ed. Conti Bizzarro: σὺ μὲν ἰσχὺν καὶ χρήματα καὶ τιμὴν ἐκ θεοῦ λαβών.

military campaign.²⁰² Isidore regarded the ruler as a judge in matters of faith, an element which Isidore probably introduced in order to push for the union of churches.²⁰³ To a certain extent, this view emerged from the use of the categories commonly applied in Byzantine imperial propaganda: as emperor of the Romans (βασιλεὺς τῶν Ῥωμαίων) and also as an imitator of God (μιμητὴς Θεοῦ).²⁰⁴ However, the rhetoricians' emphasis on the fact that the emperor received earthly power directly from God seemed to target the ecclesiastics' views of imperial authority.²⁰⁵

According to the former, the authority derived directly from God empowered the emperor to anoint his successor on the Byzantine throne, namely John VIII. For this reason, Isidore described the ceremony of John VIII's crowning by Manuel as an anointment of the son by the father-emperor without the contribution of the church.²⁰⁶ This image had echoes among late Byzantine authors, for the late Byzantine historian, Laonikos Chalkokondyles, in his account of the coronation of John VIII, stated that the latter was appointed as ἀρχιερεύς τε καὶ βασιλεύς (archpriest and emperor).²⁰⁷ In doing so, Chalkokondyles endorsed the rhetoricians' predominant attitude regarding the imperial office, seen as sacred and above all other offices including the patriarch's. Thus, it appears that their approach to the old *emperor-priest* debate differed significantly from contemporary ecclesiastics' approach.²⁰⁸

The emperor-*didaskalos*

If the above issues emerge in various forms in multiple Byzantine panegyrics, one particular imperial feature received special attention in the contemporary encomia addressed to Manuel: the emperor as a skilled rhetorician was

---

²⁰² Isidore of Kiev, *Encomium for John VIII*, PP, 3, 296.20–3, ed. Lampros: ἐπαναζεύξαντος τοίνυν τοῦ θειοτάτου βασιλέως μετά γε τῆς νίκης καὶ τῶν τροπαίων ἐκ τῆς τοῦ Πέλοπος, λαμπρῶς εἰσῄει τὴν βασιλεύουσαν, τὸν ἐπινίκιον πάντοθεν δεχομένου ἐκ τοῦ τῆς ἐκκλησίας πληρώματος.
²⁰³ Ibid. 306.
²⁰⁴ Both appellations appear in Demetrios Chrysoloras, *Comparison*, 245.13–14, ed. Lampros.
²⁰⁵ E.g. Demetrios Chrysoloras, *One Hundred Letters*, no. 32, ed. Conti Bizzarro: ἄριστε βασιλεῦ, σὺ μὲν ἰσχὺν καὶ χρήματα καὶ τιμὴν ἐκ θεοῦ λαβών, τοῖς μὲν ἔρεισμα τοῖς δὲ χρηστὴ δόξα τοῖς δὲ θησαυρὸς ἄσυλος ἐγένου, διαθεὶς ὃ πέπονθας ἐπὶ τῇ χαρισαμένου μιμήσει.
²⁰⁶ Isidore of Kiev, *Panegyric*, PP 3, 166.7–9, ed. Lampros: καὶ χρίει τὸν καὶ πρὸ τοῦδε προσήκοντα τῇ βασιλείᾳ βασιλέα.
²⁰⁷ Laonikos Chalkokondyles, *Histories*, vol 1. 192.18, ed. Darkó.
²⁰⁸ Dagron, *Emperor and Priest*, 319.

praised not only as the author of a great many texts but also as a teacher, a *didaskalos* of his son and his subjects.[209] As mentioned, most rhetoricians in the emperor's proximity had a pedagogical focus and were also highly regarded *didaskaloi* of grammar, rhetoric or philosophy. The first occurrence of Manuel as *didaskalos* appears in Demetrios Kydones' early letters and the term survives until late in the panegyrics for John VIII and Constantine XI, where orators continued to remind their addressees of their father's, Manuel II's, intellectual and pedagogical skills. In these texts, the encomiasts commented on Manuel II's influence on the moral and intellectual education of his sons and emperors. Thus, the emperor's pedagogical focus remains a unique feature of late Byzantine panegyrics.

To be sure, to a certain degree this feature corresponded to the conventional and heavily used notion of the philosopher-king. By any standards, the image of an educated emperor was not at all new among the Byzantines, who borrowed it from the ancient tradition of praise for rulers. Demetrios Kydones noted that it was not uncommon for emperors to adorn their office with intellectual lustre.[210] As a matter of fact, many late Byzantine emperors cultivated their intellectual skills: Theodore II Laskaris was a prolific philosopher and writer, Andronikos II composed philosophical treatises, and John VI Kantakouzenos, Manuel's grandfather, wrote extensive orations, theological treatises and even a historical autobiography.[211]

But if the image of philosopher-king retained a special place in many imperial eulogies,[212] a rather conventional feature of the imperial orations, it is noticeable that, in Manuel's case, authors often drew a sharp distinction

---

[209] E.g. Demetrios Chrysoloras, *One Hundred Letters*, no. 77, ed. Conti-Bizzarro: τῷ κράτει λόγων ἐστέφου μᾶλλον ἢ ταινίᾳ καὶ διαδήματι.

[210] Demetrios Kydones, *Letters*, no. 397.20–1, ed. Loenertz: τὸν τὸ κοινὸν σχῆμα τῇ σοφίᾳ κοσμοῦντα.

[211] Earlier, in the twelfth century, Niketas Choniates ironically commented on the efforts of the emperor Manuel I Komnenos to demonstrate his wisdom along with his other skills necessary for governing: 'It is not enough for most emperors of the Romans simply to rule [. . .] but if they do not appear wise, godlike in looks, heroic in strength, full of holy wisdom like Solomon [. . .] they think they have suffered a grievous wrong'; Niketas Choniates, *Histories*, 209–10, trans. in Magdalino, *Empire of Manuel I Komnenos*, 10.

[212] Kydones' letter 438 addressed to the emperor in 1393 bears in the manuscript the title Τῷ φιλοσόφῳ ('To the philosopher'). See Demetrius Chrysoloras, *One Hundred Letters*, no. 29, ed. Conti-Bizzarro; *Anonymous Panegyric* (Vat. gr. 632), ed. Dendrinos, 449.266: οὕτω καὶ βασιλεύων ὑπερβάλλει φιλοσοφίᾳ καὶ φιλοσοφῶν οὐκ ἀφίσταται στρατηγῶν.

between rhetors and philosophers.²¹³ In the imperial orations under scrutiny here, the authors added to the Platonic notion of the philosopher-king the representation of the emperor as *rhetorician*, often with its associated meaning of *didaskalos*.²¹⁴ In his panegyric, Isidore extolled the role of rhetoric in a ruler's education:

> On the one hand, it (rhetoric) brings together grammar and poetics by which it trains the speech and confers sweetness and pleasantness on speech, while removing lexical barbarisms and solecisms, and on the other hand, it brings history and offers precepts and admonitions, urging the listener to good deeds and turning him away from evil moral habits. [. . .] It also educates and trains (ῥυθμίζει καὶ παιδεύει) by philosophical arguments and abstract speculations.²¹⁵

The same image of an emperor-rhetorician added to that of the philosopher-king is manifest in the anonymous panegyric of cod. Vat. gr. 914 (1403).²¹⁶ The author praises the emperor for having acted as a teacher in Constantinople at a time when many deemed education unimportant:

> Because, despite its brilliance, this great city of yours also lacked teachers, which represented a great loss for those who longed for education and among others to me, you immediately gave us a teacher (διδάσκαλον) as medicine, which is a very good deed.²¹⁷

Then, towards the end of the panegyric, the anonymous author clarifies the difference between philosopher and rhetorician and praises the emperor for his literary skills:

> When you act as emperor you also speak as a rhetorician (ῥητορεύεις), and when you speak as a rhetorician, you act as the best emperor; you teach philosophy with Plato, and when speaking philosophically you speak

---

²¹³ In using the notion of rhetor when praising Emperor Manuel, they seem to have eliminated the negative connotations of the rhetorician's trade conjured up by Mazaris (*Mazaris' Journey to Hades*) or John Chortasmenos (*Moral Counsels*, in *Briefe*, 238–40, ed. Hunger). Demetrios Chrysoloras contrasted the emperor's sincerity with the rhetoricians' hidden agendas: ἔτι διαλέγεται καθεστῶτι μὲν βλέμματι [. . .] οὐ δεινότητι λόγων, ὡς ῥήτορες ἢ σοφισταί, παρεπιδεικνύμενος, ἀλλὰ τὴν ἐν τοῖς νοήμασι διηρευνηκὼς καὶ διερμηνεύων ἀκρίβειαν (Demetrios Chrysoloras, *Comparison*, 236.15–19, ed. Lampros).
²¹⁴ E.g. Anonymous, *Funeral Oration on Manuel II*, 449.270, ed. Dendrinos.
²¹⁵ Isidore of Kiev, *Panegyric*, PP 3, 171.7–24, ed. Lampros.
²¹⁶ In Anonymous, *Two Panegyrics*, 707.13, ed. Polemes. Cf. ibid. 708.13: βασιλεῖ θειοτάτῳ καὶ φιλοσοφοτάτῳ.
²¹⁷ Ibid. 709.77–80.

as a rhetorician. Both <the art of rhetoric and of ruling> were offered to you, in a divine manner, I take Hesiod here as your witness. [. . .] Yet clearer evidence of the truthfulness <of these statements> are your writings which are by no means inferior to Libanius's texts, and which are more pleasant than the music of Terpandros from Lesbos.[218]

The panegyrists' scrutiny of the emperor's literary activity was not merely incidental or conventional but often stretched over substantial passages of text. Apart from the above example of the anonymous panegyric of Vat. gr. 914, many instances reflect a similar attitude. In his *Comparison*, Demetrios Chrysoloras identified the emperor's intense rhetorical activity as the feature which differentiated him from other rulers.[219] In order to strengthen the force of this laudatory imagery, he also lists the emperor's works:

He creates new kinds of speeches, he rejoices in skilful literature. What are the reasons for which he does so? For the people's benefit and because ignorance flourished here. What has been previously said is confirmed by the great number of different kinds of letters, admired for their unusual arrangement and style; by his learned chapters of exhortations which surpass the letters on account of their vigour and number; and by the various orations, both numerous and extensive, some of which deal with natural matters, while some are filled with theological discussions. Among the emperor's theological writings one finds several against the Persians, several others against Western literati, some texts with a moral character and joy, and others appropriate for funeral laments or monodies. I will not speak here about metrical verses, hymns and rhetorical descriptions, which would bring no little benefit both to you and to those happening to listen to them; the accomplishment of both the ideas and the words is piety. Only a ruler can be deemed worthy of such a prize more important than any other in the world.[220]

Despite its exaggerations, the passage indicates that Manuel intended his texts to have a strong impact on contemporary audiences. According to Chrysoloras, by authoring and circulating this multitude of texts, the emperor aimed at dissipating his subjects' prevailing ignorance (ἀλογία). Furthermore,

---

[218] Ibid. 710.105.
[219] Demetrios Chrysoloras, *Comparison*, 234, ed. Lampros: ὁ δὲ νῦν αὐτοκράτωρ πολλοῖς μὲν ἀγαθῶν ὑπερβαίνειν οἶδεν ἀληθείᾳ πολλούς, λόγῳ δὲ καὶ σοφίᾳ πάντας.
[220] Ibid. 232.8–26.

Chrysoloras states, the emperor's rhetorical abilities held more significance than his 'being born in the purple':

> And it is clear that, since he reached the first summit of true happiness, he crowned himself with the power of words rather than with the imperial diadem, and he put on a purple garment of rhetoric which is much better than that which he put on in the palace.[221]

Although scholars have completely overlooked the pedagogical dimension of the imperial system of virtues,[222] a survey of the panegyrics dating from the Palaiologan period indicates that only Manuel retains this feature. In his speech delivered upon the emperor's return from the Peloponnese, John Chortasmenos offers an insight into the kind of moral education Manuel provided to his son, John.[223] Isidore's panegyric juxtaposes the position of the emperor with that of the teacher and insists on the emperor's role in his son's theoretical and moral education:

> <Manuel II> guided and initiated him into the mysteries, into the precise principles of the doctrines, into the sublimity of theology, into the depths of theoretical thinking, and into any type of moral or philosophical virtue.[224]

Similarly, Manuel Chrysoloras praised Manuel as a teacher for his brother Theodore:

> You became a teacher not only of military strategies but also of virtue and of all good things. And you acted as a teacher not only by using words but also by your deeds, so that you yourself call that one <i.e. Theodore> your student and child. For you are his brother and teacher (ἀδελφὸς καὶ διδάσκαλος) in all the virtues, whether in his speech or his deeds.[225]

Further evidence for Manuel as a teacher-rhetorician comes from sources dating from various moments of his life. Kydones praised the emperor's encyclopaedic education.[226] Early on, in a letter addressed to young Manuel, who

---

[221] Ibid. 232.23–6.
[222] See for instance Barker, *Manuel II*, 133. When listing the virtues and characteristics of Isidore's panegyric, Schmitt overlooks the function of *didaskalos* in his list of virtues; 'Kaiserrede und Zeitgeschichte', 219.
[223] John Chortasmenos, *Panegyric*, in *Briefe*, 199–225, ed. Hunger.
[224] Isidore of Kiev, *Panegyric*, 171, 25–8, ed. Lampros.
[225] Manuel Chrysoloras, *Epistolary Oration*, 130.26, ed. Patrineles and Sophianos.
[226] Demetrios Kydones, *Letters*, no. 82, ed. Loenertz.

had just fled Constantinople and settled as ruler of Thessalonike, Demetrios Kydones exhorted him to become a real teacher for his subjects. In this sense, Kydones used the term specific term of *trainer*, παιδοτρίβης.²²⁷ Furthermore, like the anonymous author of Vat. gr. 914, Isidore also mentions that upon his return to Constantinople after the trip to the West, Manuel dealt with both literary and administrative activities:

> And, as it was needed, having firmly secured that city [Thessalonike], he comes back to Constantinople and, on the one hand, he engages in delivering and writing learned speeches, and, on the other hand, he governs and administers the political and imperial apparatus, and takes care of everything in the city, embellishing the city's monuments. Sometimes he discusses with the philosophers and rhetoricians, while at other times he sits with the judges and decides upon judicial matters.²²⁸

Arguably, this notion of an emperor-rhetorician stemmed from earlier opinions about the role of oratorical skills acquisition and education in Byzantine political transactions. In the Palaiologan period, this idea began to surface in the texts of early fourteenth-century scholars, like Theodore Metochites or Thomas Magistros, who in their texts approached political issues and showed awareness of the fundamentals of political theory.²²⁹ By the mid-fourteenth century, in the introduction to his admonitory *Oratio de non reddenda Gallipoli*, Kydones voiced his view on the orator's social and political function at a time when the Byzantines had to cope with major threats.²³⁰ This was not a singular statement for, in a letter dating from 1382 and addressed to Manuel, Demetrios Kydones also argued that rhetoricians have a better grasp of various situations and therefore rhetoric can be useful in influencing social phenomena.²³¹

Thus, based on the evidence we can gather from the late Palaiologan encomiastic literature, fulfilling didactic duties was a key feature of Manuel's imperial image. According to many rhetoricians, teaching (διδακτική) was not to be regarded as just another imperial virtue, but could impact Byzantine society

---

[227] Ibid. no. 220.
[228] Isidore of Kiev, *Panegyric*, PP 3, 165.6–10, ed. Lampros.
[229] Theodore Metochites, *Miscellanea*, ch. 96, where the Byzantine scholar indicates knowledge of Aristotle's *Politics*; Thomas Magistros, *On Kingship* and *On Polity*: see Gaul, *Thomas Magistros*, 134–44.
[230] PG 155, 1015: ἐπεὶ δὲ τὸ μὲν εὐτυχεῖν καὶ μεγάλα πράττειν ἡμᾶς ὑπολέλοιπεν ἤδη, πεπράγαμεν δὲ οὕτω κακῶς, ὥστε τοῖς παρ' ἡμῖν ῥήτορσιν ἔργον εἶναι τῶν προτιθεμένων ἀεὶ κακῶν τὸ κουφότερον ἐξευρίσκειν.
[231] Demetrios Kydones, *Letters*, no. 236, ed. Loenertz.

because it brought benefits for both ruler and subjects.²³² Finally, in his comparison, Demetrios Chrysoloras reiterated this idea, that the knowledge and the stimulus for education provided by the emperor can lead to a fortunate and stable situation:

> Democritus and Anaxagoras are highly admirable among the wise men. I admire them even more than other valuable possessions. Yet the emperor of today seems much more admirable (θαυμασιώτερος), as he prompts many others towards the study of philosophy, he prefers the elevation of thought to intellectual negligence, he offers precious things and does not destroy them, in order that he himself and others would benefit and thus from needy people become prosperous again.²³³

Conclusion

The above analysis indicates tight connections between the emperor and the rhetoricians who were active in his shadow. Manuel himself cultivated these ties and sought to create a rhetorical community of lay courtiers more attentive to the ruler's rhetorical skills. He acted as patron of most of these scholars, whom he offered material support or court positions. The texts which authors like John Chortasmenos, Demetrios Chrysoloras, Manuel Chrysoloras and Gemistos Plethon dedicated to him point to the emperor's central position within this circle. Although the rhetoricians in the emperor's entourage looked increasingly to the world outside Constantinople (the Gattilusioi's Lesbos, Mystras, Thessalonike or Italy) and although the great Ottoman siege of 1394–1402 produced a rupture in rhetorical activities, they continued to support Manuel's position of authority by following the traditional tenets of Byzantine imperial ideology. Even young Plethon's imagined *politeia* set at the centre of its governing system the idea of an absolute monarch. At the same time, Plethon's proposed alternative ideal polity was probably generated by an increased awareness of the dangers Byzantium faced and by contemporary concerns to find political solutions for safeguarding the state. Such concerns were not new and can be traced back to the texts of earlier Palaiologan authors: Theodore Metochites, Thomas Magistros or Demetrios Kydones. After all, many connections tied

---

[232] Demetrios Chrysoloras, *One Hundred Letters*, no. 63, ed. Conti Bizzarro: ὁ νοῦς κέκληται καὶ λογισμός, τούτῳ μόνῳ προσχρώμενος εἶ, καὶ διδακτικὴν ἔχων ἅπασαν ἀρετὴν εἰς τελείωσιν ἄθλων ἥκεις πίστει τῇ πρὸς θεόν.

[233] Demetrios Chrysoloras, *Comparison*, 230, 12–17, ed. Lampros.

the early fourteenth-century to the early fifteenth-century scholars and rhetoricians.[234]

Another observation that arises from the study of these rhetoricians' activities and texts is that due to the support of the emperor, they set themselves in stark opposition to the ecclesiastics. If both groups preached wealth redistribution as the solution to the social problems affecting Byzantine society, they also had many issues on which they disagreed. Unlike the ecclesiastics, most imperial rhetoricians called upon the necessity of an alliance with the Latins as the sole solution to the problem for defending the state. They also grounded their notion of Byzantine identity in the historical past: either on an ancient Hellenic core of values or on the representation of Byzantium as the direct descendant of ancient Rome. Even the political utopias that emanated from the members of these two groups differed fundamentally: if Joseph Bryennios promoted the idea of a state ruled by Orthodox universalism, Plethon imagined an ideal polity and regarded himself as a new Lykourgos in a new Sparta.[235]

In their treatment of imperial authority, the rhetoricians maintained the idea of the ruler's omnipotence. They supported Manuel II in promoting his son, John, as co-emperor and cultivated the sacrality of the imperial office. To a certain extent, their attachment to Manuel II Palaiologos and to the imperial absolutist idea can be correlated with their individual immediate concerns: the emperor was still one of the major patrons of literary activities and could also provide positions at court or other benefits deriving from his largesse. In this respect, John Chortasmenos's letters asking Manuel II for material support suggest the continuous need of imperial protection. On the other hand, remarkably, most of the rhetoricians' texts added to the standard set of imperial virtues one particular image: the emperor as eloquent rhetorician and educator of both his son and his subjects. By stressing the pedagogical and the rhetorical dimension of the imperial persona, these rhetoricians reworked the old idea of the philosopher-king into an idea of emperor-rhetorician who acted as a teacher in a quest to improve his governing. Finally, their intense activity in promoting the emperor is indicative of the emperor's efforts to cultivate court-rhetorical activities, a situation which contrasted with his father's, John V's, approach.

---

[234] E.g. Plethon's claims to have held Metochites in high esteem; Siniossoglou, *Radical Platonism*, 89.
[235] See Shawcross, 'New Lycourgos'.

Part II

Other Voices, Other Approaches: Manuel II's Political Writings

Introduction to Part II

The previous chapters revealed information about the social and intellectual milieu in which the emperor tried to articulate a new political voice. In the following chapters, I offer an analysis of the strategies the emperor used in the construction of his messages identifiable in four major political texts which arose from Manuel's preoccupation with the internal and external affairs of the empire: the *Dialogue* (Ἠθικὸς διάλογος περὶ γάμου); the *Foundations* (Ὑποθῆκαι βασιλικῆς ἀγωγῆς); the *Orations* (Λόγοι); and the *Funeral Oration* (Ἐπιτάφιος λόγος). Along with this analysis, the present part of this study also provides an interpretation of Manuel's ideological stance and construction of authority in light of his rhetorical texts and against the background of the contemporary political landscape.

Further Methodological Considerations

The four texts mentioned above have in common a complex web of political references reflecting the challenges to Manuel's reign, such as the dynastic conflicts of the late fourteenth century, the appointment of his successor to the throne, and the political situation of the Peloponnese. The focus of my inquiry is the practice of rhetoric, and more specifically the strategies whereby the author turned his writings into an ideologically effective tool to disseminate political messages. Even if only several of his texts were performed orally, the public character of Manuel's texts is attested by their dissemination within *theatra* or the networks of late Byzantine literati. The rationale for this part is therefore twofold: on the one hand, political rhetoric is prominent among the emperor's writings; and, on the other hand, the scholarship on Manuel's reign and literary activity has been dominated by historical approaches that privileged biographical and source studies.

In the attempt to map the emperor's strategies of persuasion operational at several key moments of his reign, I argue that, in so far as these political texts are concerned, Manuel operated changes within the tradition of the rhetorical genres he approached and to a certain extent subverted them; in this way his texts served his efforts to project the image of a different kind of ruler concerned with the cultivation of learning among his subjects. As Chapter 7 argues, this image reflected a shift in the understanding of politics not as a means of ameliorating one's situation but rather as civic engagement for the community's benefit. Each of these four texts is unique in its genre or approach and each illustrated a particular moment in Manuel's career as emperor.

In selecting these texts from the emperor's considerable and varied œuvre I operated with two criteria: their political topic and their degree of dissemination. Their analysis will proceed on two levels. First, I will deal with formal and structural issues by looking into their contents and genre; and second, I will be concerned with the rhetorical strategies employed by the author in adjusting the rhetorical templates used in conveying his messages. This analysis will allow me to determine the typology and the different modulations of the authorial voice.

Such an investigation, which takes account of the texts' conventions and functions, requires preliminary clarification of two major notions essential for the construction of political messages: genre and authorial voice. While many modern scholars have dismissed genre and author as obsolete categories of interpretation, I would rather agree here with Jonathan Culler that they remain fundamental for the creation of meaning, since they offer 'a set of literary norms to which texts may be related and by virtue of which they become meaningful and coherent'.[1] In particular, the concept of genre has undergone significant changes and re-evaluations over time. More often than not, genres have been conceived of in terms of literary forms, such as dialogue, letter, oration, chronicle, etc. Yet, as Margaret Mullett noted, the Byzantine system of genres cannot be regarded exclusively as a system of forms transmitted from antiquity; also to be taken into consideration are the 'rhetorical types which provide the occasion, function, status, and transactional relationship between the implied speaker and the implied recipient'. These types represent the literary expression of the great human experiences, such as birth, death, power, career and education.[2] Taking into consideration these two components, Mullett argues that in Byzantium genres were created when 'the rhetorical types met the axis of forms'. Following this model,

---

[1] Culler, 'Towards a theory'. Similarly, Hirsch argued that it is generic boundaries which make the critical reading of a work possible by providing a matrix against which to set an interpretation; Hirsch, *Validity*, 68–126.
[2] Mullett, 'Madness of genre', 236.

in the present part of the study I understand genre as a literary category reflecting both a social function, such as teaching or deliberating on political issues, and the form of a text; it is the latter aspect which also signals its relation to a body of other writings. Such a definition of genre will necessarily include echoes from reader-response criticism, and particularly from Jauss's notion of horizon of expectation, defined as 'the objectifiable system of expectations that arises for each work in the historical moment of its appearance, from a pre-understanding of the genre, from the form and themes of already familiar works, and from the opposition between poetic and practical language'.[3]

Another important concept which will underpin my analysis is that of authorial voice, a topic that has recently come into scholarly focus.[4] I understand authorial voice as an overarching literary construct which reveals the authors' standpoints mediated not only by their own statements but also by the ways they organise the rhetorical material or by the text's most conspicuous stylistic choices. As a combination of representational codes, the authorial voice has the function of an agent within the text, responsible for imparting judgements on situations, events or ethical values. Thus, the scope of my inquiry will be broadened by asking how the 'author function' strengthened the emperor's arguments and, conversely, how in some cases the speech functioned in fact primarily as a vehicle to support a particular authorial profile. The notion of authorial voice will be understood in a post-structuralist frame as a non-stable and changing aspect across the texts of the same author.[5] To that extent, it will appear that Manuel II strove to construct for himself multiple, shifting, authorial voices which he used as alternatives in order to further produce and convey political messages.

Finally, concerning the rhetorical strategies employed in these texts, the principles of Byzantine rhetoric will serve as an additional hermeneutic tool, since categories like the invention or disposition of arguments can influence textual meaning. From this point of view the question of the rhetorician's adaptation of his subject matter to widespread rhetorical practices cannot be ignored. More significantly, the analysis of rhetorical strategies will help in an understanding of the unstated, unaddressed concerns. As rhetoric in Byzantium was a shifting landscape, Manuel, like many other rhetoricians, was concerned not only with saying something, but also with repositioning it. And, by being repositioned, rhetoric came to provide new ways of interpreting political realities.

---

[3] Jauss, *Toward an Aesthetic*, 22.
[4] E.g. Papaioannou, *Michael Psellos*, 27–128; Pizzone, 'Introduction'.
[5] Such post-structuralist approaches interrogated the correlated elements of authorial voice, such as author, reader and text. See Harvey, *Ventriloquized Voices*, 5–6.

An Overview of the Emperor's Rhetorical œuvre

A brief overview and discussion of Manuel II's texts is of relevance here since many earlier writings provided the material and themes for his later, more extensive texts. With few exceptions,[6] scholars have tended to emphasise the 'useless' rhetorical sophistication of the emperor's texts, understood only by an educated elite, and considered that most of them were devoid of historical information.[7] Thus, in his monograph, John Barker dismissed Manuel's literary activity as lacking substance,[8] whereas George Dennis's statement regarding the emperor's letters, despite later retractions, echoed the views on Byzantine literature of a past generation of scholars.[9]

Throughout his career, Manuel cultivated the image of a literatus capable of appreciating and enjoying the subtleties of elaborate rhetorical compositions. In his letters, the emperor expressed his view on the importance of practising literature as both pleasure and benefit:

> The study of literature is befitting (προσῆκεν) rather for one who is not completely ignorant of writing than it would be either for rustics or for the expert writers. A lamp, in order to be of any use, must be given to one who is still capable of seeing, but is not in the direct sunlight.[10]

He sought to approach most genres favoured by his contemporaries. Indeed, a look at the emperor's œuvre reveals that the list of his works resembles the writings of contemporary authors, who approached a similar range of genres.[11] The early letters sent by Demetrios Kydones, his mentor, suggest that the emperor benefited from a complete rhetorical education which, at the first stage, entailed the production of several rhetorical exercises. Because of his rhetorical skills, Kydones compared Manuel with a new Demosthenes.[12] A substantial part of Manuel's literary production was theological in nature, which

---

[6] Khoury remarked on the emperor's care to write in an elaborate and embellished style: *Manuel II Paléologue*, 14–15.

[7] An exception is Dendrinos's edition of the treatise *On the Procession of the Holy Spirit*, which tries to contextualise two of Manuel's theological texts by looking into the circulation of books and ideas in the late Palaiologan period. See also Trapp's discussion of the *Dialogues with a Muslim* in historical context and the context of doctrinary polemics: Manuel II, *Dialoge mit einem Perser*, 11–62, ed. Trapp.

[8] Barker, *Manuel II*, 402.

[9] Dennis, in Manuel II, *Letters*, xviii: 'There is a fundamental dishonesty: while living in one world, they speak from another.'

[10] Manuel II, *Letters*, no. 5.12–15, ed. Dennis.

[11] A complete list of Manuel's texts was provided by Dendrinos, *Annotated Edition of 'On the Procession of the Holy Spirit'*, 430–46.

[12] Demetrios Kydones, *Letters*, no. 262, ed. Loenertz.

prompted Hans-Georg Beck to label the emperor a *Theologe auf dem Thron*.[13] Manuel was attached to Orthodox teachings despite his close friendship with Latin converts like Kydones or Manuel Chrysoloras. Manuel authored three lengthy apologetic texts in which he defended the positions of the Byzantine church: *Dialogues with a Muslim*, *On the Procession of the Holy Spirit*, and the above-mentioned letter addressed to Alexios Iagoup also on the procession of the Holy Spirit.

Another category of texts included liturgical texts, prayers and homilies. Most of them were delivered on various religious feasts or upon important occasions such as the delivery of the city from the Ottoman siege. The prayers represented instances of displaying Orthodoxy, as in the *Morning Prayers*, a confession of faith dedicated to his son, or of encouragement in difficult situations addressed to the Mother of God (Κανὼν παρακλητικός). The homilies represent a significant part of his literary output, as Manuel is one of the very few Byzantine emperors whose sermons have been preserved.[14] We have four homilies preserved under his name: the *Homily on the Dormition of the Theotokos*, *Homily on St Mary of Egypt*, *Homily on St John the Baptist* and *Homily on the Nativity of Christ*.

Owing to his involvement in the dynastic conflicts of succession to his father, John V, Manuel authored several texts with political content in the decades preceding his access to the throne. In chronological order, the first one was an *Admonitory Oration to the Thessalonians*.[15] It was delivered in 1383, when the pressures of the Ottomans during the siege of Thessalonike were mounting. On this occasion, Manuel put forward arguments drawn from the history of the city as well as arguments that had to do with the Thessalonians' freedom.[16] The *Admonitory Oration* mirrors the preoccupations of fourteenth-century authors of deliberative orations, such as Demetrios Kydones' *Oratio de non reddenda Gallipoli*.[17] In addressing the popular assembly (ἐκκλησία τοῦ δήμου) of the Thessalonians gathered in the church of St Demetrios,[18] the future emperor used a highly elaborated style despite the fact that probably most educated individuals did not remain in the city

---

[13] Beck, *Kirche und theologische Literatur*, 789.
[14] Apart from Manuel II, we have extant homilies from Leo VI and Constantine VII Porphyrogennetos in the ninth and tenth centuries.
[15] Manuel II, *Admonitory Oration*, 290–307, ed. Laourdas.
[16] A summary of the main points of the oration is available in Laourdas's edition (302–5) as well as in Dennis, *Reign of Manuel II*, 81–4. On a contextualisation of Manuel's ideas of freedom in this speech see Angelov, 'Three kinds of liberty', 320–2.
[17] On Kydones' deliberative orations see Ryder, *Career and Writings*, 41–9.
[18] Most probably the *archontes* of the city, the members of the senate and other representatives of the population in the city; Laourdas, in Manuel II, *Admonitory Oration*, 303–4.

during the siege.¹⁹ Demetrios Kydones praised the author's refined, Demosthenic expression in this oration.²⁰ This text, although cognate with the emperor's political writings during his reign, remains different with regard to two major aspects: first, its plain deliberative character, which suggests that it was performed following intense debates about the conditions of a peace treaty with the Ottomans. This renders the oration an important testimony to the limits of Manuel's authority in Thessalonike. Second, the oration throws light on the relation between the city of Thessalonike and the central authority in Constantinople which, at that point in his political career, Manuel defied.

A further text, the *Panegyric on the Recovery of His Father from an Illness*, delivered in 1389, was intended as a way to ask forgiveness for Manuel's multiple instances of disobedience and attempts to gain pre-eminence in the succession contest.²¹ In terms of genre, Manuel's panegyric is one of the very few instances of an oration with such a title in late Byzantium. As has been noted, 'it is not entirely clear whether Manuel follows Hermogenes and refers to the genre of the oration, or simply implies that the oration was pronounced at an official gathering'.²² After describing the miracle of the emperor's recovery, Manuel turns to John's role in defending the state from the barbarian Ottomans. His aim was obvious: to underline the Ottoman threat at a time when Emperor John V was trying to reach a favourable peace with them.²³

The above enumeration of the emperor's texts indicates that Manuel's literary output was not only vast but also varied. In addition, the emperor took care to collect and circulate his writings in a coherent and unitary form. With the help of several of his acquaintances – Isidore of Kiev, Makarios Makres and Joseph Bryennios – he revised his texts and attempted to produce definitive editions of his compositions, which he included in four manuscripts similar in layout and decoration and dedicated to his son: Vindob. phil. gr. 98, Crypten. Z δ 1, Vat. Barb. gr. 219 and Vat. gr. 1619.²⁴

---

[19] Tinnefeld, 'Intellectuals', 157.
[20] Demetrios Kydones, *Letters*, no. 262.22–5, ed. Loenertz.
[21] Manuel II, *Panegyric*, ed. Boissonade. The panegyric was also analysed by Çelik, *Historical Biography*, 142–7.
[22] Toth, *Imperial Orations*, 179.
[23] Manuel II, *Panegyric*, 231–2, ed. Boissonade.
[24] See Dendrinos, *Annotated Edition of 'On the Procession of the Holy Spirit'*, lx. After the 1420s these manuscripts reached Bessarion's library. See also Kakkoura, in Manuel II, *Orations*, 191–306.

The Emperor's Political Texts

Having briefly outlined the late Byzantine literary landscape, the contemporaries' horizons of expectation and Manuel's œuvre, I will now turn to the analysis of the emperor's political texts written during his reign. This group of texts can be divided into two broad categories. The first included texts with an official character: letters issued by the emperor's chancellery addressed to various states and often concerned with issues of foreign policy and regional trade;[25] and official documents such as prostagmata or chrysobulls granting rights to various individuals or monasteries. All these texts, most probably elaborated by the emperor's officials,[26] comprised references to the several tenets of Byzantine propaganda: the emperor as the embodiment of law, his generosity, and the necessity for the emperor to respect the church and synodal decisions.

This official approach to political matters emerging from statements of an official nature was considerably enhanced and refined by several texts which dealt with a related set of ideological issues. Unlike other texts of his which often alluded to political issues, these texts were constructed around a political meaning. They can be differentiated from the emperor's literary production and from the body of official documents on the basis of further criteria: their elaboration in a highbrow literary style and their circulation within a restricted circle of literati. In addition, they were later on collected in a single manuscript, the Vindob. phil. gr. 98, dedicated to John VIII, the emperor's son and successor. This luxurious codex, written on vellum and produced in the imperial milieu, belonged to the above-mentioned series of four manuscripts that included all of the emperor's writings.[27] This attempt to collect revised versions of his texts indicates the emperor's wish not only to underline the idea of the legitimacy of his successor but also to provide his son with the theoretical tools necessary for governing a state. As a matter of fact, the heading of the contemporary manuscript Vindob. phil. gr. 42, which reproduced the Vindob. phil. gr. 98 and included all these texts,

---

[25] For instance, the letter addressed to the Senate of Venice in which Manuel requested that Venetian merchants stop giving support to local traders who evaded customs duties (*kommerkion*); see Chrysostomides, 'Venetian commercial privileges', 354–5.

[26] We know only that Manuel Chrysoloras wrote the diplomatic letters addressed to the king of Spain. See Marinesco, 'Manuel Paléologue', 192–202.

[27] MSS Vindob phil. gr. 98 and 42 were analysed and dated by Hunger, *Katalog*, 205–7, and Mazal, *Byzanz*, 117–18.

points to the overall conception of the manuscript as an advisory book for his son:

> Admonitory book of the most pious Manuel Palaiologos addressed to his most beloved son and emperor, John Palaiologos. It includes the following: epistolary preface of the ensuing chapters, a hundred chapters with an acrostic, a protreptic speech on the study of literature, etc.

In this category can be included three very short texts that touch on political matters: *Psalm on Bayezid*, condemning the sultan's attacks on Constantinople;[28] a *Prosopopoiia* on *What Tamerlane Might Have Said to Bayezid*);[29] and an *Oration to his Subjects*. The first two, which could be considered as a pair, mark the fall of his arch-enemy, Bayezid.[30] The *Psalm* was written in the manner of a biblical text and parallels to a large extent the language of the Old Testament's Psalms. Yet these parallels also show the freedom which the emperor took in using his prototypes. Thus, while he took several passages from the Psalms, he was also keen to elaborate on them under the new political circumstances.[31] The other short poem is essentially a learned *psogos* that heaps scorns on Bayezid and exhorts the Byzantines to fight for their nation, the fatherland and the emperor.[32]

Still, apart from these short pieces of writing, four other texts deal extensively with questions of ideology in a far more elaborate form and style. Since these four texts pose numerous problems of form and content, it is worthwhile to investigate them not only in terms of their historical and ideological content but also in terms of their form and strategies of constructing political messages. This is what the following chapters will attempt to do.

---

[28] Manuel II, *Psalm on Bayezid*, ed. Legrand.
[29] Manuel II, *What Tamerlane Might Have Said to Bayezid*, ed. Legrand.
[30] Both were dated to the time of Manuel's return to Constantinople after his journey to Paris; Barker, *Manuel II*, 517.
[31] Compare οἱ πεποιθότες εἰς αὐτόν (l. 24, ed. Legrand) with οἱ πεποιθότες ἐπὶ κύριον (Psalm 124); δότω δόξαν ὁ λαὸς αὐτοῦ (l. 23) with δότε δόξαν τῷ Θεῷ (Psalm 67) // εἴδοσαν πάντες οἱ λαοὶ τὴν δόξαν αὐτοῦ (Psalm 96); ὁ Θεὸς ἡμῶν εἰς αἰῶνα αἰῶνος (ll. 4–5) with ὁ δὲ Θεὸς βασιλεὺς ἡμῶν πρὸ αἰῶνος (Psalm 73).
[32] Manuel II, *Psalm on Bayezid*, 104, ed. Legrand: τούτους δὲ γενναίους ἄνδρας αὐτοὺς δεικνύναι ὑπὲρ γένους, ὑπὲρ πατρίδος, ὑπὲρ τοῦ κρατοῦντος αὐτοῦ.

3

The Deliberative Voice: The *Dialogue with the Empress-Mother on Marriage*

The first text in chronological order, the *Dialogue with the Empress-Mother on Marriage*, corresponds to a strategy of conveying political messages that is characterised by a sense of conversationalism and intimacy between the two interlocutors, the emperor Manuel II and his mother Helena. Despite its apparent domestic topic and its careful rhetorical construction, a political message of dynastic succession on the Byzantine throne underpins the text. In the present chapter, I will deal with the strategies involved in the construction of this message: Manuel's approach to the genre of dialogue and the interplay of demonstrative and deliberative topics.[1]

The dialogue was written around 1396, during the first years of the long Ottoman blockade of Constantinople which was to last until 1402.[2] The manuscript evidence analysed by Athanasios Angelou indicates that the author thoroughly revised the text and included it in the already mentioned manuscript Vindob. phil. gr. 98, dated after 1417.[3] The revised version, purged of the overly negative statements against his then enemies, was most probably intended to serve as encouragement addressed to his successor, John VIII, to marry and procreate.[4] This hypothesis is confirmed not only by the fact that, by the time of this final revision, John VIII had assumed full power in Byzantium as co-emperor, but also by the fact that MS Vindob. phil. gr. 98 also comprised other texts specifically dedicated to John VIII, such as the *Foundations* and the *Orations*.

Owing to its vividness of expression, the dialogue seemingly reflects a real and rather less formal dispute between the emperor and his mother

---

[1] On the genre of dialogue in Byzantium see Cameron and Gaul, *Dialogues and Debates*.
[2] The year 1396 is the *terminus ante quem* of the dialogue. See Angelou in Manuel II, *Dialogue*, 20.
[3] See Dennis, in Manuel II, *Letter*, xx–xxvi.
[4] On the political context of the dialogue see Dąbrowska, 'Ought one to marry?'

concerning marriage.⁵ Helena's uneasiness at Manuel's reluctance to marry was probably real since her son married very late in 1392, at the age of forty-two and only after he became emperor.⁶ By Byzantine standards of imperial marriages, this was at a very late age.⁷ In addition, other pieces of evidence suggest that such a dialogue might have taken place. The image of a well-cultivated woman ascribed to the character of his mother corresponds to reality. Helena Palaiologina Kantakouzene, the daughter of John VI Kantakouzenos (r. 1347–54) and the wife of John V Palaiologos, was a writer herself. In one of his letters dated to the early 1350s, Demetrios Kydones praised the young princess for the ἐπινίκιοι λόγοι (speeches of victory) she composed in honour of her father's victories.⁸ Her role in organising meetings of the circles of late fourteenth-century Byzantine literati can hardly be overestimated. On the one hand she participated in the debates related to the hesychastic movement supporting Gregory Palamas, and especially his close friend, the Patriarch Philotheos Kokkinos (1300–78).⁹ On the other hand she patronised and sponsored the activity of anti-hesychast scholars like Demetrios Kydones. The latter, who openly opposed Patriarch Philotheos, documented Helena's patronage in six letters addressed to her, in which he acknowledged the material and intellectual benefits he had received from her.[10]

As in the case of his other texts, Manuel dedicated the *Dialogue* to his mentor, Demetrios Kydones, to whom the emperor sent it together with a letter in which he asked for further comments.[11] But in 1396, by the time Manuel finished and sent the composition, Kydones was very old, and, unlike in other cases, there is no reaction from him. Although we do not have sufficient information regarding the performance of the dialogue in a *theatron*-like gathering, several allusions to an audience indicate that the dialogue was read

---

[5] Angelou, in *Dialogue*, 56–7.

[6] See Reinert, 'Political dimensions'.

[7] Since many of them served as pawns in political exchanges, the members of the imperial family married young. John V Palaiologos married at the age of sixteen, while Helena, his wife and Manuel's mother, married even earlier, at the age of twelve.

[8] Demetrios Kydones, *Letters*, no. 389, ed. Loenertz, dated to the period between 1347 and 1352.

[9] Philotheos Kokkinos dedicated a theological treatise to her, *On Beatitudes*, most probably in order to acknowledge Helena's efforts to promote hesychasm. However, her attitude regarding the union of the Orthodox and Catholic churches must have been rather moderate; see Halecki, *Empereur de Byzance*, 117.

[10] In letter 222, Kydones states that he received many gifts and positions in the imperial court. He acknowledges Helena's actions in other letters as well (nos. 25, 256, 134, 143, ed. Loenertz). See Kianka, 'Letters of Demetrius Kydones'.

[11] Manuel II, *Letters*, no. 62, ed. Dennis.

publicly.¹² On the other hand, the fact that Manuel revised and recopied the text after 1417 in a different manuscript indicates that he envisaged its significance beyond the immediate purpose of recitation in a courtly gathering.

Contents and Structure

The debate of the *Dialogue* concerns the question whether marriage is necessary and useful for rulers. Manuel argues against his mother that marriage does not necessarily benefit an imperial career. In spite of his reasoning, based on his experience accumulated during the turbulent second half of the fourteenth century, in the end, the emperor accepts his mother's arguments on the political advantages of married rulers and concedes defeat as if in an athletic contest.¹³

The dialogue is divided into an introductory conversation (ll. 1–300) and the discussion proper on the utility of marriage in an emperor's life. In the beginning Manuel entices his mother into the discussion by alluding to past instances of deceit he sometimes used in conversations with her. She responds to the challenge and a short exchange of opinions on the morality of deceit in specific situations follows. After the introductory exchange of sophisticated questions and replies, Manuel arrives at the main topic of discussion and ironically blames Helena for deceit when admonishing him to get married.

> I believe you recall, Mother, how you used to praise the bond of marriage, whilst sometimes I took the opposite line [. . .] I confess it was not without suspicion that I listened to your words. Nevertheless, I was persuaded (ἤκουόν σου τῶν λόγων): I did get married and quickly looked upon children. But I was not able to eliminate with the blessings of marriage all the everyday cares of married life.¹⁴

Sceptical about the benefits of matrimony, the son then demands further explanations, stating that Helena's arguments resided mostly in all mothers' desire to see their grandchildren grow up.¹⁵ In order to clarify his position, he suggests discussing the issue of marriage on the basis of twelve rhetorical

---

¹² For instance in *Dialogue*, 102: ἥδιστον γὰρ φαίνεται πᾶσι τὸ θεατὰς καθεζομένους ἢ πραγματικῶς ἢ λογικῶς πολεμοῦντας οὑστινασοῦν καθορᾶν.
¹³ Ibid. 116.
¹⁴ Ibid. 70. In this chapter I will use the translation provided by Athanasios Angelou in his edition.
¹⁵ Ibid. 72: τοῦτο πάθος εἶναι μητράσι προὔργου ποιεῖσθαι υἱέων παῖδας ἰδεῖν.

topics, six final and six circumstantial.[16] The final ones were *right* (τὸ δίκαιον), *legitimacy* (τὸ νόμιμον), *honour* (τὸ ἔνδοξον), *benefit* (τὸ συμφέρον), *possibility* (τὸ δυνατόν) and *consequence* (τὸ ἐκβησόμενον). The circumstantial were *person* (τὸ πρόσωπον), *matter* (τὸ πρᾶγμα), *time* (ὁ χρόνος), *place* (ὁ τόπος), *manner* (ὁ τρόπος) and *cause* (ἡ αἰτία).[17]

Genre

In terms of form, the choice of a dialogue with a rather domestic topic for conveying a political message may seem unusual. Unlike for many other literary genres, the Byzantines had no handbook with prescriptions on how to write a dialogue. The only functional distinction that seem to have operated among the Byzantine writers of dialogues was the one between Platonising/philosophical and Lucianic/satirical.[18] Although a connection with the new kinds of dialogue developed by humanist writers cannot be established by any means, Manuel's text reveals several interesting parallels. Just like the humanists, the emperor combined rhetorical art with political matters, while the private sphere also takes up considerable space.[19] In doing so, Manuel came closer to dialogues like the contemporary *Mazaris' Journey to Hades*, where issues like negotiations of court positions are mixed with matters of the dialogists' private lives. Ye, what makes the *Dialogue* stand out is the dramatisation of the subject matter and the disposition of its arguments, slightly different from that in other contemporary Byzantine learned or theological dialogues. Manuel's characters frequently use short interventions; they address the arguments pertaining to the utility of marriage without many embellishments or excursuses and their remarks follow a predefined line of argumentation. By contrast, in the mid-fourteenth-century *Dialogue between the Rich and the Poor*, the author, Alexios Makrembolites, leaves almost no room for dramatisation, despite the topic involving ordinary characters. His preoccupation with maximising the 'poor's' argumentation turns the 'rich' into a bogus interlocutor. One would also expect an approach more oriented towards orality in the Palaiologan vernacular dialogues like the *Poulologos* or the *Entertaining Tale of Quadrupeds*; however, these popular texts too juxtapose long discourses displaying their authors' political views.

---

[16] Ibid. 315–19.
[17] See Aphthonios, *Progymnasmata*, 41–6, ed. Rabe.
[18] Kazhdan, 'Dialogue', in *ODB*, 1.618.
[19] This was usually identified as a central feature of humanist dialogues; see Rigolot, 'Problematizing'.

Constructing Dialogic Authority

The contents of the dialogue, as well as the author's formal choices, suggest that the emperor not only mastered the skills of rhetorical composition but credited rhetoric with the power to exert significant political influence. This reliance on rhetoric, as it will be pointed out, emerges in most of his subsequent writings. In the following section I will deal with aspects of rhetorical composition in the *Dialogue*, and try to analyse how Manuel combined deliberative and demonstrative rhetorical strategies that pertained to advice and criticism regarding different acts of ruling in order to convey his message of legitimate dynastic succession.

From the outset, Manuel emphasised the role of rhetorical topics in understanding and representing human life in general.[20] Nonetheless, despite the avowed dependence on rhetorical topics, both interlocutors agree that the debate on the benefits of marriage needs further clarification. Helena hesitates about exclusively using these topics and suggests that a lot more is needed for persuasion.[21] In his turn, Manuel implies that one needs an efficient method in order to prove the benefits of marriage.[22] Yet, even if the discussants do not specify what they mean by this additional method, the way in which the twelve rhetorical topics are treated might shed more light on this issue. Thus, contrary to the purported reliance on the treatment of each of these topics, their proposed systematic debate only partially guides the discussion. Some of the twelve topics are dealt with far more extensively than others, and often arguments are replaced by long vituperations or emotional outcries which fall short of the requirements of a debate purportedly conducted in rigorous terms. The final topics, namely right, legitimacy, honour, possibility and consequence, are hastily treated each in a paragraph, while the circumstantial ones, namely person, matter, place, manner and cause, receive a single paragraph altogether.[23] The result is that most of the topics are dismissed irrelevant to the matter.[24]

Following this separate treatment of the twelve topics, only two of them, one final (benefit) and one circumstantial (time), are thoroughly discussed.

---

[20] *Dialogue*, 78.
[21] Ibid. 78: ἀλλὰ καὶ πολλῶν ἂν δέοιο τῶν βοηθησόντων σοι λόγων.
[22] Ibid. 78: συντομωτέρα μέθοδος.
[23] The topic of *right*: 80; the topic of *legitimacy*: 81; the topic of *honour*: 81; the topics of *possibility* and *consequence*: 84. Then, at one point, Helena does not hide her rush to get over any collateral discussion: 'Well, let us dispense as quickly as possible with the other hexad'; ibid. 84.
[24] Ibid. 80: ἵνα μὴ εἰς λαβυρίνθους ὅπερ ἔφης ἐμπίπτωμεν.

In terms of benefit, Manuel states that marriage brings additional worries to a statesman, for it is known that a ruler's craft already entails a long series of troubles.[25] In her reply, Helena argues that having children can thwart attempts at usurpation to a significant degree. Manuel then proceeds to the consideration of the last circumstantial topic of time. He notes that the current circumstances of the Byzantine state are exceptionally difficult:

> But if a ruler's affairs are not going well, if his days seem doomed, if everything is against him, if he is being tossed about by anarchy, not by winds – which is the sort of thing that has happened to myself – a person like this, mother, would have done better not to marry and give himself up to endless anxieties.[26]

The discussion under the headings of benefit and time give Manuel the opportunity to spell out his view on the general situation of the Byzantine state, and in particular, on John VII's attacks on Byzantium's legitimate authority. This intervention about his nephew is by far the longest reply in the text, which makes it resemble a fully fledged harangue.[27] It is worthwhile to look in more depth at this philippic-like passage, for Manuel's embedded speech against John VII deviates from the main course of the text both thematically and stylistically: in this section the conversation avoids the previous exchanges of mutual flatteries, rhetorical technicalities and clear-cut arguments pertaining to the rulers' ethics and social responsibility. On the contrary, here the emperor's attitude changes completely: the author reveals an emotional and tense mood while he paints a gloomy and dispirited picture of his personal situation as ruler of a crumbling state.[28] Several powerful images inspired by the rhetoric of panegyrics are noticeable. For instance, he uses the metaphor of the state as a ship,[29] a well-known rhetorical *topos* capitalised on by many authors of the so-called princely mirrors. Manuel used it here on purpose, partly for the contrast with the consecrated meaning, and partly to accommodate the image of his enemies as pirates. Accordingly, John VII is likened to one of the fierce pirates who attacked the ship and also to the savage Cyclopes living in cages, more dangerous than the mythical one, in Manuel's wording.[30] The emperor accuses his nephew of trying to replace him

---

[25] Ibid. 86, 201.
[26] Ibid. 94.
[27] Ibid. 96.
[28] Ibid. 94.
[29] Ibid. 97.
[30] Ibid. 98: εἰσὶ δέ ἄρα νῦν πολλοὶ κύκλωπες ἐν τῷ βίῳ, ἀγριώτεροί γε ἐκείνου πολλῷ.

on the Byzantine throne with the help of the Ottomans and, for this purpose, Manuel reminds his audience that, previously, John VII had been caught with a contractual letter signed by the Ottomans. In addition to this proof of his nephew's treason, the emperor further develops the passage by piling up a long list of negative epithets and statements. According to this lengthy portrayal, the attention which John receives exceeds by far the attention Manuel pays to Bayezid, the Ottoman ruler who reduced Constantinople to the status of a vassal state.[31]

In light of these observations about the construction of the message, it is not far-fetched to say that this passage was written not simply as a reply in a conversation on marriage, but rather as a *psogos*. Manuel seemingly used elements of *psogos* demonstrative literature in order to present the reverse image of his own political choices and administration. He chose this strategy as he probably also wanted to stress the differences of approach concerning the question of an alliance with the Ottomans. It was his father and predecessor, John V Palaiologos (r. 1354–91), who, after failing to secure sufficient help from the papacy, oriented himself towards closer ties with the Ottoman sultan Murad. The Ottoman ruler offered support to John when he tackled Andronikos IV's rebellion in 1376–9. But the consequences of the collaboration with this threatening neighbour were dire for Byzantium, which became a vassal state and began to pay an annual tribute. In contrast, Manuel took a different position and, as pointed out in the first chapter, continued to seek ways to establish contacts with the Western Christian powers.

The denunciation and criticism of John VII's claims of imperial rule suited a more general attitude towards imperial authority reflected in the lack of praise for the emperor in the course of the dialogue. Noticeably, praise for the emperor's deeds does not emerge from his mother's interventions either. If, on the one hand, the dialogue represents the ruler in negative terms – Manuel in denial of the benefits of marriage and John VII as rejecting the legitimate succession – Helena, on the other hand, is pictured as a close and outspoken counsellor rather than as her son's panegyrist. To a certain extent, this picture matched the real Helena, since she belonged to a group of Palaiologan princesses or empresses who became involved in the politics of their time.[32] Moreover,

---

[31] Bayezid is only once referred to, as 'the drunken satrap' (σατράπης μεθύων), and then in connection with John's betrayal.

[32] Participation in the political arena was not uncommon for late Byzantine imperial mothers either. John V's mother, Anna of Savoy, acted as regent for him and fought against the usurper John VI. The preserved evidence indicates Helena's involvement in the state's affairs. In one of the letters addressed to her, Demetrios Kydones gave an account of her involvement in the same rebellion led by her son Andronikos IV between 1376 and 1379.

significantly, in the first years of Manuel's reign, she stood by him and acted as his close counsellor and supporter. In the dialogue, Helena conceives of married life as a central feature of social and political activity, especially when she asserts that there are two ways of leading a social life (πολιτικὸς βίος): alone or with a wife.³³ In her view, the main reason for urging her son to marry is that in this way he will avoid quarrels over succession to the Byzantine throne. It was usual for Byzantine emperors to appoint co-emperors from among their progeny at some stage in their lives. Hence, Helena seems rather inclined to stress that a successor would strengthen Manuel's position in power by rallying even more supporters for his rule. Otherwise, John VII would easily lure the courtiers to follow him, a much younger ruler. As a result of his mother's political stance, in the dialogue the author frequently refers to the instances when he received advice from Helena. Thus, terms from the semantic sphere of exhortation, like παραίνεσις, παραινέω, συμβουλή, σύμβουλος and συμβουλεύω, surface frequently in this relatively short text.

Several other elements underpin the advisory character of this text as well. The interlocutors discuss topics which define deliberative rhetoric, such as benefit (τὸ συμφέρον), arguably one of the central topics in the theory of deliberative oratory.³⁴ Notably, the entire conversation starts from a half-serious interrogation about the value of Helena's advice on marriage. The empress's answer strengthens the deliberative turn of the dialogue:

> It should be said that, as far as I am concerned, I have never given you any wrong advice whatsoever: only the advice which is right for you at the right time. And I will do my best to demonstrate that I was not at all to blame for urging (παραίνεσις) you to marry.³⁵

Helena's hortatory attitude permeates the entire dialogue. Even if she agrees with Manuel's complaints of the multifarious menaces against him and against the empire, the empress continues to support the view that marriage is instrumental in maintaining stability and by no means detrimental to state affairs. At times her role in the conversation seems to outweigh the emperor's and, ultimately, it is from within this advisory standpoint that the image of the ideal ruler unfolds. On the basis of her advice for marriage, Helena makes several suggestions as to political action. According to her, the ruler should

---

³³ *Dialogue*, 76.

³⁴ In his influential division of rhetorical genres from *Rhetoric* 1358b–1359a, Aristotle asserted that deliberative rhetoric deals primarily with benefit, sometimes also translated as expediency.

³⁵ *Dialogue*, 86.

be the model for the social conduct of his subjects.³⁶ Therefore, instead of admonishing his subjects, she claims, a ruler should rather act decisively when necessary in order to have his subjects act themselves in the same way:

> One may have all the military experience in the world and one may be the very best orator; one may be wiser and more brave than Alexander and Cyrus; one may surpass all others of the older generations, themselves distinguished for their practical advice; but once a person judges best to stay at home, not sharing risks and hard work with those he advises, he is unlikely to gain any advantage for himself at all: you know at least as well as I do – you can certainly argue from experience!³⁷

Along these lines, according to Helena, the emperor's subjects play an important role in outlining the emperor's identity:

> You see, you cannot be in a position to regulate well (καλῶς ῥυθμίζειν) the lives of your subjects, unless you show yourself as though having been all shaped up before, giving no foothold anywhere to people who have nothing better to do than exert themselves hunting around for a chance to incriminate rulers – and as it seems many such men our country produces.³⁸

Nonetheless, at this point, Manuel questions this model and thereby subverts the ruler's ideal image which Helena has tried to carefully construct. While he accepts his mother's suggestions, he further broadens this theoretical perspective on the statesman's agency, according to his own political experience. In particular, the discussion of virtue in leadership and the degree to which rulers represent models for their subjects allows him to put forward a view with a somewhat Machiavellian touch:

> Men whom themselves are very far from being virtuous, through some form of violence and through terror and trickery, do try to lead all their subjects to virtue; they know that this way it will be better for their authority and they will enhance it. Still they are going to meet their doom for what they have done, but with a milder penalty, nevertheless in view of what they have not neglected.³⁹

---

³⁶ Ibid. 88.
³⁷ Ibid. 88–90.
³⁸ Ibid. 68.
³⁹ Ibid. 91.

Essentially, Manuel asserts that the ruler need not be virtuous but must only urge his subjects to exercise virtues, since the subjects' virtues and not the emperor's bring prosperity to the empire. For the author, who, in this passage, connects the cultivation of virtues to political expediency, being truly virtuous and only appearing virtuous in front of the subjects are two equally legitimate states. Thus, due to his more substantial political experience, the emperor's stance, unlike his mother's, was dictated less by theoretical and general issues. Virtue, Manuel argues, is a perfect aspect of the moral life (τελεώτατον) but humans are imperfect beings and they can only attempt to attain it.[40]

These differences between Helena's more theoretical view on the ruler's craft and Manuel's position inspired by the late fourteenth-century situation of Byzantium suggest that, in fact, by subtly playing demonstrative and deliberative topics against each other, the *Dialogue* set in opposition two roles of authority in matters of political government. The two interlocutors' distinct views on how to construct a ruler's socially viable representation are further reflected at the level of dialogic authority. If in the beginning, Manuel appears to control the discussion (ll. 1–65), after the preamble, it is actually his mother who checks the flow of the debate and asks the questions (ll. 66–651). Still, at the end of the text, the emperor arrives at the point where he voices his concern with the present circumstances and with the function a ruler is expected to fulfil (ll. 652–1009). Eventually, in his last intervention, even if he admits defeat, he does so rather ironically by alluding to the economic downturn:

> Come on, then, as the winning argument is on your side, let us present the prize (στέφανος). It will not be, though, a golden award as we said earlier. Golden crowns are at present in short supply: but everybody is eager for one and there is the danger it might be stolen during the ceremony. Let the award then be of roses and branches, so that the victor may go home with the prize still in his possession.[41]

Thus, in effect, in the *Dialogue*, the author's voice emerges from the confrontation between two distinct dialogic voices which the emperor tries to harmonise so that the message of dynastic legitimacy emerges more clearly. The authorial voice is further modulated at the level of style by bridging the intimacy of orality and highbrow literacy expressed in the use of the circumstantial and the final topics (ll. 463–753). He combines the elements of a day-to-day conversation with the technicalities of rhetorical argumentation.

---

[40] Ibid. 92.
[41] Ibid. 98.

The allusions to familiar situations, the mutual flatteries between a mother and her son, and Manuel's playful attitude from the beginning and from the epilogue reveal a vivid conversation. And while highbrow literacy surfaces in the interlocutors' learned allusions,[42] orality is also perceivable in the ways the author constructs large sections of the dialogue in the form of a rapid succession of interventions of questions and answers.

Conclusion

The *Dialogue* features a rather informal approach to the problems of dynastic succession during a period of prolonged Ottoman blockade. Notably, when one would have expected more praises addressed to the emperor in a text performed publicly, the author combines deliberative and demonstrative topics on the basis of which he outlines several traits of the representation of imperial power in late Byzantium. Thus, here he presents a dramatised version of his political messages whereby the emperor pictures himself as defending his choices and arguing against possible criticisms regarding his social responsibility. The analysis of the demonstrative and the deliberative approaches in the text allows for a partial reconstruction of Manuel's political strategies and, ultimately, of his style of government. Praise for decisive action or for political design was left aside in favour of a deliberative stance and a more applied discussion of concrete situations that provide suggestions for future action, even in the form of criticism of his actions. This early approach to the ruler's conduct, as will be shown in the following chapters, was to be further elaborated in other more extensive texts.

---

[42] E.g. references to Plato (ibid. 520, 547 and 671), Homer (ibid. 618, 682), or Euripides (ibid. 653).

4
The Didactic Voice: The *Foundations of an Imperial Education*

Another type of authorial voice used for conveying political messages arises from the didacticism which can be associated with two of the emperor's most extensive texts: the Ὑποθῆκαι βασιλικῆς ἀγωγῆς (*Foundations of Imperial Education*) and the so-called *Orations*. The two texts are connected in multiple ways, particularly in that both appear to construct a didactic-authoritative voice as a key element of Manuel's authorial persona. The two works also explain each other very well. In both the *Foundations* and the *Orations* Manuel drew on a multifaceted tradition of ethical writing whose separate pieces he strove to assemble in a continuous text. In terms of their contents, they complement each other, as in the case of the discussion of *human nature* in the *Foundations*, which served as background for elaborating further notions in the *Orations*. The connection between the two texts surfaces at a formal level as well: if the *Foundations* opens with a prefatory letter which alludes to the *Orations*, the seven orations end with an epistolary epilogue which covers the problematics raised in both pieces of writing. In addition, both compositions allude to each other: the prefatory letter mentions the *kephalaia* and the *paraineses* of the seven *Orations*, while in the *Orations* the contents of the *Foundations* are referred back to several times.[1]

Likewise, in the *prooimion* of the seventh oration Manuel states that he envisaged the *Foundations* and the seven λόγοι as a continuum, possibly part of a fully fledged project of political and ethical education for his son.[2] As the emperor himself suggested several times, within this larger didactic project

---

[1] E.g. *Foundations*, 156, 425a.
[2] Ibid. 528d.

the *Foundations* played the role of a preliminary stage of moral education meant to entice his son to further moral perfection:

> For, since in those chapters I strove to shape your personality (φύσις), as one might say, <here> I stirred up your mind to strive for the better and, in all possible ways, I carved up the love for good deeds in your soul.[3]

Such passages show that the function of both the *Foundations* and the *Orations* was to provide a systematic instruction to the young son and co-emperor John in various moral problems. In this form, the *Orations* and the *Foundations* resemble another contemporary writing, by Joseph Bryennios: this hitherto unedited writing of a didactic nature, titled *The Garden* (Ὁ κῆπος), was also divided into two distinct sections, one theological and another practical-theoretical, which had both a preface and an epilogue in the form of letters.[4] On the other hand, the two texts also present significant differences of form: the first, the *Foundations*, is divided into a hundred short paragraphs or *kephalaia*, whereas the second, the *Orations*, takes the form of seven successive moral-philosophical lectures. Because of these differences of I will discuss them separately.

The present chapter dealing with the *Foundations* proposes reflecting on two questions: whether the text of the *Foundations* was conceived as a collection of pieces of moral advice that differed from other kindred texts, be they 'princely mirrors', *centuria*, *kephalaia* or gnomologies; and how to understand the ways in which the arguments, imagery and abstract analogies of the gnomic utterances were combined in order to reflect a didactic authoritative voice. In answer to these questions, I will try to document the techniques and elements of persuasive speech used in Manuel's *Foundations* and argue that they proceed from more general moral-philosophical aspects to the exposition of particular elements of demeanour. The chapter is divided into four parts: first, I will present the text's context of production; second, I will discuss its structure; third, I will explore its various generic strands; and finally, I will look into the author's concern with counselling and paternal affection, on the

---

[3] Ibid. 529a.
[4] Vindob. theol. gr. 235, f 2r–3r.
[5] In several manuscripts the text is followed by the *Orations*: Vindob. phil. gr. 98, ff. 3r–30r and its copy Vindob. phil. gr. 42, ff. 7r–39r. The other manuscripts of the *Foundations* are the following: Moscow Sinod. 458 (Vlad. 437), ff. 5r–124r (fifteenth century); Monacensis gr. 411, ff. 118r–75r (sixteenth century); Vat. gr. 16, ff. 362r–90r (fourteenth–fifteenth century); Vat. gr. 1619, ff. 188v–210v (fifteenth century); for the present volume I consulted three manuscripts: Vindob. phil. gr. 98, Vindob. phil. gr. 42 and Vat. gr. 1619.

one hand, and Byzantine kingship, on the other hand, as fundamental for his understanding of the idea of rulership.

Context of Production

The *Foundations* have come down to us in six manuscripts.[5] Like most of Manuel's texts it doubtless circulated among the emperor's friends. It is plausible that the author was influenced by other Palaiologan moralising texts inspired by Plutarch's moral thinking, especially those of Theodore Metochites.[6] The version preserved in Vat. gr. 1619 has several marginal notes by the humanist Guarino of Verona, which suggest that the text was sent for examination to Guarino, whom Manuel knew through John Chrysoloras.[7]

So far, no definite date for the composition of the text has been suggested. Scholars have proposed widely varying dates. Ihor Ševčenko dated the text between 1406 and 1413[8] while Herbert Hunger seems to erroneously connect the journey to the Peloponnese in 1414–17 with the composition of the text.[9] Athanasios Angelou dated the text to 1408, the same year as the *Orations*.[10] In the only monograph on Manuel II (1969) John Barker established the *terminus post quem* in 1406 on the basis of the reference to John's age of a μειράκιον (young boy).[11] I would like to suggest that this date is more plausible because the *Foundations* preceded the *Orations* (1408),[12] and between the two texts several years must have passed. Further allusions in the text may help us date it: the beginning of the prefatory letter[13] indicates that by the time of composition, John VIII (b. 1392) had already been appointed co-emperor, an event which, although we do not know its precise date, happened before 1408.[14] Another passage indicative of the date surfaces in ch. 4 of the *Foundations* where the emperor notes that the time has arrived for his son to choose a proper way of life: 'Know that now it is the appropriate time for you who are in full bloom (τὴν ἡλικίαν ἀκμάζοντι), to choose the best way of life, and show yourself steady in your choice.'[15]

---

[6] See Oikonomopoulou and Xenophontos, *Brill's Companion*, 310–23.
[7] See Manuel II, *Letters*, nos. 56, 60. The marginal notes belong to Vat. gr. 1619, ff. 188v–210v.
[8] Ševčenko, 'Agapetos East and West', 8.
[9] John Chortasmenos, *Briefe*, 126, ed. Hunger.
[10] Angelou, in Manuel II, *Dialogue*, 46.
[11] Barker, *Manuel II*, 344–45, 494 n. 84. The same date was accepted by Leontiades, *Untersuchungen*, 40.
[12] See Chapter 5.
[13] The opening of the prefatory letter mentions the emperor's journey to the Peloponnese: ἐν Πελοποννήσῳ σε λιπών, ἐξ Ἰταλίας ἐρχόμενος, ἦσθα δὲ παιδίον ἔτι (*Foundations*, 313a).
[14] Đurić, *Crépuscule*, 45.
[15] *Foundations*, ch. 4.

If 1406 is the correct date for the composition of the *Foundations*, then the text was written at a time of political calm, after Bayezid's defeat in the battle of Ankara in 1402. Thus, the political situation in this period was different from the time of the composition of the *Dialogue* (1396). Several explanations for the emperor's choosing to address his son at this particular moment can be advanced: first, Manuel intended to offer his son a handbook of moral conduct, since he often speaks to his son as if to a young disciple;[16] due to John's age, his son was presented as a pupil who had to learn basic norms of behaviour.[17] A second rationale for the composition has to do with the ongoing dynastic conflicts that plagued Byzantine rule in the early fifteenth century.[18] As the text assumed that John would become Manuel's successor, it is highly probable that he intended to mark and endorse the appointment of his son as co-emperor.[19] In particular, this attempt to advertise his son's position came at a time when his nephew, John VII, was also trying to advertise his son's, Andronikos V's, position as legitimate successor.[20]

As in the case of other texts by Manuel, researchers of late Byzantine history have paid little heed to his strategies of creating didactic meaning. The few scholars who have dealt with the *Foundations* have eagerly pointed out that the emperor included fragments of previous authors. However, they overlooked other more salient issues of literary construction such as the ways the author arranged this material and the conception behind the resulting hundred chapters. So far only a few brief commentaries have appeared in connection with the *Foundations*: the first in chronological order belongs to the nineteenth-century scholar Jules Berger de Xivrey, who, in his survey of Manuel's works, considered the *Foundations* 'the best known and the most interesting of the emperor's texts'.[21] More recently, several accounts have been produced which nevertheless fall short of explaining the implications of the text or the techniques used. Such are Konstantinos Païdas's book on late Byzantine princely mirrors[22] or Ioannes Leontiades' unpublished doctoral dissertation which focused on the central themes of political thought: the relationship between the earthly and the spiritual power, imperial justice or the role of courtiers in the emperor's activity.[23] A more interesting approach

---

[16] See below.
[17] See the *Prefatory Letter* (Ἐπιστολὴ προοιμιακή) of the *Foundations*, 156, 316–18.
[18] See Chapter 1.
[19] John is presented as co-emperor in the dedicatory title of the *Foundations*: βασιλεὺς βασιλεῖ.
[20] See Chapter 1.
[21] Berger de Xivrey, *Mémoire*, 32.
[22] Païdas, *Βυζαντινά κάτοπτρα*.
[23] Leontiades, *Untersuchungen*.

is provided by Siren Çelik, who integrated the text into her study of Manuel as a multifaceted personality.[24] While these studies of the *Foundations* investigated the personal and political content, they overlooked other equally important aspects such as the didactic model the work proposed. My approach will assume that this composition should be understood not exclusively within the tradition of 'princely mirrors', a term that has more to do with Western medieval productions, but in the wider rhetorical context of late Byzantine didactic literature.

Contents and Structure

Let us now look into the contents of the *Foundations*. According to its preface, the text aimed at providing a comprehensive image of human life and at leading the addressee through different stages of physical, spiritual and intellectual formation. The *Foundations* dealt with a variety of topics, most of which were common to Byzantine texts for rulers: from general philosophical observations about a ruler's moral life, to counsel about how to relax after long hectic periods.[25]

Themes of deliberation: moral advice and the image of the ruler

Like most texts of advice, the *Foundations* deliberated on issues of proper conduct or reasoning. Two broad types of *kephalaia* can be identified: on the one hand, those concerned with practical advice such as the internal and the external affairs of the state and the court; and on the other hand, *kephalaia* which provided moral and theoretical definitions.[26] In the first category can be included ch. 89 describing the strategy required to lead an army on the battlefield:

> The sign of a bad army is that it is ready to run when the soldiers hide during the day, and to attack the enemy during the night. Because they hope to defeat the enemy with the help of darkness, noise and clamour, and not by their nobility of mind or by their perseverance, and because their hopes do not reflect their undertakings and resources, they rather run away even if nobody chases them away. Therefore, you must bring

---

[24] Çelik, *Historical Biography*, 339–45.
[25] For a table with the contents and structure of the *Foundations*, see Appendix 2.
[26] Apart from these two categories, a few other chapters of the *Foundations* are placed outside the sphere of practical advice or definition of moral categories. This is especially the case with the chapters drawing on religious themes, like the divine power (*Foundations*, chs. 25, 57).

everything that pertains to your plans of victory in front of your army, so that, because the soldiers will share your plans, they will be more eager to fight together with you.

In a similar instance of advice, Manuel alluded to contemporary circumstances of conflict with both Latins and Ottomans, exhorting his son to avoid fighting Christians: 'Do not fight against Christian brothers, neither with any other people nor with a barbarian nation which has a treaty with you and desires to keep that.'[27]

Notably, however, in comparison to other popular texts of moral advice addressed to rulers, like Agapetos the Deacon's *Ekthesis* (sixth century) or Nikephoros Blemmydes' *Imperial Statue* (thirteenth century), which strove to add lustre to the emperor's image, Manuel considerably extended the scope of his chapters of counsel. Thus, in the *Foundations*, common themes of advice, like the emperor's relation to God, his subjects or the law, were underpinned by explanations of moral principles and opinions on the role of reason, responsibility and human nature. Like other pieces of didactic literature, the *Foundations* preached prudence and ideal ways of living in society, but, at the same time, it was permeated by a sense of the inevitability of fate and misfortune. The result is a mosaic of chapters where, despite passages with a political character and a sense of immediacy, passages dealing with moral principles are predominant.[28]

It was Herbert Hunger who remarked upon the deliberative topics different from those in other texts of advice. He noted that Manuel's *Foundations*, in contrast to other paraenetic texts like Kekaumenos's *Strategikon*, Blemmydes' *Imperial Statue* or Thomas Magistros's *Imperial Oration*, lacked substantial pieces of advice for practical matters of day-to-day administration, present in other texts.[29] Practical counsel emerges only in a few chapters, especially those regarding the military aspects of the ruler's craft.[30] More often, advice concerning practical issues relates to matters of behaviour in everyday life[31] or is driven by the definition of the beneficial (τὸ συμφέρον) and the harmful (τὸ βλάπτον).[32] Hunger also noted a substantial increase in the treatment of

---

[27] Ibid. ch. 56.
[28] Apart from the above-mentioned definitions of moral characters, Manuel formulates other abstract definitions: ibid. ch. 21 defines truth, ch. 78 discusses the difficulty of distinguishing clearly between good and bad, and ch. 44 defines habit (ἕξις) as a moral category.
[29] Hunger, *Hochsprachliche profane Literatur*, 164–5.
[30] *Foundations*, chs. 87, 88, 89.
[31] For instance habit (ἕξις) in ibid. ch. 44.
[32] Ibid. chs. 34, 35.

philosophical and theological notions,[33] apart from the inclusion of concepts like moderation (μεσότης), commonly used in advisory texts.[34] This situation differed from the post-1204 advisory texts which, as argued, tended to deal with practical matters.[35]

In contrast, references to ethical notions drawn from classical philosophy and integrated into the emperor's programme of education addressed to his son form the basis for further recommendations of a proper demeanour.[36] Manuel inaugurates his moral account with overarching remarks and definitions which echo the *incipit* of the theological *centuria*,[37] and in the first two chapters he addresses the problem of defining the best way of life: 'People have different ways of life: some have wisdom, education, and kindness, while others foolishness, ignorance, and cowardice.'[38]

This wide theoretical scope projected in the introductory statements underlines the construction of the subsequent topics and shapes the entire text. In contrast, similar texts, such as Agapetos's *Ekthesis*, begin in a different manner, by exhorting the emperor to honour God,[39] an *incipit* which rather resembles the openings of panegyrics. Instead, broad abstract notions like life (βίος) and nature (φύσις), or common human nature stand as recurrent notions in the *Foundations* and often constitute the background for the discussion of further topics.[40] Apart from such central notions, other theoretical

---

[33] In ibid. ch. 52 Manuel uses theological notions in order to indicate how an emperor should imitate God: πρὸς τὴν αὐτοῦ μετουσίαν, καὶ πρὸς σωτηρίαν ὁδηγῆσαι.

[34] Ibid. ch. 83.

[35] Angelov, *Imperial Ideology*, 116–82. Traditionally, the education of imperial offspring included history and advisory literature. It has been argued that in the court literature between the twelfth and the fifteenth centuries authors increasingly emphasised physical and military training as opposed to the intellectual values. See Angelov, 'Emperors and patriarchs', 85–116. Yet, in my opinion, a conclusive answer to this issue cannot be given: in the case of the *Foundations* there is little room for counsel pertaining to physical or military prowess.

[36] *Foundations*, ch. 50 reveals Manuel's strategy of integrating moral advice into a philosophical framework. The paragraph starts from the observation that people tend to forget the main purpose of an action and approach secondary purposes (ὑπάλληλα τέλη), and the author's argumentation leads to the notion of the perfect ending (τελικώτατον τέλος). In other paragraphs Manuel offers an insight into the different parts of the soul (ch. 24) and its movements (ch. 83).

[37] See Ceresa-Gastaldo, *Massimo Confessore*, 48–238; Symeon the New Theologian, *Chapitres théologiques*, 40–3 ed. Darrouzès.

[38] *Foundations*, ch. 1. Definitions of βίος resurface in chs. 2, 54 and 55.

[39] Agapetos, *Ekthesis*, ch. 1, ed. Riedinger: 'Since you possess an office higher than any other dignity, above everything, emperor, honour God who gave you this office.'

[40] The idea of the limits of nature is in *Foundations*, ch. 40 and that of the common nature in chs. 57 and 68.

concepts are introduced at the beginning of the text: choice of a certain way of life, connected to the notion of nature;[41] individual responsibility;[42] or voluntary and involuntary acts.[43] Manuel often allows for more detailed discussions of such concepts, as in the case of choice (προαίρεσις), which, according to his account, makes individuals responsible for their actions. Interestingly, it is only after providing these theoretical definitions in the first part of his *Foundations* that the author proceeds to the definition of notions such as the good and the wrong, as for instance in chs. 13 and 14.

The peculiar treatment of the topics of deliberation in the *Foundations* gains further salience in the absence of a more detailed discussion of virtues, a topic commonly held as central in most texts of advice for rulers. Yet the four cardinal imperial virtues (prudence, justice, temperance and courage), central in the construction of the emperor's authority, do not come into the author's focus. The reason for this conspicuous absence seems to reside in the author's general attitude towards the topics of deliberation: the emperor is more preoccupied with discussing the distinctions between good and wrong actions rather than providing illustrations of the different types of virtues.

The theoretical delimitations and moral themes treated in the first part of the *Foundations* and typical of moral philosophy converge in the definition of the ideal moral human character, the ἀγαθὸς ἀνήρ,[44] constantly in search of the supreme good[45] and opposed to evil (πονηρός or κακός).[46] Significantly, in a very few cases, the representation of the ἀγαθὸς ἀνήρ is juxtaposed to explanations of the nature of the imperial office and to the manner in which an emperor should act in given circumstances.[47] Instead, we are generally left with a black-and-white picture that opposes different moral characters. The ἀγαθὸς ἀνήρ becomes recognisable from a series of ideal attributes: the continuous effort to acquire knowledge for practical reasons,[48] wisdom backed up

---

[41] Especially in ibid. chs. 3 and 4. See ch. 68 on προαίρεσις and φύσις. Towards the end of the *Foundations*, ch. 99 returns to the problematic of φύσις: people are made from both matter and spirit. The notions of nature and individual choice in acting emerge in *Orations* 2 and 3, where they are treated extensively.

[42] *Foundations*, ch. 30.

[43] Ibid. ch. 25.

[44] See also the idea of best life (ἄριστος βίος) in ibid. chs. 1–2 and ch. 4: ἴσθι καιρὸν ἐπιτήδειον ὄντα σοι τὴν ἡλικίαν ἀκμάζοντι, βίον ἐλέσθαι τὸν ἄριστον.

[45] See ibid. ch. 86 on the highest form of good, τὸ ἔσχατον τῶν καλῶν.

[46] The ἄριστος/ἀγαθὸς ἀνήρ is to be recognised by his behaviour (ibid. chs. 18, 32, 70).

[47] Ibid. ch. 71 explains the concept of εὐδαιμονία (happiness), a condition for becoming ἀγαθὸς ἀνήρ. Manuel argues that a ruler does not attain εὐδαιμονία if he is only wealthy.

[48] See ibid. chs. 94, 95, 96 and especially 97 on knowledge and practice.

with natural goodness,⁴⁹ and a proper attitude with regard to situations and individuals.

Owing to this emphasis on ideal moral characters, the advice specifically addressed to John has a limited scope while his individual well-being (εὐδαιμονία) acquires little significance.⁵⁰ Common themes used in texts of advice striving to create the representation of an ideal prince, like order and hierarchy, are overshadowed by the multitude of remarks on the individual's behaviour in society and at court.⁵¹ Most often, the advice is embedded in the above-mentioned philosophical and general moral advice that shapes the idea of the best man (ἄριστος ἀνήρ). Thus, Manuel dismisses blind fortune (τύχη) as a force behind the emperor's actions, for an emperor needs to fortify himself for ruling by aspiring to a good situation (τὰ ἀγαθά).⁵²

According to this representation, the ruler's image becomes rather conventional: the emperor – an imitator of God, a righteous lawgiver or a man focused on his daily tasks. Furthermore, the ruler is seen as part of a community and for this reason Manuel advises John to show politeness and outward grace (ἀστειότης and χάρις) to other courtiers.⁵³ The emperor's magnificence (μεγαλοπρέπεια) and character (σχῆμα) imply that he should treat wisely those ranking lower in court hierarchy,⁵⁴ without irony or mendacity.⁵⁵ John should remain silent when necessary, reject flatterers and consult with his friends,⁵⁶ for, as Manuel suggests, friendship features as an important instrument of acquiring political consensus.⁵⁷

In addition to these rather conventional pieces of advice, Manuel introduces several nuances. He exhorts his son to keep track of daily benefits and

---

⁴⁹ Ibid. ch. 94: οὐδὲν σοφίας ἀντάξιον, εὐφυΐᾳ συγκραθείσης.
⁵⁰ Ibid. ch. 5: τῶν κρατούντων εὐδαιμονία.
⁵¹ Ibid. ch. 30: ἅπαντα μὲν τῆς ἑαυτῶν ἀρχῆς ἤρτηται.
⁵² On the role of fortune as a blind force that can be surpassed and is opposed by one's will, see ibid. ch. 47: Τὸ προθυμεῖσθαι γὰρ ἀνδρός. Τὸ δὲ σφαλῆναι καὶ τύχης. On the ruler's high aspirations see ch. 37.
⁵³ For Manuel as imitator of God see ibid. ch. 42: καὶ Θεὸν μιμούμενος, καὶ σαυτὸν τοῖς σεαυτοῦ μίμημα ταύτῃ παρέχων. For Manuel as legislator see ch. 51. For a further discussion of the conventional traits of the emperor's image in the *Foundations* see Païdas, *Βυζαντινὰ κάτοπτρα*, 109–238; Leontiades, *Untersuchungen*, 120–50. For the notion of the emperor as part of a community see ch. 19: πάντες γὰρ ἀλλήλων δεόμεθα, εἰ μέλλει διαρκέσειν ἡμῖν τὸ ζῆν. For the emperor's focus on daily tasks see ch. 79: ζημία μεγίστη τοῖς πράγμασιν τὸ διαχεῖσθαι τὸν νοῦν τοῖς ἄρχουσιν. On ἀστειότης and χάρις see ch. 61.
⁵⁴ Ibid. chs. 8 and 10: θεραπεύειν τοὺς ὑπὸ σὲ πάντας φίλτρῳ καὶ φόβῳ.
⁵⁵ Ibid. ch. 77: μήτε εἰρωνείᾳ συνεῖναι θέλε, μήτε ἀλαζονείᾳ συνέστω σοι.
⁵⁶ Ibid. ch. 78: τὰς γνώμας τῶν φιλούντων.
⁵⁷ Ibid. ch. 18: οὕτω καὶ κοσμίως φιλήσεις, καὶ ἐν τῷ φιλεῖν καὶ φιλεῖσθαι διαμένεις.

losses, a statement that echoes Sphrantzes' later statement that the ruler should also act as an administrator of the state.[58] Then, in two further chapters, Manuel states that even rulers should relax after accomplishing stressful tasks. A frequent topic in his letters,[59] the emperor's long walks in the garden and periods of relaxation surface in other chapters as well.[60]

Finally, a conspicuous absence in the *Foundations* is the use of heroic models, particularly since such texts of advice were often conceived also as encomia for rulers. Instead, throughout the *Foundations*, Manuel either proposes models of extreme humbleness, like the biblical Job or attempts to integrate the emperor's office into a court life populated by both friends and enemies.[61]

Structure

Despite its variety of topics, unlike other works of its kind, the *Foundations* stand as a structurally coherent text where the author has attempted to systematise several topics of advice.[62] An indication of this systematisation is that passages designed to explain moral or philosophical notions were grouped together and were separated from the commandments on how to lead a good life as a ruler in difficult times. Strikingly, Manuel's moral snippets were grouped in thematic clusters of two or more paragraphs of equal length. Thus, the *Foundations* appear to have been conceived as a coherent moral text rather than as a florilegium of independent wise statements.

A key mark of this structural coherence is the concatenation of paragraphs into thematic groups. Several examples will illustrate this compositional strategy. For instance, the first six chapters deal solely with abstract notions of moral philosophy. Within this group chapters 1 and 2 are tightly connected by dealing with a similar topic: the types of life an individual can pursue. If chapter 1 asserts a triple division of the types of life (for the good, for pleasure and for one combining both good and pleasure), chapter 2 follows up on a similar topic and deals with the best kinds of life (ἄριστος βίος). Chapters 3

---

[58] Ibid. ch. 41: Λογίζου δὲ καθημερὰν ζημίαν τε καὶ τὰ κέρδη.
[59] Pleasantry and the combination of pleasantry with more serious activities is a frequent theme emerging in his letters, e.g. in *Letters*, no. 67, ll. 71–7, ed. Dennis, addressed to Kabasilas: 'But let them tell whether it is their judgment that pleasantry must once and for all be censured, or that there is a certain time for lightness and that it should not be excluded from all those matters for which the most wise Solomon apportions a time.'
[60] *Foundations*, chs. 79 and 80. Such advice might be rooted in Renaissance literature. See Hersant, *Vie active*, 263–71.
[61] *Foundations*, ch. 38.
[62] For a synoptic list with the contents and structure of the *Foundations*, see Appendix 2.

and 4 continue the theme of the first two paragraphs and discuss the best ways of life in connection with the Aristotelian notions of common human nature and individual choice. In equally theoretical terms chapters 5 and 6 further the discussion and deal with good fortune (εὐδαιμονία), another central concept in moral philosophy, and with time (καιρός), a notion that describes the right moment of action. The following group of seven chapters, 7–13, deals with issues of general spiritual development and authority: submission to God (chapters 7–9) and obedience to the church (chapters 11–13). After these two sections, the author turns to the main topic of his text, namely moral advice on how to act in various circumstances. The discussion starts with two chapters on the moral categories of good and evil, and on the appropriate behaviour towards others (chapters 14 and 15). Following this theoretical setting, the material is divided into separate sections: chapters 16–21 on relations with individuals (trust and friendship); chapters 22–37 on the individual's right course of action converging in the idea of ἄριστος ἀνήρ. Chapters 38–93 constitute the largest section of the text and deal with various aspects of moral action which a ruler has to take into consideration: calumny, focus of mind, state of mind, temperance, cautiousness, avoidance of dissimulation, honesty, relaxation after times of intense activity, military strategy, real friendship and others.[63] The advice tailored for Manuel's son as a ruler is often intertwined with the enunciation of moral principles and of virtues commonly used in texts of advice for rulers: measure (μετριότης), the four cardinal virtues (temperance, prudence, courage, justice), the ruler as head in the metaphor of the state as a living body, the ruler-legislator, the emperor as model for his subjects and fulfilling various roles (πατήρ, ἰατρός, ποιμήν, διδάσκαλος). The last six chapters of the *Foundations* act as a conclusion to the full circle of advice, and return to the theoretical stance disclosed at the beginning.

Thus, it appears that the text's literary logic does not follow a linear pattern but rather a convoluted path: it begins with the discussion of more general concepts, proceeds to matters of practical demeanour, returns to general moral notions, and repeats ideas from the beginning so that, towards the end, the practical matters of administration can be explained in light of a coherent system of ethical values.[64] This apparently loose structure allows the author to pursue concomitantly different lines of thought and to maintain the openness

---

[63] *Foundations*, ch. 21: ἦ που φίλος σοι σαφὴς ὃς κοινωνῶν σοι τῶν ἔργων, κατόπιν τοῦ συνοίσοντος αἰεὶ τὸ χάριεν τίθησιν.

[64] For instance, the notion of individual choice resurfaces in ibid. ch. 28. Hunger noticed the repetitions in the princely mirrors as well, without, however, connecting them to an overall structure; Hunger, *Hochsprachliche profane Literatur*, 157–62.

of the text by offering the possibility of connecting these clusters in a variety of ways.

Genre

The peculiarities of content and structure underline the question of the genre of the *Foundations*, a question whose answer may shed further light on the text's intended function. Certainly, owing to its declared intent and to its multiple instances of advice, the text comes close to the popular genre of the so-called princely mirrors; yet at the same time, as pointed out above, it remains intriguing that to a large extent it also deals with the enunciation of general moral and philosophical principles, thereby departing from the consecrated models of texts of advice for rulers. It appears that, in contrast to other Byzantine authors of handbooks of good conduct such as Agapetos (sixth century), Photios (ninth century), Theophylakt of Ochrid (eleventh century), Nikephoros Blemmydes (thirteenth century) or Thomas Magistros (fourteenth century), Manuel adopted a different didactic approach. Arguably, at a formal level, this approach entailed the combination of several generic strands which drew upon various sources: *gnomologia* (anthologies/florilegia), *hypothekai* or *kephalaia* (*centuria*). A look at other texts similar in form or content can throw more light on the relationship of Manuel's text to these various traditions and help us further understand how he adapted these sources in order to shape his authorial voice. For this reason, the ensuing section not only involves the issue of sources but also explores questions of continuities across the Byzantine period, intertextuality, reliance on tradition, and self-renewal.

Wisdom and advice literature

Any discussion of the genre of the *Foundations* needs to consider the author's use of gnomic or wisdom literature, a common source for texts of advice for rulers. The text includes a great many implicit and explicit quotations from various *auctoritates*:[65] Homer or the tragedians,[66] philosophers and biblical or patristic texts.[67] In many cases Manuel reworked citations from other

---

[65] Ševčenko, 'Agapetos East and West', 8–9, and Hunger, *Hochsprachliche profane Literatur*, 158–60, noted that Manuel is the only author of a princely mirror to mention Isocrates' name (*Foundations*, ch. 15).
[66] *Foundations*, chs. 96, 33, 39, 72, 92.
[67] Ibid. chs. 10, 13, 52, 56.

sources,[68] as many of them can be found in the collections of gnomes circulating in Byzantium. For instance, in ch. 55, Manuel quoted 'a poet' with the following pithy saying: οὐκ ἔστιν εὑρεῖν βίον ἄλυπον ἐν οὐδενί. The saying can be traced to Menander,[69] who included it in his collection of *Sententiae*[70] and in the chapters περὶ γνώμης of Hermogenes[71] and Nicholas.[72] Likewise, the statement in chapter 12 (ἴσον τῷ πρὸς κέντρα λακτίζειν τὸ πολεμεῖν τῆς Ἐκκλησίας τοῖς δόγμασι)[73] was listed in fifteenth-century paroemiographic corpora.[74]

A brief look at the gnomic literature that shaped the *Foundations* is useful. In particular, two genres relied on the use of gnomic sayings: *hypothekai* and *kephalaia*, the very terms used in the title of Manuel's text. As will be argued in what follows, the features of these genres influenced the shape and content of the message of Manuel's text. The *hypothekai* represented one of the oldest denominations for collections of wisdom sayings in the deliberative genre.[75] Originating in Hesiod's epic poems, they were soon borrowed in public oratory. In *To Nicocles* (3), the oration that constituted the model of ancient and medieval texts of advice for rulers, Isocrates described his text as '*hypothekai* about how one should live' (ὑποθήκας ὡς χρὴ ζῆν) while in *To Demonicus* (5) Pseudo-Isocrates described his speech as παραίνεσις (exhortation) similar to a series of *hypothekai*. In the Hellenistic period, the *hypothekai* lost their epic and dramatic character[76] so that later on, in his *Bibliotheca*, Photios highlighted the role of the *hypothekai* in the process of education.[77]

As a popular rhetorical genre, the *hypothekai* were panoplies of elaborate wise statements with a gnomic core. Manuel's composition reflects this definition and, to a certain extent, the use of gnomes controls the flow of the

---

[68] See ibid. ch. 68 where he refers to the 'poets': ὃ μὴ φορητὸν ἡμῖν εἰπέ τις τῶν ποιητῶν ἄλλως φράσας, and ch. 16 where he alludes to rhetoricians: καθ' αὑτὸ ῥηθῆναι καλὸν καὶ τῆς τοῦ ῥήτορος γνώμης συστατικόν.
[69] Kock, *Comicorum Atticorum Fragmenta*, 3.411.
[70] Menander of Athens, *Sententiae*, 521, ed. Jäkel.
[71] Hermogenes, *Progymnasmata*, in *Rhetorical Texts*, 3.18, ed. Rabe.
[72] Nicholas the Sophist, *Progymnasmata*, in Walz, *Rhetores Graeci*, vol. 1, 24. 8.
[73] Acts 26.14.3–4.
[74] Manuel Chrysokephalos, *Centuria*, in Leutsch, *Corpus*, 7.44.1; Michael Apostolios, *Centuria*, in ibid. 6.57.3.
[75] Temporini, *Aufstieg und Niedergang*, 25.1051.
[76] Ibid. With Philo's *Hypothetikos Logos* they begin to designate didactic collections of maxims treating moral issues.
[77] Photios emphasised the role of *hypothekai* in educating youth when he states that he collected the *hypothekai* in order to educate and ameliorate characters (τινῶν ὑποθήκας συλλεξάμενος, ἐπὶ τῷ ῥυθμίσαι καὶ βελτιῶσαι τῷ παιδὶ τὴν φύσιν); *Bibliotheca*, 167.112a, ed. Henry.

Foundations. The author's favourable disposition towards gnomes is understandable in light of their key role in school exercises – *progymnasmata*:[78] as such, they were geared towards training students in practical matters that would teach the young students strategies for conveying public messages.[79]

Thus, it appears that one major element defining the genre of the *Foundations* is the reliance on gnomic sayings gathered in *gnomologia*.[80] As it has been transmitted to us, the Byzantine gnomological tradition offers the picture of a mélange of many loose ends.[81] Most *gnomologia* used by the admonitory texts cultivated a limited set of themes, sometimes grouped in sections: the divine being, soul, self-conscience, virtue, wit and wisdom, education, truth, admonition, moderation, law and justice, authority and rulers, action, well-doing, happiness, mercy, freedom and slavery, ageing, effective oratory, faithful and fake friends, desire, pleasure, richness, love of money, independence, evil, envy, drunkenness, misfortune, sorrow, anger, women, abandoned things, etc. Scattered through the entire corpus of Byzantine literature, gnomes attest a certain taste for what has been called wisdom and advice literature. Other literary genres also used gnomic sayings purely as ornaments or as powerful arguments, but rather few texts grouped them thematically or in other meaningful ways.

---

[78] The importance of gnomes and *chreiai* in the Byzantine educational system can hardly be overestimated. Aphthonios's *progymnasmata* counted the elaboration of gnomes among his main categories of exercises designed to prepare the students for public speaking. In his *Bibliotheca*, Photios highlights the importance of gnomes and *chreiai* for a broad category of readers; *Bibliotheca*, 167, 115b, ed. Henry.

[79] According to the pedagogical programmes of ancient rhetoricians like Theon or Aphthonios, students were taught to wield a maxim by expanding or compressing it. Some collections of gnomes were designed to help students learn and, for this reason, their authors arranged gnomes in the form of questions and answers which helped memorisation. However, in the case of Manuel's *Foundations* the gnomes are developed in self-standing paragraphs and the purpose seems to be not the easiness of memorisation but to further explain moral aspects of life and demeanour. Manuel seems to have followed Aristotle's discussion of γνῶμαι, where the philosopher defined maxims as general statements only about questions of practical conduct, courses of conduct to be chosen or avoided; Aristotle, *Rhetoric* 79: 1394a19ff., 1395a2ff.

[80] The multitude of gnomic collections confirm their popularity at both at the collective and the individual level. For instance, in the fourteenth century the *Synopsis of Rhetoric* (Σύνοψις ῥητορικῆς) by Joseph Rhakendytes explicitly recommends the use of gnomes in letters: ἐν ταῖς ἐπιστολαῖς χρησιμώτατα τὰ γνωματεύματα τῶν σοφῶν; Walz, *Rhetores Graeci*, 3.558.

[81] See the recent project *Sharing Ancient Wisdoms* on the medieval gnomological traditions. Available at <http://www.ancientwisdoms.ac.uk/library> (last accessed 5 April 2019).

Wisdom and advice literature in late Byzantium

The gnomic content of the *Foundations* reflected the popularity of collections of gnomes in late Byzantium.[82] Judging from the number of productions, parainetic literature enjoyed a high reputation among other rhetorical genres. For instance, MS Vat. gr. 1619, which included the *Foundations*, comprised among other things an ancient gnomology attributed to Plutarch, the *Apophthegmata of Kings and Emperors* (ff. 211r–88v).

It was not unusual for authors in Manuel's circle to gather such sayings in collections of various forms. Isidore of Kiev included among his texts a section on sentences and short citations on life, *hybris* and the effects of fear and hope.[83] Another contemporary of Manuel, John Chortasmenos, wrote a text of *Moral Counsels* (Ἠθικὰ παραγγέλματα) that mirrored the fragmentary form of the gnomic collections. However, unlike in Manuel's case, Chortasmenos's moral counsel for proper conduct relies on the enunciation of Christian truths and on his personal observations of court life. Both elements were integrated into a rather pessimistic vision of social activity in which all individuals should keep a low profile in order to succeed or survive:

> Do not cease to spend time with your fellows. But if it is necessary to speak, beware not to be the one who initiates a discussion. If a discussion is initiated by others, adopt one of the following two strategies: either remain silent with regard to what has been said, or praise and accept what has been said. For it is very dangerous to wish to contradict others on various topics.[84]

Another contemporary text, Demetrios Chrysoloras's *One Hundred Letters* addressed to the emperor Manuel II, resembles the *Foundations*. It has even been suggested that Chrysoloras intended it as a literary answer to Manuel's chapters.[85] Although there are no conclusive indications of Chrysolaras's attempt to mirror the *Foundations*, these so-called letters combine epistolary

---

[82] Collections of moral advice making use of gnomes continued to appear in late Byzantium. One of the most important sources for the assessment of Byzantine *gnomologia* is the *Gnomologium Vaticanum*, ed. Sternbach, a fourteenth-century list of ancient wise sayings drawn from various authors. As for the early Palaiologan gnomic collections with an identifiable author, we can include the *kephalaia* of Andronikos Palaiologos: fifty-three short gnomic maxims, grouped according to categories; Ozbic, 'ΚΕΦΑΛΑΙΑ'.

[83] As in MS Vat. gr. 914, discussed and described by Schreiner, 'Literarische Interessen', 211.

[84] John Chortasmenos, *Moral Counsels*, in *Briefe*, 240, ed. Hunger.

[85] Conti Bizzarro, 'Demetrio Crisolora', 10–12.

features of the repenting (μεταμελετική) type[86] with elements of panegyric,[87] and admonitory texts addressed to rulers.[88] Thus here, advice addressed to rulers takes a rather peculiar form, for Chrysoloras's *Letters* combined it with requests for apologies and praise for virtues like the emperor's generosity. Similar in the predominant gnomic form and didactic intent was Joseph Bryennios's contemporary *Treatise on Reason* (Ὑπόμνημα περὶ νοός). The subtitle indicates that the *kephalaion* form stood as the main model: κεφαλαιώδεσι χρήσεσι διαλαμβάνον, ὡς χρὴ τοῦτον καθαίρειν; and the preacher's method consisted mainly of a succession of definitions without further explanations.[89]

As for the emperor's interest in wisdom and advice literature, it is reflected in Manuel's own short list of pieces of advice, which has been preserved in only one manuscript (MS Vat. Barb. gr. 219, f. 90v) under the title *Several Words for Brevity and Peace in Deliberations* (Τοῦ αὐτοῦ ἅτινα συντομίαν ἄγει καὶ εἰρήνην ἐν ταῖς βουλαῖς). This unedited text is, in fact, a set of seven commandments, also probably addressed to his son as they retain a didactic style:

1. Μὴ ἀνακόπτειν ἀρξάμενον.
2. Μὴ μέμφεσθαι περὶ λέξιν.
3. Μὴ λέγειν τὰ περὶ ἄλλων λεχθέντα ἀλλὰ ἢ προστιθέναι ἢ ἀφαιρεῖν.
4. Μὴ λέγειν περὶ τῶν ἑπομένων, πρὸ τοῦ τὴν καθόλου δόξαν στερχθῆναι.
5. Μὴ διαλέγεσθαι πρὸς πρόσωπον, ἀλλὰ ἁπλῶς λέγειν τὰ δοκοῦντα.
6. Μὴ πολυπλασιάζειν τὸ κυρωθέν.
7. Μὴ λέγειν ἑτέραν βουλήν, πρὸ τοῦ τὴν λαληθεῖσαν λαβεῖν τέλος.

Notably, in this case, advice takes a concise form and addresses a single moral issue, while the seven commandments indicate the emperor's interest in offering guidance for one's life.

---

[86] Chrysoloras apologised for a previous verbal attack on the emperor. The μεταμελητικὴ ἐπιστολὴ category was listed by Proclus in his *De forma epistolari*.

[87] E.g. Demetrios Chrysoloras, *Comparison*. Chrysoloras's *One Hundred Letters* draws much of its substance from this previous text.

[88] Chrysoloras included quotations from authors of admonitory texts, both Byzantine and classical such as Nikephoros Blemmydes' *Imperial Statue* (Ἀνδριὰς βασιλικός), Isocrates, and Isidore of Pelusium.

[89] Several parallels between the *Foundations* and other contemporary texts of advice emerge. For instance, John Eugenikos's *Hortatory Note Addressed to Despot Theodore*, PP 1, 86, ed. Lampros, although cast in the form of a deliberative oration, draws extensively on gnomic content (ὑποθῆκαι) and moral precepts (παραγγέλματα).

Gnomes and gnomologia in the Foundations

A further brief excursus on the Palaiologan uses of gnomes and *gnomologia* may help us better understand how Manuel used gnomic sayings. Certainly, in many respects his *Foundations* resembles florilegia of gnomes, as it collected short excerpts from various collections of sayings which were subsequently expanded and reinterpreted in order to fit a more sophisticated purpose that pertained to both teaching and advertising the imperial offspring. It was also an opportunity for the emperor to display his familiarity with gnomologies, like any educated Byzantine.[90] Manuel Chrysoloras alluded to this familiarity when he described the emperor's ability to write and philosophise as sententious.[91]

Unlike in other texts, in the *Foundations*, Manuel reworked the gnomic sayings according to the textual frame intended to accommodate the emperor's didactic-intellectual exercise. Chapter 39 provides a glimpse into the writer's ambiguous attitude towards ancient wisdom. Manuel shows awareness of the ancient models yet, at the same time, also voices a personal perspective. Thus, in the epistolary preface when he states that the opinions of the precursors (τῶν ἀρχαιοτέρων τὰς γνώμας) should help build a new kind of individuals, Manuel also emphasises the role of his own views and accumulated experience.[92] In doing so, the emperor was aware that the force of gnomic phrases came from their assessing of situations, partly as statements which may have taken the form of prohibitions or commands. According to rhetorical theory, gnomic phrases had to be formulated either as proofs or as rhetorical ornamentation (*ornatus*).[93] In the first case (as proofs) they were meant to have authority, while in the second (as rhetorical ornamentation) they had a demonstrative function, adding a philosophical component to the chief line of advice. A look at Manuel's text, where gnomes occupy a limited space, reveals that such enunciations were in most cases used as *ornatus* rather than as proofs or for their authority.

One can also note a tendency towards the inclusion of gnomes in the *incipit* or the conclusion of paragraphs where they acquire more effectiveness. A

---

[90] Evidence for Manuel's knowledge of gnomic collections comes from other sources as well. A preface by Joasaph the Monk preceding the funeral oration for Manuel's brother Theodore in MS Vat. gr. 1619 counts the usage of gnomes among the emperor's most striking literary talents: πυκνοῖς τ' ἐνθυμήμασι κέχρηται καὶ καταλλήλοις ἐργασίαις, γνωμικοῖς τε ἀρίστοις (*Funeral Oration*, 17–18).

[91] For a praise of Manuel's γνωματικὴ φιλοσοφία, see Manuel Chrysoloras, *Epistolary Oration*, 93.21, ed. Patrineles and Sophianos.

[92] See the epistolary preface to the *Foundations*.

[93] Lausberg, *Handbook*, 432.

pattern of moral argumentation in the *Foundations* emerges: a thesis is stated, then its antithesis or converse, followed by a concrete case. Some chapters open with an argument-headline cast in gnomic form,[94] as in chapter 77, 'A good action is a radiant herald' (πρᾶξις καλή, κῆρυξ λαμπρὸς), which thereafter determines the contents of the entire chapter. In many cases, initial gnomes provide a canvas for the author's disquisition on moral principles. Quotations in the first line of a paragraph support the author's reflection and produce two different effects: extension, through a simple explanation of the initial phrase characterised by brevity or expressed in metaphorical language; and progression, meaning that the quotations recreate the steps of argumentation and the representational elements that led to the precept.

Such use of gnomic sayings points to a double rhythm, one part based on very short sentences and the other developed along a more discursive line of thought – allowing for more detailed argumentation and the addition of various attitudes to adopt in certain circumstances.[95] This double rhythm receives further elaboration in the *Orations*, as will be argued in Chapter 5. Thus, when looked at more closely, the gnomological content of the *Foundations* reveals an uncommon handling in comparison with contemporary texts of advice such as those of Joseph Bryennios or John Chortasmenos. In contrast with these authors and with the gnomic tradition in general, Manuel chooses to avoid discontinuity between paragraphs and to treat them in a unitary framework.

Kephalaia *and* centuria

In Byzantine literature the gnomic form was also largely reflected in the use of the form of κεφάλαια (chapters), a genre prizing conciseness[96] and particularly appreciated because of its short, abstract sentences with significant rhetorical impact.[97] Rhetorical theory discussed κεφάλαια as part of *elocutio*

---

[94] The use of short sentences remains restricted. Only in a few paragraphs do they appear in the opening phrases, e.g. in *Foundations*, ch. 22: λειμῶνας μὲν ἄνθη κοσμεῖ· καὶ οὐρανὸν ἀστέρων χοροί· τὸ δὲ φιλάληθες ἄρχοντα.

[95] E.g. ibid. ch. 23, in which Manuel produces an analogy between material and moral phenomena: ἰὸν μὲν σίδηρος τίκτει, μῖσος δὲ καὶ δόλον καὶ τὰ τοιαῦτα, ψυχὴ ζηλότυπός τε καὶ φθονερά.

[96] The ancient rhetoricians do not have much to say on the format or content of series of κεφάλαια, although they were a widely employed form.

[97] That chapters (κεφάλαια) were perceived as a form of concise expression is demonstrated by the large-scale use of the phrase 'to summarise as in a chapter' (ὡς ἐν κεφαλαίῳ), which on a simple search on *TLG* returns more than a hundred occurrences. It was used, for instance, in Manuel's *Funeral Oration*, to describe the concise account of Theodore's deeds; *Funeral Oration*, 97.3–4, ed. Chrysostomides.

and *inventio*.⁹⁸ In his turn, Manuel seems to have relied extensively on this tradition; in what follows, I will try to identify several common points between the *Foundations* and other collections of *kephalaia*, particularly contemporary ones.

Palaiologan theologians like Gregory Palamas (1296–1359) or Mark Eugenikos (1394–1445) made extensive use of *kephalaia* in dogmatic debates. Palamas's polemical work of hesychast theology bears a title that indicates both a topical and a formal division: *One Hundred and Fifty Chapters on Topics of Natural and Theological Science*. Significantly, Palamas's chapters were grouped in short series, each dealing with a particular issue: the eternity of the universe (chapters 1–2), the celestial sphere (3–7), the terrestrial sphere (8–14), natural human faculties (15–20), etc.⁹⁹ Also close in form and content to the *Foundations* were two compositions by Joseph Bryennios: *The Garden or the Anthology of Divine Cogitations or Thirty Theological Maxims and Two Hundred Ethical Maxims* (Κῆπος ἢ ἀνθολογία τῶν θείων ἐννοιῶν ἢ γνῶμαι λ΄ θεολογικά καὶ σ΄ ἠθικά) and the *Forty-Nine Chapters* (Κεφάλαια ἑπτάκις ἑπτά). As both works were written during the author's pastoral activity in Crete,¹⁰⁰ they were both addressed to broader audiences and had a didactic function: the former included a sort of encyclopaedia of various areas of knowledge (theology, rhetoric, sciences, ethics) and the second was oriented towards moralising. They also started with prefaces which argued for the necessity of presenting advice beneficial (ἐπ' ὠφελείᾳ) to daily life, and they grouped chapters according to various topics, while Bryennios's focus was theological and spiritual.¹⁰¹ Manuel himself was not entirely unfamiliar with *kephalaia*: his treatise *On the Procession of the Holy Spirit* was also divided into chapters arguing in favour of Orthodox views.¹⁰²

Unlike the gnomologies, most often transmitted anonymously, the *kephalaia* and the *hypothekai* were occasionally gathered in *centuria*, collections of one hundred paragraphs.¹⁰³ They were ascribed to an intellectual authority

---

⁹⁸ Lausberg, *Handbook*, 279.

⁹⁹ Gregory Palamas, *One Hundred and Fifty Chapters*, ed. Sinkewicz. Later on, in the fifteenth century, Mark Eugenikos used the κεφάλαια in another work of religious polemic: *Syllogistic Chapters against the Latins* (Κεφάλαια συλλογιστικὰ πρὸς Λατίνους). In the debates over hesychasm, another supporter of the movement, Philotheos Kokkinos, also used the chapter form.

¹⁰⁰ Bazini, 'Première édition des œuvres de Joseph Bryennios', 96.

¹⁰¹ Joseph Bryennios, Παραλειπόμενα, 48, ed. Voulgares.

¹⁰² Dendrinos, *Annotated Edition of 'On the Procession of the Holy Spirit'*.

¹⁰³ As were those by Maximus the Confessor, Niketas Stethatos, John of Karpathos, Ilias the Presbyter and Symeon the New Theologian.

and also included the author's perspective on the issues debated. Several parallels can be traced between the *Foundations* and the tradition of moral-theological *centuria* of *kephalaia* and *hypothekai*. For instance, Maximus the Confessor's *centuria* were preceded by a prologue[104] and had an expository character offering definitions of Christian virtues with few exhortations.[105] In the tenth century, Ilias the Presbyter gathered gnomic sayings from Maximus the Confessor and John of Karpathos in an anthology, which he expanded and divided into four parts: (1) spiritual and moral teachings; (2) prayer; (3) spiritual contemplation; and (4) the practice of the virtues. Furthermore, as noted, *centuria* fulfilled two other functions: either as a spiritual testament or as a component of an educational programme.[106] These observations, corroborated by the educational scope and the compositional structure of the *Foundations*, lead to the conclusion that Manuel might also have had in mind the model of *centuria* when addressing his son.

A princely mirror?

The scholars who have used the *Foundations* in their investigation of late Byzantine political history have unhesitatingly included it in the genre of princely mirrors.[107] Manuel's text received this label on the basis of several features shared with a number of Byzantine advisory texts addressed to young princes. Among these features, the political context of advice, its gnomic content and the models (especially Isocrates' *To Nicocles* or Pseudo-Isocrates' *To Demonicus*) have long constituted arguments in favour of connecting these texts. Moreover, the formal resemblance to Agapetos the Deacon's sixth-century *Ekthesis*, as well as its influence on subsequent texts dealing with princely education, played a major role in attaching the *Foundations* to this tradition.[108] Certainly, these similarities should not be underestimated and, to a certain extent, the Byzantine books of advice represented only avatars of Agapetos's *Ekthesis*. Yet, if we consider the particularities of the *Foundations* and the attachment to the tradition of *centuria*, the 'princely mirror' genre does not fully explain key features of Manuel's text.

---

[104] Ceresa-Gastaldo, *Massimo Confessore*, 48–238.
[105] Symeon the New Theologian also wrote two *centuria* with a similar title, *Practical and Theological Chapters* (Κεφάλαια πρακτικὰ καὶ θεολογικά); *Chapitres théologiques*, 40–186, ed. Darrouzès. The two *centuria* are supplemented by another collection of twenty-five other chapters.
[106] Kazhdan, 'Chapters', in *ODB*, 1.410.
[107] Païdas, *Βυζαντινὰ κάτοπτρα*; Barker, *Manuel II*; Kioussopoulou, *Emperor or Manager*, 178.
[108] See Baldwin, 'Agapetos', in *ODB*, 1.34.

Unlike the Western *specula*,[109] which often replaced manifestos of institutional reform,[110] in Byzantium the texts of advice for princes remained confined to a set of tenets commenting on the emperor's office.[111] More than anything else, the Byzantine *Fürstenspiegel* emphasised the ruler's relationship with God and his embodiment of law (νόμος ἔμψυχος): these values, inherited from the political thought of the Hellenistic period, found fertile ground for further development in panegyric rhetoric,[112] which prompted scholars to regard the *Fürstenspiegel* as a subspecies of the encomium.[113]

Defining the *Fürstenspiegel* genre in Byzantium remains a cumbersome task.[114] Paolo Odorico recently argued that the Byzantine princely mirror is rather an empty notion reflecting the moderns' tendency to project into a different space forms characteristic of Western literature.[115] Other scholars who have dealt with texts of advice have approached two main areas of inquiry: either spelling out their ancient sources[116] or underlining

---

[109] The Byzantines never used the term 'princely mirror', a concept coined in the twelfth century; see Bradley, 'Backgrounds'. The Western medieval *Fürstenspiegel* differed from the Byzantine advisory texts in essential aspects, even if Agapetos's *Ekthesis* acquired popularity at the French royal court; see Krynen, *Empire du roi*. From a formal point of view, in the West these texts never took the form of successive paragraphs, but were predicated upon forms like orations (e.g. John of Salisbury's *Policraticus*) or fully fledged political treatises (Giles of Rome's *De regimine principum*). Princely mirrors proved to be a popular genre in almost all geographical areas of the Western medieval world: England, France, Spain, Scandinavian countries and the Slavs had knowledge of texts providing advice for present or future rulers. See Briggs, *Giles of Rome's De Regimine Principum*.

[110] For instance, John of Salisbury's *Policraticus*, which discussed the question of the prince's political responsibility and offered justifications for tyrannicide. See Nederman, 'Priests, kings, and tyrants'.

[111] See Barker, *Social and Political Thought*, 30–50.

[112] On the tradition of princely mirrors in Byzantium see also Dvornik, *Early Christian and Byzantine Political Philosophy*, 300–20. See also Nicol, 'Byzantine political thought'.

[113] Kazhdan, 'Princely mirrors', in ODB, 3.1379–80; Païdas, Βυζαντινά κάτοπτρα, 10–12.

[114] On the difficulties of providing a clear definition of the genre see Ueding, *Historisches Wörterbuch*, 3.495.

[115] Odorico privileged the investigation of context in the analysis of the texts of advice for rulers and dismissed the genre of Byzantine princely mirrors as *une catégorie inexistante*; 'Éducation au gouvernement', 226.

[116] See Giannouli, 'Paränese zwischen Enkomion'; Hadot, 'Fürstenspiegel', 555–632. Hadot's discussion of the tradition of princely mirrors in the ancient and medieval world discusses Agapetos and Photios's *Kephalaia parainetika* from the Byzantine tradition.

the resilience of a set of political notions from Justinian to the end of the empire.[117] In an influential interpretation of Byzantine *specula*,[118] Herbert Hunger analysed the formal differences in the corpus of Byzantine texts of advice for rulers and concluded that there can be identified two categories of mirrors:[119] those following the gnomological tradition[120] and those with a coherent (*zusammenhängend*) structure.[121] With regard to Manuel's *Foundations*, Hunger conceded that the emperor transformed the small apophthegmata into elaborated paragraphs.[122] According to Hunger, the gnomic 'mirrors' reflected the flexibility and the creativity assumed by each author in adapting gnomic wisdom to the needs of his work.

This flexibility of Byzantine advisory texts was also highlighted by Günther Prinzing in a study focusing on princely mirror 'topics' integrated into other texts.[123] Prinzing discussed eighteen princely mirrors and operated a distinction between self-standing ones (*selbständige*) and integrated ones (*integrierte*). He noted the difficulties involved in the definition of a *Fürstenspiegel* genre in Byzantium and argued that in the case of Byzantine texts, a strict and widely used definition does not entirely do justice to the genre.[124] Furthermore, Prinzing asserted that in order to have a better idea about this literary form one has to look into other works treating the problem of a prince's education – fragments integrated into texts that treat other issues as well.

---

[117] Accordingly, regarding Agapetos, Paul Henry III discussed in detail Philo's influence on Agapetos (Henry, 'Mirror for Justinian'), while Ševčenko ('Agapetos East and West', 3–12) looked at Agapetos's influence on subsequent texts as well as at his popularity in late Byzantium and beyond. Likewise, the only overviews dedicated to the study of princely mirrors in Byzantium from the tenth to the fifteenth century by Païdas are limited to the presentation of the major themes present in these texts: tyranny and freedom, God and emperor, the emperor as embodiment of law, etc. Other, shorter overviews of Byzantine advisory political texts are to be found in Blum, *Byzantinische Fürstenspiegel*, and, more recently, in Angelov, *Imperial Ideology*, 116–34.

[118] Hunger, 'Fürstenspiegel', in *Hochsprachliche profane Literatur*, 158–65; Blum, *Byzantinische Fürstenspiegel*, 38.

[119] Both kinds of mirrors are divided into longer or shorter sections and cultivate similar values: the four Platonic cardinal virtues, love of God, etc. For a full account of the common values present in the Mirrors see Païdas, Βυζαντινά κάτοπτρα.

[120] In the first category Hunger included Agapetos's *Ekthesis*, Pseudo-Basil's *Admonitory Chapters* (κεφάλαια παραινετικά) and Antonios's *Melissa*; 'Fürstenspiegel', in *Hochsprachliche profane Literatur*.

[121] Thomas Magistros's *On Kingship*, Kekaumenos's *Strategikon*, Blemmydes' *Imperial Statue* and Theophylakt of Ochrid's *Imperial Education*.

[122] Hunger, *Hochsprachliche profane Literatur*, 157.

[123] Prinzing, 'Beobachtungen'.

[124] See Eberhardt's definition of 'princely mirrors', *Via Regia*, 280.

The variety of the forms of princely mirrors also relied on handling the model 'mirror':[125] Agapetos the Deacon's *Ekthesis*.[126] As suggested above, it is likely that Agapetos, when describing the imperial might, at the beginning and the end of his text was inspired by encomia.[127] Agapetos's influence in late Byzantium has been investigated by Ševčenko,[128] who noted that the *Foundations* shares with the *Ekthesis* not only stylistic devices like the division into paragraphs, the acrostic, the use of parallelisms and gnomes, but also 'a fair amount of raw material'.[129] Ševčenko convincingly argued that Manuel had a copy of Agapetos at hand, although the emperor never quoted Agapetos verbatim as Basil I did in his *Admonitory Chapters*,[130] because, in Ševčenko's view, Manuel was too sophisticated a writer and also because he probably wanted to stress the connection with Isocrates, the only author quoted in the *Foundations*.[131] Thus, albeit without further investigating the issue, Ševčenko concluded that 'Agapetos' abstract preciosity was accommodated side by side with the sentiments of a new age.'[132]

It is these 'sentiments of a new age' that underpinned the differences between Manuel's *Foundations* and the *Ekthesis*. First, the differences regarding several aspects of the respective contexts of production remain significant: at the time when Agapetos's text was addressed to him, Justinian was a mature individual who had already had several military successes,[133] and needed public confirmation for his activities, while John VIII was a teenage

---

[125] For instance, Agapetos's influence has been noted with regard to sections of Pseudo-Basil's *Admonitory Chapters* (*Κεφάλαια παραινετικά*) and to the numerous paragraphs from the sixth-century writer embedded in Barlaam and Joasaph. See Henry, 'Mirror for Justinian', 288–91.

[126] Ševčenko, 'Agapetos East and West', 5–9.

[127] See the address to Emperor Justinian in Agapetos's *Ekthesis*, ch. 1, that points to the emperor's supremacy and invincibility: τιμῆς ἁπάσης ὑπέρτερον ἔχων ἀξίωμα, βασιλεῦ; and in the last chapter (ch. 72): ἀήττητε βασιλεῦ. See also Odorico, 'Miroirs des princes', 227–33, who argues that the *Ekthesis* is a panegyric written in the context of debates on the best form of government.

[128] First, Ševčenko studied the deacon's influence on the ideology of Muscovite princes (Ševčenko, 'Neglected Byzantine source'), and second, in a more extensive study, traced the transmission of manuscripts containing Agapetos's work in both Western and, especially, Eastern intellectual and political traditions ('Agapetos East and West').

[129] Ševčenko, 'Neglected Byzantine source', 150.

[130] See *Foundations*, chs. 8, 30, 39, 60, 95; Agapetos the Deacon, *Ekthesis*, chs. 8, 25, 66, 28, 13.

[131] Ševčenko, 'Agapetos East and West', 8–9. Isocrates was quoted near the beginning of the *Foundations*, ch. 4.

[132] Ibid.

[133] Agapetos addressed the emperor in the last chapter of his *Ekthesis* (ch. 72) in the words 'invincible emperor' (βασιλεῦ ἀήττητε), alluding to his military conquests.

boy when he received the *hypothekai*. Second, there are differences pertaining to the central themes of each of the two texts. The representation of the ruler as a God-fearing Christian monarch receives different treatments. Agapetos depicted the ruler in neo-Pythagorean terms as the incarnation of God's Word, as standing in the same relation to the city as God to the world, and as the embodiment of law.[134] Interestingly, statements that refer to the ruler's omnipotence, while frequent in Agapetos, find no corresponding formulations in the *Foundations*.[135]

Remarkably, Agapetos had no observations on the church and its role, and, moreover, he did not bring explicit Christian teaching to the emperor's attention.[136] The *Ekthesis* contains little that can be considered philosophical in terms of style of argumentation or prescription.[137] It is notable that, in comparison with other political advisory texts, the *Foundations* was less formal and the author seems to have relied less on wise sayings and more on his personal experience, a strategy he emphasised in the prefatory letter.[138] A mark of this specific approach is the pessimistic touch that contrasts with the purported intention of celebrating Byzantine kingship: 'In the course of life the misfortunes are manifold. If one is hoping to find many things, he will actually come across few.'[139]

Further differences emerge with regard to Agapetos's overall strategy of presenting moral behaviour as part of the emperor's persona,[140] whereas Manuel switches these two aspects: it is ideal to acquire a moral behaviour which would then shape the emperor's activity. Agapetos further remarks that appropriate conduct is in the emperor's best interest,[141] for this is the element that ensures the emperor's redemption and checks any excesses in the absence of other formal constraints. In terms of advisory strategies, whereas Agapetos used direct address in his shorter chapters,[142] Manuel scarcely employed it. The emperor's text has a more intimate tone and bears the imprint of the speaker's political experience as well as of his fatherly position expressed in the preface.

---

[134] On Diotogenes' influence in Byzantine political theory, see Nicol, 'Byzantine political thought', 26, 32.
[135] The only reference to imperial omnipotence is in ch. 68: τιμιώτατον πάντων ἐστὶν ἡ βασιλεία, and κύριος μὲν πάντων ἐστὶν ὁ βασιλεύς. In contrast, in his text of advice for rulers, Theodore II Laskaris, another celebrated Byzantine philosopher-king, used at the very beginning of his text a triumphal image of emperorship, depicting Alexander the Great's deeds. See Tartaglia, 'Opuscolo', 187–9.
[136] Chs. 5, 11, 15 and 60 use the term 'pious', also an attribute of Roman emperors.
[137] Bell, *Three Political Voices*, 33.
[138] Manuel II, *Prefatory Letter*, PG 156, 312–16.
[139] *Foundations*, ch. 54.
[140] E.g. Agapetos, *Ekthesis*, ch. 12.
[141] Ibid. chs. 5, 8, 18, 24, 44, 60, 64.
[142] Especially the address that mentions the addressee's office: βασιλεῦ.

Further differences between Manuel's *Foundations* and Agapetos's *Ekthesis* emerge in terms of structure. While a sense of order pervades Manuel's text, Agapetos developed a rhetorical technique which combined individual notions of moral and public conduct without attempting to introduce coherence into his text. The general themes of Byzantine political theory unfold in the *Foundations* by repetition and addition of new personal perspectives. In a way these strategies had practical purposes: Agapetos did not invite Justinian to read the mirror from beginning to end but to find useful advice applicable in specific circumstances. In contrast, it appears that the *Foundations* make sense only if read from its very beginning to the end, and also as a prolegomenon to the subsequent extensive *Orations*.

The comparison with Agapetos's *Ekthesis* leads to the conclusion that Manuel's *Foundations* drew on the tradition of advisory texts for rulers, a tradition usually treated under the heading of princely mirrors. There are many similarities with Agapetos's *Ekthesis* or other texts of advice, at the level both of structure and of content. Nevertheless, the *Foundations* also shows an intention to reuse this tradition in a way that entailed the adaptation of well-known material to the text's circumstances of advertising his son's John VIII position as co-emperor.

Thus, the attachment to the tradition of *centuria* with its educational upshot and systematic arrangement of topics, as well as the marked departure from the Agapetian model, allow us to include the *Foundations* within a broader category of Byzantine advisory and didactic literature which, in my opinion, can better account for its aims and functions. Even if we cannot define the genre of *Fürstenspiegel* in terms of common formal characteristics, we can describe such texts in terms of a common intention: to educate a future emperor. The corpus of advisory literature geared especially towards conduct regulation comprises different kinds of texts: collections of κεφάλαια (Agapetos, Nikephoros Blemmydes, Photios), gnomologies (e.g. Melissa), imperial orations (Theophylakt of Ochrid), poems (Marinos Phalieros, Spaneas, Alexios I Komnenos[143]), as well as texts that combine advice cast in other forms (panegyrics, novels, military treatises, letters).[144] In terms of sources, this complicated tradition goes back to Hellenistic texts.[145]

---

[143] Mullett and Smythe, *Alexios I Komnenos*, 359–97.

[144] Elements of political advice in the manner of a 'princely mirror' appear frequently in the early letters addressed by Kydones to Manuel (e.g. Demetrius Kydones, *Letters*, no. 21, ed. Loenertz).

[145] For Agapetos alone, Frohne identified a wide range of sources: Hierokles, Isocrates, the Bible, Church Fathers, florilegia of maxims (particularly Stobaios), writers of the School of Gaza, Neoplatonic authors, Isidore of Pelusium, Philo, etc. See Frohne, *Agapetus Diaconus*, 252.

The use of sources in the *Foundations* indicates that the rhetorical forms pertaining to the transmission of wisdom were reworked to serve the purpose of a late Byzantine author. Manuel's strategy entailed the synthesis of several strands of rhetorical practice common in political texts and theological reflection. Furthermore, the compositional innovations resulting from the combination of these genres suggest that it is more useful to discuss the *Foundations* in terms of a complex text with a didactic intent, a text that escapes exact classification according to either modern or Byzantine hermeneutic rhetorical tools. In order to fully appreciate the didactic function of the text one has also to identify the major features of the author's voice. In the following section, I will analyse the authorial didactic-political voice, the key element that made the *Foundations* be perceived as an educational text with a far-reaching political message.

Authorial Voice

The *Foundations* differs from other texts of advice not only in terms of form but also with regard to its didactic strategy of conveying the author's message. The author joins together several authorial voices, one of political exhortation and another of moral encouragement, which correspond to the emperor's two roles: of political advisor and of mentor for his son. While the former role takes shape by delivering advice with regard to governance, more often it appears that the author rather adopted the point of view of a genuine teacher, *didaskalos*. Thus, the emperor's official role in advertising his successor and ideology is subsumed to the more effective roles of teacher and, to an even wider extent, to the role of a father. In this section, I will investigate the elements which shaped this didactic authorial voice: the *Foundations* as a representation of social behaviour, the author's own statements detailing his didactic approach, the systematic arrangement of the chapters, the prefatory letter as a personal document addressed to his son and successor John VIII, the style of the text which privileges rhetorical amplification, and finally the statements of other contemporary authors pertaining to Manuel's didacticism.

First, the *Foundations* stands as a representation of social behaviour, a sort of fresco of daily life intended not only for the teenage John but for a broader audience. Sometimes, concrete details of daily life surface and reinforce the emperor's didactic design: chapters 41 and 48 build their arguments on a business-oriented comparison centred on the idea of ἀγορά (market);[146] then, in

---

[146] *Foundations*, ch. 48: ἔοικε δὲ καὶ ἀγορᾷ τὰ καθ' ἡμᾶς πράγματα, καὶ ἔξεστι πρὸς κέρδος νοῦν ἔχουσι πάντα πράττειν, πωλεῖν, ἀλλάττειν, ὠνεῖσθαι.

chapter 71, when pointing to the worthlessness of immoral kings despite their wealth and power, Manuel compares his lack of value with the lives of actors: ἀλλὰ τῆς μὲν ἐξουσίας ἂν εἴη καὶ τῶν ἐπὶ τῆς σκηνῆς ὑποκρινομένων αὐτὴν πολλῷ γελοιότερος (in terms of his authority, he [the ruler] would be much more ridiculous even than the actors on stage).[147] In many cases, the audience is required to make sense of the implied didacticism, and unlike in other texts with pedagogical intent, Manuel's method entails a deliberate attempt to teach through consecutive series of contradictions. Details on his method of teaching emerge in chapters 52 and 53 when he reflects on the possibility of educating either by means of λόγος or by παράδειγμα.[148]

Second, evidence for the emperor's efforts to adopt a didactic voice comes from the epistolary preface, where he stated that the intended audience included not only his son but also the general public: 'I have delayed the delivery of the parental advice which can be beneficial to both the son and the general public.'[149] It also appears that the intended audience was limited to young people, for, in several instances, Manuel made known his didactic intent by indicating that his advice took the shape of a pedagogical project not only for his son but also for other teenagers (παῖδες, νέοι, νεώτεροι, νεότης).[150] Chapter 92 argues in favour of Manuel's interest in finding practical solutions for his son's education and distinguishes between a youth's and an adult's education.[151] Accordingly, the emperor offers examples of situations when a youth can speak up: if one is asked in public to put forward an opinion, if one has to respond to calumnies, or if he has to answer during lessons. In a similar didactic framework, in chapter 93 Manuel praises the rhetorician's abilities to speak well and persuade:

> It is best to know what is the better course of action in all the situations, to speak well (καλῶς εἰπεῖν) and in an effective manner, and to be able to wisely implant the aspiration for good deeds into the souls of others.

Acquiring eloquence had another purpose as well: it helped the ruler and teacher to gain awareness about his claims and to stay away from inappropriate actions. Thus, towards the end of the *Foundations*, the author reflects on the teacher's individuality: 'It is most shameful to be able to guide the lives of others and to keep your life unchanged.'

---

[147] In the same category can be included comparisons that involve animal representations: ibid. ch. 53 (horses) and ch. 72 (birds).
[148] See ibid. ch. 32, which proposes a definition and vision of learning.
[149] See ibid. *Prefatory Letter*, 313b, 316b.
[150] Ibid. 344d, 353a, 365d, 375d, 380b.
[151] *Foundations*, ch. 92: προσήκει δὲ νεωτέροις μᾶλλον ἢ τοῖς εἰς ἀκμὴν ἀφιγμένοις.

Third, as pointed out above, the didacticism of the author's voice emerges from the chapter arrangement and the systematic approach to ethical issues, reflecting a teacher's techniques to address a student. Moreover, in his preface, Manuel used the opportunity to set up the framework of the ensuing hundred paragraphs and sketched the two main aspects of the education of a young Byzantine prince: the pursuit of physical activities, like hunting or military preparation, and intellectual training. Manuel also outlined the main ethical principles a young emperor should follow in order to become *kalos kagathos*: having acquired physical strength, at a following stage, he should study the wisdom of ancient authors. In line with these programmatic statements, the emperor remarked that, as a father with long political experience, he can teach certain topics better than either poets or rhetoricians.[152] According to this programme of systematic education, he claims in the preface, intellectual education ranked higher than physical education.

Fourth, by and large, the emperor's strong authorial voice reflected in the prefatory letter introduces further dissonances, which reflect an intention to provide flexibility in his didactic project. The preface provides an insight into how the emperor portrayed himself in relation to his son:

> For to speak with authority (μετ' ἐξουσίας εἰπεῖν), which is very effective for school teachers, professors and anyone who strives to restore or to forge the nature of youths, is entirely possible for me. But for those (i.e. the ancient writers) it is entirely impossible, even though all wisdom is gathered into one. For how can they provide exhortations causing no fear, or in a trustful manner, or in a confident way according to the stance of an emperor, a father or a friend, given that they lack the position which inspires the lack of fear, and the imperial majesty and the friendship which grows with the intimacy between teachers and students.[153]

With its personal undertones, the prefatory letter exposes the teaching role embodied by the emperor. Here, Manuel details his proposed model of education, which, he claims, was based not only on the wisdom of the ancients but also on his own experience and failures, a statement that does not square easily with his imperial office:

> I am convinced that in so far as there is some benefit here, if you want to gain something by acting diligently, it would be easy to make plain that you are the best of the men and of the emperors. For if, as the author

---

[152] Ibid. *Prefatory Letter*, 316d.
[153] Ibid. 317a.

of this text, I am inferior to these texts, nevertheless this should not be an impediment for you in acquiring virtue; but if I find something better (since nobody was excepted from the goods that follow), you will consider that it is fitting for you to inherit this for you and you will strive eagerly to advance and improve your father's wealth and even the empire itself. As you notice my shortcoming (for they are many and great) be willing to learn something from these, setting them as a teacher for a better life and for a more secure empire. It is good that you imitate those who saved themselves from others' shipwrecks and learned their lessons from the mistakes and misfortunes of those.[154]

As a matter of fact, a look at this prologue suggests that it functioned as a didactic pact. The epistolary framework allowed Manuel to address his son in a less formal manner. In the prefatory letter, Manuel attempted to shed light on the nature of the *Foundations* and reminded young John of his privileged position in the court and of the importance of a solid intellectual education.[155] This personal approach becomes visible by comparison to other contemporary prefaces to texts of advice such as John Chortasmenos's prologue to his *Moral Counsels*. There, Chortasmenos also outlined the reasons behind, the design of and the intent of his fourteen chapters in a brief introductory text which divided advice into two major categories, spiritual and worldly:

> I will enumerate in turns in the manner of a book of precepts addressed to myself, on the one hand, those types of behaviour which are pleasant for people and which need to be maintained, and on the other hand those types of behaviour which are not pleasant to the people but which are pleasant to the wise and good God.

In contrast, whereas Chortasmenos's text focused on explaining the format of his text and the principles behind the division of advice, it is noticeable that Manuel's preface did not deal with an explanation of the types of chapters but rather focused on bonding with his son. Thus, ultimately, Manuel's prefatory letter conveyed his anxieties with regard to the educator's mission: how must

---

[154] Ibid. 317c.
[155] In offering details on the *Foundations*, Manuel only partially adhered to a tradition of such opening texts: a similar prefatory section of an advisory text can be found in Theophylakt of Ochrid's imperial speech addressed to Constantine Doukas: in the first paragraphs the metropolitan spoke about the nature and value of his speech (Λόγος εἰς τὸν πορφυρογέννητον κῦρ Κωνσταντῖνον; Theophylakt of Ochrid, *Orations, Treatises, Letters*, no. 179, 1–7, ed. Gautier).

he address the issues of the administration? As a father or as an emperor? What kind of authority would fit into the context?

The prefatory letter puts forward the idea of a strong kinship relation (πατρικὴ σχέσις) overshadowing the official tie that normally would connect an emperor and his successor.[156] The expression of fatherly affection indicated that Manuel was concerned not exclusively with adding lustre to the imperial office but also with conveying the idea of intimacy with his son. The text came, Manuel claimed, from a desire to fulfil a promise: previously, he had given his son a gift in the form of a horse and an eagle, and the moment has arrived for John to receive another more substantial present in the form of protreptic speeches (προτρεπτικοὺς λόγους) and fatherly counsels (πατρικὰς παραινέσεις), so that both John and the other listeners or readers may have a more substantial benefit (συνενεγκεῖν μὲν δυναμένας υἱεῖ, συνενεγκεῖν δὲ τῷ κοινῷ).

In tune with this presentation of the bond between emperor and son, the prefatory letter (προοιμιακὴ ἐπιστολή) gives an account of the biographical circumstances and reasons for producing the text. The letter begins *ex abrupto* with a concrete reference to the circumstances of production: after reaching the Peloponnese in his voyage to Western Europe, Manuel left his family in the peninsula under the authority of his trusted brother, Theodore:

> After I left you in the Peloponnese when I came back from Italy, you were still a little child, and as you could not attend a course of education because of your age, and because fate hindered me from spending time with you, I sought to offer you a model of education (ἐρρύθμιζον) by addressing you these following hypothekai.[157]

Then throughout this opening letter, John's image, like other representations of ideal children, acquires the realistic contours of a child who, like any boy of his age, divided his time between games and study.[158]

---

[156] On the fatherly connection see *Foundations, Prefatory Letter*, 316c. In describing the relation between the two, Manuel maintains an intimate tone. He mentions friendship (φιλία) as well as practical ways whereby John should shape his consciousness: ἔδει γάρ σου τὴν ψυχὴν ἁπαλωτέραν οὖσαν, πεπονηκυῖαν καὶ πλῷ μακρῷ, καὶ ἀποδημίᾳ γονέων δοῦναί τι διαχυθῆναι.

[157] Ibid. 313a.

[158] See Angelov, 'Emperors and patriarchs', 123–5. The preface echoes an earlier letter addressed by Kydones to young Manuel, in which the teacher expresses a veiled discontent with the young emperor's tendency to spend too much time hunting, and to neglect his studies; Demetrius Kydones, *Letters*, no. 214, ed. Loenertz.

Fifth, the rhetorical style reflected a didactic function. As mentioned, Manuel tried to accommodate his formulaic expressions in a coherent, well-ordered and persuasive piece of writing that would respond to the demands of immediate didactic use. To this end, he employed a set of rhetorical instruments, effective in his pedagogical endeavour, based on gnomic collections as well as on other literary traditions. Significantly, if in the collections of wise sayings, gnomes and proverbs functioned without any pre-configured context whatsoever, here the author introduced maxims rather in order to offer a bird's-eye view of an individual's demeanour in a hierarchic society. Three stylistic features reflected didacticism: the elaborate Atticising language; the use of figures of speech, like assonances, repetitions, antitheses and balanced contrasts; and the use of striking images that might have facilitated the memorisation of wise sayings. Again, the large-scale use of these figures of speech contrasts with similar contemporary texts of advice, like John Chortasmenos's *Moral Counsels* or Joseph Bryennios's *Kephalaia*, which avoided such figures. On the contrary, in the *Foundations*, particularly abundant are parallelisms and antitheses, marks not only of a style appropriate to the age of the addressee, John VIII, a teenage boy at the time, but also of the gnomic core of the text.[159] The accumulation of epithets sometimes used for emphasis, as for instance in chapter 48 where a string of four epithets (blameworthy, μεμπτόν; shameful, αἰσχρόν; terrible, δεινόν; and senseless, ἀνόητον) is used to condemn the idea of renouncing moral values for other benefits. In other instances, instead of an accumulation of neutral epithets defining moral obligation, nominal phrases generate emphasis, as in chapter 46: καλὸν καὶ λίαν ἐπαινετόν; or in chapter 77: καλὸν καὶ ἡδὺ θέαμα καὶ παράκλησις πρὸς τἀγαθόν. Emphasis also appears at the beginning of a paragraph when the author draws attention to his arguments, as in chapter 10: αὐτόθεν δῆλον τὸ ῥηθησόμενον· λεκτέον δή.

A major stylistic feature that differentiates the text from other similar works of advice is direct address by means of vocative and imperative, which emphasise the kinship relationship with the addressee. As a matter of fact, John's position as co-emperor appears only once, in the title;[160] instead, when turning to his son, the emperor addresses him with the epithet φίλτατε ('most beloved one'). Similarly, imperatives stand as a means of directing the young prince's attention to moral principles rather than referring to an obligatory

---

[159] Parallelisms between physical and moral aspects are to be found especially in the opening sentences of the paragraphs: e.g. *Foundations*, ch. 22, λειμῶνας μὲν ἄνθη κοσμεῖ· καὶ οὐρανὸν ἀστέρων χοροί· τὸ δὲ φιλάληθες ἄρχοντα; ch. 77, πρᾶξις καλή, κῆρυξ λαμπρός

[160] The chapters are preceded by a dedicatory inscription addressed 'by Emperor Manuel to Emperor John': Βασιλεὺς βασιλεῖ Μανουὴλ Ἰωάννῃ πατὴρ υἱῷ ψυχῆς ψυχῇ καρπὸν τροφὴν ἐμῆς τῇ σῇ ὁποιασοῦν ἀκμαζούσῃ ἧ ὁ Θεὸς εἴη κοσμήτωρ.

course of action.¹⁶¹ Yet Manuel uses imperatives and vocatives less often than do other texts of advice. Instead, more often, the indicative appears when enunciating moral principles, discussing their implications or offering prescriptions. Chapter 86, for instance, opens with three imperatives (θέλε, γίνωσκε, μὴ ἀθύμει) but continues with a verb of obligation (τοῦτο δεῖ σκοπεῖν) and employs the indicative third person singular in order to show how different individuals act to attain the supreme good (ἔσχατον τῶν καλῶν). Then Manuel frames the idea of authority in terms of moral obligation, expressed with verbs like χρῆ, δεῖ, ἀνάγκη ἐστίν, or in definitions involving an adjective qualifying a moral act, as in chapter 13: λυσιτελές γε καὶ καλὸν μηδέν τι τῶν κακῶν ἐνεργεῖν.¹⁶²

As for other figures of style, images conveyed by means of metaphors and comparisons function as catalysts which fill in the gaps between the more abstract assertions of a paragraph. Such examples surface in comparisons drawn from the common store of other texts of advice: the comparison between life and a ship,¹⁶³ silence and a fortified tower,¹⁶⁴ the ruler and the helmsman,¹⁶⁵ or physical strength combined with conscientiousness and a glorious crown.¹⁶⁶ The frequent comparisons and metaphors deploy a series of images amplifying the effects of the ethical messages. They often stand rather as pretexts for more developed pieces of advice, as for instance in chapter 58: 'The sailing master enjoys the favourable wind which gently fills the sails, while there is calm weather.' To an even larger extent, chapter 90 exemplifies the enforcement of the didactic message with metaphors. The paragraph begins with a sentence which both draws the addressee's attention and justifies the use of images in order to illustrate a moral notion: 'I would say something to someone who knows' (εἰδότι ἄν που λέγοιμι). Then a description that features animal imagery follows: 'The hunter catches the eagle with the help of birdlime [. . .] And the lion is caught in traps, but just because the lion is

---

¹⁶¹ Examples of imperatives: ibid. ch. 4: ἴσθι, ch. 38: ὔθλον ἡγοῦ and συχνὰ ποιοῦ, ch. 41: λογίζου, ch. 45: παρακελεύου τῇ ψυχῇ.
¹⁶² Similarly, another significant feature is the increased presence of potential and conditional formulations, which are absent from other admonitory texts for princes; e.g. ibid. ch. 45: ἢν ἐπιθυμῇς τελειότητος; or ch. 91: εἰ ἐπιστημόνως τις τοῖς ἀνὰ χεῖρας πράγμασι.
¹⁶³ Ibid. ch. 86: τοῖς μὲν γὰρ ὡς ἔτυχε φερομένοις, κατὰ τὰ ἀνερμάτιστα πλοῖα, καὶ ζῶσιν ἐν φαυλότητι ὥσπερ ἐν χρηστότητι [. . .] οὐδ' ἐν ἐλπίσι κείσεται τῶν κακῶν ἡ διόρθωσις.
¹⁶⁴ Ibid. ch. 92: ἡ σιωπὴ κόσμος λαμπρός, πύργος ἰσχυρὸς κεκτημένοις.
¹⁶⁵ Ibid. ch. 22.
¹⁶⁶ Ibid. ch. 53: ῥώμη σώματος συγκεκραμένη συνέσει πεπλεγμένος ἄριστα τοῖς τυραννεύουσι στέφανος.

reckless. Most often, the larks are higher than the trap so that they would not attack out of control those who offer them food.'

A further distinctive stylistic feature is the constant appeal to moral models whereby Manuel dramatises and illustrates abstract notions. He stresses the importance of illustration by means of a moral type in the very first chapter: 'People have different lives: some have prudence, education, and uprightness, others stupidity, ignorance, and wickedness.' Usually, dramatisation concerns an opposition between a positive and a negative moral individual type encountered in different forms: in chapter 25, the author builds opposition around two characters, the infamous one (ὁ κακοηθής) and the good-hearted one (ὁ εὐηθής); in chapter 86 around those who live in meanness and the reasonable ones (ζῶσιν ἐν φαυλοτήτι ὥσπερ ἐν χρηστοτήτι and ὁ λογισμοῖς ἰθυνόμενος); and in chapter 87 between οἱ φρίττοντες τὸν θάνατον ἐπὶ τῶν πολέμων and οἱ δ' ὡς τεθνηξόμενοι διαμάχονται.

Another conspicuous stylistic feature that underlines the didacticism of the *Foundations* is amplification. In chapter 27 it surfaces in the detailed elaboration of the image of a fertile land in the first half of the chapter, where the author paints the image of individuals' power to counter moral afflictions:

> Think about your heart as a fertile soil in itself which, because of the drought of our common nature, produces nothing good. Next, cleaned up by God through baptism as if by a plough and by the irrigation of the holy anointment, it became soft from the previous state of harshness, and from being devoid of any smell it acquired a pleasant perfume; it received the divine mandates as if it received the seeds of a harvest; and by the power of the cup of the Eucharist and of the holy table, it was nourished, it grew, and arriving at maturity it was saved. The weeds, the excesses and the intrigues of enemies, I believe, are no smaller than those of the dishonest people and of the daemons themselves; the recklessness of our minds provides an opportunity to sow them. Yet it is we who are careless.

Such instances of stylistic amplification contrast with the recommendations of conciseness in gnomic texts, a pervasive feature ever since the ancient rhetoricians, who associated brevity with gnomes.[167] On the contrary, Manuel expands gnomes into paragraphs that explain in detail moral notions and their connections to broader philosophical notions.

---

[167] For an overview of the major stylistic devices used in Byzantine rhetorical writing see Kustas, 'Function and evolution'.

Finally, evidence about the emperor's didactic voice adopted in the *Foundations* comes from outside the text, as many court authors contemporary with Manuel noted that the emperor played a role in his son's education. Thus, in a *Consolatory Speech* addressed to Emperor Constantine on the occasion of John's death, John Argyropoulos, suggested that John VIII had great benefit from the education provided by his father: 'Was not he (John VIII) brilliantly educated by his great father (i.e. Manuel), didn't he take benefit from him who was both father and teacher, just like Peleus drew benefit from Cheiron?'[168] Isidore of Kiev also detailed Manuel's didactic efforts to educate. His extensive *Encomium* praised John for having followed his father's advice, which, according to the panegyrist, was also a sign of the skilful emperor: 'And he (John VIII) had not only a teacher but also a father, and because of him he fills his soul with wisdom, and he beautifies the imperial office by all means, and he adorns it by all means.'[169]

Other pieces of evidence about the addressee, John VIII Palaiologos, point to the emperor's educational role. Many contemporary works suggest that he followed a regular course of education where the curriculum of ancient texts played a chief role. At the Council of Ferrara-Florence he is said to have quoted from Homer,[170] while, in his treatise *On the Procession of the Holy Spirit*, Bessarion mentions that Emperor John carried with him in Italy a volume with the works of St Basil the Great.[171] Ambrogio Traversari noted that John, while in Italy, took many books with him,[172] and later on the historian Doukas says that one of Bayezid's sons, during the years spent as hostage in Constantinople, 'was enamoured of Greek learning while with emperor John, Manuel's son, and was frequenting the school in order to set his mind to letters'.[173] All this evidence suggests that the *Foundations* could have played the role of a complementary textbook in John's education.

Given these elements that highlight a didactic intent, it becomes necessary to search for the speaker's authority and identity elsewhere and not exclusively in his imperial role. Sometimes, the author equates his experience with the

---

[168] John Argyropoulos, *Consolatory Speech*, in Ἀργυροπούλεια, 26.9–11, ed. Lampros.
[169] Isidore of Kiev, *Panegyric*, 169.10–15, ed. Lampros. Isidore then offers a catalogue of military activities John was taught by his father; 170.4.
[170] *Acta graeca concilii Florentini necnon descriptionis cuiusdam eiusdem*; ibid. 106.
[171] Bessarion, *On the Procession of the Holy Spirit*, PG 161, 326b.
[172] Ambrogio Traversari, *Letters*, no. 13, ed. Canneti and Mehus: 'vidimus apud imperatorem pleraque graeca volumina digna memoriae'.
[173] Doukas, *History*, 98, ed. Grecu. For a discussion on John's education see Gill, 'John VIII Palaeologus', 152–70; Đurić, *Crépuscule*, 87–157.

authority of ancient wisdom,[174] and, from this perspective, Manuel's text uses a basic dichotomy between teaching by experience and teaching by authority: personal experience receives increasing recognition as a valid source of parental didactic authority, to the extent that in the *Foundations*' didactic authority moves from remote texts and exemplary lives into the author's voice.[175] Thus, chapter 55 argues that people learn more from their deeds and experience than from theoretical approaches.[176] Arguably, the *Foundations* valued experience from the beginning when Manuel addressed the importance of choice and responsibility, and discussed the differences between voluntary and involuntary acts.[177]

Yet, even if Manuel indirectly presented himself as a ruler and teacher who prized experience, the text remained intensely personal and produced the impression that the precepts enunciated sprang from the emperor's life.[178] The heavy use of the first person which often identifies the source of the statement,[179] a feature missing from previous model admonitory texts,[180] indicates that the personal interference in the text, far from being incidental or simply a rhetorical artifice, engenders a shifting advisory voice which subtly combines, on the one hand, intimacy and distance, and, on the other hand, learning and experience. This shifting advisory voice is pervasive in the author's style and vocabulary as well as in his attitude towards the material he presents.

As for the fatherly stance constructed throughout the text by constant reference to an affectionate relationship with his son, it provided Manuel with a less stable but potentially more effective didactic voice.[181] It is true that the

---

[174] *Foundations*, ch. 49, highlights agreement with ancient statements: ἔμοιγε τοι παραδοξότερον ἐνταυθοῖ νομίζειν παρίσταται, οὐ ψευδομένης τῆς πάλαι δόξης. Ch. 32 discusses the relationship between theoretical knowledge and experience. Cf. also the connection between experience and ancient wisdom in ch. 24: ὡς ἄγαμαι τὸν φεύγοντα τὰς ὑπερβολάς. καὶ λόγοι μάλα σοφῶν συνιστῶσί μου τὸν ἔρωτα τουτονί.

[175] See ibid. ch. 91: εἰ ἐπιστημόνως τις τοῖς ἀνὰ χεῖρας πράγμασι, οὐδὲν κωλύσει καὶ τἀναντία εἰς ἕν τι φέρειν τῶν ἀγαθῶν.

[176] See also ibid. ch. 52: τοὺς μὲν ἄγει λόγος, οἱ δὲ ῥυθμίζονται παραδείγματι. οἱ μὲν δέονται κέντρου, οἱ δὲ χαλίνου.

[177] Cf ibid. chs. 95, 96 and 97, which draw on issues of practice and knowledge. Another proof of Manuel's didactic intent is the comparison of the youth's soul with a fertile land in ch. 27: νόει μοι τὴν σὴν καρδίαν οἱονεὶ χρησίμην γῆν τὸ καθ' αὑτὴν οὖσαν, καὶ τῷ κοινῷ τῆς φύσεως αὐχμῷ φύουσαν μηδὲν ὑγιές.

[178] See ibid. *Prefatory Letter*.

[179] The first person is frequently used in a variety of circumstances, both in expressing opinions and in emphasising moral commandments, e.g. *Foundations*, ch. 55, δοκεῖ δέ μοι; ch. 70, ζήλου μοι τούσδε; ch. 85, εἴης μοι τοιοῦτος, ὦ φίλτατε.

[180] This is the case for Agapetos's *Ekthesis* and Theophylakt's *Imperial Education*.

[181] Fatherhood: *Foundations*, ch. 18: μοι μηδένα μισήσας, τοὺς φιλητέους φιλήσεις.

model of the father instructing his son in how to lead a virtuous life in the secular world, which represented a much-used trope in Byzantine literature, reflects to a certain extent the intimacy cultivated by other contemporary authors of didactic texts.[182] One can see this at work especially in the introductory letter, where the father's persona receives a unique authority and becomes a major textual feature. This persona was ultimately associated with the emperor's political voice, for in the prefatory letter Manuel also explicitly identified himself as an educator and a moralist. By omitting to remind his audience of his imperial status he came to emphasise his advisory role as an alternative identity.[183]

Such statements reflect Manuel's subtle strategy of representing John VIII as co-emperor: by combining the categories of father and teacher into a single voice, the emperor plays with his needs as a father, on the one hand, and service to the prince as his creation, on the other hand. This results in a calculated pose designed to create the impression that transparent advice would also typify his approach in other instances of governance. The major advantage of a voice migrating between paternal intimacy and solemnity was the emperor's claim of objectivity, for in working with multiple voices the author operated a multiple and stronger self-authorisation.

Conclusion

In this chapter, I have analysed how the emperor fashions his didactic voice and how it functions. While he does not distinguish between the personal and the official-imperial voices, the didacticism of the text remains the catalyst of these one hundred paragraphs primarily dealing with ethics. Arguably, the *Foundations* combines the tradition of political advice inaugurated by Agapetos, the gnomic tradition, and the tradition of theological *centuria* providing moral and theological principles. The generic strands present in the text allow for a multifaceted authorial voice less formal than that in previous similar texts. Manuel did not aim at compressing all aspects of political wisdom into striking sentences, as is apparent in texts like Nikephoros Blemmydes' *Imperial Statue*, made of 219 short paragraphs which rarely exceed four lines, or as in Agapetos's *Ekthesis*, made of seventy-two chapters with a predominantly encomiastic character. In contrast, the *Foundations* stands as more than a

---

[182] E.g. Marinos Phalieros in the Λόγοι διδακτικοί addressed to his son. Vv. 145–388, ed. Bakker, provide advice for the son's future in a very direct way.

[183] It is for this reason that, at times, Manuel reflects on how an advisor should speak: 'For it is necessary that those who exhort pursue <in their admonitions> what is beneficial'; *Foundations*, ch. 17.

list of principles for the emperor's conduct: it is rather a complex guide for understanding, managing and implementing ethical axioms. What counted was what the author did with the material he had harvested from others, not least in injecting a degree of political realism and paternal intimacy, features absent from the court rhetoric of the period. It is for this reason that Ševčenko considered it 'the most appealing Byzantine mirror'.[184]

In re-elaborating the gnomic tradition, Manuel partly positioned himself outside the traditional tenets transmitted via other texts of advice. If we were to follow Hunger's division of princely mirrors in Byzantium, we could say that the *Foundations* belong to a space between gnomic and discursive mirrors. Nonetheless, Hunger's labelling of gnomic mirrors has certain limitations with regard to Manuel's text. Indeed, it may be that such writings are gnomic in so far as gnomes add sententiousness in many places, but to describe the *Foundations* as gnomic seems to narrow the scope of the text and to distort its function. In fact, I would suggest that one should shy away from placing the *Foundations* in the category of 'princely mirrors', at least because that fails to explain the core features of the text: intimacy and political advice. In contrast, I believe that the model provided by the collections of *kephalaia* gathered into *centuria* with a marked educational purpose plays a key role in the construction of the *Foundations*.

In the epistolary preface, Manuel declared that he addressed the *Foundations* to a very young person, his son, John, who was about to enter adolescence. This may be the chief reason why Manuel did not insist on the ideal representation of the ruler, but rather tended to outline the profile of the ἄριστος ἀνήρ. By renegotiating the terms of Byzantine admonitory texts addressed to imperial figures, the work thus embodied an intention to convey a set of moral values and practical experience into the imperial office. For these reasons, the *Foundations* can be regarded as an instrument of ordering, controlling and shaping the body of moral and political knowledge Manuel inherited. It does not only address matters of state administration but also focuses on ethics, thus becoming a preliminary stage within a more comprehensive political education. It is therefore plausible that the *Foundations* represented a text designed for an earlier age that would cover the first level of a sophisticated educational programme, while the subsequent and connected work, the *Orations*, with its more elaborate presentation of moral axioms and virtues, may have been intended for a later period. However allusive and innovative, Manuel's *Foundations* should not deceive us: it lacked substantial commentaries on practical issues, but by stressing ethics it remained one of the few ways for the emperor to act as a model in the Byzantine political milieu.

---

[184] Ševčenko, 'Agapetos East and West', 8.

5

The Didactic Voice: The *Orations* (*Seven Ethico-Political Orations*)

In two manuscripts containing Manuel's writings, the *Foundations* are followed by a series of seven orations and an attached epistolary epilogue on ethical matters.[1] Each of these orations bears an explanatory lemma, but the entire collection, dedicated to his son John VIII, has no title.[2] It was probably for this reason that they became known by a somewhat neutral and vague title, added in their first printed edition published in the sixteenth century in Basel by Johannes Leunclavius: *Orationes septem ethico-politicae*. Later, this edition was reproduced with the same title in the *Patrologia Graeca*.[3] Despite criticisms, this title reflects the contents of the orations: on the one hand, they were delivered in a political context, as the exposition of the tenets of traditional Byzantine rulership in the epistolary epilogue indicates.[4] On the other hand, an attempt to analyse them in tandem with the previous text of the moral *Foundations* is legitimate, since both texts belonged to the same manuscripts and addressed a similar set of issues on the formulation of a comprehensive moral system for the prince's use.[5]

---

[1] Vindob. phil. gr. 42 and Vindob. phil. gr. 98. Angelou argued that the Vindob. phil. gr. 98 constituted the final copy of most of Manuel's texts and included most of his corrections; Angelou in Manuel II, *Dialogue*, 19–20. Moreover, in a text addressed to Manuel, Demetrios Chrysoloras mentioned together the two texts, the *Chapters* (Κεφάλαια) and the *Orations* (Λόγοι); Demetrios Chrysoloras, *One Hundred Letters*, no. 75.1–4, ed. Conti Bizzarro.

[2] Vindob. phil. gr. 42, f. 1v, places the seven orations together with the *Foundations* under the heading *Advisory Book Addressed to His Most Beloved Son and Emperor, John Palaiologos* (Βιβλίον παραινετικὸν πρὸς ἐρασμιώτατον υἱὸν αὐτοῦ καὶ βασιλέα, Ἰωάννην τὸν Παλαιολόγον).

[3] Kakkoura completed a doctoral dissertation that includes an edition of the *Orations*. In the present chapter I use the text published in PG 156, 385–562. In addition to Kakkoura's unpublished edition, I consulted the manuscripts Vat. gr. 632, Vindob. phil. gr. 98 and Vindob. phil. gr. 42.

[4] Berger de Xivrey, *Mémoire*, 37.

[5] See also the discussion in Kakkoura's edition of the *Orations*, 191–255.

The date of the *Orations* can be firmly established between the years 1408 and 1410. First, internal evidence suggests that the *Orations* were written after the *Foundations*, where John was referred to as a μειράκιον who spent more time hunting and playing than he did studying.[6] Second, a letter addressed to Gabriel of Thessalonike, sent together with a *Homily on St Mary of Egypt* that reproduces the sixth *logos*, can be dated to late 1408–10, during the emperor's visit to Thessalonike.[7] This date helps us identify John VIII's position at the imperial court, for by that time he had already been appointed co-emperor, a fact which Manuel mentioned.[8] Thus, the years of composition coincided with a period of relative calm for Byzantium, due to the defeat of the Ottomans in the battle of Ankara.

As noted in the previous chapter, Manuel tied together the *Foundations* and the *Orations*. As in the preceding *Foundations*, in this series of orations, the emperor detailed and expanded upon similar virtues a ruler should acquire. Yet, by and large, compared to the related hundred chapters on imperial education, his treatment was conducted on different terms and frequently included more sophisticated theoretical arguments. The *Orations* focus on a reduced set of themes and concepts, and elaborate in more detail their implications and ties within a complete ethical system. They integrate the ruler's craft into a comprehensive theoretical framework based on the writer's political experience as well as on concepts borrowed from ancient ethics. In many ways, by assembling these separate texts in a compact framework, it seems that Manuel's intention was to present in a coherent shape for the use of his son not only a compilation of moral norms similar to those found in the *Foundations*, but also an extensive discussion of fundamental ethical guidelines.

To begin with, in this chapter I will argue that, despite the differences of form, the orations constituted a unitary collection and, for this reason, one should consider their interrelations as well as their distinctive features. The present chapter falls into two sections: first, I will review the contents of each of the seven orations and identify their major rhetorical features. Second, I will deal with the entire collection of orations and suggest that, despite their differences in contents and genre, collectively they form a unitary composition and that, as such, they were meant to convey a single message that pertained to the education of a young ruler.

---

[6] In the beginning of the seventh oration, Manuel refers to topics discussed in the κεφάλαια.
[7] Manuel II, *Letters*, no. 150, n. 1, ed. Dennis.
[8] Manuel addresses his son as both co-emperor and son: *Orations*, 557a: ὦ συμβασιλεῦ τε καὶ παῖ.

Formally, the *Orations* represent a unique text especially because its seven sections show the features of distinct genres. The first oration has the profile of a traditional text of advice for a young prince; the following four have the features of short treatises on ethical philosophy; and the last two are strongly inspired by the previous homiletic texts of the emperor himself. Probably due to his public office, Manuel seems less inclined to emphasise his own experience than the authors of other, similar educational writings addressed to younger individuals; for instance, Theodore Metochites in his *Ethical Oration or On Education* (Ἠθικὸς ἢ περὶ παιδείας), who spoke more openly about his experience in the service of Andronikos II.[9] Metochites' text, in the form of an unbroken oration sharing a didactic interest with the *Orations*, has more personal overtones while also stressing the pedagogical value of the transmission of intellectual experience to a younger person. On the other hand, the late Palaiologan court rhetoricians produced a significant body of texts dealing with definitions of virtues and representations of virtuous models. For instance, Solon's image as an ideal ruler surfaced in numerous panegyrics and paroemiographical collections.[10] Yet Manuel chose to utilise this tradition in a personal fashion, since he not only used the model of the Athenian ruler as a quick reference to the ruler's wisdom,[11] but also provided a detailed account of the Athenian legislator's activity,[12] whereby he indicated the centrality of this model in his political vision. There are also differences between the theoretical scaffolding of the orations and other contemporary theoretical accounts, such as Gemistos Plethon's essay inspired by Stoicism, *On Virtues*, which opens *in medias res* with the definition of virtue and proceeds to analyse each virtue in detail.[13]

The Dramatic Setting

Although the public character of the *Orations* cannot be determined with precision, much evidence about the context of their delivery comes from the texts themselves. For instance, we know that the sixth oration was performed

---

[9] Theodore Metochites, Ἠθικὸς ἢ περὶ παιδείας, chs. 1–5, 53–67, ed. Polemes.

[10] See Gemistos Plethon, *Prosphonemation for Despot Demetrios*, PP 3, 207.11, ed. Lampros; Manuel Kalekas, *Oration Addressed to the Emperor*, in *Letters*, no. 1.98, ed. Loenertz; Demetrios Chrysoloras, *Comparison*, 230.24, ed. Lampros; Michael Apostolios, in Leutsch, *Corpus*, 4.3.2.

[11] In late Byzantine encomiastic rhetoric, the figure of Solon had become a standard theme in praising the emperor's wisdom, e.g. Demetrios Chrysoloras, *Comparison*, 230.24, ed. Lampros.

[12] See first oration.

[13] Gemistos Plethon, *On Virtues*, a.1.3, ed. Tambrun-Krasker: ἀρετή ἐστιν καθ' ἣν ἀγαθοί ἐσμεν.

in a religious context after the recitation of the *Life of St Mary of Egypt*.[14] In addition, it is plausible that each oration had a different audience which was restricted to a group of learned people. Thus, the scene of the performance of the orations resembles both a school and a church: Manuel acts as both the capable rhetorician who lectures his son on the acquisition of virtues and also as the priest who insists on the acquisition of Christian basic principles (especially in the last two orations). The speaker's prominence often deflects attention from the issues discussed and points to his authority as well as to a problem of textual design, for Manuel had to strike a balance in addressing his son as well as a larger audience.

The public character of the orations emerges from the author's indications that he was addressing both John and the public. He commented as follows on the ways of transmitting his message:

> Be willing to attempt to express in detail everything that is possible to happen in this manifold and theatrical life, and all the things which life shows to us, changing the mask (προσωπεῖον) little by little and dramatising (δραματοποιῶν), sometimes because of circumstances, other times because of various pretexts and persons, and above all, because of the deep changes of our times.[15]

In the fifth oration, Manuel mentions a group of people present at the time of the performance.[16] They were not only passive listeners but were also asked to draw benefit from the seven *logoi*. In the second oration, the author summarises the aim of the collection, that is, to equally instruct both John and those who will come across these texts:

> It is necessary for us to say what we think about this issue for your pleasure and equally for the benefit of those who would come across this work.[17]

In a similar vein, Manuel alludes to a 'manifold' (πολύμορφος) and 'theatrical life' (σκηνικὸς βίος),[18] terms which suggest that the emperor had in mind the *theatra* he presided over. Yet since John VIII was the main addressee of the

---

[14] Vat. gr. 632.
[15] *Orations*, 428a.
[16] Manuel mentions those present at the delivery of the oration in ibid. 465b: οἶμαι δέ τινας τῶν παρόντων σαφέστερον ἐθέλειν ἀκοῦσαι. See also ibid. 520b: ὦ παρόντες; 437c, τοῖς ἀκούσασιν.
[17] Ibid. 441d. The beneficial aims of the texts are also unveiled in 404d–405a: ἡγήμεθα μάλα συμβαίνειν τῷ προκειμένῳ σκοπῷ μήτε πάντας ἀγαγεῖν εἰς μέσον τούς γε τοιούτους.
[18] Ibid. 428a.

orations, at times he was directly addressed, as in the sixth oration where the emperor chided John for previous mistakes (πρὸς σε γὰρ αὖθις ἐπαναστρέφω).[19] In several instances the emperor turned to his conversations with John, who had different opinions on certain matters: the address in the second and the third orations (εἰ γὰρ σιωπᾷς) suggests that previously the emperor and his son had had a conversation, probably in the same manner as the dialogue with his mother.[20]

The Contents of the *Orations*

A cursory examination of the seven sections of the text evinces major differences in terms of their contents and genre.[21] While their explanatory titles offer hints as to their rhetorical genres, it is only the first oration which indicates its genre in the title as προτρεπτικός (hortatory).[22] We do, however, get information on their genre by examining their approach to the ethical principles at stake. The following review of the main themes of the *Orations* will constitute a first step in identifying the relations between its seven sections and the position of the text within the late Byzantine literary milieu.

Major Themes in the *Orations*

Although formally the seven orations differ to a wide extent, several dominant themes emerge across all the texts. Arguably, the author's interests lay in the definitions and detailed explanations of three different moral and political

---

[19] In the sixth oration Manuel suggested that it was a reply to a previous discussion with John. See ibid. 509a: ὡς σὺ φῇς.

[20] Ibid. 484a: ἄγε οὖν, εἴ σοι δοκεῖ, συμβῶμεν ἅμα τοὺς λόγους. τοὺς γὰρ λογισμοὺς ἡμῖν εἰς ταυτὸν εἶναι νομίζω. See 481b–c, where Manuel attacks John's ways of understanding pleasure.

[21] The contents of the *Orations* are also summarised in Kakkoura's edition, 53–186, and by Çelik, *Historical Biography*, 352–63.

[22] *Oration One*: 'A protreptic oration about literature, virtue and the good ruler'. *Two*: 'That the good is loved in a natural way by everyone. The evil person is to be hated by himself.' *Three*: 'On choice and will; and that the evil does not come by nature and does not originate from outside'. *Four*: 'On pleasure (on the dangers of pleasure)'. *Five*: 'On pleasure and against what has been told (on the benefits of pleasure)'. *Six*: 'That sin is the worst thing; nobody has to despair, not of himself, not of someone else; must judge himself, but not someone else; and not hate the sinners, but have pity; and on repentance, and God's providence, and on love and philanthropy'. *Seven*: 'On humility'.

categories: virtue and sin, voluntariness and choice, and symbolic representations of kingship.[23]

Virtue and sin

As in other writings with a similar educational scope, here as well the central concern is to map significant selected virtues that will befit an individual and then define them in relation to other, broader ethical categories. These virtues do not always converge in the ideal of the good ruler, but more often refer to general ethical aspects. While all the *Orations* ultimately refer to exercising a set of virtues leading to a good character, Manuel does not construct a personal theoretical basis but instead limits himself to quoting several major authorities in the field: Plato, Aristotle and the Bible. Only the second oration provides a brief theoretical preamble to the topic by grounding the discussion of virtue in an account of nature (φύσις) and choice (προαίρεσις), thereby echoing the first chapters of the *Foundations*: human nature is good per se, it is shared by all individuals,[24] it is always in search of cognate good actions and always avoiding what is contrary to the good.[25] Therefore, Manuel concludes, it is only through one's choice that some actions become praiseworthy and virtuous, while other individuals fail to distinguish between evil and good.[26]

In this account of virtues Aristotle's influence is pervasive. His position on almost all topics of moral philosophy in Byzantium was regarded as authoritative: nature, virtues, agency, reasons for action, criteria for right actions, emotions, moral perception, etc.[27] Following this Aristotelian scheme, the process of exercising various virtues culminates in the acquisition of happiness

---

[23] The quoted examples to follow come from different sections of the *Orations*: *Oration I*, 385a–409b; *Oration II*, 409b–419d; *Oration III*, 419d–441d; *Oration IV*, 441d–461c; *Oration V*, 461d–483a; *Oration VI*, 483b–527b; *Oration VII*, 527c–557a; *Epistolary Epilogue*, 557b–561a.

[24] Manuel identifies an overarching nature in ibid. 409c: ἡ πάντων μὲν ἀρχὴ καὶ ὑπεράρχιος φύσις, πάντων δὲ δημιουργὸς καὶ συνέχουσα καὶ εὖ ποιοῦσα δύναμις. The notion of a common human nature is also used in the discussion of the sixth oration on despair and the obligation not to judge others.

[25] Ibid. 412c: τὸ συγγενές ζητοῦσα καὶ τἀλλότριον ἅπαν φεύγουσα.

[26] Ibid. 412d: μέγα δὲ κἀκεῖνο νομίζουσιν ὅτι θαυματοποιοὺς καὶ μίμους καὶ ὀρχηστάς, σμήνη τε κολάκων, καὶ ὑβριστῶν ἔθνη, καὶ παρασίτων ἑσμὸν καὶ τοὺς ἄλλους τοὺς τοιούτους εὖ ποιεῖν δύναται.

[27] Beginning with the twelfth century, as suggested by Anna Komnene's programme of commentaries commissioned for George Tornikios and Michael of Ephesus, Aristotle's *Nicomachean Ethics* gained in popularity; Frankopan, 'Literary, cultural and political context'. For the Palaiologan period we know of paraphrases of the *Nicomachean Ethics* by George Pachymeres and John VI Kantakouzenos; Benakis, 'Aristotelian ethics', 67–9.

(εὐδαιμονία), another topic hotly debated by the ancient schools of philosophy. This concept was approached dialectically by opposing the opinions of those who wrongly believed they had acquired happiness and the truly happy ones (εὐδαίμονες). Manuel argues that true happiness can be attained only by choosing the right course of action and education:[28] as in the preceding *Foundations*, the virtuous person who has attained happiness embodies the ideal individual (ἀγαθὸς ἀνήρ) acting for and through virtue.[29] Often Manuel defines this ideal individual as useful and worthy (χρηστὸς), thus reflecting his primary concern of providing examples of virtuous actions.[30]

Manuel also sets the discussion of fundamental virtues and vices in the framework of the ruler's responsibility to provide models of behaviour. The assumption of Manuel's discussion of virtues is that they have to be understood as the building blocks of a moral-political system, since he refers to a system of virtues (ἀρετῶν ἅπαν σύνταγμα).[31] Such ways of defining virtues highlight the idea already present in the *dispositio* of the matter of the *Orations* that some virtues are more valuable than others. One instance of the hierarchical order of virtues is the representations of Christian virtues like humility (ταπεινοφροσύνη),[32] the road to ethical perfection (ὁδὸς καὶ πέρας); Christian love (ἀγάπη), the origin of all virtues;[33] and moderation (μετριοφροσύνη), a reflection of the previous two.[34] Among these three virtues, Manuel regarded humility as the most significant: 'Had one acquired all virtues, he would draw no benefit for himself, unless he previously acquired humility, since this one only lightens and guards all other virtues.'[35] Manuel did not promote ταπεινοφροσύνη exclusively as a Christian virtue reflecting one's simplicity

---

[28] *Orations*, 416b: οἱ δ' ἀγαθοὶ [. . .] τῇ προαιρέσει τὴν εὐδαιμονίαν λογίζονται.
[29] See the account of Solon in the first oration and the sixth oration, 493b.
[30] E.g. *Orations*, 417b: δι' ἐντελέχειαν πράξεων μοχθηρῶν μήτ' ἐθέλων χρηστός.
[31] Ibid. 540a. Manuel often provides details about his hierarchical system of virtues. See also his statement about *love* as the mother, root and foundation of all virtues, Ibid. 541d: ἔστι μὲν ἡ ἀγάπη μήτηρ τε ἅμα καὶ τροφὸς καὶ ῥίζα καὶ κρηπὶς ἄντικρυς τῷ τῶν ἀρετῶν συστήματι.
[32] Ibid. 529a: τὸ δὲ ὕστατον εἰπεῖν περὶ τῆς πάντα ἀγαθῆς ταπεινοφροσύνης οὐ κατὰ τύχην γέγονεν, ἀλλ' οὕτω δόξαν ἀκόλουθον εἶναι.
[33] Ibid. 540c: ἀρχὴ γὰρ δήπουθεν ἡ ἀγάπη τοῦ τῶν ἀρετῶν ἐστι κύκλου. ἡ δὲ μετριότης τὸ τέλος.
[34] Ibid. 540c. Moderation or measure (μετριοφροσύνη) is present throughout the *Orations*, especially in the praise of Solon, in the presentation of positive pleasure and in the last oration.
[35] Ibid. 529a. A definition of humility is provided at the end of the oration, 541d: ἔστι δὲ ἡ ταπεινοφροσύνη οἱονεί τις ὁδὸς καὶ πέρας καὶ ὅτιπερ ἂν γένοιτο ἢ νοοῖτο ἔρεισμα καὶ φυλακτήριον ἀκριβὲς πάντων ἑξῆς τῶν καλῶν, λῆξις τε τῶν ἀρετῶν καὶ ἀνάπαυσις καὶ σωτήριος λιμήν.

of behaviour, but also as a virtue befitting a ruler.[36] Contrary to the multifariousness of sin, humility possesses a uniform character (μονοειδής), and gives meaning to order (τάξις) and hierarchy.[37] Yet, Manuel's vision of a hierarchy-like structure of virtues was not the only way to understand them, for he also projected the image of a full circle of virtues, with Christian love and moderation as the main landmarks.[38] This image, comparable to the definition of humility as concomitantly a road and an end, supplements the hierarchical perspective and provides the reader with the possibility of approaching and understanding the system of moral virtues in multiple ways.

Unlike the ancient philosophers, Manuel contrasted virtues with sins and not with vices. Following a similar educational purpose, sins are also hierarchically ordered, with discouragement (the sixth oration) and judgement of others' shortcomings (seventh oration) at the top of this scale.[39] He explains the wrongfulness of ἀπόγνωσις (despair) by reference to the truth of the Christian revelation.[40] The causes of moral evil and subsequently of moral mistakes are then identified in ignorance and indifference, as opposed to knowledge, listed in the first oration as one of the ruler's essential virtues:

> This evil originates in deceit and errors: it grows out of ignorance and recklessness which nourishes and expands the evil.[41]

In addition to these sets of virtues and sins, Manuel approached other virtues as well. He problematised his account of virtues and admitted that virtue cannot be encountered in pure forms but is always mixed with other attitudes, thereby alluding to the inherent problems of the office of the emperor, who was supposed to display an image of moral perfection. Furthermore, he emphasised that rhetorical skills should be exercised in public life, an idea that was not new to Byzantium.[42] His attitude contrasted with the one emerging

---

[36] In a similar vein, Isidore of Kiev's *Panegyric* mentioned humility as a central imperial virtue.
[37] On the use of uniformity, see *Orations*, 537b. On order and hierarchy, see ibid. 537d: τοὺς ἀκριβῶς τὴν τάξιν διατηρήσαντας.
[38] Ibid. 540c: ἡ ἀγάπη τοῦ τῶν ἀρετῶν ἐστι κύκλου.
[39] The contrasting vices are φθόνος and ζῆλος, See ibid. 500b: φθόνου γὰρ ἐγκαθημένου ταῖς ψυχαῖς, οὐ ζήλου τὸ τοιοῦτον κακόν.
[40] Ibid. 493b: πῶς οὖν οὐκ ἔξω φρενῶν ἐστιν, ὁ τὴν σωτηρίαν ἀπογινώσκων, τῶν ἀπεγνωκότων μὲν δι' ἑαυτοὺς καὶ τὰς πράξεις, χρησταῖς δ' οὖν ὅπως ζώντων ἐλπίσι δι' αὐτόν γε τὸν Σωτῆρα, καὶ ἅπερ οὗτος πέπονθεν ὑπὲρ ἡμῶν σταυρωθείς;
[41] Ibid. 436a.
[42] Earlier, John Sikeliotes argued that rhetoric is a crucial part of the sciences, and particularly of political science; Sikeliotes, 'Prolegomena in Hermogenis librum περὶ ἰδεῶν', in Rabe, *Prolegomenon Sylloge*, 393–420.

from several fourteenth-century texts where rhetoric combined with knowledge and wisdom did not seem to have an imperial function. For instance, Demetrios Kydones acknowledged only an ornamental role for rhetoric in exercising political authority: 'And the emperors themselves take pleasure in adorning their office with wisdom and learning.'[43]

Finally, an aspect that distinguishes Manuel's treatment of virtues from similar accounts, whether in panegyrics or in other more systematic treatises, is that the system of virtues developed throughout the *Orations* does not comprise any explicit reference to the traditional four cardinal virtues of a ruler. Due to this conspicuous absence, it is likely that the emperor did not intend the text as a traditional book of education for a future ruler, a princely mirror, as it were, but rather aimed at supplementing and renewing an old system of virtues.

Voluntariness and choice

Following Aristotle's treatises, the *Nicomachean* and the *Eudemian Ethics*, the *Orations* treat the system of virtues within a discussion of the voluntary character of actions and individual responsibility. Manuel adopted this model of ethical philosophy and ascribed responsibility of action to the agent and less to the circumstances.[44] He argued that actions originated in the individual's choice. Responsibility and voluntariness were both derived from the notion of a good human nature (φύσις), a concept already treated in the *Foundations*.[45] In addition, the discussion on voluntariness in the third speech is not a general disquisition of free will but rather appears as an attempt to ground other theoretical and practical issues such as the acquisition of virtues.

A key distinction operated in the *Orations* with regard to human will is between plain voluntary acts (τὰ ἑκούσια σαφῶς) and acts against will (τὰ ἀκούσια).[46] While, in defining these two categories, the emperor relies on Aristotle's authority, he further focuses on identifying criteria for distinguishing further types of involuntary[47] acts (τὰ οὐχ ἑκούσια) like those generated by

---

[43] Demetrios Kydones, *Letters*, no. 397.20, ed. Loenertz. In another letter (406.3–5) addressed to John VI Kantakouzenos, Kydones refers to the pleasures of rhetoric without any reference to its use in public.
[44] *Orations*, 440a.
[45] The notion of a common nature is employed especially in the third oration on choice and will, e.g. ibid. 441a: ἡ φύσις δὲ πᾶσι κοινή, καὶ τὰ ταύτης ἡμῖν κοινά [. . .] ἡ μὲν γὰρ φύσις ἐν ὅροις μένει, καὶ προαιτήσεται πρὸς Θεὸν καὶ τοὺς ἀνθρώπους.
[46] Ibid. 428c–432b.
[47] The vocabulary for describing voluntariness draws on Aristotle, as Manuel acknowledges; ibid. 432b: Ἀριστοτέλους δὲ τοῦτο φωνή· οὕτω γὰρ ἐκάλεσε τὰ ἀμφιρρεπῆ καὶ μὴ παντελῶς καθαρεύοντα τοῦ τε ἑκουσίου καὶ ἀκουσίου.

lack of information or by constraint,[48] which can still be motivated.[49] Such are the cases of the individuals in power who, because of their unrestrained will, act swiftly in certain circumstances without paying heed to consequences.[50] In contrast, voluntary acts take place with full knowledge of consequences and by choice.[51] Again, Manuel refers to concrete cases, insisting on a particular category of voluntary acts, namely cases of people aware of their mistakes,[52] who nevertheless afterwards blame circumstantial factors, such as drunkenness and momentary excess (ὕβρις).

Apart from these broad categories, the emperor introduces a further category, 'mixed voluntary actions' (τὰ μιξοεκούσια), a distinction intended to solve the difficulties of establishing solid criteria for voluntary and involuntary actions. This category mirrors the previous statement on the impossibility of acquiring virtues in a pure form. In all instances, Manuel recommends maintaining a middle path between actions with positive or negative outcomes and relying on knowledge and choice.[53] It is ignorance of the benefits of our actions, Manuel claims, that distorts individual choice.[54] Accordingly, judgement based on will and knowledge which derives from deliberation and learning (βουλὴν καὶ μάθησιν, 440b) will always generate a correct choice.[55]

Symbolic representations of kingship

In a text addressed to a young emperor, one would expect frequent allusions to classical models of kingship. Yet the symbolic representations of kingship remain sporadic, with a few mentions of legendary rulers like Alexander, Cyrus or Samson only as shadowy terms of comparison.[56] Instead, as in the *Foundations*, Manuel's approach to kingship emphasises his personal experience and relies less on prophetic or mythological models: 'I say this not as someone who

---

[48] Aristotle had already identified these two conditions, ignorance and force, which remained central in philosophical and legal accounts of responsibility: βία καὶ ἀνάγκη; *Nicomachean Ethics*, 1110a1–b17.
[49] *Orations*, 424a.
[50] Ibid. 429a.
[51] Ibid. 428d: λέγω τὸ καὶ πᾶν ἑκούσιον τῆς προαιρέσεως γίνεσθαι.
[52] Ibid. 432a: ὥστε τὸ πᾶν εἰργάσατο γνώμῃ.
[53] Ibid. 433c: ὁπόσον τι τῆς γνώσεως ἢ τῆς προαιρέσεως μίξομεν τοῖς ἐφ' ἡμῖν πράγμασιν.
[54] Ibid. 437d: ἄγνοια τὸ κακόν, εἰ δεῖ συντόμως εἰπεῖν.
[55] Ibid. 433 c. Cf. 440c: ἡ δὲ κρίσις προαιρέσεως.
[56] There are rather few mentions of such figures as Nestor or Solomon: e.g. ibid, κἂν οὕτω τὴν σαυτοῦ ψυχὴν ἀσύγκριτον ἀποφήνῃς, ὡς εἶναι μὲν τῆς Νέστορος καὶ Σολομῶντος φρονιμωτέραν, εἶναι δὲ τῆς Ἀχιλλέως καὶ Σαμψὼν ἀνδρειοτέραν, γέμουσάν τε ἀρετῶν.

gives oracles, nor as a prophet. For, to give oracles was Teiresias' mission, and the gift of prophesying belonged to David.'[57]

Although Manuel constantly emphasises the virtues required by the emperor's position, the representation of kingship remains problematic, given that the author's primary intention was rather to provide a general ethical training. In doing so, Manuel envisaged political action within an ethical frame. For this reason, it is only the first and the last of the orations that explicitly include elements of a model ruler, while the other orations provide a theoretical background and a normative approach to his son's behaviour. In the first oration, the model envisaged by Manuel was constructed upon the conflicts which opposed the Greeks of classical antiquity to the peoples of the East, thereby drawing a parallel with the contemporary conflict between the Byzantines and the Ottoman Turks. The oration contrasts Croesus's excessive accumulation of wealth with Solon's moderation accompanied by good reasoning.[58]

Significantly, the model of rulership emerging in the first oration draws on negative representations of several eastern rulers: Gyges, Croesus and Xerxes, criticised for their irrational choices: 'Thus, this irrational multitude of barbarians was defeated by a small army who was worthy of many rewards.'[59] Croesus, Manuel continues, preferred to amass wealth which he misleadingly took for happiness; Gyges came into power through magic and deception; and Xerxes was driven by the desire to conquer foreign lands and was unable to use the huge military forces of his empire. In contrast, the Athenians led by Solon honoured peace, instead of desiring to acquire land: 'In this way, the Athenians who possessed all kinds of virtues were honoring peace instead of many plots of land.'[60]

Apart from the two orations, the epistolary epilogue also focuses on the ruler's image.[61] The epilogue serves to express a traditional Byzantine idea of rulership and to highlight a tenet central for an audience familiar with the imperial office: the emperor is God's representative on earth and should act accordingly. Far from adding anything new, this perspective rather reflects a preoccupation with integrating this text into the tradition of Byzantine political writing and emphasising the emperor's position and subjects' expectations. Ultimately, Manuel seems willing to attach his personal experience and his knowledge of moral and philosophical tenets to the Byzantine imperial tradition.

---

[57] Ibid. 405d.
[58] Ibid. 392a: πενία μετ' ἀρετῆς τιμιωτέρα τῶν πλούτῳ κομώντων ἐκείνης ἄνευ.
[59] Ibid. 392d.
[60] Ibid. 392d.
[61] See ibid. 560c for an extensive discussion of the notion of kingship.

Having identified the major topics discussed in the *Orations*, in the following section I will discuss the methods of advice employed in each of the seven orations.

The *Orations*: Summary and Form

First oration

The first oration can be firmly integrated into the genre of protreptic orations.[62] Owing to the fact that its main purpose was to provide advice to a young co-emperor, protreptic elements in the form of moral prescriptions are pervasive in the collection. Yet since this is the only oration which the author specifically ascribes to a rhetorical genre, an excursus into the functions of this literary form is helpful in assessing Manuel's didactic strategy.

Originating in texts of classical philosophy, protreptic discourses aimed at changing habits and at winning a young student for the study of philosophy.[63] It was a common belief that protreptic orations were meant as a primary stage all students were supposed to go through in their *paideia*. In theory, after the protreptic stage came the stage of direct advice (παραίνεσις) where the students learned how to lead their lives.[64] As far as we can grasp from the extant protreptic literature, there was no preferred form for such texts, which could equally take the shape of public orations, letters, dialogues or anthologies. Michael Apostolios, a fifteenth-century Byzantine teacher, described proverbs as λόγοι προτρεπτικοί (hortatory speeches),[65] while in a Christian context Nikephoros Kallistos Xanthopoulos, a fourteenth-century ecclesiastic writer, equated protreptic compositions with admonitory orations.[66] They only adhered to a common set of rhetorical techniques intended to persuade and expose major aspects of philosophy to someone from outside the field in search of a broad education. Commonly, the *protreptikoi* advocated a wide range of preoccupations, from intellectual

---

[62] Λόγος προτρεπτικὸς εἰς λόγους, καὶ περὶ ἀρετῆς καὶ ἀγαθοῦ ἄρχοντος: 'A protreptic oration about literature, virtue and the good ruler'.

[63] Porter, *Handbook*, 120–5.

[64] See Schenkeveld, 'Philosophical prose', 204.

[65] See the definition by Michael Apostolios, who describes proverbs as statements useful for the soul; Leutsch, *Corpus*, 2: παροιμία ἐστὶ λόγος ὠφέλιμος, ἤτοι βιωφελής [. . .]· ἢ λόγος προτρεπτικὸς παρὰ πᾶσαν τοῦ βίου τὴν ὁδὸν χρησιμεύων.

[66] Nikephoros Kallistos Xanthopoulos, *Historia Ecclesiastica*, 4.33.42: καὶ πρὸς Ἕλληνας δὲ αὐτῷ λόγος ἐγράφη προτρεπτικός.

to military ones. The preserved *protreptikoi* indicate that while the label had been used rather loosely, at the same time, they continued to emphasise a philosophical training.⁶⁷ Despite the popularity of the genre in antiquity, with the disappearance of the old philosophical schools, in Byzantium the interest in protreptic speeches decreased.⁶⁸ Another factor leading to their disappearance was the fact that other rhetorical genres, such as homilies or catechetical texts, began to replace them. On the other hand, in the Palaiologan period exhortations to the study of philosophy echoing the ancient protreptic orations continued to be written. Demetrios Kydones wrote a long text on the study of philosophy as a means to escape the fear of death.⁶⁹ Earlier, Theodore Metochites composed a fully fledged protreptic oration addressed to a young student who had neglected his education and dedicated himself to other preoccupations, *An Ethical Essay or On Education* (Ἠθικὸς ἢ περὶ παιδείας). Metochites' speech highlighted the utility of philosophy and history.⁷⁰

In so far as the first oration is concerned, Manuel only partially adhered to this long standing tradition. Even if he placed this text in the category of advice for intellectual training, he added a twist: he substituted the traditional study of philosophy with an exhortation to acquire necessary rhetorical skills useful for government. 'There is nothing more beneficial for the rulers than to know how to speak well', he states at one point in the oration.⁷¹ Moreover, he used fewer of the injunctions and imperatives that were usual in protreptic literature, and instead he listed, as the chief methods of didactic approach, the use of *chreiai*, analysis and comparison.⁷² This approach entailed connecting various episodes (διηγήματα)⁷³ which

---

⁶⁷ Epicurus's *Letter to Menoeceus* dealt with both *protreptikoi logoi* and *parainesis*: the writer admonished the young student to pursue the study of philosophy. In another influential and popular *Protreptikos Logos*, Iamblichus brought together extracts from ancient philosophers, especially Aristotle's *protreptikos*, whereby he tried to convince his disciples of the need to philosophise (φιλοσοφητέον)'; *Protrepticus*, 3–126, ed. Pistelli. See also Themistius's protreptic speech advocating philosophy for the people of Nicomedia; *Orations*, 97–111, ed. Downey and Schenkl.
⁶⁸ For a more detailed account of the *protreptikos* in Byzantium, see Polemes, 'Εισαγωγή', 15–49.
⁶⁹ Demetrios Kydones, *De contemnenda morte*, 16.5–10, ed. Deckelmann: τὸ γὰρ φρονεῖν καὶ νοεῖν καὶ τοῖς θείοις καὶ ἀσωμάτοις συνάπτεσθαι; and 16.25–39.
⁷⁰ Theodore Metochites, Ἠθικὸς ἢ περὶ παιδείας, 44–8, ed. Polemes.
⁷¹ *Orations*, 385a.
⁷² Ibid. 385a; cf. the method of σύγκρισις in 408d.
⁷³ The connections between various parts are often highlighted, and likewise the beginning of an argument, e.g. ibid. 405d: καὶ σκοπείτω τις ὡδί.

illustrated a positive model (παράδειγμά τι) of action and a hypothetical model of government (ἐξ ὑποθέσεως):

> Such an emperor or omnipotent ruler of a community with a vigorous soul will be the saviour of his people, and highly beneficial, since he would be knowledgeable of the best course of action at all times and in all circumstances.[74]

Manuel departs from the protreptic tradition in another way as well. Unlike in the ensuing six orations, he refrains from drawing on abstract arguments. Instead, the oration relies on several Herodotian episodes contrasting models of rulership which typify an idea of political wisdom (πολιτικὴ ἐπιστήμη): the meeting between Solon, the Athenian legislator, and Croesus;[75] Xerxes' campaign against Greece;[76] and the story of Gyges, the Lydian king.[77] The key suggestion resulting from these stories is that wisdom and reason, reflected in the enlightened model of Solon, prevail over sheer force. As a result, by combining all these Herodotian episodes with moralising statements in a historical-mythographic fabric,[78] Manuel puts forward the model of a ruler who has to be prudent, efficient and wise.[79]

Second and third orations

In the second oration, the focus shifts from symbolic and mythological representations of model rulers to abstract notions of moral philosophy. In terms of subject matter and formulation, these speeches constitute a distinct group in the collection, different from the inaugurating protreptic lecture and the last two homilies.[80] By and large, they echo the genre of philosophical essays defined as prose monologues on selected theoretical problems.[81] Yet they

---

[74] Ibid. 404c–d.
[75] The story of Solon's meeting with Croesus, in Herodotus's version, had a long career in Byzantium, e.g. in John Tzetzes, *Chiliades*, 1.4–54.
[76] *Orations*, 389d–401d.
[77] Ibid. 401d–404c.
[78] See ibid. 396c: τοὺς δ' οὐκ ἀρκοῦντας ἀκολουθεῖν, τούτους δ' ἐς κόρακας.
[79] Ibid. 405a.
[80] For instance, the link between the second and the fourth and fifth orations on pleasure is established by using the same categories of individuals (οἱ ἀγαθοὶ and οἱ φαῦλοι) who generate conflicting definitions of the moral good: οὗτοι καὶ τοὺς φαύλους ἀνθρώπους ἀγαθοὺς νομίζουσιν εἶναι, καὶ τοὺς ἀθλίους εὐδαίμονας [. . .] ὁ βίος δὲ αὐτοῖς τρυφῆς καὶ πλέον οὐδέν; ibid. 412c–d.
[81] Ierodiakonou, 'Byzantine Philosophy', in *Stanford Encyclopedia of Philosophy*. Available at <http://plato.stanford.edu/entries/byzantine-philosophy> (last accessed 25 April 2019).

cannot be fully integrated into the tradition of philosophical writing, given that they are tuned to the protreptic tone of the first and the last two orations. For this reason, in these four *Orations* Manuel supplements the discussion of theoretical themes with explanatory examples of how several categories of individuals understand notions like the moral good (τὸ ἀγαθόν).

The author frequently claims that, in formulating his moral counsel, he relies on working philosophical definitions borrowed from other authoritative sources, especially ancient philosophers like Plato and Aristotle, or, less frequently, the Scriptures.[82] Concepts drawn from Aristotle's *Nicomachean Ethics*, such as actuality (ἐντελέχεια) or happiness (εὐδαιμονία), are pervasive even if they are never treated systematically.[83] In fact, the *Nicomachean Ethics* or one of its paraphrases seems to have constituted the model for these four orations, since the major concerns of the Stagirite can be identified here in an almost identical sequence:[84] the moral good, virtues, happiness, voluntary and involuntary actions, and the nature of pleasure.[85]

The second oration, which deals with the first three issues, attempts to theorise a set of norms of proper demeanour. Several contemporary examples may shed further light on the authorial role Manuel envisaged for himself and on the text's functions. Gemistos Plethon's contemporary treatise *On Virtues*, dealing with similar themes, opens with a definition of virtues and continues in distinct stages to definitions of several types of virtues.[86] Since Plethon's declared aim was to treat with precision the topic of virtues, he divided them sharply between general (γενικαί) and special (εἰδικαί).[87] A section of the treatise titled *Division of Virtues* (Διαίρεσις τῶν ἀρετῶν) describes virtues in an abstract fashion, according to clear-cut criteria and not according to the context of political action:

> The general virtues are prudence, justice, courage and wisdom, while the special ones are fear of God, good judgement – derived from prudence, holiness, statehood, kindness – derived from courage, and moderation, freedom and decorum – derived from wisdom.[88]

---

[82] See *Orations*, 417c: κατὰ Πλάτωνα; 420c: κατὰ τὴν Γραφήν.
[83] Ibid. 417b: δι' ἐντελέχειαν πράξεων μοχθηρῶν.
[84] Benakis, 'Aristotelian ethics'.
[85] See the similar order of chapters in the *Nicomachean Ethics*.
[86] Gemistos Plethon, *On Virtues*, ed. Tambrun-Krasker: ἀρετή ἐστιν ἕξις καθ' ἣν ἀγαθοί ἐσμεν. See Aristotle, *Eudemian Ethics*, 1219a32: ἡ δ' ἀρετὴ βελτίστη ἕξις.
[87] Gemistos Plethon, *On Virtues*, a.2.1, ed. Tambrun-Krasker: ῥητέον δὲ αὖθις δι' ἀκριβείας μᾶλλον περὶ αὐτῶν, ἀρξαμένοις ἀπὸ τῆς ἀτελεστάτης, ἐπὶ δὲ τὴν τελεωτάτην κατὰ φύσιν ἰοῦσι.
[88] Ibid. b. 14.17–21.

Chronologically slightly later, Cardinal Bessarion writing on virtues used a similar Aristotelian philosophical perspective in his treatise *On Substance: Against Plethon* (c. 1450).[89] When dealing with definitions of moral categories, both Plethon and Bessarion assumed a style characterised by technical precision and oriented towards argumentation and not towards the application of theoretical definitions to an individual ethos. By contrast, Manuel did not comply with the rules of a philosophical, systematic style of writing, as precise theoretical distinctions are rare.[90] He treated them in a fashion developed from his political experience. Claiming authority over the ensuing statements and outlining his personal view about the ruler's virtues, the emperor geared the text towards personal reflection right from the opening statement of the oration: '*I consider*, and I think that everyone agrees, that not only the earnest and good men but also the wicked and the evil ones hate wickedness on account of their nature.'[91]

The oration is divided into two distinct but related parts: first, on moral good and evil, and second, on virtues and their aim, which is happiness. Manuel dramatises the opposition between moral good and evil by contrasting the views of those who hate knavery and are good, on the one hand, with, on the other hand, the opinions and views of the φαυλότεροι.[92] This strategy allows him to avoid the intricacies of philosophical argumentation and focus further on adding moral glosses about various categories of individuals. Therefore, it is not the concept of good that matters here, but rather the construction of moral individual characters.

In a similar vein, the third oration deals with theoretical aspects concerning the notion of a common natural good. Manuel takes another step in his argument about a virtuous life and, as in the *Foundations*, introduces notions borrowed from Aristotle's *Ethics*:[93] voluntary, involuntary and non-voluntary actions, as well as the conscious choice of the course of life:

> It remains therefore, to argue why some people act in some way, while others act in a different way, although we have a similar nature. And we say that this happens because of our different choices.[94]

---

[89] Bessarion, *On Substance: Against Plethon*, ed. Mohler.
[90] E.g. *Orations*, 420b: ἀρετὴ γὰρ ἀνενέργητος (not actualised or realised), ἀμωσγέπως ἄκοσμος (somehow disorderly).
[91] Ibid. 410b.
[92] Ibid. 413a: αὗται μὲν οὖν αἱ κρίσεις τῶν φαυλοτέρων περὶ τὸν ἀνθρώπινον βίον.
[93] On voluntary and involuntary actions see Aristotle, *Eudemian Ethics*, 1223a21–7.
[94] *Orations*, 421a.

Given the complexity of his argumentation, more than in the previous orations, Manuel draws on Aristotle and Plato as major sources of authority.[95] Yet the method and the aim remain similar to those of the previous oration, as he creates a dialectic contrast between philosophical notions that eventually are highlights of the representation of the perfectly moral individual.

Fourth and fifth orations

The fourth and the fifth orations deal with another topic of ethical philosophy, pleasure, which in Aristotle's *Nicomachean Ethics* was also discussed after the topic of will and voluntary actions. As in the previous orations, the argument develops in several stages and draws on strong contrasts.[96]

The fourth oration emphasises the negative sides of pleasure and, for this reason, it resembles a *psogos*, only one concerned with an emotion and not a person. Two aspects stand out: first, the author states that the negative view of pleasure does not necessarily coincide with his opinion but comes from people with a restricted definition of pleasure; and second, he personifies pleasure as a plague in a long tirade against the damages it can produce. Such negative connotations involved in the personification of pleasure break the balanced account of moral notions. The arguments of the previous sections are replaced by long vituperations, where the length and intensity of the descriptions of the damage done by pleasure contrast with the author's previous, more tempered opinions:

> Who could possibly describe its modes, its contrivances, or its versatility? For it always takes delight in cunning by which it inflicts indignities upon everyone. It is just as others represented it, 'it takes on', they say 'the mask of benefit and of the good'.[97]

The fifth oration, which deals with the same theme, pleasure, is a response to the previous essay. In terms of theoretical approach, if in the fourth oration the emperor claims to rely on the authority of Plato's dialogues, this one draws on Aristotle's balanced account of pleasure. By contrasting two different

---

[95] Ibid. 432b: Ἀριστοτέλους δὲ τοῦτο φωνή; 437c: κατὰ τὸν Πλάτωνα.
[96] Ibid. 449c–d: καὶ τὶ ἄν πρῶτον εἴπομεν; τί δὲ ὕστατον; τί δὲ μέσον τῶν ἐκείνη πρὸς ἡμᾶς γιγνομένων;
[97] Ibid. 449c. In 449d a long personification accounts for the insidious mechanisms of pleasure: δελεάζει δὲ κακοηθείᾳ ἐσχάτῃ· καὶ πᾶσι γίνεται πάντα, πρὸς ἀνατροπὴν τῶν χρηστοτέρων ἠθῶν. σύμβουλος αὐτόκλητος ἔπεισι, καὶ τὴν ῥαστώνην θαυμάζουσα, κακίζει πάνθ' ἃ δίδωσιν ἀγῶνα σώμασι καὶ ψυχαῖς, νοσοποιὰ ταυτὶ καλοῦσα.

views on the same topic, Manuel appears to employ the dialectic method on a large scale. He emphatically states his theoretical position immediately after the preamble:

> I contend that pleasure is good for those who want to be good, and for those who make use of it in an appropriate and honest way (σεμνῶς), it is a vital element in our lives, and by no means harmful or immoral, unless we want to abuse it.[98]

Thus the chief goal of the oration is not only to present another alternative view on pleasure but to offer a complete lesson about how to deal with various kinds and aspects of pleasure. A more balanced account of pleasure, Manuel now claims, has a practical purpose, namely to help people regain the path of righteousness.[99] In doing so, the author marks a break with the previous theoretical *logoi*, for here he provides a detailed list of norms of practical behaviour along with an exposition of practical solutions on how to act in circumstances that involve passions and emotions.[100]

Sixth oration

By far the longest in the series, the sixth oration[101] is sharply divided into two parts: first (484a–505a), a homiletic section on the 'greatest of all sins', despair,[102] and second (505a–528c), a direct admonition to young John that further explores themes like divine love and mercy. The demarcation line between the two sections of the oration emerges in the address to the son: 'for now I turn back to you (πρὸς σὲ γὰρ ἐπαναστρέφω)'.[103] The two distinct and

---

[98] Ibid. 464c.
[99] Ibid. 464a: βούλομαι δὲ τινος πλάνης ἐλευθεροῦν ἐνίους, ἤδη πειρώμενος προασφαλίσασθαι τοὺς ἀκροατάς, ὡς μὴ πειραθεῖν ἑτέρας πλάνης.
[100] See ibid. 505c: δεῖ γὰρ καρτερώτερον διαμάχεσθαι τοῖς τῶν ἐχθίστων ἰσχυροτέροις.
[101] The sixth oration features a long explanatory title: 'That sin is the worst thing; nobody has to despair, not of himself, not of someone else, must judge himself, but not someone else; and not hate the sinners, but have pity; and on repentance, and God's providence, and on love and philanthropy.'
[102] The theme of despair was not a new topic for Manuel, who dealt with it also in his *Homily on the Dormition of the Theotokos*. Written after recovery from an illness, this latter homily is an exhortation against fear of death and the distress provoked by the numerous torments in one's life, taking the image of the Mother of God as a model of how to deal with suffering. See *Homily on the Dormition of the Theotokos*, 562–6, and the *hypothesis* (543.19–24) of the homily (ed. Jugie).
[103] *Orations*, 505a.

loosely connected parts, of equal size, may constitute a reason for the unusual length of the oration, more than double the size of the others. In motivating the extent of the second part Manuel states that the significance of the topic demanded a lengthier account: 'I will multiply the oration, as I see that the suffering took hold on you.'[104]

As for the aims and the content of the sixth oration, they can also be evaluated by looking at its fate: after it was written and delivered as part of the 'ethico-political' series, the emperor reused it verbatim in a homily on St Mary of Egypt delivered on the occasion of a religious feast (1408–10). In the *prooimion* of the homily which followed the recitation of the vita of St Mary of Egypt, Manuel established a close connection with the sixth oration.[105] This interrelation with the *Homily on St Mary of Egypt* suggests that the text was geared towards a genre that differed from that of the previous orations. Thus, the sixth oration included features particular to a homily, such as an appeal to Christian doctrinal truths and the inclusion of far more biblical quotations than in the previous orations. The topics approached (sins, despair, judgement of others, forgiveness, mercy, redemption, benevolence) featured extensively in Byzantine homilies. In comparison to previous texts, this oration relied on the Christological model of rulership[106] and did not teach by presenting new perspectives or contrasting arguments, but projected a model of behaviour within a set of the already-known truths of Christian doctrine. Furthermore, the authority of the Bible and of the patristic authors replaced Plato and Aristotle.[107]

The author's focus moves within a range of topics that includes a discussion of Christian tenets and representations of divine acts[108] as well as an ideal model of earthly rulership reflecting divine πρόνοια.[109] In the first section the emperor wraps the previous ideas on moral good, will and emotions in an explicit Christian framework.[110] Yet, despite the shift in theoretical orientation, connections with other orations in the collection still emerge. Continuing the fifth oration's preoccupation with identifying ways to apply theoretical norms to daily behaviour, the emphasis now falls on concrete

---

[104] Ibid. 505c.
[105] Vat. gr. 1619, f. 15v.
[106] See *Orations*, 560c.
[107] Ibid. 505a: οἱ γὰρ πολλοὶ τῶν ἀνθρώπων, φησὶν ἡ χρυσὴ Γλῶττα, τῶν μὲν ἰδίων ἁμαρτημάτων συνήγοροι γίνονται, τῶν δ' ἀλλοτρίων κατήγοροι.
[108] Ibid. 512c.
[109] Ibid. 513b: οὐδεὶς ἀπόβλητος τῷ δημιουργῷ, οὐδεῖς ἐν λήθῃ τοῦ προνοοῦντος πάντων ἑξῆς.
[110] Statements like the one in ibid. 496c: ψυχῆς γὰρ θάνατον δεῖ νοεῖν τὸ κεχωρίσθαι Θεοῦ are absent from previous orations.

steps to avoid damaging emotions like despair, instead of dwelling upon representations of concepts. Concomitantly, Manuel states *expressis verbis* the aims of the oration: to advise all to acknowledge their sinful nature and to repent.[111]

Likewise, the second section includes concrete references to individual moral faults.[112] For instance, Manuel speaks in detail of the necessity of providing service for others (θεραπεία), most probably an allusion to the fact that John had to repent of previous mistakes. Such statements further outline the broad framework of an ideal imperial representation that is developed in the ensuing section.[113] This framework not only had a didactic purpose[114] but also provided compositional unity to the entire collection, as indicated by the references to the ensuing section.[115]

Seventh oration

The topic of the seventh oration, the virtues of humility and love, connects the text with the previous oration in another disguised homily. As in the preceding text, the oration constructs an ethical argument in two distinct phases: first, a presentation of Christian precepts (533c–d), and second, a direct address to John openly criticising his behaviour. Having expounded ethical issues and because this final oration strives to sum up the entire collection, Manuel alludes more frequently to the kinship connection with his son and formulates the political-moral upshot of the *Orations*. The proem implies that this text represented a conclusion of the entire collection of both the orations and the *Foundations*: 'This affection of mine for you generated these many speeches together with a letter (i.e. the opening letter of the *Foundations*).'[116] Furthermore, as in the sixth oration, here the method of advice marks a shift from the previous orations: illustrative stories or argumentation based on ancient philosophers disappear, since, as Manuel states, his intention was to confront John's deeds with a broad range of fundamental Christian principles:

[111] Ibid. 525b.
[112] Ibid. 497a: εἴτε γὰρ νωθεία τίς ἐστι τὸ διαβαλλόμενον, εἴτ' ὀλιγωρία πρὸς τἀγαθόν, ἢ ὅ τί περ ἂν τῶν ὁπωσοῦν οὐ καλῶν.
[113] Ibid. 513c–516b.
[114] Ibid. 528a: καὶ διὰ ταῦτα τοῖς πᾶσιν ἂν παραινέσαιμι [. . .] ἐπὶ τὴν ἀρίστην ὁδὸν ἐπιστρέψασιν.
[115] The last passage connects the sixth oration to the following one by approaching φιλανθρωπία and ἀγάπη as divine virtues, and ends in the fashion of a homily.
[116] *Orations*, 529c–d.

And the Saviour made it clear when he addressed his disciples in the following words: You can do nothing without me. There will be no need of words for me, nor of the ancients, nor of the moderns, with which to indicate the truthfulness of the <divine> doctrine. I will not make use of examples, nor of syllogisms.[117]

The first section offers an account of the highest virtue, humility, mirroring the *incipit* of the previous oration, which dealt with the 'worst of sins'.[118] Then it proceeds to a related topic and extends the discussion to another Christian virtue, love, by summarising the previous discussion on humility:

Having thus spoken, it is also necessary to speak in a more concise manner about the other virtue, that is love, which can be defined as mother and nourisher, root and foundation for the system of virtues, a guide for all those who proceed towards virtue.[119]

After the account of humility, Manuel turns to the means of attaining these virtues. Like the previous one, the oration includes a direct address to his son, John.[120] The first step in providing counsel consisted in correcting John's erroneous beliefs, which he held with regard to other people lower in rank and made known probably after a dialogue with the emperor.[121] Thereafter, the address turns into open criticism as John is advised to repent of his actions. Although it is not entirely clear how literally this advice was to be taken, the public assessment of the co-emperor's behaviour was probably meant to create the image of an emperor deeply concerned with his son's and successor's education: 'But you my beloved, be humble and mourn, for you have to be aware that you are not willing to be good.'[122]

Even if Manuel does not provide further details about which actions require repentance, from the above allusions it is likely that they had to do with treating the courtiers in an irreverent manner. It is for this reason that the final section includes advice as to the kind of behaviour John should avoid: 'Since

---

[117] Ibid. 548d.
[118] Ibid. 533d–536a. See also 541b: ἀγαθὴ γάρ ἐστι καθ' αὑτήν, ὡς εἰρηνικὴ καὶ πραοτάτη, ὃ δὲ Θεοῦ ἐστιν ἴδιον.
[119] Ibid. 541d.
[120] Ibid. 545b: ἀλλ' ἐρεῖς, ὦ φίλτατε.
[121] Ibid. 552d: ὥστε σοι καὶ ταῖς θέσεσι διαμάχεται, οἷς γε δοκεῖς αὐταῖς ἐπαμύνειν, καὶ γίγνεται πάντοθεν σαφές, ὡς ἔστιν ἀγαθὸν ποιεῖν καὶ μὴ ὑψηλοφρονεῖν. ἄτοπον ἄρα σοι τὸ συμπέρασμα καὶ κατὰ τόνδε τὸν λόγον.
[122] Ibid. 533b.

you do everything well, do not act arrogantly. For you do not acquire authority because of evilness towards someone else but because of your deeds.'[123] Thus, in this final oration, it is the attitude (τρόπος) that is the key element which determines the success of one's actions, for 'one must not be high-minded, even if he reached the highest authority'. [124]

The epistolary epilogue

As in the preceding *Foundations*, so in the *Orations*, Manuel included an additional text in the form of a letter that details the reasons for putting together this collection of essays. Yet if in the prefatory letter of the *Foundations* Manuel established a relationship based on the kinship tie, here the manner of address is more formal, probably because the text was meant for a wider audience and the emperor wished to assert his authority more vigorously. As a matter of fact, panegyric elements dominate this final section of the *Orations*. However, by projecting the image of a ruler empowered by God,[125] this epilogue stands as a surprising conclusion appended to a collection of seven orations which avoid references to the emperor's omnipotence.

Unlike in the previous orations, the epilogue provides few pieces of direct counsel to John but points to the necessity of following longstanding moral precepts. It is here that Manuel operates a distinction between the 'new better law' promoted by himself and the 'old law':

> For I sit on this throne and I am now addressing to you these exhortations which are better than the ones of the previous times in so far as they reflect a new law and a new grace. If you wish, one can say that if those <exhortations of the old> reflect the shadow of the law, mine represent a true mandate (τῆς ἀληθείας κήρυγμα). The seat upon which I find myself now is better than the one of the olden times and it supersedes it by far, since (if I am not too daring) it mirrors God's authority.[126]

Thus, the epilogue, despite its distinct mode of expression, reveals the author's purpose and reasons behind the choice of subject matter in his orations: the combination of narratives, notions of ancient ethics and Christian

---

[123] Ibid. 533c.
[124] Ibid. 548b: ἀκτέον δὴ τὸν λόγον ἐπὶ τὸν τρόπον, ᾧ ἄν τις πράξας τὸ ἀγαθὸν.
[125] Manuel draws a parallel between his experience and that of Moses in the Old Testament; ibid. 560c: εἰ γὰρ καὶ θεόθεν ἀμφοτέροις τὰ τῆς ἀρχῆς, ἐμοί τε λέγω καὶ τῷ Μωσῇ (καὶ γὰρ κἀκεῖνος ἡγέμων καὶ διδάσκαλος).
[126] Ibid. 560a.

principles was meant to serve as a sort of *vade mecum*, a book with extensive practical and theoretical moral teachings to be transmitted from a father to his son.

Between Teaching and Preaching: Constructing the Genre of the *Orations*

Having presented the contents of these seven texts, in what follows I deal with the genre of the *Orations*, which, arguably, must be regarded as a coherent, homogeneous text.[127] As indicated above, a functional definition of the genre has to consider two elements: the form of the text and the rhetorical type which provides the composition's occasion and function. In size and comprehensive scope, the format of a collection of seven successive orations relies on an approach distinct from that of a fully fledged oration. This approach entails multiple ways of linking speeches and generating an impetus towards totalisation usually implied in didactic cycles. Inter- and intra-textual echoes proliferate, as Manuel's variations on the moral and philosophical themes interact to modify or further qualify the commonplaces of imperial behaviour.

I suggest that the thematic and stylistic coherence of the *Orations* allow us to regard these seven orations as a diatribe, a form of speech popular in antiquity and defined as a group of lectures or orations on a moral theme characterised by vividness and immediacy in language.[128] Aside from homilies, sometimes gathered in thematic collections,[129] polemic speeches on Christian doctrinal issues,[130] deliberative orations and occasional educational treatises, there is virtually no similar example of didactic prose that would envisage a wide range of topics subsumed to a didactic intention.

---

[127] See the succession of arguments which Manuel mentions in ibid. 465b: ἔτι καὶ μᾶλλον συστῆσαι καὶ τῇ τῶν λόγων ἀκολουθίᾳ ἐν διαφόροις ἐπιχειρήμασι.

[128] For an overview of the diatribe as literary genre, see Stowers, 'Diatribe', in Ueding, *Historisches Wörterbuch*, 627–33. See also Porter, *Handbook*, 202.

[129] Collections of texts with a similar function can be identified in the homilies of Philotheos Kokkinos (*Three Homilies on Beatitudes*) and Isidore Glabas (*Four Homilies for St Demetrios*).

[130] This is the case with the collection of four speeches by Makarios Makres (*Four Orations for Those Offended by the Success of the Infidels*, in *Macaire Makrès et la polemique*, ed. Argyriou), contending through theological arguments and biblical passages that the achievements of the Ottomans on the battlefield were temporary. Nevertheless, despite the fact that all four orations draw on plain advice for maintaining the Orthodox faith, Makres' orations lack internal cohesion, as each of the speeches deals with a separate topic and the author does not link the speeches.

Even if such literary productions were quasi-absent in late Byzantium, we can relate the *Orations* to the genre of the diatribe with a certain degree of precision. A brief look at the history of the genre will support this statement. In the sense current in antiquity and the Middle Ages, diatribes stood for a tradition of productions typical of the Hellenistic period by authors like Bion of Borysthenes, Plutarch and Dio Chrysostom.[131] In ancient literary theory diatribes, treated as a paraenetic counterpart of protreptic, dealt with practical matters.[132] Besides, diatribes presupposed continuity despite the strict division into a series of speeches which cut across several themes simultaneously. Their chief intention was to guide disciples through several stages of moral progress. In antiquity, teachers and public orators addressed diatribes to a limited group of students and not a large public. The authors of diatribes, particularly popular in the Hellenistic period, did not restrict themselves to a single school of thought but often combined various themes. On the other hand, diatribes were by no means lessons of philosophy for the masses: a large popular audience would probably not have understood Epictetus's lectures, except for students at an early stage of their philosophical training.

The lectures included in a diatribe were commonly used for introducing philosophical themes or for establishing contact with a non-specialist but educated audience. For their didactic purposes, authors of diatribes relied on deliberative techniques such as direct address or the heavy use of rhetorical figures: parallelisms, isocola, antithesis, comparisons or anecdotes.[133] In their quest for expediency, authors of diatribes avoided difficult philosophical topics and approached a standard list of subjects: poverty and wealth, passions and emotions, self-control, fear of death, and divinity.[134] Hermogenes held a similar view on diatribes as handbooks of ethics meant to imprint the speaker's character on the listener's judgement.[135]

As noted above, Manuel constantly emulated philosophers who dealt with topics like moral good, pleasure or virtues. Yet he avoided a polemical approach. Because of the absence of vehement contentions for a certain point of view, the tone remains moderate throughout the seven texts, in a move

---

[131] See Oltramare, *Origines*, 39.
[132] Ibid. 45.
[133] Porter, *Handbook*, 123. Sometimes diatribes used the Socratic technique of leading students into contradiction in order to correct them afterwards. In fact there was a close connection between diatribe and philosophical dialogue, another genre popular in the Palaiologan period. Boyle argued that diatribe evolved in classical antiquity as a popularisation of the philosophical dialogue; Boyle, *Rhetoric and Reform*, 45.
[134] Boyle, *Rhetoric and Reform*, 50.
[135] Hermogenes, Περὶ μεθόδου δεινότητος, in *Rhetorical Texts*, 5.5, ed. Rabe.

which goes against the profile of the deliberative orations, seeking not to exacerbate emotions. In the *Orations* Manuel adopted a civil ethos, reflected in the presentation of argumentation *in utramque partem*, as the chief means to arrive at moral truth. Often he backs the authority of philosophical principles with his own appraisals, and once he claims to have exhausted a topic.[136] Such treatment contrasts with deliberative orations where speakers abide by the decision of an assembly. Manuel's judgement, as he often argues, is individual and conciliatory; for instance, he concedes that both those who say that pleasure is *pathos* and those who strive to attain it are right.[137]

In light of these observations, despite the pervasiveness of authoritative ideas originating in the writings of Plato and Aristotle, the orations are to be understood neither as a philosophical work nor as a preparation for philosophy. Instead, by and large, philosophy becomes the handmaiden of rhetoric, the main instrument of persuasion available for a future emperor. Conversely, rhetoric becomes the major instrument and medium of transmitting principles of good conduct. The arrangement of topics suggests that the more theoretical sections constitute the basic ingredient in a larger context that guides the listeners towards the end of the didactic programme included in the *Orations*. Thus, Manuel begins with the profile of the ideal virtuous ruler, while the following four philosophical orations disengage from this representation of the ideal ruler, offering very little actual guidance on aspects of the ruler's craft. The seven orations can thus be read as a continuous text in seven chapters proposing a path which one is invited to follow up to the peak of the supreme virtue: the Christian humbleness of the seventh oration, which echoes Solon's humbleness portrayed in his conversation with Croesus in the first oration. Eventually, as stated in the epilogue, the whole set of moral arguments developed throughout the *Orations* is included in a traditional Byzantine perspective on kingship, which emphasises the relation between emperor and God.

The unity of the *Orations* as a diatribe surfaces at other levels as well. Based on their contents and methods of approaching the subject matter, they can be roughly grouped into three categories: the first oration with its preoccupation with the emperor's image stands alone; the following four orations tend to explore and explain theoretical concepts drawing on the classical philosophical and rhetorical tradition; and finally, the sixth and the seventh orations are more prescriptive and draw on the Christian tradition that provides their theoretical background. Yet, as the proem of the sixth oration indicates when

---

[136] See *Orations*, 441b: δεῖ δέ, οἶμαι, τὸ πᾶν εἰπόντας συντεταγμένως καὶ συντόμως, ἐνταῦθα στῆσαι τὸν λόγον.
[137] See fifth oration.

referring back to the previous discussion on pleasure, these three groups are formally connected:

> In the preceding lecture on pleasure, I have offered several arguments in its favour. Having discussed the nature of pleasure, now it is necessary, I believe, to discuss despair, if we were to fulfil our duty. For, on the one hand, it is due to the abuse of pleasure that sins appear in our souls; and, on the other hand, from frequent sins there comes despair.[138]

Manuel never used a specific term to designate his work, only the general term λόγοι. Yet he offered several hints with regard to the overall design of the *Orations*. Thus, the sixth oration includes a motivation for the process of putting together the seven different rhetorical pieces. According to Manuel, the discussion of 'despair' emerged as part of a lengthier text, an undertaking (ἐγχείρησις) planned beforehand to comprise a string of texts meant to be read together.[139] In the same vein, frequently, the term τὸ προσῆκον (appropriateness) is mentioned as the emperor's real impulse for writing an admonition for his son. Even if Manuel does not offer a full insight into what this might have meant for the audience, it can be inferred that it was tied either to the duty of educating the son or to that of writing in a manner that would fit the demands of the multifaceted collection of *Orations*.[140]

Manuel also offered a series of reasons for his global approach to presenting the system of virtues and the ways to attain them. This is the case with the explanations for the inclusion of philosophical digressions necessary in order to complement the regular course of instruction in the second oration:

> For it seems to me that I would prefer to philosophise rather than to provide you with moral principles of education. The form of the present oration forces me to highlight many divisions and subdivisions, and many degrees, and to reveal a certain scale of these.[141]

This passage indicates the author's awareness of his pedagogical mission. Such an approach, entailing the breaking down of substantial theoretical

---

[138] *Orations*, 484b–c.

[139] Ibid. 484b.

[140] Another formula frequently employed by the author to describe the *Orations* is 'the form of the speech' (τὸ σχῆμα τοῦ λόγου, ibid. 404c), which suggests that he had a clear idea of the shape the collection of speeches should take. On the one hand, this shape entailed successive stages in developing its argument, and on the other hand, it excluded details which the author considered irrelevant for his pedagogical aims.

[141] Ibid. 428d.

themes into smaller parts is most visible in the third oration where, by emphasising the unity and didactic function of the text, the unity and the didactic function of the *Orations* as a whole are also suggested:

> These statements can be made about obvious voluntary and involuntary actions. On non-voluntary actions (this is Aristotle's opinion) I make a similar statement. And, in support of the statements which will be made here, I will recall now something that I said previously.[142]

The didacticism and unity of the *Orations* are also reflected at the level of style. Manuel tunes his speech to the appropriate approach and method for effective presentation, for sometimes, as he states, his ideas have to be explained at length, and in other instances they need brevity.[143] The author's interplay with various stylistic categories used in each of the seven texts also functions as a catalyst for maintaining the coherence of the different parts of the text. A certain tension between a neat logical argumentation employing concepts of classical philosophy and a will to instruct permeates the text of the *Orations*. In the third oration, before beginning a more sophisticated presentation of ethical concepts, Manuel insists that he does not intend to produce confusion in his attempt to clarify sharp logical divisions and subdivisions already employed by philosophers like Plato, Aristotle and others.[144] With regard to notions like voluntariness he admits that the ancient philosophers have already produced complete accounts and that his task remains only to briefly expose the foundation of moral demeanour and to instruct.[145] Moreover, the sort of speech (σχῆμα τῆς ὁμιλίας) and the onset of the text (ὁρμὴ τοῦ λόγου) will not allow him to present all the details of the ethical problems in the debate. These observations indicate that Manuel was aware of both the function and limitations of his *Orations*, as an original text.

In all seven orations, Manuel adopts a style radically different from that of the *Foundations*, where the restrictive form of the chapter (κεφάλαιον) compelled him to put to work a limited range of stylistic devices. As a result, several important differences from the *Foundations* render the didactic scope of

---

[142] Ibid. 432b.
[143] On the various approaches to presenting a speech see ibid. 428b–c: καὶ γὰρ καὶ τὸ σχῆμα τῆς ὁμιλίας, καὶ ἡ τοῦ λόγου καταρχὰς ὁρμή, εἴργει τοσοῦτον ὑπερεκτείνεσθαι, πάσαις ἑπόμενον ταῖς παρεκδρομαῖς, κἂν ἀναγκαῖαι τὸ κατ' αὐτὰς λέγεσθαι. See also ibid. 541d: εἰ δὲ δὴ καὶ τοῦτο χρέων ἐστι, συνελόντας ἡμᾶς εἰπεῖν ὡσπερεὶ κεφαλαιωδέστερον.
[144] Ibid. 428a: Manuel states that he will not explain the concept of voluntary actions, and that he will try to be as explicit as possible in order not to induce confusion (ἰλιγγία).
[145] Cf. ibid. 464d: ἡμῖν ὁ λόγος διὰ βραχέων αὐτίκα δείξει.

the *Orations* more specific. Thus, in the *Orations*, the sententious style of the *Foundations* gives way to a more discursive one and the speaker claims to adopt the stylistic virtue of clarity (σαφήνεια), which allows him to pass quickly through a larger body of theoretical material.[146] While quotations from the Old and the New Testament abound in the sixth and the seventh orations, *gnomologia* and collections of proverbs receive much less attention.[147] A reduced use of gnomes and sententious style allows for more authorial interventions, which usually enforce the authority of the emperor's didactic voice.[148] These changes in the style of address correspond to a better-modulated pedagogical function which in turn reveals the author's strategies of self-representation.

Yet, just as in the *Foundations*, so here one of Manuel's major concerns was to create a functional and rounded *dispositio* of the material in each oration.[149] The above summary of the contents of the orations indicates that the author attempted to produce well-shaped and coherent compositions. A mark of this strategy is that the epilogues wrap up the contents of each oration and sometimes offer an insight into the topics of the following oration.[150] Similarly, in the second oration, the concluding passage echoes the statement at the beginning of the oration.[151]

In fact, the first five orations follow a similar pattern, which includes an initial declaration concerning the contents, three topics for discussion by confirmation and refutation, and a conclusion. This common design entails that the presentation of the topics is usually set in the opening of the oration.[152] In order to construct arguments more extended than the restrictive length of a paragraph, Manuel often summarises previous arguments or anticipates ensuing controversies, techniques which provide the text with a rhythm specific to

---

[146] Few maxims originating in *gnomologia* were used here: e.g. καὶ ὁ τὸ σπέρμα παρασχών, αὐτὸς τῶν φύντων αἴτιος (Ibid. 432b), quoted from Demosthenes, *On the Crown*, 159.4.

[147] See *Orations*, 424d: καὶ συλλαμβάνονταί μοι ταυτησὶ τῆς ἐννοίας, οἵ τε σοφοὶ τῶν παλαιοτέρων καὶ τῶν καθ' ἡμᾶς ἱεροί τινες ἄνδρες.

[148] See ibid. 440c: ταῦτα δὲ ἡμῖν ἔδει δειχθῆναι, καὶ γέγονε κατὰ τὴν ἡμετέραν ἰσχύν.

[149] Cf. the reference to the combining and chaining of ideas, ibid. 449c: καὶ τί ἂν πρῶτον εἴποιμεν; τί δὲ ὕστατον; τί δὲ μέσον τῶν ἐκείνη πρὸς ἡμᾶς γιγνομένων; πῶς ἄν τις ὅλος, τοὺς ἐκείνης τρόπους, τὰς μηχανάς, τὰς ποικιλίας ἐξείποι;

[150] Ibid. 441b: δεῖ δέ, οἶμαι, τὸ πᾶν εἰπόντας συντεταγμένως τε καί συντόμως, ἐνταῦθα στῆσαι τὸν λόγον.

[151] Ibid. 420c.

[152] Thus, the preamble of the first oration lists the ensuing sections of the essay in the first oration. See ibid. 404c: ἀποδεικνύναι πειρᾶσθαι ταῖς παραθέσεσιν, ὡς ἄρχουσιν ἐθέλουσιν ἀγαθοῖς εἶναι πάντων ἄμεινον ἂν εἴη. See another instance when Manuel delimits the sections of the discourse: ibid. 460b: ἕως ὧδε τὰ περὶ τῆς ἡδονῆς ἔσται, ἐπεὶ μὴ δεῖ περαιτέρω.

a didactic handbook. For this reason, marks of continuity between the various topics, such as bridging statements that signal connections between important arguments, appear regularly, thereby providing a smooth transition between the major points for discussion.[153]

In addition to the usual arsenal of rhetorical devices (e.g. argumentative questions or summarising statements), Manuel's didactic method continuously oscillates between the brevity necessary for approaching a wider variety of themes[154] and the inclusion of a wealth of details meant to clarify certain complex topics.[155] As a result, three pervasive modes of organising the topics of advice appear throughout the seven texts. In the first mode, the organisation of the didactic-moralising material relies on arguments from justice and advantage. The second mode draws on a comparative presentation: argumentative points are developed through illustrations referring to separate and contrasting times, places or groups of individuals with different opinions. Finally, in the third mode, Manuel makes use of direct pedagogical appeals in the form of castigations, criticisms or references to concrete instances of public behaviour.

Thus, it appears that the seven *Orations* were not intended as a series of unconnected seven texts. On the contrary, the apparent indeterminacy of this collection of markedly different types of orations allowed for a greater freedom in the use of philosophical or theological themes. Thereby, if we cease looking at the orations in isolation as instances of unambiguous categories, and instead search for their connections, we acquire a better insight into their cohesiveness, and their internal changes, reversals and development.

Authorial Voice: Teaching the Son and Admonishing the Emperor

As suggested above, the formal differences between the seven orations indicate that the author approached ethical and political advice in multiple ways. Several types of approach can be distinguished: illustrative examples, philosophical argumentation, appeal to Christian principles, and displaying instances of personal experience. Even if no oration relies on a single type

---

[153] E.g. the frequently used σκοπῶμεν δὲ.

[154] *Orations*, 469a: ὥσθ' ὅπερ ὑπισχνούμεθα δείξειν, ἀγαθὸν εἴληφε τέλος, Θεοῦ συναιρομένου, βράχεσι λόγοις;

[155] See ibid. 460b on the length of the discussion on pleasure: οὔτε γὰρ ἐς τἀκριβὲς ἐλθεῖν μοι δοκεῖ ῥᾴδιον εἶναι τὸν περὶ ταύτης λέγοντα, οὔτε τὸ μῆκος θέλοντα φεύγειν, τὰ κατ' αὐτὴν καθαρῶς εἰπεῖν δυνηθῆναι.

of approach, each of the seven texts depends on a dominant compositional and methodological mode that reflects the author's peculiar didactic voice. In what follows, I will try to map the major constituent elements and modulations of the authorial voice as expressed here.

From the outset, it appears that having assumed the goals of a diatribe writer, Manuel proved to have fully undertaken the role of a teacher (διδάσκαλος). All seven orations include frequent formulas of address to John as a son, whereas only once, in the seventh oration, is the official title βασιλεύς used. These formulas attest that, despite the public character of the texts, the emperor wished to include the advice he was giving in the sphere of kinship as well. An 'I–you' relationship pervades the *Orations* and this is the chief way in which Manuel maintained the teacher/disciple roles, the more advanced talking to the novice and through him to a wider readership. Along these lines, especially in the sixth and the seventh orations as well as in the epistolary epilogue, Manuel often emphasised that the teachings he presented came from himself.

In doing so, he set himself in contrast with ecclesiastical authors of homilies who assumed didactic stances according to which only the Holy Scriptures could incarnate the authorities which generated moral teachings.[156] On the other hand, the emperor came close to the model of intellectual mentorship envisaged earlier by Demetrios Kydones. In their intense correspondence, apart from the customary praise for imperial generosity, the scholar exhorted Manuel to pursue a rhetorical education, and at the same time criticised his student's political errors or excesses, whenever required by the circumstances.[157] From this perspective, with the inclusion of castigations and admonitions, the orations seem to have been designed to win John's respect for his father.

If the often reiterated primary aim of the *Orations* was to teach, the object of teaching was not an ordinary topic which students had to learn in school. The author's primary task (τὸ προκείμενον),[158] as he often claimed, pertained to the inculcation of moral principles by means of both precursors' authority and the speaker's experience. This urge towards teaching did not emerge only

---

[156] The contemporary homilies of Isidore Glabas avoid mentioning the authorial self or the preacher as fulfilling the role of a *didaskalos*. Glabas's case indicates that he took a rather impersonal perspective on teaching, unlike Manuel, who provides direct counselling to his listeners. Isidore Glabas shows this stance in both his sermons and letters: δι' ὧν ἂν εἰς μαθητὰς τοῦ κοινοῦ διδασκάλου καὶ Δεσπότου τελοῖμεν; *Homilies*, 1.6.4, ed. Christophorides.

[157] See the episode of Manuel's rebellion in Thessalonike.

[158] Cf. δέδεικται μέν, ὡς ἡγοῦμαι, τὸ προκείμενον ἡμῖν ἱκανῶς καὶ τὸ πέρας ὁ λόγος εἴληφε προσῆκον αὐτῷ (*Orations*, 420d).

in selected orations but informed the entire collection, regardless of the topics approached. It surfaced especially in the first oration, a protreptic speech, and in the last one, where the didactic function was set in explicit terms.[159] They indicate that the aim was not just to put on display the value of a moral way of life, but to provide means of attaining it by correcting flawed behaviour.

This sort of teaching required a teacher with special abilities. Like any concerned teacher, Manuel shows his acquaintance with the topics approached and that he has travelled at least some way along the path he is revealing to John. As in the *Foundations*, Manuel combines two positions of authority in the relationship with John and the rest of the audience: those of the ruler and of the father-tutor. If, as noted above, he states that the text was envisaged for a wider audience and for the common benefit of society, he also insists on presenting John as the main addressee of this piece, pointing to a parallel father–son type of relationship. It is only at the beginning of the seventh oration that Manuel projects the image of an affectionate father,[160] while in most instances, direct address from a paternal perspective is used in order to strengthen a programmatic statement and to provide further backing for his advice. As he often remarks, he is also aware of the necessity of undertaking these two major roles.[161]

By this account, as in the *Foundations*, Manuel weaves together the two standpoints, of the emperor and of the father, in a sole didactic framework which he reinforces with two elements associated with his didacticism. First is the pedagogical approach which he creates by treating the subject matter in a systematic way and by arranging the various themes according to a scheme that would become easily understandable for his young son. This didactic method entails not only the use of models circulated by authors like Herodotus, Aristotle and Demosthenes, most probably already studied by John earlier on, but also Manuel's self-promotion as a model emperor.[162] Second, he conveys moralising messages with an impact on both his son and the extended

---

[159] See *Orations*, 548c: [. . .] ὡς ὁ λόγος ἤδη ἔφθη. τοῦτο δὲ τοσούτῳ κακὸν ὥστε καὶ τὸν Χρυσορρήμονά που διδάξαι βέλτιον σαφῶς.
[160] Ibid.: σὺ δέ μοι πάντως, ὦ φίλτατε, καὶ τὸ περὶ σὲ μέγα φίλτρον, ὑπόθεσίν μοι τοῦ τολμήματος ἤδη πῶς γέγονε.
[161] Manuel develops the idea of his two roles (father and educator) in ibid. 462d: ὥστ᾽ ἐμοὶ τοῦτο προσήκει οὐ μόνον ὥσπερ τοῖς ἄλλοις, ἀλλὰ καὶ μετὰ διπλῆς τῆς προσθήκης· τοῦτο μὲν διὰ τὸ σχῆμα, τοῦτο δὲ καὶ διά σε, δι᾽ ὃν γε δήπουθεν ἐμαυτὸν εἰς τουτονὶ τὸν ἀγῶνα καθῆκα, μηδὲ τοῦ καιροῦ παντάπασιν ἐπιτρέποντος [. . .] βούλομαι δέ τινος πλάνης ἐλευθεροῦν ἐνίους, ἤδη πειρώμενος προασφαλίσασθαι τοὺς ἀκροατάς, ὡς μὴ πειραθεῖεν ἑτέρας πλάνης ἔκ τε τῶν ἄρτι λεχθέντων, κἀκ τῶν ἤδη ῥηθησομένων.
[162] Ibid. 464a.

audience of his texts. Thus, within this didactic framework, Manuel leads his son and the audience through different stages of moral education.[163] The definitions and distinctions reflecting a didactic approach do not represent just a series of abstract statements: ultimately the purpose of this collection remains that of finding the aims and social function of moral education.[164] For this reason, whenever philosophical or theological issues surface, a moralising normative ending is also added.

Despite these similarities, in terms of the type of didactic model cultivated in the *Orations*, there are several marked differences from the *Foundations*. The will to instruct, which pervades the *Orations*, depends not on a store of Hellenic and patristic wisdom in the form of precepts for the noble young man, but on more substantial pieces of advice. Most often, advice encompasses a great many aspects: from enticing the young son to acquire public rhetorical skills to following strict rules of behaviour inspired by Christian doctrine. Thus, the moral instruction of the *Orations* emerges as more elaborate than that in the *Foundations*, which rather stood for a prescriptive account for an early stage in moral teaching. A conspicuous difference is that the exhortation to the acquisition of rhetorical skills for political action put forward in the first oration[165] has no equivalent in the *Foundations*. Similarly, the representation of humility as the supreme imperial virtue and the idea of a divinely inspired ruling authority are absent from the *Foundations*.

Advice for John takes several shapes, such as direct address attached to a theoretical account, rhetorical questions,[166] imperatives,[167] exemplary stories and, most often, statements indicating appropriate or inappropriate demeanour.[168] In more elaborate forms, advice pertains to negative traits of John's behaviour or to his opinions, as in the lecture on pleasure.[169] The admonition inserted into the debate over the nature of pleasure testifies to a possible previous dialogue between the emperor and his son.[170] Often, castigations inserted

---

[163] This method is unveiled in ibid. 465b: ὅθεν δὴ διὰ πλείονων ἐκθέμενος τὸν λόγον, ὀρθῶς γε ἔχον δείξω τὸ δόγμα.

[164] Ibid. 432 a–b.

[165] Ibid. 389b: Manuel explicitly advises John to consult Herodotus's *Histories* in order to improve his knowledge and understanding of the ruler's craft.

[166] E.g. ibid. 497a.

[167] E.g. ibid. 504b.

[168] E.g. ibid. 424b: ἀλλὰ σπουδῇ καὶ καρτερίᾳ μεγίστῃ τὰ κακὰ διαφεύγειν δύνασθαι. Or 437d: ἄγνοια τὸ κακόν, εἰ δεῖ συντόμως εἰπεῖν.

[169] In this lecture Manuel advises John to free himself from harmful feelings; ibid. 473c–d: σὺ μὲν γὰρ, ὦ τάν, ὡς ἔοικε, σαυτὸν αἰτίας ἐλευθεροῖς, καὶ τὴν ἀκρασίαν οὐδὲν λογίζῃ καὶ τὴν ἐθελούσιον κίνησιν παρ' οὐδὲν τίθης.

[170] Ibid.

THE DIDACTIC VOICE: THE *ORATIONS*   193

into the expository theoretical sections reinforce advice: as mentioned, in the seventh oration the author's advice turns into outright criticism of John's behaviour. Here didacticism and moralisation converge in Manuel's rebuking of John for having judged other individuals inappropriately.[171]

The didacticism that underlines the author's voice is further signalled not only by the continuous effort to provide advice but also by the lack of praise for John's qualities, in a text that was probably delivered publicly and was supposed to advertise his son as successor. On the contrary, as noted above, John was rather criticised, an attitude that contrasts with other public rhetorical addresses.[172] As a result of this effort to express a strong personal voice, it appears that the author-emperor used the opportunity not to praise his son but to reveal elements of an ethos useful both for the co-emperor in his early youth and for his subjects.

Other modulations of the author's voice can be grasped through an inquiry into the methods of constructing his educational message. Manuel's chief strategy does not differ from that of other Byzantine authors who organised their topics into antithetic patterns reflecting symmetry and proportion. Yet if in most rhetorical public orations the climax comes near the centre of the work, with a slight fall of intensity thereafter, the *Orations* accumulates arguments and representations so that the climax comes at the end of the collection.[173] Furthermore, this climax finds expression in the presentation of a hierarchic system that proceeds from lower to higher cardinal virtues. It is important for Manuel to outline several general considerations before making concrete observations on his son's behaviour, in an attempt to make John more receptive to his didactic discourse. It is equally important to introduce these general considerations towards the end of the speech, particularly to demonstrate that Manuel's observations are linked to the problems outlined

---

[171] Ibid. 512c. In the second oration Manuel chides those who refuse to follow the path of righteousness, οἱ πονηροὶ καὶ φαῦλοι, and expands the action of moral good and evil to the entire community. Due to their knowledge and education, the ideal individuals (οἱ ἀγαθοὶ ἄνδρες) can identify what is related to them (συγγενές) or not (417a).

[172] Kydones' earlier letters to the young Manuel offer a different perspective, which included a multitude of eulogies. Even if it was customary for a court official to praise an emperor, Kydones' relationship with Manuel, which entailed criticism as well, does not entirely explain the praises he was addressing to his much younger disciple. Moreover, the *mesazōn* encouraged Manuel to improve his leadership skills at a time when he was struggling for power with his father, John V. In a letter sent from Constantinople to Manuel, while in the Turkish camp, Kydones exhorted Manuel to become a model ruler for his subjects, whereas in the *Orations* John was far from being represented as a model of kingly behaviour; Demetrios Kydones, *Letters*, no. 220.18–22, ed. Loenertz.

[173] Kennedy, *Cambridge History of Literary Criticism*, 1. xiv–xv.

in the previous speeches. There is also a difference of tone within the sections of the *Orations*. Thus, the conclusion of the seventh oration and the epistolary epilogue are triumphant, while the other texts are in general much more balanced in their presentation of arguments and counsel.[174]

Alongside hierarchy, there can be grasped a further strategy to round off the seven different texts and to offer the possibility of a different, 'circular' reading of the whole. This strategy becomes visible in the parallels between the first and the last orations, the only ones that openly consider the best ways to govern. In the first speech, Solon plays the role of the model ruler who defended Athens with few resources by using appropriate principles of political administration, which entailed the selection of a group of ἄριστοι from among the equal members of the community. The representation of Athens as an egalitarian democracy contrasts with the wealth, *hubris* and insolence of the Eastern empires. In the last oration, which puts forward the virtue of humility as the ruler's fundamental quality, Solon's image as a moderate and humble leader among his peer ἄριστοι re-emerges, this time in Christian dress.

Climax and circularity, embedded in the structure of the *Orations*, find an echo in the different identities the author assumes.[175] The rhetorician's engaged 'I' yields to the impersonal stance of the imperial office asserting itself transparently, especially in the epistolary epilogue: Manuel orchestrates a variety of roles as disguised teacher, mythographer and philosopher, all of them predicated upon two social functions, emperor and father, which he often switches.[176] The audience is expected to perceive how individual speech genres reinvent conventional themes and how they reshape their features against the tradition of public admonitory speeches. The audience is thus led through a labyrinth of intersecting roles assumed by the author and, for this reason, the emperor's relationship with it acquires a fluctuating dynamic. Manuel has to show flexibility because he will probably encounter several types of educated audiences: some appreciate protreptic speeches, others philosophical ones and others again homilies. Depending on the textual level of his lessons and on the various teaching roles, Manuel is either engaged or distant: his commentaries are, in turns, generous or parsimonious, benevolent or judgemental, and scholarly or clerical-spiritual. By revealing these multiple perspectives

---

[174] Terms like μετρίως, πρέπον and προσῆκον, which emerge frequently, convey an idea of equilibrium applied to both the form and content of the *Orations*.

[175] See *Orations*, 529a: καὶ δή μοι τελεσθέντος τοῦ πρὶν διαύλου, ὥρα κἀκείνοις χαρίζεσθαι, καί σοι τὸ δέον ἀποπληροῦν.

[176] Manuel emphasises the role of the emperor-father's experience in shaping his son's opinions; ibid. 464b.

on virtues – theological, philosophical or derived from experience – Manuel instantiates the problems inherent in the political paradigm itself: the emperor stands as a model, yet it is difficult to make the person who holds the office become a perfect man, an embodiment of so many virtues.

Also as a reflection of Manuel's shifting roles, which allow him to move from argumentation and figural representation to prescriptive language, several modulations of genres appear to unfold in the *Orations*. His oratorical combinations include the discourse of classical paradigmatic historiography, contemporary conflicts, philosophical arguments and homiletic exhortations. The mix of these genres reflects an intention to create a distinct didactic voice, if not to subvert their core generic features: the homilies, for instance, reinforce their didactic meaning when combined with pagan mythological knowledge and with public castigations addressed to the young co-emperor.

In the case of the first oration, I have already indicated that as a protreptic oration, it does not offer advice for the pursuit of philosophy, as one would have expected, but points to the significance of rhetoric. The result of this change of interests may have been surprising for the readers of protreptic speeches which are usually focused on the education of philosophers. At the same time, one should consider the emperor's intention of offering a realistic representation of what was expected from a ruler, mostly political wisdom (πολιτικὴ ἐπιστήμη) and a set of practical virtues helpful in coping with the increased influence of other social categories. Yet the emphasis on rhetoric does not hinder the effective communication of the emperor's political messages. The roles of the philosopher and of the rhetorician were interchangeable, with a tendency to emphasise the value of the latter.

Combining past and present authorities constituted another major strategy to effectively communicate ethical principles applicable to present circumstances. As pointed out, Manuel often quoted authors like Plato, Aristotle, Demosthenes, Herodotus, the evangelists and the Church Fathers. Yet the relationship with past authors of texts of ethics remains ambiguous. One can detect traces of dissatisfaction with this tradition, especially when Manuel questions the method of excerpting from different authors.[177] This dissatisfaction comes from his intention to break off with the tradition and foreshadows a distinct view on the emperor's role.[178] Often, Manuel argues from his experience and designs plans for future actions. Even the earlier *Foundations* are

---

[177] Ibid. 532a: πολλῶν δὲ ὄντων καὶ μεγάλων τῶν περὶ ταπεινοφροσύνης προειρηκότων καὶ ἐν τοῖς πάλαι, καὶ ἐν τοῖς νῦν, οὐδεὶς οὐδέπω τὸ πᾶν εἴρηκε.

[178] See the distinction between νέα and παλαιὰ νομοθεσία in the *Epistolary Epilogue*, 560a.

quoted as a valid source of inspiration for moral models, equal to other texts of advice.[179] He insists on the validity of his authorial methods and indicates his attempts to add a personal contribution, not just reproduce old ideas. The author's interventions trigger changes in the account of ideal imperial behaviour common to other imperial authors, and in the disposition of the material in the orations.[180] Mastering persuasive skills is openly included in the list of kingly virtues, while humility, another virtue that does not appear in other, similar texts of advice for young rulers, appears at the top of this system. Thus, even if Manuel modestly claims that he has not added anything new, eventually, in the concluding sections of the orations, he appears to be keen to emphasise his political experience as well as rhetorical achievements.[181]

Conclusion

Far from being a text focused on kingship, the *Orations* are rather geared towards the presentation of the individual's acquisition of moral values. The correlation between ethics, the rulers' virtues and rhetorical skills is certainly framed in a tradition that originated in the writings of the rhetoricians of Hellenistic and Graeco-Roman times.[182] Yet in Manuel's case, through the development of the idea of a special kind of imperial behaviour, the presentation of moral virtues reflects, on the one hand, such a tradition and, on the other hand, an insight that could only have come with practical experience. Drawing on multiple philosophical sources, this formulation of imperial behaviour is based on the ideal of tolerance, with strong bonds of friendship and values such as education and moderate enjoyment of life.

The seven orations establish a tight connection with the preceding work, the *Foundations*, with which they share several themes. I suggest that the two texts are intended as a sole textual unit and function as a single work in the form of a moral diptych, with an epistolary introduction in the *Foundations* and an epistolary epilogue in the *Orations*. Moreover, a number of allusions in the *Orations* refer to the subject matter of the *Foundations* and create an interlacing pattern that weaves together their two moral-political 'plots'.

---

[179] The *Foundations* receive an authority equal to that of the biblical or ancient authors in *Orations*, 429b: καὶ συλλαμβάνονται μὲν ταυτησὶ τῆς ἐννοίας, οἵ τε σοφοὶ τῶν παλαιοτέρων καὶ τῶν καθ' ἡμᾶς ἱεροί τινες ἄνδρες. ἀκήκοας δέ τι καὶ παρ' ἡμῶν περὶ τούτων σαφέστερον εἰρηκότων ἐν τῷ ἑξηκοστῷ δευτέρῳ τῶν πρὸς σε μοι κεφαλαίων.
[180] For instance, *Orations*, 545d: ἐρῶ δὲ τὸν ἐκείνου σκοπόν, οὐ τὰ ῥήματα.
[181] Ibid. 441c: ταῦτα δὲ ἡμῖν ἔδει δειχθῆναι, καὶ γέγονε κατὰ τὴν ἡμετέραν ἰσχύν.
[182] Morgan, *Literate Education*, 146–50, 228, 267.

This concatenation, combined with the absence of an official prologue in the *Orations*, invites readers to consider these two texts in tandem and interpret their patterns of repetition and variation. From this perspective, the function of the collection emerges as twofold: first, to further the investigation of some of the themes approached in the *Foundations* and offer details on issues discussed there; and second, to publicly blame John VIII for previous acts of misbehaviour.

The *Orations* and the *Foundation* also share an intention to educate, and for this purpose they use various strategies: narrative accounts, discussions of philosophical concepts and homiletic style. What unites them is the mechanism of protreptic rhetoric which Manuel puts to work in combination with parainetic elements, in an attempt to subvert the rhetorical genres addressing questions of rulership. As in other texts of his, while the author is aware of the borrowings from ancient philosophers' texts, he is also keen to point out elements of his experience that are reflected in the style he adopts for addressing his son. Manuel applies old concepts to new situations so that different views on the ruler's virtues will throw light on the problems inherent in the construction of an ideal representation of kingship. In the context of late Byzantine court rhetoric, the seven orations stand as an experimental text, especially due to their generic differences and the strategies of combining multiple rhetorical forms. The *Orations* mix narrative and biblical imagery with sharp philosophical argumentation inspired by ancient authors; homiletic and philosophical styles; protreptic and apologetic. Above all, Manuel also shows awareness of his political experience and individual authorial skills.

These observations suggest that the author invites the audience to consider the orations as parts of a meaningful whole, rather than to see them as separate writings. Like most Byzantine homilies or texts of advice the *Orations* combine both Christian and pagan elements in various moulds. Such literary polyphony contributes to the success of the orations and adds the possibility of more than one reading. Moreover, like other Byzantine anthologies or collections of different literary genres, Manuel's *Orations* has its own method of bringing order into a loose body of subject matters, classifying various orations, invoking thematic similarities and designing a cohesive unity.[183] They are connected in a form which can be described both as circular and as progressing from argument to argument. Thus, the *Orations* begins with a text on the ruler's virtues (first oration), then further explains

---

[183] For a discussion of the methods of anthologising poems used by Byzantine authors, see Lauxtermann, *Byzantine Poetry*, 75.

the fundamentals of these virtues (second to fifth orations) and, in the end, turns back to the ruler's cardinal virtues, adding a final, deeper, Christian ideological statement (sixth and seventh orations). On this account, Manuel configures his literary voice as that of an author with a coherent œuvre reflecting a particular political identity and not simply as an author of various texts performed on various occasions.

6

The Narrative Voice: The *Funeral Oration on His Brother Theodore, Despot of Morea*

In 1418 the humanist Guarino of Verona, a former student of Greek in Constantinople, commented in a letter upon a funeral oration which the emperor Manuel II had written on his brother, Theodore, despot of the Morea (1382–1407).[1] Guarino praised the emperor's literary skill with the following words:

> The emperor himself once sent me a very kind letter together with a funeral oration on his brother, which he wrote; the oration is delightful, ample and admirably interwoven with beautiful words and gnomic expression (*verborum et sententiarum ornatu*).[2]

In the same letter, Guarino mentioned that he had asked his friend Ambrogio Traversari to translate the text into Latin or Italian,[3] thus echoing a request made by the emperor.[4] Despite the emperor's optimism regarding this translation project, the reasons why Manuel intended to circulate his text in the West remain unknown. Was he attempting to advertise his literary skills in the intellectual milieu of humanist Italy or was he trying to convey a message about his political options in a wider European context, at a time when he was

---

[1] Guarino studied Greek with Manuel Chrysoloras in Constantinople for several years. See Cammelli, *Dotti bizantini*, 131–9.
[2] Guarino of Verona, *Letters*, no. 94 addressed to his friend, Nicolaus, ed. Sabbadini. See Ambrogio Traversari's remarks on the oration in his *Letters*, II.292, ed. Canneti and Mehus.
[3] Ibid.: 'hanc ipsam ad fratrem Ambrosium nostrum mittam', 'I will send this <oration> to Ambrosius, our brother.' On Ambrogio Traversari and his relation with Guarino see Stinger, *Humanism*.
[4] Manuel II, *Letters*, no. 60.167, ed. Dennis: 'In return for the favor I am doing you, read it and then show it to those you know if you could add to the author's reputation. You could also translate it into Latin or into your own language.'

seeking Western help to defend Byzantium?[5] Whether the first or the second option holds true, Guarino's letter suggests that the oration was considered interesting enough for an audience outside the literary circles of Constantinople, already well aware of the emperor's literary skills.[6]

If the Byzantine literati appreciated the text for its literary merits, the *Funeral Oration* on Theodore also summed up the main tenets of the emperor's political outlook present in his other texts. It stood for a different modality of conveying political messages that pertained to events in the history of the early fifteenth-century Peloponnese. Indeed, despite its resemblance to an encomium on another imperial offspring, an overarching discourse of legitimisation and justification of a certain course of political action pervades this oration, which documents the tumultuous history of the late fourteenth-century Peloponnese.

Given this text's underlying political dimension, the present chapter will analyse the major formal aspects relevant for the praise addressed to Theodore I Palaiologos, by focusing on the extensive narrative of events which the emperor included in the oration. Based on this analysis, it will be suggested that the author constructed the commemorative oration for his brother around an idea of the emperor's strict control of the affairs in this remote region of the Byzantine Empire. Like the previous chapters, the present chapter will be divided into several sections that will highlight the major literary aspects of the text: first, I will examine the contexts of production and then its contents, arranged according to the rules of the genre of the *epitaphios logos*; second, I will analyse the narrative; and finally I will discuss the authorial voice emerging from this text.

Contexts of Production

So far, Manuel II's *Funeral Oration* has sparked little discussion among scholars of Byzantine literature. This situation is somewhat unusual, considering that many historians like Julian Chrysostomides, the editor of the *Oration*, noted its importance as a historical document for the medieval Peloponnese.[7]

---

[5] See Patacsi, 'Joseph Bryennios'.

[6] Manuel promoted his rhetorical skills in order to project the image of a highly educated ruler. His panegyrists often praised him as a teacher. See Makarios Makres, *Funeral Oration for Emperor Manuel*, in Sideras, *Byzantinische Grabreden*, 306.3–4; Demetrios Chrysoloras, *Comparison*, 235.23–5, ed. Lampros.

[7] Much of the information on the history of the Morea comes from Manuel's *Funeral Oration*; Zakythenos and Maltezou, *Despotat grec de Morée*, 1.125–65; Necipoğlu, *Byzantium*, 235–58. Chrysostomides remarked that the *Funeral Oration* 'is one of the most significant documents in a period of Byzantine history, which is scantily documented'; *Funeral Oration*, 27. See Loenertz, 'Pour l'histoire du Péloponnèse', 234–56; Page, *Being Byzantine*, 249–58.

Indeed, the text provides a considerable amount of information pertaining to individuals and events which shaped the history of the region.[8] Nevertheless, close observation of other aspects of this text, like its cultural-literary setting or its performative context, may take us a step beyond the sheer reconstruction of Morean history in the late fourteenth and early fifteenth century and help us appreciate the underlying reasons for the emperor's actions in the Morea.[9] The present chapter will, therefore, follow a slightly different path and focus on Manuel's *Funeral Oration* as a literary document of the late Palaiologan period.

The *Funeral Oration* on Theodore was written around the year 1410[10] and was dedicated to Manuel II's younger brother, appointed as despot of the Byzantine province of the Morea in 1379. The two brothers enjoyed a very close relationship, as attested by their collaboration in common military actions and their common friends.[11] Theodore's rule was marked by long conflicts with the Latins, the Ottomans and the local Byzantine *archontes*, yet, at his death in 1407, owing to his diplomatic efforts and to the favourable international conditions, the situation in the province was relatively stable.[12] According to the lemma of the text, Manuel delivered a short version in Mystras in 1408.[13] The text of the oration is also included in codex Vindob. phil. gr. 98, a de luxe manuscript that was produced in the Constantinopolitan court milieu and presents similarities with other manuscripts dedicated to Manuel's son John.[14] The extended version, copied by Isidore of Kiev, was performed only later in Mystras in 1415. The delivery of the final, long version constituted a lavish demonstration of imperial authority, as Isidore of Kiev, a close friend of both

---

[8] In the first monograph dedicated to Manuel's works, Berger de Xivrey had already noted that it had a markedly historical character; *Mémoire*, 41.

[9] The most important monograph is the two-volume book by Zakynthenos and Maltezou, *Despotat grec de Morée*. The most recent treatment is in Necipoğlu, *Byzantium*, 235–84.

[10] Chrysostomides in *Funeral Oration*, 29. On the date of the speech see also Manuel Chrysoloras, *Epistolary Oration*, 40–8, ed. Patrineles and Sophianos.

[11] Between 1382 and 1387 Theodore and Manuel planned an alliance against the Ottomans; Dennis, *Reign of Manuel II*, 114, 119. Demetrios Kydones and Manuel Kalekas, two members of the emperor's literary circle, addressed letters to Theodore. In Kalekas's letter 29, he describes his relationship with Theodore in very affectionate terms: 'Can you imagine how much I desire to see it? You know how passionately I yearn to be able whenever I should wish to see him whom I regard as myself?' See Manuel Kalekas, *Letters*, nos. 15, 16, 49, ed. Loenertz.

[12] See Chrysostomides in *Funeral Oration*, 1–25.

[13] On the date of the first performance of the oration see Chrysostomides in *Funeral Oration*, 30.

[14] See the description of the manuscripts provided in Kakkoura's edition of *Orations*, 191–254.

the emperor and Guarino,[15] recounted in a letter addressed to Manuel. Isidore noted the impressive size of the audience as well as the performer's efforts to recite in a way that would reflect the complexity of the text:

> And when the date of the oration came and the anniversary of the day of the year on which the one praised moved from the earthly world, a ritual took place on that day, in the presence of our excellent and most brilliant despot, and also of the metropolitan and of the Senate as well as of selected people from the ecclesiastical hierarchy. All the members of the *dēmos* were also present: all people came together to be part of the audience in higher numbers than the spectators of the Olympic games. It seemed appropriate that the funeral oration be read before the ritual, and the messenger of the book was summoned for this purpose. [. . .] Good Gazes read the first part in a quiet and even mode, raising his voice little by little to a piercing tone, inasmuch as it was needed and the order of the *logos* demanded.[16]

As in the case of most of his texts, the emperor circulated the *Funeral Oration* among the members of his literary court. No fewer than five commentaries on this text have survived, pointing to the popularity the emperor wished to win for the speech. Thus, Plethon wrote a preface (προθεωρία) in which he lists the issues discussed in the *Funeral Oration* and gives short descriptions of the main units of the text.[17] A certain monk, Joasaph, wrote a shorter preface which he entitled *On the Character of the Oration* (Περὶ τοῦ χαρακτῆρος τοῦ λόγου).[18] In addition, several manuscripts contain three other short notes in prose or verse, by the emperor himself, by Matthew Chrysokephalos and by a certain Demetrios Magistros.[19] The most substantial commentary, which belonged to Manuel Chrysoloras, was written in the form of an encomium on the emperor's literary skills and provides detailed comments on the different aspects of the *epitaphios*:[20]

---

[15] Guarino of Verona, *Letters*, nos. 2.930a and 930b, 678–80, ed. Sabbadini. Most likely Isidore also helped the emperor with writing the oration. See Manuel Chrysoloras, *Epistolary Oration*, 38–9, ed. Patrineles and Sophianos; Chrysosotomides in *Funeral Oration*, 29.

[16] Isidore of Kiev, *Letters*, nos. 66.24–67.17, ed. Regel.

[17] For a translation of Plethon's preface to the *Funeral Oration* see Appendix 3.

[18] Joasaph the Monk, *On the Character of the Oration*, in *Funeral Oration*, 70–1.

[19] These five pieces, among which Plethon's is the most extensive, are included in Chrysostomides' edition; *Funeral Oration*, 67–72.

[20] The exact title of Chrysoloras's text is unknown, although it was doubtless addressed to Emperor Manuel II; Manuel Chrysoloras, *Epistolary Oration*, 50, ed. Patrineles and Sophianos. Commenting on the emperor's literary achievements in the *Funeral Oration* Chrysoloras says: σὺ δὲ τὸν βίον τούτου διελθών, βασιλικῆς τε καὶ πολιτικῆς παιδείας τύπον ἔφηνας καὶ οὐκ ἐκείνου μόνον στήλην ἀλλὰ καὶ οἷον δεῖ τὸν ἄρχοντα ἁπλῶς εἶναι ἀνδριάντα ἔστησας, ὃν πάλαι μὲν ἔδειξας ἐν σεαυτῷ, αὐτὸς πλάστης καὶ τεχνίτης τούτου καὶ εἰκὼν γενόμενος; ibid. 64.26–30.

adherence to and departure from the established model of funeral orations, the personality of the deceased person, the participants in the commemoration, etc. Chrysoloras listed a wide range of the oration's qualities. He started with power, beauty and honour (δύναμις, κάλλος and ἀξίωμα) and finished with precision, intensity, majesty, inventiveness, diversity, order, coherence, etc.[21]

The Rhetorical Template and the Compositional Structure of the *Funeral Oration*

As with any *epitaphios logos*, one of the chief functions of the oration was to praise Theodore, the emperor's brother and deceased ruler of the Morea. Yet it is also true that the extent and the variety of the other elements included in the text infuse the oration with new meanings which go beyond sheer eulogy. In this section, I will proceed to identify and analyse the author's strategies and techniques that were used in building political messages. I envisage here two major aspects which pertain to the author's craft: first, the use of a rhetorical template enunciated long before, and, second, the narrative of events in the Peloponnese which, in my opinion, is decisive for formulating and conveying an imperial message. Both these aspects highlight the issues which Manuel constantly plays against each other in this oration: the portrait of his brother, the history of the Peloponnese, and his own involvement in the politics of the region.

The ancient theory of topoi *and the* Funeral Oration

The principles enunciated by the ancient theory of rhetoric represent a valuable hermeneutical device for understanding this text. Most of all, they enable one to chart with a certain degree of precision the changes of form, content and attitude which were effected by the revival of classical models.

Funeral orations held a prominent place in both the society and the literary culture of the Hellenic world. Ever since Thucydides' rendition of Pericles' speech commemorating the death of the Athenian heroes, texts of this kind had been constantly produced and copied as models.[22] The Athenian historian established a model which combined elements from two other genres: panegyric and biography. As a result, this double determination, reflecting a

---

[21] Ibid. 74.31–75.28: ἀκρίβεια, δεινότης, σεμνότης, μεγαλοπρέπεια, ἐπίνοια, τὸ ποικίλον καὶ πυκνὸν καὶ καινὸν τῶν νοημάτων, τάξις, συνέχεια, τὸ οἰκεῖον καὶ τὸ καθαρὸν τῆς λέξεως, τὴν διαλάμπουσαν διὰ πάντων ὥραν.

[22] Other notable funeral discourses are treated by Dionysius of Halicarnassus in his *Art of Rhetoric* VI.1–4.

set of ethical standards and a historical treatment respectively, left deep traces in the fabric of the genre. The implications of this double determination have been extensively treated by Laurent Pernot in a comprehensive study which is also relevant for the present analysis.[23]

A cursory look at the corpus of extant funeral orations reveals a variety of ways to approach the event of an individual's death. Thus, depending on circumstances, some authors focused more on praising the dead person's character, while others preferred to spice up the encomium with a more detailed account of the individual's activities and of their effects on the current state of affairs. In addition, funeral orations included compulsory sections meant to express their authors' grief and sentiments of loss. Especially in the introduction and the epilogue, they included elements borrowed from another popular funerary genre, the monody, which was a shorter piece of writing dedicated to mourning a person. In contrast, as Manuel Chrysoloras noted, a funeral oration had several functions, including a pedagogical one.[24]

The inclusion of the *epitaphios* in Menander's Περὶ ἐπιδεικτικῶν indicates that the prevailing view was to regard funeral orations as pieces of demonstrative rhetoric.[25] Menander's discussion of *epitaphioi* under the heading of encomia touched upon various aspects of the genre like its history, performance and typology. In addition, the rhetorician gave details on the arrangement and the content of each chapter to be included in a funeral oration. In Byzantium, Menander's rules were used as guides for several kinds of speeches, while their audience is well attested by a significant number of extant manuscripts. As a matter of fact, most of the late Palaiologan funeral orations, such as Makarios Makres' and the anonymous *Funeral Oration on Manuel II* (Vat. gr. 632) largely followed these prescriptions.[26]

In light of these preliminary observations with regard to the genre of *epitaphioi*, the first stage of my discussion of the literary and rhetorical strategies used in this oration will consist of a summary of the oration based on an overview of the ways in which the author complied with the rules of the genre which he adopted. Thus, the ancient theory of *topoi*, defined as thematic rubrics according to which facts were arranged, provides an appropriate and coherent conceptual framework. The model, established long before by

---

[23] Pernot, *Rhétorique de l'éloge*, 1.110–37.
[24] Manuel Chrysoloras, *Epistolary Oration*, 71.10, ed. Patrineles and Sophianos: καὶ πολλὰ δὲ ἄλλα τῶν χρησίμων ἐν τοῖς ἐπιταφίοις λόγοις παιδευόμεθα.
[25] Menander Rhetor, *Treatises*, I (Γενεθλιῶν διαίρησις τῶν ἐπιδεικτικῶν), 418.6–422.4, ed. Russell and Wilson.
[26] Makarios Makres, *Funeral Oration for Emperor Manuel*, 309–26, in Sideras, *Byzantinische Grabreden*; Anonymous, *Funeral Oration on Manuel II*, 441–51, ed. Dendrinos.

Isocrates' *Evagoras* and subsequently theorised in other rhetorical treatises, presented the following succession of units:[27]

- parents of the praised individual;
- country;
- birth;
- childhood: physical and moral qualities;
- adult age: the period up to the coming into power and the period of rule;
- general comparison with heroes of the past;
- *makarismos* (blessing).

Following this structure, the *Funeral Oration* makes use of a similar string of basic elements.[28] At the outset of his oration, Manuel states that his speech remains subject to the canons of the panegyric:

> The established norm of panegyrics lays down that before honoring the dead with praise, his country and parents should also be acclaimed, especially when they are indeed men of significant virtue and great fame.[29]

This passage, which leaves no doubt regarding the nature of the *Funeral Oration*, stands as a short definition of panegyric as it was accepted by any educated Byzantine. With this statement Manuel seems to wish to indicate that he is avoiding novelties and that he is following strictly the prescriptions enunciated in late antiquity, and consistently assumed by Byzantine writers of *epitaphioi*. From this point of view, the *Funeral Oration* does not present any peculiarities. It deals with the family, education, virtues, deeds and death of Theodore, despot of the Morea, and accordingly it is divided into the following sections: a proem (προοίμιον), accounts of fatherland (πατρίς), family (γένος), nurture (ἀνατροφή), education (παιδεία), ways of living (ἐπιτηδεύματα), deeds (πράξεις) and comparison (σύγκρισις), concluding with *topoi* typical of funerary speeches: lamentation (θρῆνος) and consolation (παραμυθία).[30]

---

[27] The scheme is presented and discussed in Pernot, *Rhétorique de l'éloge*, 1.137.
[28] The order (τάξις) of compositional rubrics is strictly respected throughout the oration, according to most generic precepts. Manuel alternates these emotional sections with narrative or descriptive units which entirely neglect Theodore's figure. And with regard to another rhetorical category, ἀκολουθία (the succession of compositional sections), transitions are usually marked by anticipating the content of what is to come.
[29] *Funeral Oration*, 79.6–10. The translations used in this chapter are from Chrysostomides' edition of the *Funeral Oration*.
[30] Also listed in the introduction to the edition by Chrysostomides; ibid. 27.

The first segment of the speech, the proem, establishes an emotional contact with the audience.[31] This section is closely connected with the following part, the intention (πρόθεσις),[32] which bridges the two succeeding sections and explains the nature of the following section, the nobility (εὐγένεια) of the deceased. While Manuel admits that a panegyric should eulogise the nobility of family and place of birth of the individual under focus, he introduces a slight modification as he plainly asserts that this rule was superfluous,[33] since all knew that his fatherland was the great city of Constantinople.[34]

As a consequence of the insistence on private emotion, in the end, Constantinople gets a very brief encomium which includes only praise for the fame of its founder, Constantine.[35] It is also worth noting that, by contrast, Isidore of Kiev's panegyric addressed to Manuel's son John included an extensive praise of the city which stood as a core part of the entire panegyric.[36] As for Theodore's parents and ancestors, they are treated in a few lines that stress their role as emperors in an uninterrupted series of rulers.[37] Manuel's partial overlooking of details pertaining to his brother's nobility (εὐγένεια), also noted by Manuel Chrysoloras in the *Epistolary Oration*,[38] mirrors a rather rare habit among ancient authors of panegyrics. Menander himself rebuked those authors who, when praising emperors, started their eulogy *in medias res*.[39] From this point of view, Manuel seems to have wished both to comply with the rule of a proper encomium and to instil the idea of Theodore's significance in state hierarchy.

The ensuing rubrics, education (παιδεία) and nurturing (ἀνατροφή), which touch on the despot's personality, receive more attention than the previous ones. This rubric begins with the account of his earliest age.[40] Theodore's qualities were twofold: intellectual (he excelled in rhetorical

---

[31] Ibid. 75.1–79.5.
[32] Ibid. 79.6–24.
[33] Ibid. 81.4: περιττόν.
[34] Ibid. 81.5–6.
[35] Ibid. 83.13–30. This is not the case with Isidore's *Panegyric*, which describes the city's glorious past. Further on the praise of Constantinople, see Rhoby, 'Stadtlob und Stadtkritik'.
[36] Isidore of Kiev, *Panegyric*, PP 3, 136.14–154.31.
[37] *Funeral Oration*, 83.31–85.20.
[38] Chrysoloras also noted that the emperor overlooked the parents; Manuel Chrysoloras, *Epistolary Oration*, 95.1, ed. Patrineles and Sophianos.
[39] Menander Rhetor, *Treatises*, II, 370, 9–10, 12–28, ed. Russell and Wilson. Pernot discussed the few cases of ancient panegyrists who neglected to treat εὐγένεια; *Rhétorique de l'éloge*, 1. 258–9.
[40] *Funeral Oration*, 85.21: ἐτράφη μὲν βασιλικῶς, ἐκ παίδων δὲ ἐδείκνυ τὴν εὐφυίαν.

studies)⁴¹ and physical (he had proven military abilities).⁴² Such values were also echoed in other contemporary pieces of writing. Demetrios Kydones and Manuel Kalekas addressed Theodore in several letters written in the usual elite idiom, which leads one to the conclusion that he possessed the educational background of an upper-class Byzantine.⁴³

As in the previous rubrics, there is little novelty in the discussion of virtues (ἀρεταί)⁴⁴ where Theodore is portrayed as wise, righteous, courageous, unswerving⁴⁵ and, above everything, temperate and maintaining moderation in his actions.⁴⁶ More substantial than the previous rubrics, the section of ἐπιτηδεύματα⁴⁷ follows the usual generic prescriptions as well:⁴⁸ it embraces the despot's way of life, the attitude adopted in various situations and towards certain people, the career envisaged since youth, his conduct and ethical disposition. All in all, so far, the author's attitude is unsurprisingly highly laudatory.

It is the section on actions and deeds (πράξεις)⁴⁹ which was theoretically meant to illustrate Theodore's excellence and which occupies the largest part of the oration. According to his own statements,⁵⁰ Manuel does not recount all of his brother's deeds but operates a selection of facts beginning from the period before the arrival in the Peloponnese and up to the recovery of the major strongholds in the region previously sold to the Knights Hospitaller. This section abounds in details of Theodore's deeds and of other episodes from Peloponnesian history: the rebellions of the local *archontes*, the settlement of a significant Albanian population in the region, the Ottoman

---

⁴¹ Ibid. 85.24–87.3.
⁴² Ibid. 87.10–87.22.
⁴³ E.g. Demetrios Kydones, *Letters*, nos. 293, 313, 322, 336, 366, 414, 421, 425, 427, 442, ed. Loenertz. On Theodore's education, ibid. no. 322: χάρις σοι καὶ τοῦ γράψαι καὶ τοῦ μετὰ κάλλους τοῦτο ποιῆσαι. γὰρ στρατιώτῃ μᾶλλον ἢ ῥήτορι τοιαῦτα γράφειν προσῆκε.
⁴⁴ *Funeral Oration*, 87.23–89.21.
⁴⁵ Ibid. 87.24–5.
⁴⁶ Ibid. 89.1–21.
⁴⁷ This section is not about the office, but about the usual conduct of the young individual. As the πράξεις were reserved to the adult age, the ἐπιτηδεύματα would be considered as revealing a character and a moral disposition (ἦθος, τρόπος, προαίρεσις).
⁴⁸ Menander defines it as: ἔνδειξις τοῦ ἤθους καὶ τῆς προαιρέσεως ἄνευ πράξεων ἀγωνιστικῶν; Menander Rhetor, *Treatises*, II, 384, 20–1, ed. Russell and Wilson.
⁴⁹ Ibid. 97.3–211.12. Concerning the πράξεις, the dominant view has usually been the one formulated by Cicero, who recommended that panegyrists should praise only the most recent deeds; *Partitiones Oratoriae*, 75. See Menander Rhetor, *Treatises*, II, 391, 26–7; 415, 19–21, ed. Russell and Wilson.
⁵⁰ *Funeral Oration*, 97.3–5: 'So far we have spoken only briefly and we think that we have thoroughly proved that your Despot's nature deserved great praise.'

attempts to increase their influence in the region, the negotiations with the Latins, and, most of all, the temporary sale of Byzantine cities to the Hospitallers. Although it follows chronological order, it does not end with the despot's death, which occurred at the time of a long series of negotiations leading to the pacification of the peninsula.

After the πράξεις comes the comparison (σύγκρισις) with the ancient heroes.[51] Roughly, this rubric supports a division into two parts: one dealing with Theodore's deeds, comprising a comparison with a series of Homeric heroes and with his ancestors; and a second part which deals with his fatal illness. The latter comparison triggers a further parallel to Job's sufferings.

The lamentation (θρῆνος),[52] in fact an integrated monody, is primarily a description of the mourner's feelings. The emperor enhances this section with a dialogue between the author himself and the members of the audience asked to offer emotional support to the emperor in expressing his grief. The use of the dialogue in a funeral oration might indicate the influence of the homiletic tradition, the only oratorical genre which included occasional conversations between the performer and the audience.[53] The final section, the epilogue (ἐπίλογος), corresponding to the peroration, includes the usual blessing (μακαρισμός) and an exhortation addressed to the audience to endure the loss with dignity.

Having identified the main rubrics of the rhetorical template in use in the *Funeral Oration*, I will now turn to look briefly into the ways in which Manuel handles these rules in the praise of his brother. In broad terms these rhetorical rules were connected with two major categories of rhetorical practice: *inventio* and *dispositio* of subject matter. As Menander had already noted in the Περὶ ἐπιδεικτικῶν, orators often exercised freedom in complying with these rules.[54]

One way leading to the identification of authorial peculiarities in terms of *inventio* and *dispositio* is to look at the choice of details provided in the main section of the text, Theodore's πράξεις. Doubtless, the author selected only a limited number of episodes purged of any negative implications for the despot's activity. The most striking element which he does not mention is the alliance with the 'barbarian' Ottomans against the powerful local Byzantines. The selection of details goes hand in hand with the sequence

---

[51] Ibid. 211.13–233.14.
[52] Ibid. 233.15.
[53] Cunningham, 'Dramatic device'.
[54] E.g. the use of formulas like ἔξεστί σοι, οὐδὲν κωλύει, ὡς ἄν τις βούληται in Menander Rhetor, *Treatises*, II, 382.4; 384.3; 404.29. For the discussion on the orator's liberties see Pernot, 'Règles et liberté de composition', in *Rhétorique de l'éloge*, 1.251–3.

of *topoi*: like many other orators who adjusted the rules according to their subject matter,[55] Manuel eliminates from his encomium entire rubrics, such as γένεσις or τύχη.

As for the length of the oration, it must first be noted that, while epideictic speeches had no set limits,[56] funeral celebrations were commonly regarded as a genre of reduced length. Monodies, the other major funerary type, were strictly limited to 150 lines. The primary reason for cultivating brevity was certainly the chagrin of the participants in the ceremony. Late Palaiologan funeral orations comply with this model of brevity.[57] However, in the present case, it appears that Manuel draws equally on the genre of imperial orations (βασιλικοὶ λόγοι), which had no limit for developing their constituent *topoi*.[58] Consequently, the oration often expands in directions that depart from the exclusive presentation of Theodore's personality: it praises the Knights Hospitaller for their bravery, it rebukes the Ottomans as savage barbarians and it highlights aspects of the political context of Theodore's actions. Nonetheless, despite its considerable length, the speech retains its oral character, emerging from the references to a group of listeners present at the public delivery of the oration.

So much for the analysis of the *inventio* and *dispositio* of the *topoi* in this speech. The arrangement of rubrics indicates that the oration closely follows a conventional scheme. However, as suggested above, the most substantial rubric, the way of life (ἐπιτηδεύματα) and the deeds (πράξεις), receive a very different treatment which, arguably, illustrates a tendency towards altering the genre of funeral orations by Manuel himself.

The Narrator and the Narrative

Habitually, these two sections (ἐπιτηδεύματα and πράξεις) included several narrative vignettes that highlighted the virtuous character of the deceased person.[59] The account of an individual's deeds represented the main feature

---

[55] Pernot gives a long series of examples of omissions of *topoi*: for instance, the family is omitted by Dion XXVIII, 9; XXIX, 2–3; Aristides, *Eteones*, 3; *Panegyric of Kyzikos*, 23; the fatherland by Aristides, *Alexander* 5; Pernot, *Rhétorique de l'éloge*, 1.156.

[56] Lucian, *On Authority*, 18: οὐκ ἔστιν αὐτοῦ μέτρον νενομοθετημένον.

[57] Makarios Makres, for instance, wrote a brief funeral oration on the emperor. MS Vat. gr. 632 includes another rather brief funeral oration for the emperor.

[58] Chrysostomides also noted that Manuel's *Funeral Oration* was not based exclusively on the tenets of ἐπιτάφιοι but also borrowed from the βασιλικοί; in *Funeral Oration*, 28.

[59] See the contemporary *epitaphios* on Manuel II; Dendrinos, 'An unpublished funeral oration on Manuel II Palaeologus', 441–51.

which differentiated *epitaphioi* from monodies or consolatory orations (παραμυθητικοὶ λόγοι), shorter pieces of funeral rhetoric delivered straight after the death of an individual in the form of a lamentation. Notably, in the case of the *Funeral Oration* these narrative constituents take on extended dimensions, which render Manuel's text one of the lengthiest examples of its type in Byzantine literature.[60] There is yet another feature that distinguishes Manuel's *epitaphios* from other, similar productions. Thus, while the text is centred on the representation of Theodore's image as a just and capable ruler, the author also reveals two other aspects reflecting his experience as emperor: his role in the development of events in the Morea and a brief history of the area as part of the Byzantine state.

Indeed, Manuel provides a wide range of details regarding not only his brother's activities but also the political history of the despotate.[61] In doing so, he operates a careful selection of what he presents as relevant political and military events.[62] As a result, only several major episodes receive more attention: the rebellion of Andronikos IV in Constantinople in 1376–9, the pacification of the Morea after the arrival of Theodore in 1382, Bayezid's attempts to increase his influence, the meeting of the regional Christian leaders in Serres (1393), and the sale of Peloponnesian strongholds to the Knights Hospitaller (1400).

Understanding Manuel's strategy of integrating the rhetorical and ideological elements of an encomium in a narrative thread requires a close reading of the account of events embedded in the oration. Drawing on concepts from the domain of narrative theory, in what follows I will focus on two aspects: the narrator and the narrative technique employed in order to fuse the different reports of events from the history of the Morea into a single, yet multifaceted, story.

From the outset, it should be noted that, in many ways, the narratives included in pieces of public oratory still form a puzzle for the student of ancient Greek and Byzantine rhetoric. Such narratives have been constantly overlooked by scholars who have focused primarily on categories central to the rhetorical analysis usually employed in the investigation of oratorical texts: argumentation and manipulation of technical categories such as figures of

---

[60] Sideras described Manuel's oration as the longest Byzantine funeral oration; Sideras, *Byzantinische Grabreden*, 316.
[61] For the use of the term 'despotate' see Loenertz, 'Origines du despotat d'Épire', 361.
[62] Also noted by Manuel Chrysoloras, *Epistolary Oration*, 111.6–10, ed. Patrineles and Sophianos.

speech or *topoi*.⁶³ A case in point that illustrates the treatment of narratives in Byzantine oratorical texts⁶⁴ is a recent volume on Byzantine narrative.⁶⁵ While it touches on narratives included in texts intended for public performance in religious contexts, it deals exclusively with narrative genres par excellence, such as history and hagiography. A rather singular study on the oratorical narrative by Oliver Jens Schmitt investigated the historical content in Isidore of Kiev's *Panegyric Addressed to Emperor John VIII*. However, while the study acknowledges the role of narrative in this extensive late Byzantine imperial oration, it is limited to a presentation of the historical information and does not further explore the orator's narrative strategies.⁶⁶

The narrator

Before proceeding to the investigation of the ways in which these related episodes are connected into a single narrative, I will first consider how the emperor fashions himself as a narrator. Certainly, Manuel was not an innovator in rhetorical techniques: authors of epideictic rhetoric resolved the tension resulting from the use of both narrative accounts and literary portraits either by relying on chronological accounts or by classifying deeds in time of peace and war according to the cardinal virtues.⁶⁷ Manuel Chrysoloras noted the paradox of the *epitaphioi* which, despite their sad topic, still had to be pleasant for the listeners: 'Funeral orations are not only just, good, and useful, but also enjoyable and capable to generate delight.'⁶⁸

---

[63] Another reason for marginalising the study of narratives in oratory could be that speeches have been judged as non-narrative texts. However, just as many narratives include non-narrative elements, so speeches often embed sophisticated narratives. In fact, in antiquity speeches were already treated together with the *genus mixtum* of narrative. In his *Rhetoric*, Aristotle assigned a central position to narratives in his theory of internal arrangement of speeches, τάξις. Aristotle listed διήγησις together with other major speech units – preface (προοίμιον), proof (πίστις) and epilogue (ἐπίλογος) – and conceived of it as a highly argumentative element.

[64] Perhaps due to these difficulties in the analysis of oratorical narratives, only recently have scholars begun investigating them more systematically. For instance, the volume edited by de Jong, Nünlist and Bowie, *Narrators, Narratees, and Narratives*, has a chapter discussing the features of narratives used by ancient orators like Demosthenes, Lysias and Isocrates in their texts for purposes of argumentation in civil trials; Edwards, 'Oratory'.

[65] Burke, Betka, Buckley, Hay, Scott and Stephenson, *Byzantine Narrative*.

[66] Schmitt, 'Kaiserrede und Zeitgeschichte'; Leonte, 'Visions of empire'.

[67] Pernot, *Rhétorique de l'éloge*, 1.134–40.

[68] *Funeral Oration*, 73.1.

For his part, Manuel openly embraces a chronological approach. We are fortunate to have the author's post-factum remarks on the production of the text, remarks which highlight the chief role of narrative in the funeral oration. The emperor's letter to Manuel Chrysoloras, whom he was asking for feedback on his composition, alluded to the methods of writing an *epitaphios* and revealed the author's poetics of praise by means of narrative. The emperor states that in a laudatory text the account of one's deeds is more eloquent than a sheer enumeration of qualities:

> For we consider it exactly the same thing to give a detailed account of the life of good men and by that very fact to adorn them with praise directly. That praise, to be more precise, which the account of a person's deeds evokes is undoubtedly greater than the simple statement that the man in question was brave, intelligent, and possessed of all other virtues.[69]

Likewise, other contemporary authors noted the presence of a narrative voice.[70] The preface of the funeral oration included in MS Vindob. phil. gr. 98, by Gemistos Plethon, notes that Manuel recounted events from the recent history of the Morea as well as Theodore's activities.[71] Another commentator on the oration, Joasaph the monk, also highlights the author's extensive use of narratives of events in the Morea embedded in the eulogy of Theodore.[72] Finally, Manuel Chrysoloras's *Epistolary Oration* (1415) mentions the unusual inclusion of details from the history of the Peloponnese.[73]

Apart from these observations, at the beginning of the oration, the emperor addresses the question of the role of narrative strategy in the economy of praise. He introduces the section dealing with Theodore's deeds in the Morea with a brief explanatory preface:

> So far we have spoken briefly and we think that we have thoroughly proved that your Despot's nature deserved great praise. [. . .] I shall not recount everything he did, since the magnitude of his achievements prevents me from expatiating on each one singly, and their number – for they are

---

[69] Manuel II, *Letters*, no. 56, ed. Dennis.

[70] In his letter to Manuel, Isidore of Kiev noted that upon hearing the *epitaphios*, the participants had the impression that they had visualised Theodore's deeds. See Isidore of Kiev, *Letters*, no. 67.21–2, ed. Regel.

[71] For a translation of Gemistos Plethon's preface, see Appendix 3.

[72] Joasaph the Monk, *On the Character of the Oration*, in *Funeral Oration*, 12–14.71.

[73] Manuel Chrysoloras, *Epistolary Oration*, 85, ed. Patrineles and Sophianos: καὶ περὶ τῶν ἐκείνοις τὰς ἀφορμὰς τῆς δυνάμεως καὶ τοῦ βίου παρασχόντων θεοφιλῶν ἀνδρῶν καὶ τίνων εἰσὶν οὗτοι ῥύακες οἱ παρ' ἡμῖν.

innumerable – makes it impossible to describe them all in proper sequence. My failure to detail them at length is, I believe, contrary to your wishes, for I know, and am entirely convinced, that just like those who yearn to see the portraits of their beloved ones, so you long to see this man's entire life, all of which is worthy of admiration. [. . .] From the many and fine and great deeds which you all know to have been accomplished by him – who not long ago was still among us but now alas is the subject of our tears – I shall, as I have said, only actually mention a few of his achievements and this in a very brief manner. Nevertheless these deeds will show clearly that the man who achieved them was a true benefactor to mankind, to whom he brought great honor.[74]

Essentially, this brief *ars narratoria* says that the emperor does not intend to present exhaustively the events in Theodore's life, because such an attempt would require the tools of a proper historian and Manuel claims that it is more important to reflect on Theodore's virtues. Furthermore, Manuel insists that a story like Theodore's needs to concentrate only on few of his basic (καίριον) achievements, indicative of his 'soul's desires for good'.[75] Nonetheless, the text does not entirely mirror these initial programmatic statements, as the ensuing section brings in multiple elements specific to a historical account. On the contrary, once he begins to reveal the story the author openly adopts a different method:

We must certainly relate *everything and in detail* (πάντα καὶ ἕκαστα), all the evils which the cities here suffered from the neighbouring Latins and the Turks when they attacked either by land with cavalry or by the sea with pirate vessels. In this way, the land of Pelops was being destroyed.[76]

The narrative confirms this tendency. Indeed, even if throughout the account the narrator remains aware of the difficulties resulting from the inclusion of narrative vignettes in a piece of epideictic rhetoric,[77] he amasses numerous details, implications and justifications of actions.[78] These elements

---

[74] *Funeral Oration*, 97.3–25.
[75] Ibid. 99.4–7.
[76] Ibid. 115.7–13.
[77] Ibid. 151.22–5: 'It is impossible to describe in a panegyric the ways and means by which he escaped, showing how much the Sultan deserved to be spat on.'
[78] The account includes many details regarding the geographical background. The story line progresses through different locations: Constantinople, the Peloponnese, Corinth and Serres. Minute details of the location of events are provided, such as the river Spercheios where Theodore was kept captive in Bayezid's camp; ibid. 149.30.

do not always add further information regarding Theodore's personality but instead emerge as parts of a larger representation of local political history. It is for this reason that, in his conclusions, the author insists that he has relied on all the possible objective facts which aimed at offering multiple clarifications[79] and to provide an overview of the situation in the Peloponnese.[80] In addition, he does not organise his narrative episodes according to a list of his brother's virtues, as was the case in most panegyric texts,[81] but follows the chronological order of events.

Accordingly, Manuel's narratorial voice takes on the features of a raconteur, rather than of a historian.

> But I am compelled to speak more clearly, as far as I am able, and in the course of my narrative (διήγησις) to set out step by step the account of the circumstances surrounding this particular undertaking. It is imperative to show clearly because of whom it was contrived and how as a result of this drama things took a turn for the better.[82]

Manuel not only constantly pictures himself as an omniscient storyteller, but also emerges as a participant in the Peloponnesian saga. Three episodes illustrate his involvement.[83] First, during Andronikos's rebellion when Theodore was held captive in prison, Manuel claims to have played a major role in the dynastic drama of usurpation. He agrees with his father on letting Theodore out of prison but criticises John V for several other decisions. Second, in the episode of the reunion of the most important Byzantine leaders summoned by Bayezid in Serres, Manuel stresses his awareness of his brother's plans and his support for Theodore in his heroic rejection of Bayezid's request for total submission. Third, Manuel asserts his knowledge and approval of another of his brother's major political moves, namely the sale of Morean strongholds to the Knights Hospitaller. At a closer look, it emerges that these three instances provide most of the elements used for Theodore's representation.

---

[79] Ibid. 173.6–8: 'Moreover I ought to demonstrate more clearly (σαφέστερον) how extensive the disaster would have been had not the situation been dealt with in this way.'
[80] Ibid. 129.7–9: 'I wish to speak of things in general rather than of particular individuals.'
[81] Pernot, *Rhétorique de l'éloge*, 1.172.
[82] *Funeral Oration*, 181.27–30. Cf. 97.6–7.
[83] An instance of Manuel's expression of his involvement in Moreote affairs appears when he is relating the circumstances in which Theodore undertook his office in the Peloponnese: 'and so in accordance with his father's decision, his mother's advice and my own, my brother came to you, although it was hard for him to tear himself away from my father'; *Funeral Oration*, 113.13–16.

In terms of narrative theory, the emperor's systematic 'intrusion' into the story indicates the homodiegetic relationship of the narrator with his account, meaning that he identifies himself as a character in his story world.[84] Following the same terminology of narrative theory, the narrator of the *Funeral Oration* can be described with the following attributes: (1) internal – he participates in the activities he recounts; (2) primary – there are no other narratives related by characters in the account; (3) overt – he controls and frequently intervenes in the development of the story; (4) omniscient – he appears to know all the details of the story; (5) omnipresent – there are no other narrators; and (6) dramatised – he frequently presents his feelings with regard to the events and engages his audience in the story.

It is important to understand the author's strategy of defining himself as a narrator because from such a perspective he offers motivations, distributes responsibilities for actions and makes use of his authority in order to describe situations or characters. Thus, the narrator's strong voice interferes with the account in order to shape the connections between the different stages of the story. His metanarrative interventions have different purposes: they signal the swings between biography, eulogy and history,[85] they speed up the narrative flow, anticipate information as proleptic statements or simply offer off-track comments on events.[86] The variety and frequency of narratorial interventions also underline the narrator's direct involvement in the story and suggest a strict control of its course.

---

[84] The concept of the homodiegetic narrator was introduced by Genette, *Narrative Discourse*, 212–62. Genette described the homodiegetic narrator as closer to the action than heterodiegetic narrators, who stand outside the story world.

[85] E.g. in *Funeral Oration*, 133.1: 'But let us take up our speech and follow events in proper order'; or in 167.13: 'let us resume our speech so that we proceed in good order' (εὐτάκτως).

[86] Here are several examples: marking ellipsis of information to be filled by the audience, e.g. *Funeral Oration*, 105.14: 'I shall keep silent as to how this came about for it would be superfluous to speak of it'; 123.20: 'As for the prince's extreme arrogance which was exposed by these events I will keep silent'; 139.28–30: 'Therefore being so disposed he accepted a piece of advice – I will not say from whom; let it be from the devil whom he bore in his soul'; commentaries marking paralipsis, 149.8–9: 'He succeeded in doing so, as my oration will soon show'; interventions commenting on the structure of the narrative, intended to signal the beginning of a section or to speed up the rhythm of the story, 111.3: 'Let us take up our story'; 133.1, 'Let us take up our speech and follow events in proper order'; authorial interventions, 163.19: 'I shall not speak any more about myself, nor shall I draw out my speech by lingering on details and events which took place in that long absence abroad'; 191.9: 'I hesitate to say this'.

Reflecting this strong narrative voice, the narrator's focus does not remain fixed on Theodore's figure but often shifts to his own person, that is, the emperor's, or to events from the history of the Peloponnese. By and large, the changes of focus are marked with conclusive or introductory comments.[87] For instance, after presenting the motives behind Theodore's temporary and slightly compromising alliance with the Knights Hospitaller, the account goes on with a passage suggesting the impact of the despot's actions on the region's capacity to repel further attacks. Thus, the passage opens with a statement squaring off the previous remarks, and likewise, in another passage, Manuel uses the same strategy of changing the focus of the story by turning his attention from his brother to Bayezid.[88]

The narrative of events

Having identified the aspects of the narrator's voice, I will now address the nature of the narrative of events in the *Funeral Oration*. The account of Theodore's deeds there offers wide scope for narratological analysis, since, in quantitative terms, narrative occupies more than half of this fairly long text. The two topical narrative sections, ἐπιτηδεύματα (achievements) and πράξεις (deeds), are not isolated from one another but are connected *thematically* – they present facts connected to the political milieu of the late fourteenth century; *structurally* – their connections are clearly marked;[89] and *chronologically* – the actions presented in the πράξεις section follow immediately on the ones in the ἐπιτηδεύματα. Therefore they can safely be judged as a single narrative unit. Nevertheless, the accounts included in the two sections differ in two respects: first, the ἐπιτηδεύματα section reflects Theodore's behaviour towards his parents and family,[90] while in the πράξεις, the intention is to reflect more on his military achievements.[91] Second, in the ἐπιτηδεύματα Manuel recounts only one event which is ostensibly intended to reveal Theodore's character and loyalty towards his brother and the legitimate emperor, John V. This event dates from the time when the despot was living in Constantinople and took

---

[87] Examples of concluding remarks are frequent: ibid. 159.19: 'These are the facts and they are known in many corners of the world'; 199.12: 'Such was the enemy and such were his schemes'; 127.34: 'Enough!'
[88] Ibid. 197.15.
[89] Ibid. 109.6–7: 'Our speech must proceed to succeeding events.'
[90] Ibid. 109.4–5: 'these two instances have revealed what sort of man he was to his parents, to us and to the other members of his family'.
[91] Ibid. 109.8–9: 'our speech must proceed to succeeding events touching only on a few of those which have the power to reveal his virtue'.

part in the dynastic conflict in which Andronikos IV rose against his father and the rest of the family over the succession to the Byzantine throne.[92] On this occasion, Manuel provides numerous details regarding the actors in the rebellion, which took place between 1376 and 1379, when members of the Palaiologan ruling family were imprisoned.[93]

Given this type of information, the story included in the ἐπιτηδεύματα section, with its emphasis on Theodore's character, functions as a preamble to the following chapter, which unfolds the narrative of the despot's πράξεις during his rule in the Morea. The narrative does not cover the whole spectrum of the complicated political implications of his local rule, but is limited to a discussion of several landmark moments for the Byzantine state: the pacification of the region in the first years of Palaiologan rule by diplomatic and military actions; the rising power of the Ottomans, who were beginning to pose a threat to the fragile despotate of Morea; and the sale of several strongholds to the Knights Hospitaller, with the aim of protecting these from a potential Ottoman attack. Owing to this selection of events, it appears that Manuel designed a linear story, an epic where the element that matters appears to be the exemplarity of the hero: Theodore leaves the embattled city of Constantinople and arrives in the Morea with a mission to reassert Byzantine control over a region where Latins and local lords have already created an autonomous provincial political order. This initial moment is signalled in 101.1: 'Our troubles had piled up and the disasters of our misfortune had reached the climax.'[94] Following this story line, after two decades of military efforts punctuated by victories and defeats, the Peloponnese seems indeed to have returned to stability. Again, the moment of the happy ending is marked in the text even if it coincides with the despot's death: 'So a lasting peace was signed' (καὶ δὴ σπονδῶν γενομένων ἰσχυροτάτων).[95]

Based on these statements, the narrator seems to have envisioned an action progressing from an unfortunate situation to a more favourable state of affairs under the beneficial influence of Theodore's virtuous deeds. Surprisingly enough, these commencing and concluding remarks do not mention Theodore, suggesting that what matters for the narrator from the beginning is the progress of a sequence of episodes and not primarily the development of characters. Such a linear story thread rather resembles a historian's approach,

---

[92] Barker, *Manuel II*, 24–50.
[93] *Funeral Oration*, 101.1–103.9.
[94] See also the initial statement in the section dedicated to the situation of the Morea; ibid. 111.4: 'The situation in the Peloponnese was grave.'
[95] Ibid. 207.5.

and yet Manuel was, above all, an experienced public speaker who, constrained by the *kairos* of the speech, has to keep story and heroic portrait in balance. An answer to this question can be provided if we look not only at the episodes themselves but also at the messages and representations at stake, which may help us understand the specificities of a rhetorician's approach to historical information.

As previously indicated, three issues seem to matter in this story: the representation of Theodore as an arduous military leader and skilled diplomat; the fashioning of Manuel's self-image as capable ruler of the Byzantine state; and the very recent history of the despotate of Morea as part of the Byzantine state. For each of these aspects, the author creates a different narrative strand or plot, with the result that they provide a multilayered account where the different representations of the protagonist, the emperor and the historical province of Morea, while autonomous to a certain extent, often mirror each other.[96]

Naturally, the most extensively documented of these three narrative strands of the *Funeral Oration* follows the trajectory of Theodore's achievements. As protagonist of all four major episodes he remains in the narrator's focus. Manuel outlines his profile in the laudatory preamble, where he describes Theodore as an educated and generous brother.[97] These virtues are then echoed in the closure of the plot the author builds around Theodore's personality. Yet while usually in panegyrics or *epitaphioi* the individual episodes are presented under specific headings revealing categories of virtues, moral or physical, Manuel does not attach his brother's virtues to particular episodes. After the proem, the plot follows the steps of Theodore's early career in Constantinople. The first major event in his life, as Manuel recounts it, was the rebellion of Andronikos backed by the Genoese. During the rebellion, Theodore had to leave Constantinople and take up office as despot in Thessalonike. Yet the despot-to-be did not want to leave his brother in prison and chose to stay against the will of the father-emperor. It is at this point that the plot constructed around Theodore's personality intersects with Manuel's plot of fashioning an imperial image, as the emperor suddenly shifts the narrative focus from the despot to himself.

A brief outline of each of the three narrative strands may make for a better understanding of their connections as well as their points of departure or closure.

Outline of Theodore's narrative
111.4–16: Theodore is appointed despot of the Morea but delays his travel to the province because his mother is in captivity.

---

[96] For an overview of theoretical approaches to story and plot, see Abbott, 'Story, plot, and narration', 39–50.
[97] *Funeral Oration*, 95.13.

113.15–16: Theodore arrives in the Peloponnese with the approval of his mother, father and Manuel himself.

115.24–7: Theodore is warmly received by the locals in the Morea.

117.2–30: Theodore meets resistance from the local *archontes*.

135.30–1: At Bayezid's request, the despot goes to Serres. There, he meets his brother Manuel and other Byzantine leaders.

147.9–25: Theodore agrees to surrender Monemvasia and Argos to the Ottomans.

149.9–11: Theodore sends letters approving the Ottoman occupation of Argos.

149.12–20: With the approval of other legates, Theodore secretly sends his trusted men to slow down the surrender of Argos.

149.24–151.18: Theodore flees Bayezid's camp near the river Spercheios and marches to Argos in order to arrive there before the Ottomans.

167.9–12: Back in the Peloponnese, Theodore conceals his plans of safeguarding the despotate.

181.3–30: Theodore initiates secret negotiations with the Knights Hospitaller regarding the cession of certain Byzantine strongholds.

183.10–12: Theodore invites the Hospitallers from Rhodes and reaches an agreement with them.

185.3–4: Theodore assumes that the benefits of his plan will be understood by the rest of the Moreotes.

197.28–31: Confronted with growing discontent regarding his decision to sell the cities to the Hospitallers, the despot tries to persuade his supporters that this action was appropriate.

199.13–33: Following agreement with the Hospitallers, Theodore signs a peace treaty with the Ottomans.

207.17–22: Closure: 'it is true that at first the difficulties came upon him suddenly and often with violence. For his virtues, God's reward came in the form of great success.'

While reporting on Theodore's actions, the narrator gradually builds another, parallel narrative strand that traces the emperor's direct involvement in the internal affairs of the Morea. Once Theodore has left the city for the remote province of the Peloponnese, Manuel wishes to project the image of a ruler concerned with the well-being of other parts of his empire.[98] Moreover, in terms of character status, Manuel presents himself not in a minor role or as

---

[98] His involvement in the affairs of the Morea finds expression in his sole preserved letter addressed to Theodore. Manuel recommends Kananos for a position close to Theodore in the Morea, after Kananos supported the emperor against John VII: Manuel II, *Letters*, no. 13.34–6, ed. Dennis.

a helper, a position which he assigns to the Knights Hospitaller, but rather as another protagonist.[99]

Outline of Manuel's narrative

113.15–16: Manuel together with his father approves of Theodore's appointment as despot.

135.4–5: Summoned by Bayezid, Manuel arrives in Serres, where he meets Theodore.

139.14–16: While Manuel is in Serres, his nephew, John VII, enters Constantinople, thus threatening the stability of the empire. In addition, John VII receives Bayezid's support.

149.16: Manuel is one of the few whom Theodore informs about his intention to simulate the surrender of Argos.

163.2–165.9: Manuel presents himself as Theodore's only hope at a time when Ottoman pressures are increasing. However, the emperor is unable to help his brother, for he is away travelling in search of military support against the same Ottomans. Due to the difficulties encounters during his voyage, he limits himself to advertising his brother's difficulties in asserting his authority in the region.

167.19: Manuel consents to the cession of Corinth to the Knights Hospitaller.

171.27–30: Closure: Manuel consents to Theodore's invitation to the Hospitallers to defend Byzantine fortresses. He connects the beneficial intervention of the Hospitallers with the support received from them during his conflicts with John VII.

These two narrative strands which often run in parallel, of Theodore and of his brother the emperor, are connected by a common theme: the plan to bring peace to the Byzantine Morea. These two threads are further framed by another narrative strand, that of a brief history of the Morea in the late fourteenth century.[100] Thus, when at the outset of the story Manuel states that his wish is to speak of things in general rather than of individuals,[101] he turns his attention to the big picture, that is, the situation of the Morea. The same strategy emerges in the conclusion of the section on Theodore's πράξεις, where the emperor shifts the focus from his brother to the context of the Peloponnesian peninsula.[102] In the same passage, by identifying the Morea with his audience of Moreotes, the narrator emphasises the role of the

---

[99] On the theory of narrative characters, including the position of the helper in relation to the opponents and the protagonist, see Greimas, *Structural Semantics*, 207.
[100] On framing in narratives see Altman, *Theory of Narrative*, 17.
[101] *Funeral Oration*, 129.7–9.
[102] Ibid. 211.13–14.

community in his story: 'I refer to the animate and rational Peloponnese, indeed to you gentlemen whose integrity of character has preserved a monument in everlasting honor of him.'[103]

This statement, which converts the primary audience into participants in the story, is of a piece with the rest of the text, which discusses the various aspects shaping the history of this Byzantine province: the situation on the ground before Theodore's arrival,[104] factors influencing the interior and exterior affairs of the despotate, and even the ideological implications of actions like the alliance with the Knights Hospitaller. Thus, arguably, the narrative strand which reveals the history of the Morea consists of a series of interconnected narratorial snippets integrated into a chronological sequence centred on a confrontation between the Byzantines and their enemies. The outline of this plot provides a picture of how these episodes combine.

Outline of the Morea narrative

115.7–10: The Peloponnese had initially suffered losses due to Kantakouzenos's rebellion. Pelops's land has been utterly destroyed (κατετρίβετο).

119.3–5: Kantakouzenos's death brings peace to the peninsula.

119.12–25: With Theodore's approval, ten thousand Illyrians settle in the mountainous regions of the peninsula for reasons of defence.

133.6–12: Background information concerning the situation in the Peloponnese before Theodore's arrival: the local Byzantine *archontes* allied with the Ottomans and controlled the peninsula.

133.13–24: Stalemate in the Ottomans' schemes to invade the peninsula and possibilities for Ottoman action.

135.2: Bayezid's plans to eliminate the Byzantine leaders by summoning them all to Serres has direct implications for the situation in the Morea.

- 141.6: The sultan orders a eunuch to kill the Byzantine lords.
- 141.15: Bayezid tortures second-rank officials.
- 141.20: Bayezid sends Manuel home in order to detain Theodore afterwards.
- 143.6: Bayezid moves southward. He passes through Macedonia and Thessaly and camps in central Greece.
- 143.13: Omur, one of Bayezid's generals, is sent to demand Argos and other places in the Peloponnese. Monemvasia and the neighbouring villages had already been occupied.

---

[103] Ibid. 213.4–6.
[104] Ibid. 111.4: εἶχε τὰ πράγματα κακῶς τῇ Πελοποννήσῳ, ('the situation in the Peloponnese was grave').

153.3–6: Theodore's escape from Bayezid's trap triggers a series of fortunate events in the Peloponnese and beyond, especially in Attica.

157.2–19: In the aftermath of Theodore's flight, Bayezid tries to minimise this personal defeat and retreats. During the retreat he plunders Thrace and sends an army against Theodore.

157.23–159.17: The Peloponnesians besiege the Ottoman possessions in the region close to the Isthmus of Corinth. In their turn, the Ottomans receive help not only from the sultan's army but also from many local Byzantines.

161.17–29: A group of local Byzantines sides with the Ottomans.

167.14–20: The Hospitallers enter the plan to defend the peninsula from the Turks. They have been already present in the region when they undertook the defence of Corinth.

177.24–179.2: Negotiations for the sale of Moreote strongholds to the Hospitallers.

185.5: Claiming that not all the details of the deal between Theodore and the Hospitallers have been revealed publicly, certain Moreotes express disagreement.

187.4–9: The Byzantines' alliance with the Hospitallers prompts the sultan to give up his plans of conquest.

193.33–195.2: In the meantime, the international political context makes the situation in the Peloponnese worse.[105]

203.23–30: Locals attack the strongholds now held by the Hospitallers, unaware of Theodore's designs.

203.30–205.14: The attacks on the Hospitallers stop. A peace treaty is signed between the Byzantines and the Hospitallers.

207.1–7: Following the conclusion of this last conflict between the Moreotes and the Knights, the Ottomans offer Theodore a truce. They only demand that the Hospitallers should go back to Rhodes, in their territories: 'A lasting peace is signed and he brought the war to an end to your considerable glory.'

209.11–211.1: Closure: The Hospitallers hand the Moreote strongholds back to the Byzantines. The whole business is achieved honourably (ὑγιῶς) and without further conflicts.

---

[105] 'For the enemy possessed a great force, coupled with a hostile disposition and a crafty mind, while all the Albanians, Bulgars and Serbs were already conquered and a great army had been routed at Nicopolis. I refer to the army assembled by the Hungarians, Germans, and western Franks whose names alone were sufficient to make the barbarians shudder. However our allies failed.'

So much for the three narrative strands brought together in the account of Theodore's achievements. The author's strategy of combining these details in a multilayered account of the history of the region is further substantiated at other levels of the rubrics of ἐπιτηδεύματα and πράξεις: the representation of the narratees, style, characters and motivation of actions. First, the author envisages his audience not only as listeners to his oration but also in terms of intradiegetic narratees; that is to say, they are often represented not only as active listeners but also as characters internal to the account.[106]

It is the oration's prologue that first addresses the narratees and establishes a parallelism between the emperor's attitude and his audience: they were both hit hard by the calamity of Theodore's death. Manuel notes the 'tears, laments, and all the other signs of mourning'.[107] He mentions that the wish and even the reproaches of the listeners 'who have received benefits from the hands of this greatly mourned man' became the main reason for the delivery of the commemorative oration.[108] This paragraph, as well as the following ones pointing to Manuel's reasons for performing his brotherly duties, creates familiarity between the author and the listeners. Moreover, direct address effaces hierarchical differences:

> I ask you to forgive me, for his loss has left me half-dead and I have scarcely the strength to accomplish what you would welcome.[109]

If this first conventional contact with the audience takes place in the προοίμιον, it is noticeable that Manuel continuously engages with his audience.[110] Direct address is used not only to reinforce familiarity, but also more specifically to create a consensus between those present and the speaker, as happens when explaining Theodore's intricate plan to involve the Hospitallers in Moreote affairs: 'Are there any among us who object to the stage and the mask?'[111]

This active engagement with his audience emerges in other instances as well, owing to the fact that most probably among those to whom the oration

---

[106] In narrative theory the narratees are defined as the primary audience of the narrator, and distinct from the actual reader. See Herman, *Cambridge Companion to Narrative*, 279.
[107] *Funeral Oration*, 75.16–17.
[108] Ibid. 75.10, 75.12–14.
[109] Ibid. 77.2.
[110] He has in mind both listeners and readers, Ibid. 249.32: 'I do not feel that I have made a fitting conclusion. I ask forgiveness for my inadequacy from those of you present here and from those who might by chance at some time read this oration.'
[111] Ibid. 189.7.

was addressed there were also many of Theodore's collaborators.[112] Manuel gives his audience credit for the knowledge of many events in which Theodore was involved and of the reasons for his choices. This again can be regarded as a rhetorical strategy, but its frequent use indicates that there existed a certain 'intimacy' between the speaker and his listeners, an intimacy which eventually, in the epilogue, is substantiated by his engagement in a real dialogue with the listeners.[113]

Yet the fact that Manuel sets out a series of events as already known by the audience, while constantly refreshing his audience's memory, generates a series of interesting implications. Given the fact that the narratees most probably know all the details of Theodore's activities in the Morea, there is only one element which the emperor can add to this knowledge, namely a slightly different explanation but, at the same time, the official account of already-known events. Furthermore, this shared knowledge of events, as well as the interests of both the despot and the listeners, prompts the emperor to represent the narratees as agents of historical change and individuals who shared similar ideals:

> You had a deep longing for peace even though there seemed very little likelihood of it. You obtained a full peace, far better than that previously enjoyed and bringing with it considerable prestige.[114]

In other instances, the narratees' representation as responsible participants in the events affecting the region is reinforced by questions which, albeit posed in a rhetorical fashion, are intended to establish the correctness of Theodore's course of action:

> What just grounds for complaint, then, did he give his accusers? Would it be easy for any of his slanderers to draw on their usual repertoire? [...] Would it not sew up any mouth whose only use was continually to speak foolishly? Were not his achievements full of common-sense, probity, and knowledge of statecraft (πολιτικὴ ἐπιστήμη)?[115]

These observations on the narratees' role allow us to make further observations regarding the strategy the emperor employs here: thus, first, he establishes emotional contact with the listeners, who in any event have been playing

---

[112] See above, Isidore's letter addressed to Manuel.
[113] *Funeral Oration*, 235.20.
[114] Ibid. 187.23–189.6.
[115] Ibid. 197.17–25.

a key role in regional politics and in the Byzantine landscape. At the following level, he concedes an extensive knowledge of events on which an official interpretation is superimposed. And finally, based on this already-established familiarity, the author seems to build in the following sections a certain sense of community of knowledge and action.

Second, at the stylistic level, the use of paratactic style as a marker of fast developing action is notable. Parataxis, backed up with the use of the historic present and of rhetorical questions, is most visible in the episode of the sale of Corinth, when the speed of the developing action prompts Manuel to compare it to a dramatic act, a δρᾶμα.[116] Apart from adding an original element to his narrative technique,[117] the persistent use of theatrical terminology in this final section of Theodore's πράξεις[118] adds further meaning to the entire story: Manuel describes not only his brother's drama but something more significant: the dramatic and rapidly changing course of the history of the Morea. Another feature of Manuel's style emerges in the heavy use of rhetorical questions.

Third, at the level of characters, the dramatic conflict is built on the basis of a tripartite scheme of typological actors: hero/protagonist – enemy – helper.[119] These typological distinctions reflected the late Byzantine principles of imperial ideology and conduct in foreign affairs. It is the reason why, in constructing his characters, Manuel privileges explicit instead of implicit characterisation and cultivates ideas like dynastic excellence in ruling, Ottoman barbarity in customs and the Latins' similarity of religious belief. However, ambiguities are not absent from the story, as the author plays with the features of a hero-protagonist, which Manuel undertakes when referring to his own actions in the Peloponnese.

For obvious reasons, Theodore stands as the most elaborated character, an incarnation of perfect moral and military duty. Emerging as Manuel's character doublet, he strikes a balance between the justice he shows to all social groups and loyalty to his family, especially his parents.

---

[116] Ibid. 181.27–8: 'But I am compelled to speak more clearly (σαφέστερον), as far as I am able, and in the course of my narrative to set out step by step the account of the circumstances surrounding this particular undertaking.'

[117] At one point the entire development of events is likened to a theatrical representation: ibid. 187.1–2: ταῦτα [. . .] τελευτήσειν εἰς ἀγαθὸν τὸ δρᾶμα ('his drama would have a happy ending').

[118] There are numerous allusions to dramatic acts: ibid. 167.12: τὸ δρᾶμα δηλώσομεν; 185.3–4; 185.6: ἐν ἀγνοίᾳ τοῦ δράματος; 187.1–2: ταῦτα [. . .] τελευτήσειν εἰς ἀγαθὸν τὸ δρᾶμα; 187.11: τὸ δὲ δρᾶμα ὕμνητο καὶ ἡ σοφία τοῦ ποιήσαντος; 191.5: δηλονότι τὸ ἡμέτερον τοῦτο δρᾶμα ἄριστα μὲν διανοηθέν; 189.7: σκηνὴ καὶ προσωπεῖον; 193.14: οὐδὲ δράματι καθαρῶς ἔοικε τουτὶ τοὔργον; 193.25: τοῦ δράματος ἕνεκα.

[119] Herman, *Cambridge Companion to Narrative*, 607–40, 66–79.

Most often, Theodore's virtues are discussed in connection with his actions in service of the Peloponnesian community.[120] His care for the community's well-being takes the form of martyrdom:

> Indeed of his own free will he became a martyr and surrendered himself for the sake of the many, and endangered himself and went through painful experiences and suffered ignominy.[121]

Owing to the narrative outlook, the common comparisons with biblical and classical models are rarely used. David is mentioned only once,[122] as is Odysseus.[123] Far more developed are the instances stressing the despot's power of reasoning, which further supports his characterisation as a ruler capable of conducting complex negotiations:

> He was possessed of powers of reasoning which would have befitted men like Plato or Alexander, he was a father to you, a friend, a teacher, a provider, a guardian, a ruler, one who while he lived both in action and in name admirably acted as physician, shepherd, steersman and in many other roles which succor men and improve situations and, in short, lacked no virtue.[124]

Likewise, Theodore's representation as a politician who calculates with practical wisdom,[125] and who acts only according to his vision, has a particular thrust:

> But he was not like those people who perceive only what is before their eyes. On the contrary more than any other man he looked ahead into the future and continually took care of everything.[126]

To a large extent, Theodore's heroic portrayal relies on his conflicts with a multifarious enemy. His brother, Andronikos IV, the first antagonistic figure in

---

[120] *Funeral Oration*, 187.14–15: 'and it was a pleasure to see the rejoicing Despot among the rejoicing subjects'.
[121] Ibid. 155.6–7.
[122] Ibid. 113.13.
[123] Ibid. 145.24–6: 'this new Odysseus the ever good and inventive man had experienced many and various wanderings'.
[124] Ibid. 135.24–7.
[125] Ibid. 179.22–3: πλήρης φρονήσεως; 203.28–9: φρόνησις, ἐμπειρία περὶ τὰ πολιτικὰ, ἐπιστήμη. At 181.3–30 the negotiations for the sale of the despotate reveal that Theodore took into consideration all political factors, both internal (the discontent of the local population) and external (the rise of the Ottomans).
[126] Ibid. 171.5–8.

the story, receives brief treatment, despite the fact that his rebellion had dire consequences for Byzantium. It is possible that the narrator wants to retain a certain consistency in cultivating the idea of the perfection of the ruling family. It is also possible that Manuel feared that the insistence on Andronikos's rebellion would prompt the audience to think of similarities with his own rebellion in Thessalonike (1382–7).

Another major enemy character is Matthew Kantakouzenos's son who opposed Theodore upon his arrival in the Morea. Yet his portrait is far from monotone and includes several ambiguities, perhaps again due to Manuel's hesitations to throw a negative light on his mother's family:

> In a word, though his courage may have been misplaced and he fought for an unjust cause, in other respects he was not ignoble and he had a subtle and infinitely resourceful mind.[127]

Also among the enemies, one should include the Byzantine deserter *archontes*. They are represented in dark tones as opposing the legitimate central authority, in a way that makes them seem much more dangerous than other adversaries.[128] The arguments against the local elite have mainly religious grounds. Manuel is surprised that Orthodox Christians questioned the authority of the state[129] and, most of all, they are disparaged for allying with the pagan Ottomans:

> There were a number of individuals not all of whom belonged to the common people or were considered to be of low rank who joined the enemy [. . .] They became for us an incurable calamity. I do not know what you would call them: Romans and Christians on account of their race and baptism, or the opposite because of their choice and actions?[130]

Yet the character who receives by far the most detailed representation as an enemy is Bayezid. At many points in the narrative, the narrator heaps long series of negative epithets upon him. Previously Manuel's lord, Bayezid is constructed here as Theodore's main opponent. In stark contrast to Theodore's encomium, Bayezid's portray stands as a virulent *psogos*. Manuel was fully aware of his intentions and methods from the time of the exile in Asia Minor

---

[127] Ibid. 117.23–5.
[128] Ibid. 125.22–127.30: 'But what is worse certain noblemen, who against all decency were against us were found among the prisoners.'
[129] Ibid. 131.16: 'It was impossible for them to preserve their confession and faith in Christ inviolate. Why? Because in their union with Christ they promised absolute loyalty to him and enmity against the demons and yet afterwards they did the opposite.'
[130] Ibid. 161.17–29.

and from the six-year siege of Constantinople. First, the sultan is scolded for being of a different religion;[131] from this position he stands as the 'agent of Satan' (ὁ τῷ Σατὰν ὑπηρετούμενος),[132] an Αἰθίοψ,[133] since he could not tolerate a Christian ruler.[134] Second, he is an immoral and essentially weak ruler, 'a schemer of deceit by nature'[135] and fearful of Latins.[136] Third, Manuel reprimands him for his barbarity, and from this point of view he is the σατράπης,[137] the ruler of Asia,[138] a Persian tyrant (τὸν τύρραννον Πέρσην)[139] and a barbarian (τὸν βάρβαρον);[140] unlike Theodore, he cannot control his anger.[141] Fourth and most frequently, Bayezid is described as a savage beast[142] or as a negative character from Greek mythology. Thus, he acts like a snake (ὄφιν ἐκεῖνον),[143] a δράκων (serpent),[144] a gaping beast (τὸν κεχηνόντα θῆρα);[145] 'he put on a sheepskin though he was a downright wolf'[146] and, by donning the skin of a lion or a fox, he exchanged the one for the other;[147] he had an innate ferocity (ἔμφυτος θηριωδία);[148] 'this most hostile monster attacked our possessions and, according to the habit of swine when they sharpen their fangs, he goaded them on and was, in turn, urged on by them'.[149] 'In his heart, he was a Cyclop with impiety instead of blindness, shamelessness instead of a cave. Indeed the sultan was a shepherd, but not of sheep like those of the Cyclop but of men who did not differ from beasts';[150] in addition, he was 'the man whose jaws gaped like Hades, who desired to swallow us all up

---

[131] Trapp counts the passage in the *Funeral Oration*, 128–31, as a part of the polemic between Christians and Muslims; Trapp, 'Quelques textes', 448–9.
[132] *Funeral Oration*, 135.5.
[133] Ibid. 141.15.
[134] Ibid. 127.32.
[135] Ibid. 135.6.
[136] Ibid. 185.20.
[137] Ibid. 135.30
[138] Ibid. 127.31.
[139] Ibid. 153.7.
[140] Ibid. 197.25.
[141] Ibid. 157.19.
[142] This is also a general description of all the enemies, e.g. ibid. 127.22–5: εἰς τοὺς ἐχθροὺς καὶ μετὰ τῶν λύκων γενομένων.
[143] Ibid. 187.2.
[144] Ibid. 149.6.
[145] Ibid. 153.21.
[146] Ibid. 209.4
[147] Ibid. 135.8.
[148] Ibid. 197.13–14.
[149] Ibid. 127.33–4.
[150] Ibid. 145.3–6.

in them'.¹⁵¹ Eventually, when Bayezid is deceived by Theodore, Manuel represents him as a tamed creature:

> Having changed from a wild beast into a bleating lamb, he who previously howled fiercer than the wolves now looked like a tamed wild beast.¹⁵²

The final typological character present in the oration, the *helper*, just as in the case of the *enemy*, takes a variety of forms, even if they only have a meteoric appearance. The first helpers in chronological order are Theodore's parents: his mother, Helena, is described as a political counsellor close to Manuel. For instance, she knows and approves of Theodore's plan to flee Bayezid's camp and to sell the city of Corinth. His father, John V, is pictured in more ambiguous terms. Apart from several favourable references in the section dedicated to Theodore's nobility of family and in the narrative,¹⁵³ the senior emperor is present in a sole episode, that of Andronikos IV's rebellion. On the other hand, his absence from the following episodes speaks volumes. For the first ten years of Theodore's despotate in the Morea, John V was alive, active as ruler of the state, and surely aware of the implications of his son's activities in the Morea. We do not know to what extent he controlled the course of the policy in this region. What is known is that during the 1380s he had a conflict with Manuel, who disobeyed his father and proclaimed himself ruler of Thessalonike. Hence probably emerged this representation of John V. Thus, at one point during Andronikos's putsch, the emperor, his wife and Manuel himself decide that Theodore should get out of prison and go to Thessalonike as despot. But soon thereafter John changes his mind, and this seems to be presented rather as a weakness, as it occurs in the very last moment of the preparations.¹⁵⁴ Even if Manuel concedes that this change of plan was due to his own illness and Theodore's wish to help his brother, he also emphasises that the alternative of letting Theodore out of prison was better.¹⁵⁵

Still, the helpers par excellence seem to be the Knights Hospitaller. The first encounter with them occurs in 167.14–20. Manuel forges a positive

---

[151] Ibid. 139.4–6.
[152] Ibid. 155.24–6.
[153] Ibid. in the εὐγένεια section and in 113.24–6: 'he was sent forth most excellently fortified and supported by his father's and indeed also by his mother's and everybody's prayers'.
[154] Ibid. 101.7–10.
[155] Theodore himself seems to have been against this decision, which the author outlines in quite strong language: ibid. 103.4–5: 'So he [Theodore] sat with his eyes fixed on the ground, thinking of a cruel executioner [i.e. John].'

image of the Knights, in contrast with the previous negative traits ascribed to the Latins' activities in the region:

> There was a community in Rhodes composed of men who had vowed to the Saviour chastity, obedience and poverty and who had also promised to fight those who strove against the Cross, and they were accustomed to bear the sign of the Cross on their clothes, weapons, and flags.

As can be seen from the passage just quoted, in the Hospitallers' case, Christian faith played a crucial role in choosing them as allies. Thus, they are friends and Christians (φίλοι καὶ χριστιανοί),[156] they keep their vows to stand by their faith[157] and 'would give all their wealth to achieve great deeds for the glory of Christ'.[158] Their declared intention to occupy the entire Peloponnese was motivated by their will to defend the Christian faith in the Mediterranean, where they had already expanded their sway. In addition to representing a fearsome military force,[159] the Hospitallers, unlike other Latin peoples, were 'well disposed toward Byzantium'.[160]

Despite these positive characteristics, ambiguity persists in the portrayal of the Knights Hospitaller. One must never forget, Manuel says, that they were Latins, and that their friendship was rather circumstantial. Thus, eventually they are pictured as the least oppressive solution to the Morea's problems,[161] while they seem to have caused trouble in the region:

> It seems to me that I have been incorrect in describing them as helpers and saviours. Even if the people of the Peloponnese preferred the Hospitallers [. . .], yet they could hardly be called 'saviours and helpers' if they only delivered us from the enemy's yoke to place us against our will under their power.[162]

Not only do the Ottomans and local landlords opposed to Theodore receive extremely negative characterisations, but even the Hospitallers, who seem to play the role of the protagonist's helper, in the end are slightly criticised on ethnic grounds.[163]

---

[156] Ibid. 171.1–25.
[157] Ibid. 169.13–15, 175.6.
[158] Ibid. 175.7–21.
[159] Ibid. 185.28–30: 'it was rather that Bayezid feared that the Hospitallers, who were stronger than we were might harm the adjacent cities to the Peloponnese'.
[160] Ibid. 169.1.
[161] Ibid. 195.31–2: κακῶν γὰρ δὴ προκειμένων τὸ μὴ χεῖρον βέλτιον.
[162] Ibid. 199.33–5.
[163] Ibid. 177.1–4: 'occasionally, on a small pretext they recklessly set themselves in motion and once they start it is hard to hold them'.

Fourth, at the thematic level, the author inserts proleptic enunciations and provides elaborate justifications of the eventful history of the peninsula,[164] elements which introduce a sense of unity to the account. Thus, Manuel's narrative does not always look back to past events but also anticipates actions by projecting the image of brighter times for the Peloponnese. Occasionally, the narrator includes prolepses indicating a better course of events or pinpointing possible alternative actions. For instance, the alliance with the Hospitallers allowed for an interval of peace and of planning for future times:

> And this is what makes us hope that one day good fortune may change and desert them (i.e. the Ottomans), siding with us, as it did in the days of our forefathers.[165]

Motivation for actions covers a large section of the oration as it supports the enunciation of various political options. It takes a multitude of forms, from the utter vilification of the enemies of the Morea to complex lines of argumentation which occupy long paragraphs of text.[166] More detailed argumentation, which finds an echo in judicial oratory, is provided in two different cases: the settlement of Albanian immigrants in the Peloponnese,[167] and the invitation addressed to the Knights Hospitaller to undertake the defence operations of strategic military outposts in the peninsula.[168]

---

[164] With regard to Manuel's style of argumentation, Chrysostomides noticed the humanist terms, the clarity and the originality; in *Funeral Oration*, 27. See also Isidore of Kiev: 'therefore, some celebrated the harmony of your words (ὀνομάτων ὥραν), your style (τὴν συνθήκην τῶν λέξεων), the beauty of your expression (τὸ τῆς φράσεως κάλλος), and the order of the arguments (τὴν τάξιν τῶν ἐπιχειρημάτων)'; Isidore of Kiev, *Letters*, no. 67.17–19, ed. Regel.
[165] *Funeral Oration*, 161.5.
[166] On the uses of motivation in narrative see Herman, *Cambridge Companion to Narrative*, 65.
[167] Manuel inserts this episode after describing the situation prior to Theodore's arrival as desperate. The 'Illyrian' immigration is presented as a fortunate and unique event, despite the fact that it was opposed by a large part of the indigenous population. On early Albanian settlers in the Peloponnese, see Vranoussi, 'Deux documents'. The argumentation for the appropriateness of Theodore's consent with regard to the foreigners' settlements is supported by the Albanians' inherent ethnic virtues: they are skilled warriors and always keep to their oaths (*Funeral Oration*, 123.4–7).
[168] The emperor opens his argumentation by presenting the background of the situation, noting that, by that time, the Ottomans were plundering continental Greece. Then he lists three major arguments for the alliance with the Hospitallers: the general unfavourable situation not only in Byzantium but also in the West (*Funeral Oration*, 193.33–195.2); the Ottomans' fear of the Hospitallers; and the Hospitallers' ramifications and good connections in the Western world (ibid. 167.21–173.28). These arguments coincided with Theodore's arguments for selling the despotate (ibid. 197.14).

Finally, a considerable number of references to the emperor's narrative emerge in texts penned by contemporary authors. In their prefatory texts Plethon and Joasaph the monk remark the inclusion of numerous details pertaining to Theodore's actions.[169] Yet the most elaborate comments pertaining to the emperor's narrative treatment of an encomium belong to Manuel Chrysoloras. In his extensive *Epistolary Oration*, he notes the novel approach introduced by the emperor in treating the topic of his brother's death.[170] According to the emperor's ambassador, the praise of the deceased person must rely on the deep knowledge of details in the life of the individual eulogised:

> It is necessary that he (the speaker) is knowledgeable of the life and deeds of those whom he praises. For if one praised another for his military or political deeds, but the one praised were neither a general nor a political man, he would say nothing in accordance with his deeds.[171]

Chrysoloras also underlines the importance of history in the *Funeral Oration*:

> And it is possible to find history in this text as well as accounts of the lives of men; most of the oration deals with such topics. In addition, there is praise and narrative of these, as well rebuking of evil deeds. And there we learn about directions and regulations and about the government and we witness wars and military actions.[172]

The catalogue of literary achievements also includes a small section on the narrative:

> That he deals well with the narrative accounts, with the antitheses and the refutations; that he was familiar with the examples and the changes in actions and the resemblances. And for each of his well-shaped statements, he offered many explanations and arguments.

Following these general observations Chrysoloras often notes that the author made use of detailed narratives in his praise for Theodore:

> Since the topics of the speech often required a narrative approach, you spoke about this one <Theodore> in much detail.

---

[169] See Appendix 3.
[170] Manuel Chrysoloras, *Epistolary Oration*, 61.7–9, ed. Patrineles and Sophianos: σὺ τοίνυν, ὥς περ καὶ ἄλλα πολλὰ καλὰ τῶν παλαιῶν, καὶ τὸ βασιλεὺς δὲ καὶ στρατηγὸς οὕτω καλῶς δύνασθαι λέγειν καὶ τοῦτο ἀνεκαίνισας.
[171] Ibid. 66.5–9.
[172] Ibid. 71.10.

Chrysoloras also praises Manuel for not mixing features of monodies into an *epitaphios* and notes that other authors did so wrongly.[173] Finally, he tries to explain the selection of facts employed by Manuel[174] and emphasises that the author praised his brother by looking at his brother's actions.[175]

Authorial Voice

I will end my discussion of the *Funeral Oration* with several observations on the authorial voice adopted here. As in the other texts analysed so far, here as well the author's individuality is strongly represented. Arguably, as the analysis of the different plots has shown, Manuel adapts the genre of the *epitaphioi* to his needs and introduces numerous elements of self-portrayal by representing himself in various ways, and especially as narrator and actor in the events of Moreote history. These roles that Manuel incarnates when writing the text were also noted by Manuel Chrysoloras in his commentary:

> You fulfilled your task in many ways. First, as a brother to a brother, second, as a good ruler to a just ruler, third, as a virtuous individual to someone who is striving eagerly to acquire virtue, and finally as a lord and emperor towards someone who made no little effort for the defence of his country and nation.[176]

A further mark of this adaptation, the dichotomy between plain praise for the brother and a biased account of the state of affairs in the Morea, which

---

[173] Ibid. 75.28–30: ἀλλ' οὐδὲ σοὶ ἔπρεπεν, ὅπερ ἐν τοῖς τοιούτοις οἱ πολλοὶ ποιοῦσι, γυναικείας οἰμωγὰς καὶ ὀλολυγὰς μιμεῖσθαι καὶ διὰ τοῦτο, ἐπεὶ κατὰ τὸν μονωδιῶν νόμον.

[174] Ibid. 80.25: ἀλλὰ πολλὰ τῶν μεγάλων καὶ ἃ μόνα ἄλλοις ἂν ἤρκεσεν ἀσμένως εἰπεῖν, ἑκὼν παρέλιπες ὑπὸ μεγαλοψυχίας· καὶ εἴρηκας δὲ μὴ πάντα δεῖν λέγειν ἐφεξῆς, καλῶς τοῦτο λέγων. ἐκεῖνο μὲν γὰρ πένησι συμβαίνει λόγοις· πενίας γὰρ ἐν πᾶσι τὸ ἀκριβολογεῖσθαι καὶ μέχρι τῶν σμικροτάτων παρεκλέγειν, ὅταν ἀπὸ λυπρῶν καὶ ὀλίγων τί ποιεῖν βουλώμεθα. ὅταν δὲ ἀφθόνοις ἔχωμεν τοῖς ὑποκειμένοις χρῆσθαι, ἔστι τὰ μὲν παραλαμβάνειν, τὰ δὲ τουτων καὶ ἀπορρίπτειν, ἔστιν ὅτε καὶ αὐτὰ μεγάλα, μηδὲν σμικρολογούμενον.

[175] Ibid. 83.2: καὶ πολλὰ δὲ χρήσιμα ἐπὶ τοῦ ἀνθρωπίνου βίου, τοῦτο μὲν πρὸς τύχην, τοῦτο δὲ πρὸς ἦθος καὶ ἀρετήν, οὐ καθόλου μόνον ἀλλὰ καὶ καταμέρος, τοῦτο δὲ πρὸς ἐπιτηδεύματα καὶ πράξεις τούτους ἐπ' αὐτῶν τῶν πράξεων ἐμφαίνειν.

[176] Ibid. 99.18. Furthermore, according to Chrysoloras, Theodore saw Manuel as his teacher and master: ἄλλως γὰρ οὐδ' ἂν ἦν μαθητὴς καλὸς οὐδὲ παῖς καλός· καὶ τὰ καλὰ δὲ πάντα ἐκεῖνα πέπραχε σὺν σοι, ὥς περ χορευτὴς ὑπὸ κορυφαίω· [. . .] τὸ γὰρ παρὰ τοιούτου καὶ τοιαῦτα μαθόντα οὕτως ἀκριβῶσαι τέλειον ἐκεῖνον δείκνυσιν. εἰ γὰρ Ἀχιλλεῖ τὸ παρὰ Χείρωνος τὰ πολεμικὰ μαθεῖν ἔπαινον φέρει, πηλίκον ἐκείνῳ τὸ παρὰ σοῦ τοιαῦτα παιδευθῆναι;

seemingly had implications for the general situation of Byzantium, is reflected in the ways Manuel modulates his authorial voice in this text. On the one hand, when dealing with the portrayal, be it encomiastic or critical, the author's voice becomes highly emotional. Overall, however, this emotional voice does not influence the representation of the main course of action, which seems to unfold independently from the rest of the oration.

On the other hand, as I have already suggested, Manuel adopts a voice that allows him to construct narrative plots which recount not only the exemplariness of the hero and the heroic ethos but also the late fourteenth-century political situation of the Morea. Certainly, these elements do not combine in a history proper, or in chronicle-type writing. Accordingly, when dealing with such topics, Manuel creates a language that uses the heroic past for legitimising contemporary issues. The author is not a historian, but rather assumes the voice of a story-teller. This voice nevertheless retains strong political overtones pertaining to problems of dynastic continuity and defence against centrifugal forces such as the Ottomans, Latins and independent Byzantine landlords. Furthermore, this voice seems tuned to the process of narrativisation of public orations that took place in late Byzantium,[177] and also to the tradition of ancient speeches in the forensic genre. The texts of the ancient Greek orators included narrative accounts clearly marked by metanarrative interventions and various other types of concluding remarks. The narrative accounts of the forensic orations were divided into several sections dealing with different thematic aspects or temporal stages of the story. There as well, the narrators are internal and overt and often comment on the events recounted, while the narratees are addressed on a regular basis and invited to judge a situation based on the narrator's presentation of facts.[178] As Manuel's purpose is to convey a political message which defends his own political position in the late Byzantine political sphere, it is not far-fetched to say that in forging his authorial voice he consciously makes use of this particular tradition of judicial rhetoric in his poetics of praise.

Conclusion

The above analysis has suggested that the encomium for the deceased brother was integrated into an account of the affairs of the Morea. Manuel appears to have tried to emulate the traditions both of the panegyric oration and of the epic/chronicle. The subject matter, the praise for his brother, is treated

---

[177] On narrativisation in Byzantium, see above.
[178] Edwards, 'Oratory', 317–53.

in the form of a narrative account, and to a large extent the author is precise about the events he recounts. By this account, the unit dealing with the despot's achievements was conceived not as a mere list of glorious deeds illustrating Theodore's virtues but as a string of interconnected episodes, truly an account of the Morea and not only of the brother. Certainly, these elements do not combine in a composition resembling a historical chronicle. They are primarily intended not just to describe military situations but also to convey a political message, as various stylistic devices such as the configuration of a strong narrative voice or the use of criticism indicate. As it stands, based on the peculiarities of the author's literary strategies, this narrative of Theodore's deeds takes the form of a sanitised, official account of events which puts forward a message with wide ideological implications within the late Byzantine political context.

The *Funeral Oration* is thus the most ideologically driven text the emperor composed. To a certain extent, narrative and ideology have a similar function. They both involve the acceptance of an authoritative, integrative explanation of actions that orders the world and provides meaning, often manifesting itself as a sort of canonisation. This chapter has examined the form and contents of the narrative included in the *Funeral Oration*, by highlighting the dichotomy between plain praise for Theodore, the author's brother, and an official account of the state of affairs in the Morea. The emperor-narrator engages rhetorically in a dialogue with the political elite of the Morea, and introduces elements altering the function of funeral orations, in order to advertise a political statement of dynastic authority in a situation determined by several important military and social factors, which were specific not only to the region but also to Byzantium at large. By and large, these elements corresponded to the developments within the literary milieu of late Byzantine Constantinople.

Although the story is chronologically structured, its three plots run at different paces and intersect with each other only at certain points in the text, as in the case of the meeting in Serres or the episode of the sale of Moreote strongholds to the Knights Hospitaller. In such cases, it appears that the narrator is more interested in weaving different plots than in depicting characters, who, in any case, never attain a fully fledged profile but remain rather schematic.[179] For this reason, the narrative of events looks at Theodore's ethos from a different angle only partly correlated with the long lists of virtues enunciated in the

---

[179] One can easily discern here Propp's famous functions of various characters: the hero (Theodore and Manuel); the enemy (the Latins, the Ottomans, and local Byzantine individuals); the helper (the Hospitallers and the Albanians). See Propp, *Morphology*.

introduction and peroration. Likewise, closure of the narrative is avoided or deflected until the situation in the Morea becomes politically and socially stable.

More than two decades ago, Julian Chrysostomides, the editor of Manuel's oration, confidently opened the historical introduction of the text in the following way: 'The theme of the funeral oration is Theodore Palaeologus Porphyrogennetos, Despot of Mystras, and his deeds which he performed as ruler of the Despotate between the years 1382 and 1407.'[180]

Doubtless, Theodore represented the central figure of the text and was portrayed as the hero of many episodes. But it is no less true that, from Manuel's perspective, he stood for something else: a younger brother acting always in accordance with his elder brother's will, and thereby an embodiment of the ideal local ruler loyal to the authority emanating from the city. The study of the narrator's perspective reveals that the construction of Theodore's personality is not the sole concern of the text, which still manages to follow all the steps required by a funeral oration. Manuel tries to tune his expression of grief to a message that would soothe the concerns of the Moreotes loyal to Constantinople by eloquently framing the rhetorical representation of his brother in a wider picture of regional history. The Byzantine and the Italian readers of the text, like Manuel Chrysoloras and Guarino of Verona, were probably right to admire the literary merits of the text, yet the emperor's skilful integration of narrative into praise also involves a far-reaching statement of his political outlook.

---

[180] Chrysostomides in *Funeral Oration*, 15.

7

Towards a Renewed Vision of Imperial Authority

The texts analysed in the first six chapters of this volume seem to legitimate, authorise or justify the actions and attitudes of two major social groups: the ecclesiastics and the rhetoricians. This chapter will deal with the political messages which the emperor set forth in his rhetorical compositions written at moments of significant political changes: the *Dialogue* during the siege of Constantinople (1394–1402), the *Foundations* and the *Orations* at a time marked by the rule of John VII in Thessalonike (1403–8); the composition of the *Funeral Oration* coinciding with the recovery of Byzantine rule in the Peloponnese (1407). Chronologically, the texts belong to a period that saw both the threat of the imminent loss of Constantinople and the relative calm generated by the Ottomans' retreat at the beginning of the fifteenth century. Manuel's texts indicate flexibility in adapting his messages to the political developments on the ground.

The social and political circumstances of the early fifteenth century forced Manuel to advertise his intentions and reassert his role on the Byzantine political stage. While in the previous chapters I dealt with the literary and rhetorical aspects of the emperor's political texts without treating in detail the entire range of implications of the problems raised, in this chapter my aim is twofold: first, to discuss Manuel's ideological stance considered from the viewpoint of his political message; and second, to argue that one of the most important elements of his insignia of power and of his political message consisted of a conception of rhetoric as a civic activity intended to ameliorate both the act of ruling and his subjects' lives. Ultimately, this aspect will help us rethink the representation of Byzantine imperial power in the last decades of Byzantine history and its relation to rhetorical culture. In addition, I will address the question of what this ideological stance might suggest for political and intellectual developments in late Byzantium. Eventually, these findings will allow us to evaluate Manuel's similarities and differences in terms of the imperial vision conveyed by other Byzantine emperors with intellectual preoccupations.

The present analysis will follow in the footsteps of the previous chapters. On the one hand, I assume that the emperor's central ideas emerged as a reaction to several key political and social phenomena: the disputes with the church, the Ottoman threat and the dynastic conflicts with John VII. On the other hand, previously discussed rhetorical markers such as genre and authorial voice will help us understand Manuel's discursive strategies whereby he introduced innovations or illustrated general trends of Byzantine ideology. Eventually, this analysis will reveal the terms which Manuel negotiated with an audience that included individuals with different backgrounds and interests. The analysis will also highlight his strategies of presenting an idea of rulership acceptable to the two main groups competing in Byzantium: the hard-line Orthodox and the Latinophile.

Before I proceed to the discussion proper, a look at the emperor's understanding of the Byzantine political sphere is needed. Just like other contemporary authors, Manuel, in his political texts which have been hitherto analysed, showed a certain degree of political realism reflected in his awareness of the decline in state authority, as alluded to in his arguments against marriage[1] or in the letters expressing his hopes for Western support.[2] Manuel was also aware that the lack of economic means persisted from the reign of his father, John V. Voicing this awareness of economic troubles in a letter addressed to Kydones, Manuel tried to reconcile his former mentor with the emperor-father accused of not having paid him the due salary on time:

> Now don't tell us that it is easy for an emperor to give a thousand staters and to give that amount frequently when it is difficult for him to assert his power over the nation, which in a way he has been serving for quite some time. That is the way things are by the nature of the situation.[3]

Likewise, the author's ironical remarks in the final passage of the *Dialogue* disclosed the emperor's perception of the dire political situation:

> Come on, then, as the winning argument is on your side, let us present the prize. It will not be, though, a golden award as we said earlier. Golden crowns are at present in short supply.[4]

---

[1] *Dialogue*, 70–2.

[2] Manuel II, *Letters*, no. 16 to Kydones, ed. Dennis, in which Manuel describes how he was forced to participate as a vassal in the Ottoman military operations.

[3] Ibid. no. 12 (trans. Dennis). See also Demetrios Kydones, *Letters*, no. 70.8–10, ed. Loenertz, rebuking the emperor John V over his salary.

[4] *Dialogue*, 117.

Alongside these remarks about contemporary circumstances, Manuel's texts arguably represented elements within a wider process of creating a politico-didactic persona. They not only reflected his political experience but also indicated his understanding of the contemporary political arena. In the first speech of his *Orations* Manuel discussed the notion of political wisdom (πολιτικὴ σοφία) and noted that ancient legendary rulers like Odysseus, Nestor and Solon possessed it, while Croesus, the Lydian king, did not.[5] As for his awareness of the variations within the political system, Manuel seems to have favoured the idea of a comprehensive governing body, a system that would have included a council of *aristoi* with the emperor as *primus inter pares*. This idea resulted from another passage in the first oration which extolled the benefits of Solon's leadership by means of an institutional system.[6]

The passage implies a connection between the ruler and his advisors, a group which to a large extent coincided with his literary court. Further on, Manuel asserted that Solon surpassed the others not on the basis of his financial or military resources but exclusively because of his practical wisdom.[7] The image of the Athenian legislator was especially popular with Byzantine historians and panegyrists who admired his insights. The twelfth-century historian Niketas Choniates used Solon's image of a wise man in order to criticise the political situation in Constantinople before its sack in 1204, when the citizens did not heed warnings about the upcoming tyranny. Likewise, in Manuel's case, the appeal to Solon's representation alludes to a contemporary situation when local and Italian merchants' political influence overwhelmed the emperor's authority. This image also stands as an example of Manuel's strategy of approaching contemporary issues within a framework dominated by symbolic representations and theoretical considerations. For, as I have pointed out, in his political texts Manuel used several fundamental ethical notions and themes: voluntariness, choice, pleasure, good and evil. Arguably, by engaging with philosophy, as a political thinker he also created a synthesis of various political ideas. This synthesis, which was centred on the idea of defining imperial authority, also included the other topics which contemporary authors, ecclesiastics or lay rhetoricians, approached: the social divide, the representation of enemies and friends, and Byzantine identity.

---

[5] *Orations*, 388d.
[6] Ibid. 388b. Cf. *Foundations*, ch. 84, on the importance of close friends in the administration: τὰς γνώμας ἔχοντι τῶν φιλούντων.
[7] *Orations*, 388 on Solon: οὗτος ἀνὴρ προὔβη πρὸς ἄκρον σοφίας, τῷ τιμᾶσθαι ταύτην παντὸς χρυσίου.

Society and Social 'Classes'

Unlike in the texts of the rhetoricians and of the ecclesiastics, the emperor's observations on the divisions in Byzantine society are rather scarce and follow the conventions of imperial propaganda.[8] Such statements portray the ruler as a benefactor of his subjects, regardless of their social class. One would have expected more allusions on the divisions within Byzantine society in Manuel's letter collection, and yet his letters included few concrete pieces of information on social realities. Only rarely does the emperor mention the state's economic hardships. Thus, in a letter from the early 1400s the emperor referred to the lack of private and public funds in both Constantinople and Thessalonike.[9] In another letter, addressed to Kydones, the emperor echoes his mentor's concerns with the social and economic troubles of Byzantium:

> I have the impression that, without your realizing it, the general misfortunes nearly dragged you away from the letter you were beginning to the composition of a tragedy, a reaction which I myself am now on the verge of sharing.[10]

Thereafter, in a letter addressed to Patriarch Euthymios which described the situation in the Peloponnese, Manuel remarked that the conflicts within Moreote society originated in the social divisions therein.[11] On other occasions, he seemed to couch allusions to the economic conditions in rhetorical parallels, as in the epilogue of the *Dialogue* or in the first of the *Orations* where he rebukes Croesus for having amassed too much wealth.[12] If, overall, it appears that the emperor excluded the topic of social differentiation, he addressed more often the topic of benefits shared by Byzantine society as a whole. This idea of society was described in abstract terms as a body of subjects who follow the ruler's model:

> But all subjects will regulate (ῥυθμίσουσι) their own life, not on the basis of what the ruler may say but directly on what he may do; looking at his actions as if upon an exemplar, they will be stimulated to imitate him; and they will indeed follow him in all his pursuits.[13]

---

[8] E.g. *Foundations*, ch. 9. Cf. Agapetos's *Ekthesis*.
[9] Manuel II, *Letters*, no. 34, ed. Dennis, addressed to Manuel Chrysoloras.
[10] Ibid. no. 21 (trans. Dennis).
[11] Ibid. no. 51.
[12] *Oration* I.
[13] *Dialogue*, 89.

As a result, the notion of common interest, expressed in terms like *public affairs* and *benefit* (τὸ κοινόν, τὸ συμφέρον), is encountered more frequently than in other contemporary authors.[14] To a certain extent a conventional element of Byzantine imperial propaganda, the frequent allusions to the common benefit of the people echoed Plethon's utopian republic, where the citizens' responsibility towards the common welfare was particularly emphasised.[15] This notion appears especially in the *Foundations* where the emperor reminds his son of the necessity of acting in accordance with the interests of most citizens.[16] It appears therefore that the social differences were masked by an appeal to the common good and an approach to various social categories as subjects of the emperor.

Enemies and Allies

The identification of enemies and allies in Manuel's texts had a particular significance as the emperor, more than other contemporary authors, connected it to the theme of political freedom.[17] The emperor's presentation of allies and enemies reflected both his political realism and his longstanding views on the non-Christian enemies of the state. In the *Foundations*, Manuel admitted that the Byzantines were surrounded by more powerful peoples.[18] First, aware of the changes in the regional balance of forces, Manuel seems to adopt the idea that the Byzantines ceased to represent a regional force and that potential allies were to be treated with more caution. The official letters addressed to Western chancelleries make clear the position of subordination which the emperor adopted with regard to other regional power brokers. It may be for this reason that he avoided the use of derogatory denominations for the surrounding peoples which could have provided support in the defence against

---

[14] E.g. *Foundations*, Prefatory Letter, 314b: συνεγκεῖν δὲ τῷ κοινῷ. Cf. ibid. ch. 19: πάντες γὰρ ἀλλήλων δεόμεθα; ch. 42: καὶ πρὸ τοῦ ἰδίου καλοῦ εἰς τὸ κοινῇ συνοῖσον ὁρῶν; ch. 43: καὶ ὁ τὸ ἴδιον θέμενος πρὸ τῶν κοινῇ συμφερόντων πρὸς ἑαυτὸν ἐφέλκεται ταυτηνὶ τὴν εἰκόνα.
[15] Gemistos Plethon, *On Virtues*, a.2.40, ed. Tambrun-Krasker: πολίτῃ πρὸς πόλιν.
[16] E.g. *Foundations*, ch. 37: ἡ πρὸς τὸ κοινῇ συνοῖσον ἐπιμέλεια.
[17] Among the many examples of discussions of freedom see ibid. ch. 29: πολλῶν γε θρήνων ἄξιον, ἐξουσίαν εἰληφότας τέκνα Θεοῦ γενέσθαι, ἔπειτα δουλεύειν ἐθέλειν; Manuel II, *Admonitory Oration*, 302.20: δρῶμεν τοίνυν, ὦ ἄνδρες, πάντα, ἀνεχώμεθα πάντων ὑπὲρ τῆς ἐλευθερίας; and Manuel II, *Letters*, no. 4, ed. Dennis, on freedom in Thessalonike. Further on the idea of freedom in late Byzantium see Angelov, 'Three kinds of liberty'.
[18] *Foundations*, ch. 26: νόμιζε μηδένα ἀνθρώπων καὶ τῶν τὴν μείζω δύναμιν κεκτημένων. Cf. Manuel II, *Admonitory Oration*, 300.32, ed. Laourdas: ἀλλὰ πολλῷ προέχει ὁ ἐχθρὸς εἴς τε χρήματα καὶ γῆν καὶ συμμαχοῦντας καὶ στρατιάν.

the Ottomans. Instead, the Albanians, or Illyrians, as he describes them in the *Funeral Oration*, appear as a brave and virtuous people, loyal to the Byzantine despot of the Peloponnese, Theodore I. Such a characterisation was radically different from Kydones' negative opinions on other neighbouring peoples, the Bulgarians or Serbs:

> Well then, to have the Illyrians, in addition to the forces of the Peloponnese which in themselves were not small, was of the greatest assistance. He arranged all this according to his own plan and far surpassed the expectation of others. For if a small additional assistance helps to tip the scales, what could not be achieved by a substantial force which was also experienced in warfare?[19]

Second, Manuel's view on an alliance with the Latins emerges as more nuanced than in the accounts of the Ottomans. Thus, the preface of his treatise *On the Procession of the Holy Spirit* suggests that the emperor did not wish to attack the Latins' faith, but his goal was to expound and defend the Greeks' doctrine of the procession of the Holy Spirit: 'This treatise was not written against the Latins; for it belongs to someone who needs to defend a position rather than to someone who wishes to attack others.'[20] Such a positive attitude towards the Latins' faith also emerges in one of his letters where he praised the Latin liturgy and spirituality.[21] The conciliatory attitude towards the Latins in theological matters was paralleled at the political level. In the *Funeral Oration* Manuel presented the Knights Hospitaller in positive terms when Theodore sold them the major Peloponnesian strongholds:

> There was a community in Rhodes composed of men who had vowed to the Saviour chastity, obedience and poverty and who had also promised to fight those who strove against the Cross, and they were accustomed to bear the sign of the Cross on their clothes, their arms, and banners.[22]

Although in the same *Funeral Oration* he also expressed concerns vis-à-vis other groups of Latins, overall the emperor maintained a positive attitude.[23]

---

[19] *Funeral Oration*, 120–2 (trans. Chrysostomides). Cf. the remarks on the Bulgars, Serbs and Hungarians; ibid. 191–3.

[20] Dendrinos, *Annotated Edition of 'On the Procession of the Holy Spirit'*, 1.

[21] Manuel II, *Letters*, no. 30, ed. Dennis, addressed to Constantine Asanes (1396), in which he compares the Latin 'sacred rites' with the Orthodox 'hymns and readings'.

[22] *Funeral Oration*, 166 (trans. Chrysostomides).

[23] Ibid.: 'We are not so wretched, spineless or stupid as to prefer those strangers (i.e. the Latins) to ourselves.'

He further testifies to this position with the letters he sent from the West to scholars and courtiers in Constantinople, where he expressed optimism about the response of Western rulers to his requests for military help.[24]

In contrast, the attitude towards the Ottomans emerges as completely different, despite the fact that Manuel had often conducted negotiations with the Ottomans and enjoyed their benevolence. Around 1391, his long theological treatise composed of twenty-six dialogical episodes on the differences between Christianity and Islam showed that the emperor, despite his awareness of the traditional Byzantine view on Islam,[25] had made the effort to understand the basics of the enemy's religion. The dialogue featured a conversation between the emperor and a *müderris* (teacher), most often on friendly terms. One section, however (*Dialogue* no. 5), provided historical and political arguments against the military successes of Bayezid and the Ottomans, which, to some extent, resembled Makarios Makres' series of homilies about 'those scandalised by the successes of the infidels'.[26] Nevertheless, this approach to Islam in the *Dialogues* disappeared from the emperor's subsequent writings, which all included long passages that vilified the Turks as an ethnic group.[27] Manuel specifically addressed two short texts against the Ottomans, both written after the end of the siege of Constantinople (1394–1402). The first one, titled *Some Remarks the Leader of the Persians and the Scythians Might Have Made to the Proud Tyrant of the Turks (Bayezid) Who Talked Grandly and Insolently*, was an *ethopoiia* that ridiculed Bayezid for his defeat. The second was titled *Psalm about the Saracen Thunderbolt, when God Looked upon His People and, through his Enemies, Slew Him Who Was a Beast in Every Way*.

In the *Funeral Oration* Manuel overlooks the Turkish help received by his brother Theodore during the conflict with the local *archontes*; moreover, the emperor offers an extremely negative account of the Ottoman invaders who were beginning to show their interest in occupying the Byzantine province of the Peloponnese.[28] Manuel again focused on Bayezid, whom he addressed in a virulent *psogos*.[29] Then a veiled criticism of the Ottomans surfaces in the

---

[24] Manuel II, *Letters*, no. 39, ed. Dennis, sent from Paris in 1401.
[25] Manuel was aware of John of Damascus's writings against Islam; Khoury, *Manuel II Paléologue*, 42.
[26] *Dialoge mit einem Muslim*, no. 5, ed. Förstel. After an account (54–9) of ancient Greek and Roman glorious deeds, the Persian declares himself convinced that Islam was no better than Christianity (63).
[27] E.g. Manuel II, *Letters*, no. 31, ed. Dennis, addressed to Kydones, in which the Muslims are portrayed as God-haters and Muhammad is presented as a false prophet.
[28] See the inscription of Parori; Loenertz, 'Res Gestae'. For the translation of the inscription, see Leonte, 'Brief "history of the Morea"', 417.
[29] *Funeral Oration*, 186, 206.

Orations where Manuel relates the story of the defeat of the Persian armies by the far fewer but better-organised Athenians.[30]

Equally hostile, in the emperor's view, were the Byzantine *archontes* who opposed his authority. First, in the *Dialogue*, Manuel included another *psogos* against his nephew John VII, condemned for his claims to legitimacy and for his alliance with the Ottomans that led him to attack the emperor.[31] Then, in the *Funeral Oration*, Manuel blames the Byzantines who sided with the Ottomans in the attempt to oust Theodore.[32] Certainly, the attacks on the regional landowners had to do with the emperor's efforts to project the image of his imperial authority as in control of the elites active in remote provinces. Yet, in contrast to this attitude towards the rebellious *archontes* who in 1416 sabotaged the emperor's plan to rebuild the Hexamilion wall, Manuel cultivated the idea of a group of close allies active at the court in Constantinople. This group of court allies, within which can be included his 'literary court' represented in the letters, was well reflected in his political texts. The *Dialogue* presented Helena Kantakouzene, his mother, as a close collaborator in matters of governance. The *Foundations* and the *Orations* drew heavily on the significance of the ruler's court counsellors. If in the *Foundations* the advice addressed to John VIII is more straightforward,[33] in the *Orations* it is couched in the account of the Athenian legislator and ruler Solon. Thus, in the first of the seven *Orations* the author stresses that the legendary statesman of the seventh century BC was only a *primus inter pares*, the appointed leader of a group of equally powerful individuals.[34]

Markers of Byzantine Identity

Turning to Manuel's understanding of Byzantine identity, it is remarkable that the emperor's references to Hellenism were rather rare, despite the trend of self-identifying as Hellenes known to have existed in the Palaiologan period. Only in the early *Dialogues with a Muslim* does the heritage of ancient Greece appear more prominent, while in other instances it was reduced to quotations of ancient authors like Pythagoras or Isocrates.[35] Instead, like the previous Byzantine rulers, the emperor continued to

---

[30] *Oration* I.
[31] *Dialogue*, 129.
[32] *Funeral Oration*, 127.
[33] *Foundations*, ch. 55.
[34] *Orations*, 388.
[35] *Dialoge mit einem Muslim*, no. 5, ed. Förstel; *Foundations*.

emphasise the Byzantines' Romanness.³⁶ At the same time, unlike in the ecclesiastics' case, the references to the Byzantines' Hellenic origins were less present in discussions of political contexts, although Manuel did refer to the ancient Greek background.³⁷ Only in the first *Oration* did the emperor suggest a parallel between the Byzantines and the ancient Greeks who also fought against the peoples of the East. Nonetheless, ever since his earliest texts, the *Panegyric* addressed to his father and the *Admonitory Oration to the Thessalonians*, he had placed the Roman foundation of the state at the core of Byzantine identity.³⁸ The emperor identified the Byzantines with the Romans as he repeated several tenets of official propaganda that also emphasised the glorious Roman past. From this point of view his writings resembled the court rhetoricians' panegyrics. It is therefore not far-fetched to say that this political aspect was emphasised ever more strongly in direct proportion to the decline of the state, as if he sought to reassert what no longer seemed so obvious about the empire of the Romans.

Yet Manuel's representation of the Byzantines did not entirely function according to propagandistic needs, but also owed much to his political realism. No longer did the emperor cultivate the idea of ethnic exceptionality or describe his people as the chosen people, but rather referred to them as another Christian people equal with others. One is tempted to explain this attitude on the basis of the Treaty of Gallipoli (1403), which had stipulated the formation of a Christian League including the Byzantines, the Genoese and the Serbs.³⁹ The major shift in the attitude towards ethnicity came from the comments the emperor made on the population of Albanians/Illyrians which settled in the Peloponnese at the beginning of Theodore's rule. Unlike Kydones, who regarded the neighbouring Christian peoples as barbarian, Manuel praised them for their austere lifestyle as well as for their loyalty.⁴⁰

On the other hand, if the comparisons with other neighbouring peoples diluted the idea of Byzantine uniqueness, Manuel promoted an idea of fatherland (πατρίς) as a distinctive political entity, limited to Constantinople and

---

³⁶ See the analysis by Page, *Being Byzantine*, 249–70. Page argues that, although Manuel uses the term 'Rhomaios' less than other authors like John Kantakouzenos, his terminology of Romanness confirms the primarily political content observed in earlier writers.
³⁷ E.g. Isocrates, Pythagoras and Homer in the *Foundations*.
³⁸ Manuel II, *Admonitory Oration*, 297, 21, ed. Lourdas. See the address in Manuel II, *Panegyric*, 228, ed. Boissonade: ὦ ἄνδρες Ῥωμαῖοι.
³⁹ See Chapter 1.
⁴⁰ See above.

echoing the Western city-based polities.⁴¹ Some scholars have rightly argued that this notion reflected a process of territorialisation of the fatherland; that is, authors began to operate with an idea of a state defined within strict territorial boundaries and not as an *imperium sine fine*.⁴² This emphasis on national and ethnic connotations embedded in Manuel's idea of πατρίς differentiated it from the notion of Christian fatherland held by ecclesiastics like Bryennios and Symeon of Thessalonike, both concerned with eschatological and universalist meanings.⁴³

Renewal of Imperial Ideology in Manuel's Texts

Having discussed the major topics of Manuel's political discourse, I will now turn to the final concern of this chapter: the emperor's conception of imperial authority, seen as both self-representation and evidence for his response to the social and political challenges effected by contemporary power brokers. As noted in the previous chapters, the construction of imperial authority represented the backbone of the political texts studied so far.⁴⁴ Viewed against the backdrop provided by other, similar contemporary writings, Manuel's politically charged texts written during his reign seem to provide an answer to two questions about the political history of late Byzantium: what the emperor stood for and how his style of government can be defined.

The construction of a distinctive imperial representation with Manuel at its centre can be understood from two viewpoints: within the framework of official manifestations of power and as a result of the emperor's attempts to adjust imperial propaganda to new realities. According to this double-layered model of analysis, first, one notes that the late Byzantine representation of imperial power remained to a certain extent unaltered. Manuel's coronation ceremony, performed at the same time as his marriage on 12 February 1392, was not much different from previous ceremonies, as described in the account preserved by an anonymous Greek short chronicle and by the Russian

---

⁴¹ *Funeral Oration*, 111: ὑπὲρ τῆς πατρίδος τε καὶ τοῦ γένους καὶ τῶν φυσάντων, and 161: οὓς οὐκ οἶδα ὅ, τι καλέσετε, Ῥωμαίους καὶ Χριστιανοὺς διὰ τὸ γένος καὶ τὸ βάπτισμα. Earlier, in a letter, he appeals to Kydones to come back to Byzantium, his fatherland: 'you should cling to the fatherland no less firmly than the octopuses to the rocks' (τῆς τε πατρίδος ἔχεσθαι οὐχ ἧττον ἢ τῶν πετρῶν οἱ πολύποδες); Manuel II, *Letters*, no. 12.18–19, ed. Dennis. On the comparison between Manuel's ideas and contemporary processes in the Italian cities see Kioussopoulou, *Emperor or Manager*, 235–44.

⁴² Kioussopoulou, 'Hommes d'affaires byzantins', 15–21.

⁴³ Kioussopoulou, *Emperor or Manager*, 160–82.

⁴⁴ Chapters 3–6.

pilgrim Ignatios.⁴⁵ Likewise, the official documents issued by Manuel's chancery reflect his adherence to timeless imperial models.⁴⁶ Here Manuel used the same formulas as in more fortunate periods of Byzantine history when they better reflected the extent of the emperor's authority. In addition to external markers like the ceremonial and the formulaic language of official documents, the emperor's rhetorical texts included several of the standard principles of Byzantine imperial ideology. Many chapters of the *Foundations* and especially the epistolary epilogue of the *Orations* draw on old assumptions. There, the emperor described himself as supreme ruler, God's vicar on earth⁴⁷ or legislator.⁴⁸ Likewise, the passages on imperial authority drawn from Byzantine law codes and written on the last folio of MS Vindob. phil. gr. 42, which included Manuel's political texts, are indicative of the role of the old ideological values in the emperor's political theorisation. Significant in terms of the continuity of Byzantine political thought are also the distinctions between legitimate ruler (βασιλεύς) and tyrant (τύραννος)⁴⁹ and the fact that in the *Dialogue* and the *Foundations* Manuel also embedded the image of the state as body, where the emperor stands as the head and other political groups represent the limbs.⁵⁰

---

⁴⁵ This was a short chronicle of the monastery τοῦ Λειμῶνος (Lesbos) published by P. Schreiner, *Chronica Byzantina Breviora*, I. 104, *Chronik* 10. Yet this has to be used with caution since it seems that it was based partially on Pseudo-Kodinos and John Kantakouzenos, containing the rubrics and texts of prayers for the ceremonies in Hagia Sophia in which the emperor took part. See Schreiner, 'Hochzeit und Krönung', 76.

⁴⁶ Notions like justice and philanthropy that are present in Manuel's texts can all be found in the *prooimia* of imperial documents throughout the Byzantine period. From the time of Eusebios they had been elements of the Byzantine imperial idea, that is, of the concept of the emperor as God's representative on earth. It is characteristic of the continuity and consistency of Byzantine imperial ideology that several parallels can be drawn between Manuel's texts and imperial speeches of the sixth century. Like Manuel, his predecessors insisted on the idea of the emperor's responsibilities towards his subjects and his accountability to God for his policies. On the continuity of imperial virtues in Byzantium see Hunger, *Prooimion*, ch. II, 114, 123, 143; Hunger, 'Philanthropia'.

⁴⁷ *Orations, Epistolary Epilogue*, 560c: τί οὖν δὴ τὰ τοῦ Θεοῦ πρὸς ἡμᾶς; οὐ δημιουργός; οὐ πατήρ; οὐ βασιλεύς; οὐ προνοητής; οὐ διδάσκαλος;

⁴⁸ *Foundations*, ch. 51: νομοθέτης μὲν ὁ βασιλεὺς καὶ κριτὴς τῶν ὑπ'αὐτὸν ἀναδέδεικται. Further on principles of imperial propaganda see Païdas, *Βυζαντινά κάτοπτρα*, 1–20; Leontiades, *Untersuchungen*, 92–134.

⁴⁹ On the distinction between emperors and tyrants see *Foundations*, ch. 85: ὁ βασιλεὺς ἐννόμως ζῶν, καὶ νόμοις ἄγων τοὺς ὑπ' αὐτόν, καθάπαξ ἐναντίος ἐστι τοῖς τυραννεῖν ἐθέλουσιν, οἳ νόμον ἀπαράβατον ἔχουσι τὰς ἑαυτῶν ἡδονάς.

⁵⁰ *Foundations*, ch. 43. Cf. *Funeral Oration*, 206–8: 'For this champion, your Despot, with whom you fought, he as head, you as limbs, succeeded in two things, though he would have been content had either one or the other had been successful, for both were excellent.' See also Païdas, *Βυζαντινά κάτοπτρα*, 150–6.

Particular attention was paid to the relationship between the imperial and ecclesiastical authorities, where the emperor favoured the previously dominant view of the ruler's pre-eminence.[51] In the *Foundations* the author plainly advised his son to regard the church as a mother, guide and collaborator:

> Above everything, you must honour the church. This is your mother, your nurse, your teacher, creator, anointer, road, and guide, and collaborator, and calling (μήτηρ, τίτθη, διδάσκαλος, πλάστης, ἀλείπτης, ὁδός, καὶ ὁδηγός, καὶ συνεργός, καὶ παράκλησις) towards what is best and most stable.[52]

If this piece of advice concerned more the spiritual aspects of his son's rule (τὰ πάντα πνευματικά), in the epistolary epilogue of the *Orations*, Manuel proclaimed the pre-eminence of imperial rule over priestly authority. He also indicated the terminological distinction between the two: the first is imperial dominion (βασιλεία), conceived as full power coming directly from God, and the second is mere authority (ἡγεμονία), which the priests have received from Moses:

> Thus, I sit on a throne which imitates God's throne (τὸν Θεὸν εἰκονίζοντος), while the priests, and the Pharisees sit on Moses' seat. This <latter> is less important than ours. And let no one accuse me of boldness or stubbornness. For I do not compare myself to Moses, who had the power to see God (how could I?), I only compare the positions. Let us look more closely. For both I and Moses derive our authority from God (for that one too is sovereign and teacher. These are from God, since any kind of authority is divine, according to the Apostle); but imperial authority (βασιλεία) is greater than simple rule (ἡγεμονία), as the newer teachings are more authoritative than the older, just as they depend on the New Testament. Thus, my stance towards you far exceeds not only the stance of the priests and Pharisees towards the Jewish people, but also Moses' pre-eminence over all those.[53]

These statements in the epistolary epilogue resemble other references to the emperor's role in deciding on matters of faith, like the one in the *Dialogue*.[54] Certainly, in stating the emperor's pre-eminence over church and clerics in the conclusion of a text which dealt with anything but ecclesiastical

---

[51] Especially dominant in authors of the twelfth and the thirteenth centuries: Theodore Balsamon and Demetrios Chomatenos.
[52] *Foundations*, chs. 11 and 12.
[53] *Orations, Epistolary Epilogue*, 560b–c. On the connections between the emperor and God see also *Foundations*, ch. 9: ἀποδίδου γοῦν αὐτῷ τῷ Θεῷ τὸ χρέος ἅπαν εἰς δύναμιν.
[54] *Dialogue*, 695–8: ἄρχοντος δὲ καὶ βασιλέως [. . .] καὶ τὰ τῆς πίστεως.

authority, Manuel expressed his opposition to the ecclesiastics' claims of authority in earthly matters. His assertion of the secular ruler's higher status clearly contrasted with Symeon of Thessalonike's opinions expressed in his liturgical texts on the patriarch's omnipotence.

Yet, second, the construction of a distinctive representation of imperial power during Manuel's reign can be regarded from a different point of view as well, for even if Manuel relied on the formulaic language of imperial propaganda expressing longstanding ideological principles, the question remains whether such statements of imperial ideology can always be taken at face value. The answer depends on the analysis of the emperor's treatment of several key aspects common to imperial ideology. In Chapters 3–6 I have already argued that Manuel made a number of modifications within the genres of the texts he composed during his reign: he used dialogic orality and irony in order to counteract the imperial claims of his nephew John VII; he used the forms of *kephalaia* and diatribe to create a multilayered didactic-moralising text; and he included a fully fledged brief history of the Morea in the funeral oration for his brother Theodore. In what follows, based on this previous analysis, I will argue that these modifications must be understood in the context of Manuel's efforts to redesign the idea of imperial office so as to respond to the political challenges described in the first chapter of this volume. These efforts, converging in a process of the renewal of imperial representation, become apparent at three interconnected levels: his deliberative stance; the treatment of virtues; and the representation of the emperor as rhetorician and teacher-*didaskalos*. In addition, in the same framework of renewing imperial authority one can include his efforts to assert his influence within the church, as reflected by his liturgical and homiletic texts.

The first step in understanding Manuel's efforts to redesign the imperial representation concerns his general approach to oratorical genres, an issue which has already been partially discussed above. A look at Manuel's œuvre indicates that many of his texts include exhortations as to how to deal with specific occasions or about a ruler's moral and political stance.[55] The early *Admonitory Oration to the Thessalonians* was an attempt to persuade reluctant local *archontes* to reject the Ottomans' terms of surrender, an event which eventually took place in 1387. Manuel drew on a series of deliberative topics that brought into the foreground the notion of one's liberty as a reflection of ancient Greek and Roman glory.[56] The *Foundations* and the *Orations* were

---

[55] E.g. in *Foundations*, ch. 72, he distinguishes between those who rule, have authority (ἀρχή) even over large territories and populations (like the 'Scythians') and those who are fortunate (εὐδαίμονες) and are emperors (βασιλεῖς).

[56] Manuel II, *Admonitory Oration*, 298–9, ed. Laourdas.

conceived as exhortations for the moral betterment of his son, John VIII. As mentioned above, the exhortations included in both texts were often underlined by the idea of effectively acting according to a goal that would bring benefits to the community. Thus, in both texts Manuel frequently used terms like benefit (τὸ συμφέρον), damage (τὸ βλαβερόν) and profit (τὸ λυσιτελές), all markers of deliberative rhetoric.[57] Based on such remarks as well as on exempla and gnomic sayings, the author then puts forward recommendations or admonitions. In another, much shorter text, the *Oration to His Subjects*, the emperor urges the addressees to follow his moral commandments for an ascetic life and to show courage in defending the state and its ruler.[58] In the *Funeral Oration* the exhortation is also transparent: the praise addressed to Despot Theodore as representative of the ruling family also stands as an invitation addressed to the local *archontes* to acknowledge the central authority in Constantinople.[59] The emperor's reliance on topics of admonitory rhetoric seems to owe much to a trend in Palaiologan oratory preoccupied with identifying solutions to the problems faced by the empire.[60] Arguably, Manuel placed his texts within this trend, thereby echoing contemporary rhetoricians' deliberative productions.

One notch down, there can be identified the emperor's peculiar treatment of a common topic in admonitory literature: the system of princely virtues. This is a topic which, as previously noted, reveals a great deal of information about the priorities of the interest groups active at the Byzantine court.[61] We have already seen that, in general, when praising the emperor, the panegyrists used a series of virtues common in imperial rhetoric. The four cardinal imperial virtues of prudence (φρόνησις), courage (ἀνδρία), justice (δικαιοσύνη) and wisdom (σωφροσύνη) occupied a central place in their texts.[62] Manuel is no exception to this rule, and yet his system of virtues underwent significant alterations. First, in the *kephalaia* of the *Foundations*, he introduces a systematic arrangement of virtues. As I have pointed out,[63] the emperor

---

[57] On these terms as markers of deliberative rhetoric see Olmsted, 'Topics'. See *Foundations*, ch. 26: [...] δύνασθαι βλάψαι καὶ τὸν φαυλότατον, μὴ συγχωροῦντος τοῦ κρείττονος, ἢ δι' ὀργήν, ἢ πρὸς τὸ ἡμέτερον ἀφορῶντος συμφέρον; ibid. ch. 35: ἱέραξ, ἵππος, ἰχθὺς κατὰ λόγον, οὐ σὺν λόγῳ τὰ συμφέροντα πράττειν πεφύκασιν; ibid. ch. 41: λογίζου δὲ καθημερὰν ζημίαν τε καὶ τὰ κέρδη.

[58] Manuel II, *Oration to His Subjects*, PG 156, 561–2: τούτους δὲ γενναίους ἄνδρας αὐτοὺς δεικνύναι ὑπὲρ γένους, ὑπὲρ πατρίδος, ὑπὲρ τοῦ κρατοῦντος αὐτοῦ.

[59] *Funeral Oration*, 211–13.

[60] See Chapter 2.

[61] Angelov, 'Byzantine imperial panegyric', 55–70.

[62] For the use of the cardinal virtues in medieval Western intellectual tradition, see Bejczy and Nederman, *Princely Virtues*.

[63] See Chapters 4 and 5.

used a moral-philosophical outlook which determined the value of all virtues, be they physical-military, intellectual, spiritual or political. Inspired by Aristotle's *Ethics*, Manuel distinguished between voluntary and involuntary actions, to which he added a further personal category of mixed voluntary actions (μιξοεκούσια).[64] Within this philosophical outlook, Manuel added several other virtues: moderation (μετριότης), love (ἀγάπη) and humility (ταπεινοφροσύνη).[65] Certainly, these were not new for the authors of panegyrics. Nonetheless, the emperor, by attaching them to the cardinal virtues, signalled his intention of renovating the system of imperial virtues so that it would reflect his philosophical-moral outlook as well as his political strategy, often seeking reconciliation between opposing views.

The theoretical treatment of virtues did not represent the major concern of the *Foundations*; it was rather the *Orations* which expanded and refined the discussion on this topic. The *Orations* replaced the *Foundations*' treatment of virtues with the elaborate construction of an exhaustive system of virtues, conceived not only as core elements of an ethical-philosophical system but also in a hierarchical order. The view which pervades this composition is that, according to Manuel, in a ruler's life, some imperial virtues have more importance than others. Thus, the last two pieces of the *Orations* were dedicated to two virtues which the emperor specifically designates as the highest a ruler should be endowed with: love (ἀγάπη) and humility (ταπεινοφροσύνη).[66] Furthermore, the first five texts of the *Orations*, which draw on theoretical ethics, formed the basis and preparation for acquiring higher Christian virtues which, according to Manuel's view, coincide with the ruler's highest virtues. The inclusion of these among a ruler's values constituted a novelty in imperial propaganda. These two virtues, love and humility, are to be found neither in the rhetoricians' texts nor in any other rhetorical text of the Palaiologan period, except for the contemporary Demetrios Chrysoloras's one hundred letters, which emulated Manuel's texts.[67] As Manuel himself had previously authored a panegyric for his father, he was probably aware of the system of virtues used in imperial propaganda, and yet he chose to promote another set of values.

The proclamation of love and humility as fundamental imperial virtues reflected the emperor's preoccupation with ongoing political processes. By setting these two virtues at the top of his hierarchical system, Manuel addressed

---

[64] *Orations*, 432c.
[65] *Foundations*, ch. 20.
[66] Oration VII, 529a–b: ὁ δὲ τὰ καλὰ κτησάμενος πάντα οὐδὲν ἑαυτὸν ὤνησεν, εἰ μὴ καὶ τὴν ταπεινοφροσύνην προσεκτήσατο.
[67] Demetrios Chrysoloras, *One Hundred Letters*, ch. 80, ed. Conti Bizzarro: οὐδὲν ὑψηλότερον ταπεινοφροσύνης ἐν βίῳ.

the political circumstances of the early fifteenth century. The seventh oration plainly states that a more humble attitude was commendable in times of great political distress:

> Humility conceals the protectors, those who maintain order in times which do not allow us to stand without fear.[68]

In terms of political governance, several groups and individuals began to exsert influence, and hence the emperor's authority in matters of administration experienced a setback. As discussed above, in the first oration Manuel praised Solon's institutional change in the government of Athens, according to which the ruler was to become the leader of a group of *aristoi*, who upheld the right of censuring their leader.[69] This major change in the system of virtues constituted a means to signal to the other political actors that the emperor understood his new position as having an importance equal to that of other individuals.[70] On the other hand, if we take into consideration that the addressee of the orations, John VIII, was also Manuel's designated successor, it turns out that they were clearly intended to answer the educational needs of the emperor's son and co-emperor. By advocating humility (ταπεινοφροσύνη) Manuel rebuked his son for recent instances of misbehaviour. In the seventh oration, Manuel advises him to show moderation and not to boast of his achievements.[71]

The virtues treated in the two *Foundations* and the *Orations* show Manuel's effort to refine his ideas and present an integrated system of moral excellence. The texts suggest that he may be implicitly making the case for a new kind of kingly conduct, in which virtues like those celebrated in the first and the last speech were cultivated against the physical qualities of the traditional ruler, like strength and military prowess.[72] If so, an openly new political conduct gains visibility. According to this system of virtues, the ruler should make

---

[68] *Orations*, 537d.
[69] *Orations*, 538a: οὐκ ἄρα διὰ ταῦτα ἄριστος ἀρίστοις, καὶ μέγιστος μεγίστοις ἀνὴρ ἀνδράσι νομίζοιτο, καὶ νῦν γε πᾶσιν ἔτι δοκεῖ. Cf. Anonymous, *Funeral Oration on Manuel II*, 445.1, ed. Dendrinos: περαίνειν τὴν Ἀθηναίων πολιτείαν.
[70] On the new style of authority which entailed stronger collaboration with state officials, see Leontiades, *Untersuchungen*, 184. Furthermore, *Foundations*, ch. 90, equates the ruler's activity with that of ordinary people.
[71] *Orations*, 544d.
[72] This kind of heroism is somewhat different from what some scholars have asserted with regard to the political ideals of the Palaiologan period. Angelov stated that the Palaiologan ideal was predominantly militaristic; *Imperial Ideology*, 134.

use of a peaceful approach even in times of utmost distress and should adopt appropriate conduct towards his subjects.[73]

Furthermore, the outlook that shaped the *Funeral Oration* echoed this new type of political heroism preached in Constantinople. Although in the rubric of the blessing (μακαρισμός) the author compared his brother to valiant ancient heroes and in the section dedicated to his brother's deeds he refers to military deeds, Manuel constructed a narrative whose epilogue displays peace in the Morea. According to his account, the restoration of peace under Byzantine authority was achieved primarily through skilful diplomatic planning that considered the presence of different ethnic groups in the region.[74]

The emperor-preacher

Manuel's attempts to convey political messages of ideological renewal by means of public oratory were not confined to texts designed for this purpose. His liturgical and homiletic writings also had political connotations and were intended to advertise his authority. This little-known and hitherto unexplored aspect of his activity mirrors his concern for the growing influence of ecclesiastics and their attacks against imperial authority. The prayers and the four homilies often reveal Manuel's political attitudes and allude to historical events. One of these texts, the *Kanon paraklētikos* (Κάνων παρακλητικὸς εἰς τὴν ὑπεραγίαν ἡμῶν Δέσποιναν Θεοτόκον ὑπὲρ τῶν νῦν περιστάσεων/*Prayer to the Holy Mother of God for Help in the Present Circumstances*), specifically addressed an event in the history of early fifteenth-century Constantinople, namely the siege of the city in 1411 by the Ottomans. Here, the author prays for the Theotokos to defend the city against the invaders:

> We, the entire gathering of the faithful,/ Call on our Mother/ Of the supreme ruler, God./ Deliver your people from misfortunes/ And give to your city the victory against the enemies./ You can see, Virgin, there is another enemy,/ Who is attacking forcefully/ This possession of yours./ As you have previously destroyed the father of this one <i.e. Bayezid, 1402>,/ Make this one here and his army disappear.[75]

---

[73] On the idea of avoiding discord see *Foundations*, ch. 56: μηδὲ πολέμει πρὸς ἀδελφοὺς τοὺς ἀπὸ Χριστοῦ, μήτε μὴν πρὸς ὁντινοῦν, ἢ βαρβάρων ἔθνος; and *Orations*, 501b, against civil strife: καὶ κατὰ τῶν ἀδελφῶν μὴ θρασύνεσθαι, μηδὲ κατεπαίρεσθαι, μηδὲ ἀπογινώσκειν αὐτούς. On adopting a proper conduct towards others see *Foundations*, chs. 74, 77, 81–2: ἴσθι τὴν ὑπηρετῶν εἰς τὸ κοινὸν βλάβην σοὶ λογιουμένους τοὺς βλαπτομένους.
[74] See Chapter 6.
[75] Manuel II, *Kanon paraklētikos*, ed. Legrand.

Apart from the liturgical prayers,[76] Manuel's homilies[77] place the emperor among other authors of sermons like Demetrios Chrysoloras or ecclesiastics like Gabriel of Thessalonike and Makarios Makres. Although several cases of Byzantine emperor-homilists (Leo V, Leo VI, Constantine VII Porphyrogennetos, Manuel I Komnenos) can be identified, Manuel's case remains singular for the Palaiologan period. In these homilies, written in a high style for an educated audience, he explicitly made use of his religious education to develop his notion of the imperial idea. His homilies call for God's protection of the chosen emperor and his people.[78] At the same time, Manuel appears to have conceived for himself the role of a responsible guide for the people's spiritual life.[79] In doing so, he appears to have followed Theodore Balsamon's twelfth-century formulation which prescribed the emperor's right to enter the sanctuary of the church whenever he wished to deliver sermons, to bless and cense with a candelabrum (τρικήριον) which bishops used during church services.[80] On the other hand, the homilies echoed the old representations of emperors as priests. Previously, Theodore Balsamon had quoted a passage from Flavius Josephus in which the Roman emperor Tiberius styled himself 'most exalted bishop' (ἀρχιερεὺς μέγιστος), a Greek rendition of the pagan title *pontifex maximus*. Similarly, Manuel echoed Eusebios's notion of a Christian emperor-teacher (*didaskalos*) acquainted with the divine mysteries by virtue of being God's 'image' on earth.[81] Thus, by composing and delivering homilies, Manuel appears to have imitated Constantine the Great, who was the first emperor to have done so. Moreover, as in the homilies of another emperor, Leo VI (866–912),[82] the sacerdotal

---

[76] See also *Morning Prayers*, PG 156, 564–76.
[77] *Homily on the Dormition of the Theotokos*, ed. Jugie; *Homily on St Mary of Egypt*; *Homily on the Nativity of Christ*; and *Homily on St John the Baptist* (Vat. gr. 1619, ff. 15r–29v; ff30r–46v; and ff. 47r–54v respectively).
[78] Manuel II, *Homily on the Dormition of the Theotokos*, ed. Jugie, 556–7.
[79] See *Foundations*, ch. 31: τὸ μὲν ἀεὶ τὰ βελτίω τῶν χειρόνων ἐκλέγεσθαι Θεοῦ.
[80] Canon 69 of the Quinisext Ecumenical Council, in Rhalles and Potles, Σύνταγμα τῶν θείων, 2. 185, indicates that the emperor's entry into the sanctuary of the church was allowed. On Balsamon's understanding of customary law, see Simon, 'Balsamon'.
[81] Eusebios, *Life of Constantine*, I, 5: 'By him (i.e. by Constantine), God cleansed humanity of the godless multitude, and set him up as a teacher of true devotion to himself for all nations, testifying with a loud voice for all to hear, that they should know the God who is, and turn from the error of those who do not exist at all'; Cameron and Hall, *Eusebius*, 69. See also Beck, *Byzantinische Jahrtausend*, 130, with reference to the passages of Eusebios in Sansterre, *Mémoires et documents*, 131–95, 532–93.
[82] Leo VI, *Homilies*, ed. Antonopoulou. On the links to Constantine the Great consciously made by Basil I and his grandson, Constantine VII, see Dagron, *Emperor and Priest*, 206–8. Cf. Leo VI, *Homilies*, 72–9, ed. Antonopoulou.

character of the Byzantine imperial office, inspired by the royal models of the Old Testament, David and Solomon, is present.[83]

The four homilies drew on religious topics and, according to their preambles, were performed upon the religious feasts of saints or, as in the case of the *Homily on the Dormition of the Theotokos*, upon the occasion of the recovery from an illness.[84] It is possible that they were performed in the imperial palace, like, for instance, Joseph Bryennios's sermons. The homilies display not only the emperor's knowledge of intricate doctrinal issues, as in the *Oration on the Theotokos*,[85] but also his vision of a life of ascetic practice, as in the *Oration on St John the Baptist*.[86] Thus, to a certain extent, the imperial homilies shared the concerns present in the ecclesiastics' writings. And yet the emperor also took the opportunity to integrate elements of his own imperial idea into these sermons. In the introductory part of the homily on St John the Baptist the emperor depicted himself as the bridegroom (νύμφιος) of the church, and also mentioned that his son and co-emperor was present at the public delivery of the sermon.[87] This connection between Manuel's homiletics and his son, the co-emperor, is further underlined by the fact that the sixth of the seven *Orations* was actually reproduced verbatim with few differences from the *Homily on St Mary of Egypt*.[88] If occasionally Manuel shows the humility required of the speaker in such circumstances, most often he states that his power derives from God, who allowed him to govern his people.[89]

Thus, despite being limited to limited topics and occasions of performance, the homilies appear to have played a certain role in shaping Manuel's imperial image. Certainly, as his ability in dealing with theological matters had been demonstrated in other texts (the *Dialogues with a Muslim* and the treatise *On the Procession of the Holy Spirit*), through his homilies he reached out to a wider public and gained acknowledgement of his authority in matters of faith. The edifying accents of the homily together with its delivery by the

---

[83] See *Homily on St John the Baptist*, Vat. gr. 1619, f. 47r: καὶ ὅτε ταῦθ' οὕτως ἔχει, ὑποχρέω πάντες ἐσμέν, τῷ τοῦ Θεοῦ ἑπόμενοι νόμῳ, καὶ ἡγεμόνι χρώμενοι τῷ θειοτάτῳ Δαυίδ, ᾧ λίαν ἐτιμήθησαν οἱ φίλοι τοῦ Θεοῦ.

[84] For instance, the homily on the Mother of God was occasioned by the emperor's recovery from an illness. See Manuel, *Homily on the Mother of God*, 543, ed. Jugie.

[85] Ibid. VII.

[86] *Homily on St John the Baptist*, Vat. gr. 1619, f. 51r: φεύγων μὲν τὰς πόλεις καὶ τὰ ἐν αὐταῖς ἡδέα ὥσπερ ἄλλός τις τὴν ἑρμηνίαν καὶ τὰ ἐν ταύτῃ λυποῦντα, ἔχων τὴν ἔρημον πόλιν καὶ ἀντὶ πατρίδος αὐτὴν ἀσπαζόμενος.

[87] Vat. gr. 1619, f. 47r.

[88] On the differences between the two texts see Kaltsogianni, 'Zur Entstehung'.

[89] Cunningham and Allen, *Preacher and Audience*, 7–19. See Vat. gr. 1619, ff. 30r–v: πάντα γὰρ θεόθεν ἡμῖν.

emperor in person would have persuaded people of his authority. At the same time, in contrast to contemporary ecclesiastics who emphasised the distinction between the patriarch's spiritual power and the dispensable state of the emperor, Manuel's homilies and liturgical texts favoured an opposite ideology. Thus, it can be contended that the homiletic and liturgical writings served political purposes because they conveyed an ideological message of subjection to the emperor by indicating respect for religion.

The emperor-rhetorician

Still, in addition to the priestly stance, a clearer set of features pertaining to the emperor's profile emerges from his political texts. Especially, the admonitory stance adopted by the emperor, as well as the systematisation of virtues, further expands our understanding of Manuel's approach to imperial authority. Based on these aspects,[90] I suggested that the emperor adopted several shifting voices which originated in his attempt to represent himself as an emperor-rhetorician who also cultivated his representation of an affectionate and concerned father. In what follows, I look more closely into how the emperor forged this representation, which owed much to his literary preoccupations and to the performative context of the address to his son and co-emperor, John VIII Palaiologos.[91]

Manuel's letters often indicate that literary activities account for one's pleasurable pastime following periods of intense activity.[92] As noted, he represented himself as chair of *theatra* and judge in literary matters. Owing to these activities, he cultivated the role of an orator preoccupied with the refinement of his performative skills. He often makes reference to moments of acting on stage.[93] Yet, the emperor claims, such literary preoccupations also had a different function. From his earliest letters onwards, he emphasised the role of rhetorical skills in a ruler's education:

> Being an accomplished speaker is clearly preferable to being wealthy; it provides something more pleasurable than all pleasure as well as a greater glory. [. . .] A person who wishes to deliver a faultless speech must also

---

[90] See Chapters 3–6.
[91] Not only were both the *Foundations* and the *Orations* addressed to John VIII, but Manuel collected most of his texts into four de luxe manuscripts which he offered to his son (Vindob. phil. gr. 98, Vat. gr. 1619, Vat. gr. 632, Crypt. Z δ 1).
[92] Manuel II, *Letters*, nos. 9, 11, 32, ed. Dennis.
[93] See Manuel II, *Letters*, no. 30, ed. Dennis, addressed to Constantine Asanes, and the *Funeral Oration*, 188: 'Are there any among you who object to the stage (σκηνή) and the mask (προσωπεῖον)?'

consider what will please the hearers and the topics which will make them feel glorious and enviable. He must have a natural ability in addition to practice; his desire must have the assistance of intelligence and, furthermore, of the proper occasion.[94]

The above passage can be corroborated with his other rhetorical exercises apparently written for amusement purposes as well as instances of the emperor's reflections on the strategies used in writing, which reveal his preoccupation with the significance of writing in a ruler's activity.[95] Early on, in the *Panegyric* for his father, Manuel outlined the main traits of a rhetorician's craft, by commenting on what should be included in or excluded from a public oration and what kind of arguments an orator should use.[96] Such remarks in the *Panegyric*[97] foreshadowed the generic changes the emperor made in the rhetorical texts he wrote during his reign. Previously, I have argued that in the *Funeral Oration* Manuel significantly expanded the narrative section of his brother's, Theodore's, deeds. With its detailed historical information, this account, similar to a history of the Morea, motivated the emperor's intervention in the province and gave him the opportunity to display his claims to full authority even in the distant territories of the state. Furthermore, Manuel advertised the oration; he received several responses which point to his intention of disclosing his rhetorical training in a form which would make it clear that writing and performing were central elements of his activity.[98] These well-documented instances, which reveall the emperor's penchant for the use of rhetoric, evince his concerns for the role of knowledge and learning in a ruler's life. According to this often-reiterated view, an emperor must be in possession of an education based on the knowledge and wisdom of the ancients.[99]

---

[94] Manuel II, *Letters*, no. 11.2–9, ed. Dennis.
[95] For instance the *Image of the Spring on a Royal Tapestry*, 411–14, ed. Davis.
[96] Manuel, *Panegyric*, 228, ed. Boissonade: οὐδὲ γὰρ ὁμοίως τῷ μαθηματικῷ τὸν ῥητορικὸν βιασόμεθα διαλέγεσθαι. εἴτε γὰρ τῷ ῥητορεύειν ἐθέλοντι παρασταίη ἐναργέσιν ἀποδείξεσι καὶ μηδαμῇ τἀμφισβητήσιμον ἐχούσαις εἰς τοὺς ἀγῶνας χωρῆσαι, εἴθ' ὁ μαθήμασι σεμνυνόμενος ψιλῇ τῇ πιθανότητι καταχρηστέον εἶναι νομίσειεν, οὐδετέρῳ ἂν κατάλληλον τὸ ἐγχείρημα γένοιτο.
[97] Further remarks on what his studies and writing meant to him and on the necessity of neglecting them due to other activities can be encountered in his letter to Alexios Iagoup: Barker, *Manuel II*, 410–13, 528–30. See Dendrinos, 'Ἐπιστολὴ τοῦ αὐτοκράτορος Μανουὴλ Παλαιολόγου'.
[98] See Chapter 2.
[99] *Foundations*, ch. 39: χρὴ θεμέλιον ἔχοντας τῶν ἀρχαιοτέρων τὰς γνώμας τοὺς νεωτέρους, οἰκοδομεῖν εἴ τι δύναιτο.

The *Foundations* and the *Orations* further testify to Manuel's idea that education was one of the core elements in a ruler's craft. In the first oration, for instance, he compares Croesus's treasure and Xerxes' military resources with the Athenians' wisdom, and remarks that knowledge was a more important aspect than hoarding wealth or resources.[100] Such concerns were tailored to the emperor's didactic outlook, which privileged the representations of mentors concerned with ethical education and, ultimately, led him to represent himself as an emperor-teacher. As a consequence, he constantly connects intellectual activities like writing with a ruler's career:

> But if we refrain from literary activities, the fruits of our education will disappear to such an extent that we will not even be able to understand clearly the dogmas which enable us to be truly pious. With all this in mind, I continue to do some writing, not as much as I ought, but as much as the time permits, in order that I might be an example to my subjects of the love of letters, so that as they mingle so much with barbarians they might not become completely barbarised.[101]

According to this outlook, what made knowledge an effective tool in a ruler's hands was the ability to speak well (καλῶς λέγειν).[102] The emperor's firm stand concerning the acquisition of knowledge and rhetorical skills for a politically efficient language was coterminous with the central idea promoted by the emperor in the *Foundations* and the *Orations*: the process of becoming an ideal man (ἀγαθὸς ἀνήρ), a model of life that he proposes to his son John.[103] Attaining this ideal, Manuel argues, needed strict guidance backed up with discipline; therefore, he appears ready to strengthen his parental role with the role of a *didaskalos*.[104] The embedded didactic function had already been assumed in the preface to the *Foundations*, and in the *Orations*, where education appears as an element in the construction of the imperial ethos. Two passages, already quoted earlier, are telling:

---

[100] *Orations*, 385a. Cf. *Foundations*, ch. 75: learning (μάθησις) should represent a core activity for a ruler.

[101] Manuel II, *Letters*, ch. 52.29–35, ed. Dennis.

[102] It is for this reason that in the very first lines of the *Orations* Manuel entreats his son to acquire the rhetorical skills which would allow him to become a good ruler. See *Orations*, 385a.

[103] *Foundations*, Prefatory Letter, 316c: εἰ μέλλεις καλὸς κἀγαθὸς ἔσεσθαι.

[104] E.g. *Orations*, 557a: αὐτός σου τὴν φίλην κεφαλήν, ὦ συμβασιλεῦ τε καὶ παῖ, οὐ μόνον ἐνταυθοῖ στεφανῶσαι, ἀλλὰ κἀκεῖ, τῷ καλῷ στεφάνῳ τῶν μακαρίων.

For to speak with authority (μετ' ἐξουσίας εἰπεῖν), which is very effective for schoolteachers, professors and anyone who strives to restore or to forge the nature of youths, is entirely possible for me. But for those (i.e. the ancient writers) it is entirely impossible, even though all wisdom is gathered into one. For how can they provide exhortations causing no fear, or in a trustful manner, or in a confident way according to the stance of an emperor, a father or a friend, given that they lack the position which inspires the lack of fear, and the imperial majesty and the friendship which grows with the intimacy between teachers and students.[105]

I am convinced that in so far as there is some benefit here, if you want to gain something by acting diligently, it would be easy to make plain that you are the best of men and of emperors. For if, as the author of this text, I am inferior to these texts, nevertheless this should not be an impediment for you in acquiring virtue; but if I find something better (since nobody was excepted from the goods that follow), you will consider that it is fitting for you to inherit this for you and you will strive eagerly to advance and improve your father's wealth and even the empire itself. As you notice my shortcomings (for they are many and great) be willing to learn something from these, setting them as a teacher for a better life and for a more secure empire. It is good that you imitate those who saved themselves from others' shipwrecks and learned their lessons from the mistakes and misfortunes of those.[106]

Within this didactic framework which he set up, Manuel then offered hints as to the behaviour an ideal emperor and ἀγαθὸς ἀνήρ should adopt:

You should recognise the good individual not by his fate but by his attitude and behaviour. The good individual is not one who exerts his power but one who uses the power which he has at his disposal. Not one who possesses much gold buried in the ground, but one who prides himself on his friends.[107]

Interestingly, with the exception of Solon, among the paradigms of behaviour proposed in both the *Foundations* and *Orations*, one does not find any of

---

[105] *Foundations, Prefatory Letter*, 317a.
[106] Ibid. 317c. On the emperor's knowledge of different strategies of education see the citation from Gregory of Nazianz in *Foundations*, ch. 32: τοὺς μὲν ἄγει λόγος, οἱ δὲ ῥυθμίζονται παραδείγματι. οἱ μὲν δέονται κέντρου, οἱ δὲ χαλινοῦ.
[107] *Foundations*, ch. 70: the ideal ruler is to be praised not for his wealth but for the friends; ch. 71 insists on the fact that wealthy rulers must not necessarily be admired.

the legendary mythological figures of rulers common in imperial orations.[108] As a matter of fact, Manuel avoids ideal representations of imperial rule almost completely, thereby subverting the classical comparison with heroic models identifiable in other imperial orations. Instead, in the *Foundations* he mentions exclusively the model provided by the exemplary yet hapless life of Job.[109] Yet, along with such models, the emperor's didacticism surfaces especially in the systematic way in which he presents ethical notions. The strategy adopted was to proceed from basic philosophical questions or illustrations to more complex problems and principles.[110] At other times he urges his son not to indulge only in military and physical activities but to combine them with intellectual pursuits.[111] Even more, pointing to his predominant intellectual preoccupations, Manuel exhorted his son to seek relaxation in delightful gardens after moments of intense activity.[112] In addition, Manuel repeatedly offered advice on how to act in specific situations and for the proper behaviour expected in relation to his subjects.[113] Likewise, he frequently referred to the importance of one's nature and character. The most conspicuous evidence for such advice appears in the last two orations, which, as mentioned above, tried to regulate John's behaviour by means of direct address. Thus, in the conclusion of the last *Oration*, after Manuel expressed lengthy criticism of his son's acts as co-emperor, he exhorted John not to pass radical judgement on others, since the position of judge was reserved to God:

> Thus it is good and safe to give only to our Saviour the power to judge everyone and not to compare us with each other. Since this is my opinion, it has been shown in every way that nobody must be high-handed towards others. Even if some people have a high reputation, they should not mock other people, nor should they think highly of themselves: for, as it is said, the one who judges me is God. He is the one who may crown your head, oh co-emperor and son, not only here but there where he crowns the blessed ones.[114]

---

[108] This is not the case with the *Funeral Oration*, where the final *comparison* (*synkrisis*) of the deceased with the ancient heroes brings into the foreground a whole series of legendary heroes; *Funeral Oration*, 215.

[109] *Foundations*, ch. 69.

[110] E.g. ibid. chs. 1–4 on different ways of life and *Orations* II and III on notions like good and voluntariness. In both cases these initial presentations serve as the basis for further teaching.

[111] E.g. *Foundations*, ch. 53: ῥώμη σώματος συγκεκραμένη συνέσει πεπλεγμένος ἄριστα τοῖς τυραννεύουσι στέφανος.

[112] See ibid. ch. 80: οὐκ ἐστίν οὐδεῖς ἐν ἀνθρώποις, ὃς ἂν σπουδῇ διηνεκῶς χρήσαιτο· ἀλλ' ἡ φύσις ἑκάστῳ σπουδάζοντι καὶ παραμυθίας τινός ἐφίεται. See also Manuel II, *Image of the Spring on a Royal Tapestry*.

[113] As in *Foundations*, ch. 84 on οἰκεία διόρθωσις.

[114] *Orations* 7, 556d. Cf. 505a: ὁρᾷς, ὁπόσον ἀγαθόν ἐστιν ἡ αὐτομεμψία.

Similar instances of didactic advice can be encountered not only in the *Foundations* or the *Orations* but also in other, shorter texts written during Manuel's reign and dealing with counselling on specific issues of behaviour: the *Several Words for Brevity and Peace in Deliberations* (1406),[115] the *Anacreontic Verses Addressed to a Completely Ignorant and Most Garrulous Person* (1392–6)[116] or the *Oration to His Subjects*.[117]

The didactic framework of the moral advice revealed by the references to the emperor's teaching role suggests that, contrary to the assessments of previous scholarship,[118] the emperor strove to construct the image of an emperor-rhetorician, an image which retained a strong political dimension. This message involved on the one hand differentiation from previous Byzantine rulers who, like Manuel's father, had neglected the intellectual aspect of ruling. Another late Byzantine ruler, John VI Kantakouzenos, had mostly theological preoccupations which he utilised on specific occasions, without their amounting to a complete programme of imperial renovation. On the other hand, by composing a series of political texts Manuel tried to legitimise his dynastic line and his immediate successor John VIII, against the challenges of John VII's line. Furthermore, the message embedded in Manuel's texts also involved another distinction from the church, itself teacher-*didaskalos* but in spiritual issues, as stated in the epistolary epilogue:

> For if you must not disobey the priests of old and the Pharisees, because they are sitting on Moses' seat, although they transmit nothing from what I taught, it is much more appropriate that you listen to me who am teaching you what is useful, even if I might not be doing this well.[119]

This representation was distinct from the conventional representation of the ruler as philosopher-king, in that it valued highly the acquisition and use of rhetorical skills in political transactions. Other Byzantine emperors like Leo VI the Wise (886–912), who wrote numerous homilies, or Theodore II Laskaris (1221–2), author of moral and political texts, had promoted themselves as philosopher-kings. In contrast to this notion as describing the passive usage

---

[115] For a transcription of this short text, see Chapter 4, p. 139.
[116] PG 156, 575d–576d. Cf. Manuel's *Discourse on Drunkenness and Adultery*, ed. Boissonade.
[117] In the *Oration to His Subjects* Manuel adopts a didactic stance by advising his subjects about what was beneficial for them and about avoiding dangerous habits: ὡς ἐξ εὐμενοῦς ἄρχοντος πρὸς εὔνους ὑπηκόους τοὺς ἐν ἀκμῇ, PG 156, 561.
[118] E.g. Mergiali, who considers that late Byzantine intellectuals' pastimes were rather scholarly amusements and had nothing to do with political realities; *Enseignement*, 165.
[119] *Orations, Epistolary Epilogue*, 560a.

of knowledge, Manuel's conception of *logos* involved an active civic role of rhetoric in the state's life. It is, therefore, I believe, appropriate to say that this emperor-writer reworked the old version of a philosopher-king into a new mould formed according to his own preoccupations and to the concrete political challenges of his day.

These observations allow us to draw several conclusions. First, the projection of the imperial image as that of a teacher-rhetorician has to be understood in the light of the emperor's efforts to convey political messages by means of his rhetorical compositions. If in his early letters Manuel envisaged the process of writing rhetorical texts as a pleasurable activity, in his political texts he adopted a different approach. His approach was multifaceted and suggests the emperor's intention to constantly adjust his imperial vision to conditions and opportunities that appeared throughout the first two decades of his reign. Thus, his earliest political text, the *Dialogue*, supported the emperor's claims to dynastic supremacy at a time of internal strife with his nephew John VII. This tendency was consolidated in the ensuing years and found reflection in his didactic texts, the *Foundations* and the *Orations*. The later *Funeral Oration* projected the image of an emperor capable of exerting authority over distant and vulnerable Byzantine territories. Using an extended narrative, Manuel forged a different facet of Byzantine rulership concerned with military and diplomatic activities. Just as in the case of the *Foundations* and the *Orations*, here as well the medium conveying the message of political authority was a rhetorical text with educational undertones.

Second, these observations can also lead to a better understanding of the emperor's conception of rhetoric as a political instrument, different from other contemporary conceptions such as the court rhetoricians'. Both the emperor and the panegyrists embraced a wide range of meanings which boil down to two major perspectives: first, rhetoric itself is a powerful medium, and second, those who know how to handle it can effectively become powerful themselves. This understanding of rhetoric was grounded in the ancient assumption that knowledge and education empower individuals. According to many theorists of rhetoric, by learning the practical skills of literacy the educated individual also acquired the appropriate ethics and became capable of ruling the community.[120] Yet whereas the imperial rhetoricians dwell on the psychological impact of rhetoric on individuals, in his texts Manuel underscored its civilising influence on individuals and on society at large. As used by panegyrists,

---

[120] The correlation between power, ethics and rhetorical education in the Hellenistic and Roman world has been convincingly investigated by Teresa Morgan on the basis of Egyptian papyri and the theoretical texts of authors like Cicero, Quintilian and Plutarch; *Literate Education*, 146–50, 228, 267.

rhetoric highlights the power of language to distort reality by exaggerating the effects of the ruler's actions. On the contrary, Manuel used *logos* to highlight the capacity to lead and to shape worldviews. For him, as for other ancient rhetoricians, the perfect orator should be not only a virtuous man but also a ruler.

Furthermore, as a prominent member of the Constantinopolitan scholarly circle, the emperor emerged as responsible for challenging the cultural domination of the traditional panegyric. He was interested in rhetoric's potential for beneficial results and less in its power to convey personal interests. Accordingly, his political writings seem to have been designed to end political turmoil and to harmonise individual and collective interests. In contrast to the court orators' project, I suggest that Manuel's project sought to compensate for the lack of previous enlightened statesmanship and participatory citizenship after the conflicts with the Ottomans. Departing from the scholars' programme, Manuel linked rhetoric to the articulation of wise governance and civic conscience. Clearly, each programme sought to fulfil a special need: whereas the orators' programme conceived rhetoric as key to social survival and political prominence, Manuel's turned it into an expression of, and a guide to, the salvation of the Byzantine Empire. It can be concluded that if for the late Byzantine court orators, rhetoric represented a question of formal address, for Manuel, who included rhetorical training in his moral system, it represented rather an instrument of coercing political mores and practices. In his texts, rhetoric moved away from issues of praise and closer to the political present because, in his view, the mission of rhetoric was to specify common goals and to articulate widely acceptable visions.[121]

These observations allow us to assess the singularity of Manuel's vision within the broader picture of Byzantine approaches to imperial authority. Although Byzantine imperial ideology is a vast topic with many ramifications that so far have not been thoroughly investigated, studies like those already mentioned by Gilbert Dagron, Dimiter Angelov and Anthony Kaldellis gave a clearer insight into Byzantine ideas of political authority prior to Manuel's rule. Several lines of debate can be distinguished: first, the emperor's union of two powers, temporal and spiritual; second, the actual limits of the Byzantine emperor's rule, which caused frequent conflicts with other institutions; and third, the kinds of virtues that Byzantine emperors adopted or chose to project about themselves, often by means of public oratory. As indicated throughout

---

[121] Such a process was certainly not unique in the Palaiologan period, as it is observable in the texts of other, early Palaiologan authors like Thomas Magistros or Maximos Planoudes.

this volume, Manuel was aware of these themes and phenomena, which he discussed in his texts. The idea of imperial sanctity that had been elaborated earlier by Theodore Balsamon and became popular during the reign of Manuel I Komnenos continued to exert an attraction for late Byzantine rulers as well. The growing influence of new centres of power like the *dēmos* or the court of *oikeioi* made emperors rethink their strategies of decision making. Likewise, Manuel's connection with previous rulers can be detected in the imperial rhetoric which flourished under the Palaiologoi and cultivated absolutist values.

Moreover, Manuel was not the only emperor with intellectual preoccupations. Before him, Leo VI the Wise, Constantine Porphyrogennitos, Manuel I Komnenos, Theodore Laskaris and John VI Kantakouzenos had literary or philosophical preoccupations. For instance, Theodore Laskaris II wrote moral and political treatises that encapsulated his vision of political authority.[122] Others, like John Kantakouzenos, Manuel's grandfather, used their texts in order to justify their actions. Yet in the case of Manuel II Palaiologos, writing rhetorical texts was more than a means of justification or of disseminating intellectual reflections. He remains unique in the way he conceived rhetoric as a tool of civic betterment and also in the way he fashioned himself not as a philosopher-king but rather as a public orator, a new Demosthenes, as Kydones praised him in his youth. Due to his political experience and to the late Byzantine circumstances, Manuel probably became aware that his influence and authority were limited and contested. He sought to reconfigure the imperial position by changing the system of imperial virtues and by adding the lustre of ancient civic oratory. Unlike previous rulers who conceived of their intellectual preoccupations as an additional feature validating their authority, Manuel rather sought to leverage the power of rhetoric in a way that was meant to change the nature of the imperial position in Byzantium into a mediating role between the various groups vying for influence and public attention in Constantinople. Moreover, he did not see this role as limited to his reign but considered his political texts to have a far-reaching educational dimension, as he dedicated them to his son, John.

Manuel II's Imperial Vision and Style of Government

In the previous chapters, I have tried to record shifting authorial voices which the emperor used, from the *Dialogue* to the *Funeral Oration*, when addressing political issues specific to late Byzantium: deliberative, didactic and narrative. They supplement each other rather than exclude one another. From a view of

---

[122] Angelov, *Imperial Ideology*, 204–52.

polemical political discourse in the *Dialogue*, I moved to a model of education and the emperor's relation to other factors of political decision making. From questioning the dynastic order (in the *Dialogue*), I moved to attempts to reinforce political order through a different kind of political discourse (the *Funeral Oration*). The texts reveal not only the emperor's developing standpoints in his attempts to answer political challenges, but also a unique and long-term imperial ‚project that sought to establish a system of effective political communication by exhibiting his fatherly concern for his son and co-emperor. This project involved several stages with changing approaches determined by the confrontation between Manuel's outlook and the ideas of other groups competing for influence. In the first stage, the emperor strengthened his connections with the literati and frequently chaired *theatra*. The letters and the dialogic mode of his text on marriage point to the fact that during the last decade of the fourteenth century, the emperor did not have at his disposal too many possibilities of circulating his political messages except for the rather informal meetings in the framework of *theatra*. In this period (1391–9) the *theatra* seem to have resembled literary salons where debates took place and Manuel could concomitantly assume the role of a court leader and of a μαΐστωρ τῶν ῥητόρων.[123] In a second stage, which chronologically coincides with the years following the emperor's return from the West, rhetorical productions became much more numerous. Following a post-1402 trend, like other court rhetoricians, Manuel celebrated the defeat of the Ottomans as a divine omen. But if the Ottoman threat was temporarily deflected, Byzantium still had to live through a period of dual rule with John VII in Thessalonike holding the titles of *basileus* and *autokrator*. Both Manuel II and John VII had sons who had the right to inherit their fathers' throne. At this decisive moment, Manuel was quick to act: he not only appointed his son as co-emperor, but also made known his chosen successor by specifically addressing two texts to his son, the *Foundations* and the *Orations*. Publicly displayed fatherly affection thus came to play a central role in the Byzantine politics of dynastic succession. Employing a didactic stance, Manuel presented himself as his son's teacher in matters of ethics and political action, and also offered a systematic introduction to major philosophical themes. In parallel to these texts, he used the opportunity of his brother's commemoration in Mystras to modify the *epitaphios* genre sharply and make sure that by using a fully fledged narrative voice in describing Theodore's achievements, he presented himself as a defender of the Morea. The generic transformations in the *Funeral Oration*, reflected in the large-scale use of narrative, point to his intention of employing his rhetorical skills for political purposes.

---

[123] See Chapter 2.

A closer look at the genre of his political texts reveals that he had a distinct rapport with the Byzantine rhetorical tradition. In the *Foundations* and the *Orations*, texts that imitated Agapetos's *Ekthesis* and the ancient didactic diatribe, respectively, he returned to the origins of political and didactic writing. These compositions represented unique cases of reusing ancient genres, as no contemporary author seemed attracted by these kinds of texts. In this way, Manuel used the authority of Agapetos and of the ancient teachers not only to distinguish himself from other, peer writers of his time but also to strengthen his message of imperial prestige. Yet in his other political texts, the *Dialogue* and the *Funeral Oration*, generic experimentation served him to come close to the rhetorical tendencies of his time and to integrate himself into the scholarly circle whose members subsequently came to provide him with diplomatic or court services.

The emperor's efforts to adapt his imperial vision to the realities and react in publicly performed texts continued through his reign. After 1411, he delivered prayers and sermons which, alongside his previous theological and liturgical writings, suggest that he assumed a more influential position in the church. This move can be interpreted as an act whereby the emperor sought to appease if not to counteract the anti-imperial position adopted by the ecclesiastics in their discourse. Thus, although at times his politico-didactic texts concerned with issues of authority acknowledged the limits of his political authority, the emphasis on rhetorical training legitimised and authorised a different type of ruler, yet still a ruler.

When describing Manuel's style of government, scholars have often quoted Sphrantzes' statement attributed to Manuel, according to which in times of crisis, an emperor was supposed to act rather as a manager (οἰκονόμος) of political and economic affairs:[124]

> My son, the Emperor, seems to himself to be a suitable emperor – but not for the present day. For he <John VIII> has large views and ideas and such as the times demanded in the heyday of the prosperity of his ancestors. But nowadays, as things are going with us, our empire needs not an emperor, but an administrator. I am afraid that the decline of this house may come from his poems and arguments, for I have noted his propensities and what he thought to achieve with Mustafa, and I have seen also the result in what danger they have brought us.[125]

---

[124] Sphrantzes' words were echoed by Manuel himself in the *Foundations*, ch. 59, where he advises his son to manage (οἰκονομεῖν) the moments of peace.

[125] Sphrantzes, *Memoirs*, 58–60, ed. Grecu. John's poems have not been preserved and it is plausible that Sphrantzes rather alludes to the emperor's literary education and ideals of independent rule.

Certainly, as John Barker argued, the emperor's vast political experience cannot be overlooked when judging his ideological outlook. Manuel was a *basileus-oikonomos* inasmuch as he was an *emperor-hagiographer* who collected and used relics for diplomatic purposes,[126] or an *emperor-priest*, as his homiletic texts indicate. Yet the above analysis has shown that, when considering his ever-developing style of government, the role of rhetoric in his rule cannot be overlooked.[127] His prolific literary activity indicates that he also wished to add a further dimension to his rulership and to reinvent himself as a rhetorician, both like other active fellow authors and as a teacher-instructor of his son and of his subjects. On the one hand, these texts served purposes of self-promotion through self-presentation, since, with few instances of public display remaining, literary culture became an instrument of self-fashioning and one of the few means of political propaganda. In the absence of a more substantial body of court rhetoricians, the emperor undertook the role of a social-political commentator on the state situation and accordingly put forward a personal discourse on imperial authority. His interest and skill in staging and publicising himself and his policies are well documented. Unlike previous Byzantine *princely mirrors*, the *Foundations* and the *Orations* were not only tools of social control through direct advice but also advertised Manuel's dominant position in relation to the other *basileus* and *autokrator* John VII, while the *Funeral Oration* made clear that the emperor still had authority in the Peloponnese.

On the other hand, the use of several authorial voices reflecting different rhetorical approaches – deliberative, narrative, didactic – combined with his fatherly and priestly stances suggests that the emperor sought to attain a kind of social harmony. In his highly elaborated rhetorical texts, Manuel promoted the idea of a seductive authority which preserved most imperial prerogatives

---

[126] On the emperor's involvement in economic activities such as trade or tax collection, pursuits which sometimes overlapped with the aristocracy's interests, see Matschke, 'Kaiser oder Verwalter? Die Wirtschaftspolitik Manuels zwischen 1403 und 1422 und ihre Effekte', in *Schlacht bei Ankara*, 220–35. In 1407 Manuel sent several relics to Martin V of Aragon (1395–1410), after consultations with the patriarch and other Constantinopolitan nobles: 'de columna in qua ligatus fuit Salvator Noster; de lapide super quem Petrus incumbens, post ternam Christi negacionem, amarissime flevit; de lapide in quo, post deposicionem a cruce ut ungerent, positus fuerat humani generis Liberator, ac eciam de craticula super quam Sanctus Laurencius fuit assatu'; Marinesco, 'Manuel II Paléologue', 199. On his so-called relic diplomacy see Barker, *Manuel II*. Relics remained an important diplomatic tool even later on and was used by Theodore II Palaiologos and John VIII Palaiologos; Ganchou, 'Géorgios Scholarios'; Hilsdale, *Byzantine Art and Diplomacy*.

[127] Chrysostomides had already pointed to the significance of Manuel's reflective nature combined with his pragmatic and empirical knowledge when developing his political conception; in *Funeral Oration*, 12.

while admitting the growing influence of other groups. By contrast with the approach of previous rulers of Byzantium, this version of the empire helped him identify a middle path between political groups in conflict and dissipate the tensions between the hardcore Orthodox and the Latinophiles. In writing these texts Manuel sought to exercise a form of social control achieved through agreement rather than through direct and material coercion.

Furthermore, Manuel's texts reverse the representation of an emperor preoccupied exclusively with the political aspects of his position, a representation cultivated especially during his father's reign. In a hitherto unseen gesture, Manuel publicly displayed his fatherly tie with his son, in a move which turned his audience's attention to his desired successor. Manuel also subverted the image of the philosopher-king by replacing philosophical preparation with rhetorical education, focusing on providing a pleasurable experience to the readers/listeners. Finally, the image of the philosopher created by constant reference to concepts and themes drawn especially from ancient philosophers' writings was reinforced by that of a Christian preacher and of a *didaskalos* teaching his son right behaviour.

We can also draw further conclusions about Manuel's relation to the rhetoricians and the ecclesiastics. My aim here has been to map certain political discourses current during Manuel II's reign and to identify the approaches to the emperor's authority in the texts of the ecclesiastics, the imperial rhetoricians and the emperor himself. Comparison between the statements inserted into the discourse used by each group and by Manuel himself points to numerous similarities as well as differences. Regarding the growing concerns with the economic and social situation, it is remarkable that the ecclesiastics and the court rhetoricians held largely similar opinions. They identified the members of the higher echelons of the social elites, businessmen and aristocrats, as responsible for the endemic poverty in Constantinople and in Thessalonike. As for the emperor's texts, however, they do not display a similar interest in social and economic issues. The attitude to the enemies and the potential allies of Byzantium differed from one group to another: while the ecclesiastics claimed that the Byzantines should defend themselves alone, the emperor and the rhetoricians favoured the idea of an alliance with the Latins. In addition, Manuel suggested that other neighbouring peoples, like the Serbs, the Bulgarians or the Albanians, could provide help. For these peoples, he did not use the term *barbarians*, thereby echoing the provisions of the Treaty of Gallipoli in 1403 which assigned to the Byzantines a place in an alliance with other regional Christian peoples. Therefore he downplayed Byzantine uniqueness, occasionally pointing only to their Romanness, a notion also used largely by court rhetoricians. Moreover, in both Manuel's and the rhetoricians' texts the tendency was to use a territorially delimited and national πατρίς (fatherland). On the contrary, the ecclesiastics tended to use the notion of πατρίς with the universalist connotations of a community of the Orthodox (γένος τῶν ὀρθοδόξων).[128] Finally, the attitude to imperial authority was particularly radical in the texts of most ecclesiastics, who denied the emperor the claims to universal and absolute power. Orthodox clergymen envisaged a political entity where the emperor's authority was limited and could be censured by the church. On the other hand, rhetoricians cultivated a representation of imperial authority which relied on the tenets current in Byzantine courtly propaganda. In particular, they equally raised the emperor's military successes as well as his literary preoccupations. Often they described the emperor as a teacher (διδάσκαλος). In fact, this feature was one of the core elements of Manuel's construction of imperial authority since he assiduously cultivated his rhetorical skills. In his texts he assumed a didactic-fatherly stance in order to assert that his firstborn son, John VIII, was to be his successor. In other texts like the *Dialogue* or the *Funeral Oration* he reacted to the political challenges of the day, and in his homiletic and liturgical texts he envisioned the role of a priest, thus signalling his opposition to the ecclesiastics' claims of church pre-eminence.

Viewed from a wide historical perspective, these broad discursive themes indicate a conflict ongoing in the last decades of the Byzantine Empire, between the church, on the one hand, and the emperor, on the other hand, who relied on the support of the aristocracy whose interests were reflected in the rhetoricians' texts. Yet even if the emperor's political discourse had more affinities with the rhetoricians' discourse, Manuel's texts put forward a clearly distinct alternative. He realised that he needed bureaucrats and the propaganda of the court rhetoricians to strengthen the authority of the imperial administration, particularly against the ecclesiastics' claims. Nevertheless, analysis of his texts indicates that he certainly also wished to avoid becoming too circumscribed by the practices and precedents that accompanied government. It is probably for this reason that he sometimes rebuked his friend Demetrios Chryoloras for having praised him excessively.

Manuel thus appears as a unique political strategist preoccupied with the interstices of the imperial office. His main concern was the promotion of an imperial ethos distinct from that of his predecessors, and at the same time adaptation to the new realities in which the Byzantine emperor represented little more than a group leader. Often his voice engaged with the collective imagination of his audience: while being connected to a timeless history and experience, it echoed the emperor's personal experiences.

---

[128] See also the analysis by Kioussopoulou, *Emperor or Manager*, 178–80.

Conclusions

The aim of this book has been to examine the political messages conveyed in several rhetorical texts by Emperor Manuel II and determine the strategies whereby the emperor-author outlined a renewed version of late Byzantine imperial ideology. Until now, students of Manuel II's writings have investigated his texts for evidence of the political and institutional history of the last decades of Byzantine history. This kind of information surfaces especially in his letters and in the *Funeral Oration*. Yet other rhetorical texts of his, which lacked concrete data concerning events, situations or individuals, have previously been largely overlooked if not dismissed as too obscure for historical research. Nevertheless, on closer scrutiny, they present multiple pieces of evidence which pertain to the discursive construction of imperial representations at a time of significant economic, social and political transformation. These hitherto unstudied pieces of evidence allow us to get a better sense of the emperor's style of government and of the ideological assumptions underlying his actions.

The point of departure for my investigation was the observation that, as in other periods of Byzantine history, the emperor had to balance competing interest groups in order to secure his authority. As contemporary sources indicate, his political and military responses were rather calculated and commensurate with the resources he had at his disposal. More often than not, he showed a conciliatory attitude towards the conflicts unfolding both in Byzantium and in the Eastern Mediterranean. He negotiated alliances not only with the Latins but also with the Ottomans, thereby avoiding open military encounters. Alongside the agreement with his nephew, John VII, for sharing imperial power, his intense diplomatic activity, despite the lack of success, suggests an attitude of political moderation.

Manuel's political writings, despite being couched in fairly conventional terms, reflect the relations which the emperor sought to negotiate and establish with other contemporary power brokers in the church and at his court. Viewed against the backdrop of other, similar contemporary productions, his texts can provide answers to a number of questions with regard to the history of late Byzantium: what did the emperor stand for in those years? What was his style of government? What were the means envisaged for saving the state from impending destruction? They reflected the emperor's concerns vis-à-vis ongoing issues and conflicts with effects on the institutional framework, or issues such as the imperial succession, the exertion of central authority in provinces isolated from Constantinople, or the necessity to establish a balanced system of alliances with other regional influential actors.

In the first two chapters, I offered a survey of the contemporary groups that interacted with the emperor: the ecclesiastics and the rhetoricians. I documented the membership of these two groups as well as the ecclesiastics' conflicts with the emperor and the rhetoricians' support for Manuel's rule. I dealt extensively with the literati the emperor gathered at his court. I noted that the emperor maintained a strong relationship with them as attested by the intense exchange of letters taking place between him and them. After a presentation of the performances of literary writings taking place in the framework of the so-called *theatra* I focused on the major groups of the literati active in Constantinople: on the one hand, there were those oriented towards closer connections with the Latin West, like Demetrios Kydones, Manuel Kalekas, Manuel Chrysoloras, Demetrios Skaranos and Maximos Chrysoberges. They partook in common intellectual projects, such as the translation into Greek of the Dominican liturgy, as well as in coordinated diplomatic pursuits, like the attempt to regain from Venice the properties and assets of John Laskaris Kalopheros. On the other hand, the written sources present us with the image of another group of individuals who upheld strict Orthodox views, a group which includes Patriarch Euthymios II, Joseph Bryennios, Theodore Potamios and Makarios Makres. As indicated by their letters and manuscript evidence, they were connected by numerous intense intellectual exchanges. Apart from these two groups we find other individuals associated with the emperor on account of their common literary preoccupations: Demetrios Chrysoloras, John Chortasmenos and Isidore the future metropolitan of Kiev.

Subsequently, I turned to the emperor's political texts composed during his reign: the *Dialogue with the Empress-Mother on Marriage* (1396), the *Foundations of an Imperial Education* (1406), the *Seven Ethico-Political Orations* (1408) and the *Funeral Oration for His Brother Theodore, Despot of Morea* (1411). After a survey of the emperor's substantial œuvre comprising theological, liturgical and political writings, I proceeded to a close reading of each of these texts and used notions drawn from both modern literary theory and ancient rhetorical handbooks. This double perspective enabled me to analyse in more depth categories such as genre and authorial voice, which in turn support a better understanding of the topics approached in these writings and of their functions in the given contexts. In addition, in this section I contextualised these texts in historical and rhetorical terms.

Building on the investigation of the underlying social and intellectual developments as well as on Manuel's rhetorical strategies, I dealt with the emperor's ideological claims that shaped the approaches to the nature and exercise of political authority in the late fourteenth and early fifteenth centuries. I proceeded from the observation that in late Byzantium, as everywhere else, different social groups adhered to aims that suited their interests. As a result, the late Byzantine political sphere presents the picture of an arena where different political perspectives sometimes competed and sometimes intersected with each other. Thereby I discussed the specificities of the emperor's discursive representation of imperial authority. In order to identify not only the differences but also the common genealogies of these three competing visions, I dealt with four major themes of discourse shared by all authors of the later Byzantine periods: the cleavages between different segments of society and particularly between the emerging entrepreneurs and the impoverished citizens of Constantinople and Thessalonike; the approach to the question of Byzantium's alliances; the formulation of Byzantine individuality either in cultural terms as identification with Hellenism, or in religious terms as Orthodox, or within a political framework as Roman; and the conceptualisation of the idea of imperial rule. Finally, I looked at the major features of Manuel's style of government as reflected in the vision he constructed in his political texts in addition to other liturgical writings such as prayers and homilies.

The most important findings of my study I consider the following. With regard to late Byzantine political practices, one can note a process of change within the basis for decision making by the inclusion of individuals with a variety of social backgrounds: aristocrats, businessmen, ecclesiastics and at times Latins (Marshal Boucicaut, Gattilusio). Frequently some of these opposed the emperor, as became clear from the support they offered to John VII or to the Ottoman forces. This change occurred under the influence of both the aristocracy and the population, which was increasingly referred to as taking part in public gatherings meant to decide on affairs of state. In addition to these changes in the social elites and the institutional framework, the challenges to imperial authority coming especially from the ecclesiastics and from the supporters of Manuel's brother's, Andronikos IV's, lineage forced the emperor to find other supporters at the Constantinopolitan court. As a result, his strategy of reasserting control over the centrifugal forces in the empire involved his action at two levels: on the one hand, the emperor seemingly strove to balance the influence of different factions, and on the other hand, Manuel also proved to be interested in conveying his political messages to as wide an audience as possible. He attempted to create a kind of parallel court, populated by literati who were also court officials. He thus managed to preside over this court without contest and, subsequently, he could use this milieu to validate and disseminate his own political views.

The examination of the emperor's group of literati led me to conclude that the network of scholars in Manuel's entourage served various purposes. At a basic level, some of these literati, like John Chortasmenos, used this network to obtain material benefits for themselves and their families. The network was also used for cooperation amongst scholars, as the manuscript evidence indicates. It appears that authors including the emperor himself often commented on each other's texts. Manuel also actively engaged his literary friends in his political activities, as the example of Manuel Chrysoloras, teacher of Greek in Florence and later the emperor's envoy to the West, shows. A key outcome of the scrutiny of the emperor's literary court pertains to the modality in which the emperor used the scholarly circle as a platform to advertise an image of his authority. In the absence of an officially appointed μαΐστωρ τῶν ῥητόρων the emperor himself acted as an official court orator. Especially before 1403, *theatra* offered the opportunity for the emperor to broadcast his literary skills. With the temporary normalisation of the situation after the battle of Ankara, the emperor could rely on several members of this network, such as Demetrios Chrysoloras, Manuel Chrysoloras, Makarios Makres and John Chortasmenos, to write panegyrics or pieces of public oratory which extolled his military and political merits in pacifying the state. Furthermore, the importance of the emperor as a major patron of letters and promoter of literary activities in the late fourteenth century appears even more clearly through a comparison with other, similar contemporary sponsors. Owing to the decline in economic resources, the activities of patrons like Cristoforo Garatone, an Italian humanist and student of Guarino of Verona, proved rather limited in scope. In contrast, it seems that not only was Manuel II active in literary circles but he also sponsored a workshop for copying manuscripts.

The analysis of the emperor's political texts reveals that all four of his political compositions were conceived and transmitted as different ways of expressing moral and political advice: deliberative (*Dialogue*), 'gnomic' (*Foundations*), based on diatribe (*Orations*) and narrative (*Funeral Oration*). In the *Dialogue*, which draws on both orality and sophisticated rhetorical theories of topics, praise for decisive action or for a political design was replaced with a deliberative stance. In the *Foundations*, by combining the categories of father and teacher into one authorial voice, the emperor played with his needs as a father, on the one hand, and service to the prince-elect, on the other hand. This strategy had the advantage of creating a voice that moved between paternal intimacy and court solemnity. Weaving multiple voices as well as several generic strands (*centuria*, *hypothekai*, gnomic literature, 'princely mirrors'), the author created a multifaceted and stronger self-authorisation. Connected by the same intent of providing an educational model for his son, John VIII, are the seven *Orations*, the text linked to the *Foundations*. Here, the author organised the material of his seven texts with different topics in the manner of a diatribe, a form of speech popular in antiquity and defined as a group of lectures or orations on a moral theme characterised by vividness and immediacy in language. Thus it appears that the seven *Orations* were intended as something different from a series of seven orations unconnected among themselves. Noticeably, the apparent indeterminacy of this collection of different types of *logoi* allowed for greater freedom in the use of philosophical or theological themes. As a result of the configuration of the *Orations*, the educational message is constructed through an accumulation of arguments and representations which culminate in the admonition addressed to John to regard humility (ταπεινοφροσύνη) as the highest imperial virtue. In the last text I analysed, the *Funeral Oration*, Manuel appears to have emulated the traditions both of panegyric oration and of epic and chronicle. The subject matter, the praise for his brother, is treated in the form of an historical account and the author offers a wealth of details about the events he recounts. With regard to the construction of the authorial voice, I argued that the author wove into his narrative three different plots: one following Theodore's deeds in the Peloponnese; one about the emperor-author himself, who presented his actions as decisive in the pacification of the region; and one about the history of the Morea.

In all these four texts, the elaborate construction of political advice is reflected in their deliberative contents, the ethos which the emperor strove to construct, and, not least, by their inclusion in a single codex, the Vindob. phil. gr. 98, dedicated to John VIII and part of a series of four manuscripts which comprised most of the emperor's literary texts. From this viewpoint, it can be suggested that the texts were conceived as elements in a comprehensive didactic project envisaged by the emperor Manuel II. In addition, the author often subverted the common tenets of imperial representation and presented himself as a 'defeated' interlocutor in the debate of the *Dialogue*, as a teacher-rhetorician of his son in the *Foundations* and the *Orations*, and as his brother's helper in the *Funeral Oration*. Furthermore, notably, the emperor constantly suggested and explicitly stated that rhetoric

CONCLUSIONS

and the ability to speak in a persuasive manner were correlates of power. In light of these observations, his strategy of configuring a strong authorial voice can be interpreted as an attempt to persuade by means of a kind of dual authority: both as political power that strove to accommodate other power brokers and as oratorical virtue.

The analysis of political visions in late Byzantium points to several developments. Concerning the ecclesiastics' discourse, it emerges that the members of the high-ranking hierarchy like Symeon of Thessalonike or Joseph Bryennios adopted a radical position in relation to their wealthy contemporaries, whom they rebuked for the widening gap between the different social classes and for not participating in the defence of the city. These authors' discourse acquired even more radical hues regarding the authority of the emperor in the question of the patriarch's appointment. If the roots of this shift in the ecclesiastics' discourse, most evident in the treatises of Makarios of Ankara, can be traced back to the early Palaiologan period, its echoes are to be found in the texts of later church officials like Sylvester Syropoulos and Mark Eugenikos as well.

Unlike the ecclesiastics, the imperial rhetoricians continued to support the idea of the omnipotence of imperial power in Byzantium. Even Gemistos Plethon, who preached extreme political reforms that entailed a return to the values of ancient Sparta, agreed upon the appropriateness of monarchical rule. In their panegyrics, the rhetoricians praised extensively the emperor's deeds, his dynastic lineage and his direct successor, John VIII. Among the usual virtues identifiable in panegyrical texts, these authors often described the emperor as a skilled rhetorician and teacher not only for his son but also for his people. Furthermore, unlike the ecclesiastics who preached a kind of Orthodox utopia, they emphasised the Byzantines' identity reflected in their Romanness.

A slightly different picture of imperial authority emerges from the analysis of the emperor's discursive representation thereof. He reworked the ancient representation of a philosopher-king in the form of a rhetorician-king and put forward a personal version of the hierarchical system of kingly virtues, with humility (ταπεινοφροσύνη) at the top. He often pictured himself in the guise of a *didaskalos* not only of his son to whom he addressed his texts but also of his subjects, as he suggested in his very short *Oration to His Subjects*. Furthermore, his preaching activity probably indicated a tendency to absorb into his office the function specific to the church's spiritual authority.

The analysis of the three competing political discourses reveals the antagonisms emerging in the last decades of the Byzantine Empire, between, on the one hand, the church and, on the other hand, the emperor. By contrast to the orators' project, often driven by personal aspirations, Manuel's project seemingly sought to compensate for the lack of previous enlightened statesmanship and participatory citizenship, in the aftermath of the conflicts with the Ottomans (post-1402). Unlike the court rhetoricians', Manuel's vision of imperial authority linked rhetoric to the idea of best governance. Clearly, each programme undertook to fulfil a special need: whereas the orators' programme conceived rhetoric as key to social survival, Manuel's transformed it into a guide to the salvation of the Byzantine state. Thus, his rhetoric deliberately omitted praise and engaged more intensely with the political present, since, as he often argued in his texts, rhetoric's mission was to articulate widely acceptable visions.

With regard to his style of government, the exploration of the emperor's rhetorical texts allows us to draw further conclusions. Thus, the use of multiple authorial voices reflecting several rhetorical approaches, deliberative, narrative or didactic, combined with his priestly stance suggests that the emperor sought to appeal to different kinds of audiences. By relying heavily on his own elaborated rhetorical texts, Manuel seems to put forward the notion of an authority which would preserve most imperial prerogatives, despite the vigorous claims of other interest groups. This aestheticised version of the empire helped him mediate between court parties in conflicts such as the one between the Orthodox hierarchy and the Byzantine converts to Catholicism. Furthermore, through these texts, he managed to promote a sustainable level of political concord that eventually allowed him to achieve his imperial vision.

To conclude, my investigation reveals a picture of the emperor Manuel II as a political thinker concerned with the construction of a functional representation of the imperial office. He assiduously cultivated the alternative image of an emperor-writer, very much different from the image of his father, John V, who was more interested in day-to-day state administration. Yet unlike other Byzantine philosopher-kings, through his texts Manuel strove to shape a new role for the imperial institution in an environment increasingly controlled by forces like the Ottomans, the Italian merchants and the Byzantine nouveaux riches. This new role entailed the large-scale use of rhetoric, one of the very few tools which he could use in order to maintain a certain cohesion in the collapsing Byzantine political sphere. By producing different versions of his authorial voice, he engaged with the collective imagination of his audience so that the texts became connected to a recognizable Byzantine history. At the same time, his political writings echoed his personal experiences that underpinned his attempts to advertise a new imperial ethos, adapted to the new social realities in which the Byzantine emperor represented little more than a *primus inter pares*.

The present investigation of the emperor's texts in their rhetorical and socio-political contexts stands therefore as a contribution to the conceptualisation of imperial authority in late Byzantium. It may serve as a starting point for future research as well, particularly with regard to the influence of the emperor's political thinking on other rhetorical compositions, be they theological or liturgical. Another possible avenue of investigation that it may open is the study of the connections between rhetorical innovation and political transformation in the Palaiologan era. As such it may provide reference material for historians in search of discursive continuities and discontinuities with earlier or later Byzantine authors.

Appendices

Appendix 1
Members of Manuel II's Literary Circle

Name	Status in the court or in the patriarchate	Years of activity	Evidence from letters	Further evidence of connections with Manuel	Relation with members of the literary circle
Pro-Latin					
Ambrogio Traversari (PLP: 29205)	Humanist teacher	1417		Letters of Guarino	Chrysoloras, Guarino, Skaranos
Constantine Asanes (PLP: 1503)	*Theios* of John V and Manuel II, rhetorician	1396	Addressed by Manuel	*Mazaris' Journey to Hades*	Kydones, Chrysoberges, Kalekas
Demetrios Kydones (PLP: 13876)	*Mesazōn*, ambassador, teacher	1370–96	Addressed to Manuel Addressed by Manuel	*Dialogue* dedicated to Kydones	Chrysoloras, Chrysoberges, Skaranos, Asanes, Euthymios, Bryennios
Demetrios Skaranos (PLP: 26035)	Ambassador	1390–1430		Letters of Kalekas and Kydones	Kydones, Chrysoberges, Chrysoloras, Asanes
Guarino of Verona (PLP: 4324)	Teacher, humanist	1400–20	Addressed by Manuel	Letters of Chrysoloras, Isidore of Kiev, Guarino	Chrysoloras, Isidore of Kiev
Jacopo d'Angeli	Humanist	1390–1415		Letters of Kalekas	Kalekas, Chrysoberges
John Chrysoloras (PLP: 31160)	Teacher, ambassador	1390–1420		*Epistolary Discourse* to co-emperor John VIII, letters of Guarino	Chrysoloras, Guarino
Manuel Chrysoloras (PLP: 31165)	Teacher, ambassador	1390–1415	Addressed by Manuel	*Comparison*, *Epistolary Oration*	Kydones, Chrysoberges, Kalekas, Chortasmenos, Chrysoloras, Asanes

(Continued)

Name	Status in the court or in the patriarchate	Years of activity	Evidence from letters	Further evidence of connections with Manuel	Relation with members of the literary circle
Manuel Kalekas (PLP: 10289)	Teacher, theologian	1390–1403	Addressed to Manuel	Kalekas's *Apologia de fide sua* addressed to Manuel	Kydones, Chrysoberges, Chrysoloras, Asanes
Maximos Chrysoberges (PLP: 31123)	Theologian	1380–1415		Letters of Kydones	Kydones, Chrysoberges, Chrysoloras, Bryennios
Strict Orthodox					
Constantine Ivankos (PLP: 7973)	Teacher	1390–1410	Addressed by Manuel	Praise for rhetorical skills (Manuel)	Nicholas Kabasilas, Simon
David (PLP: 5008)	Hieromonk, spiritual father	1415	Addressed by Manuel	Manuel, *Confession Addressed to His Spiritual Fathers upon the Recovery from an Illness*	Makarios Makres
Euthymios (PLP: 6268)	*Hegoumenos* of Stoudios monastery, patriarch (1410–16)	1390–1416	Addressed by Manuel	Collaboration on Manuel's *Kanon paraklētikos*, the controversy over the metropolitan of Moldavia	Makarios Makres, Bryennios
Gabriel (PLP: 3416)	Metropolitan of Thessalonike		Addressed by Manuel	Collaboration on Manuel's *Homily on St Mary of Egypt*	Makarios Makres, Joseph Bryennios
Joseph Bryennios (PLP: 3257)	Priest, theologian, court orator	1390–1430	Addressed to Manuel	*Homilies* (performed in the emperor's presence in the imperial palace)	Kydones, Patriarch Euthymios, Manuel Pothos, Manuel Holobolos,
Makarios Makres (PLP: 16379)	*Hegoumenos* of the Pantokrator Monastery; monk at the Vatopedi Monastery; theologian; diplomat	1400–1430		Poem addressed to emperor Manuel and Despot Andronikos (1416); monody on the emperor (1425); copyist of the emperor's texts	Bryennios, Hieromonk David, Gabriel of Thessalonike
Manuel Pothos (PLP: 23450)	Judge (*krites*)	1380–1400	Addressed by Manuel	Praise II for rhetorical skills (Manuel)	Kydones
Michael Balsamon (PLP: 2118)	*Protekdikos, didaskalos katholikos*	1390–1415	Addressed by Manuel	Praise for rhetorical skills (Manuel)	Kydones, Chortasmenos
Nicholas Kabasilas Chamaetos (PLP: 30539)	Theologian	1370–96	Addressed by Manuel		Kydones

APPENDICES 283

Name	Status in the court or in the patriarchate	Years of activity	Evidence from letters	Further evidence of connections with Manuel	Relation with members of the literary circle
Simon (PLP: 25382)	*Protos* of Mt Athos	1400–10			Constantine Ivankos
Theodore Kaukadenos (PLP: 11561)	Teacher, tutor	1380–90	Addressed by Manuel	Participation in *theatron*, tutor of Manuel's sons	Kydones, Chortasmenos
Theodore Potamios (PLP: 23601)	Teacher, theologian	1400–18	Addressed to Manuel Addressed by Manuel	Praise for rhetorical skills (Manuel)	Kydones, Pothos, Chrysoloras, Bryennios, Isidore Glabas
Other					
Demetrios Chrysoloras (PLP: 31156)	*Mesazōn*, theologian	1390–1416	Addressed to Manuel Addressed by Manuel	*Comparison*, *One Hundred Letters*	Nicholas Kabasilas, Chrysoloras
Demetrios Pepagomenos (PLP: 22359)	Copyist, imperial secretary	1415–52		*Monody on the Death of Cleope Malatesta*	Chortasmenos, Bessarion
Frangopoulos (PLP: 30084)	Protostrator, *katholikos mesazōn* in the Morea	1392–1438	Addressed by Manuel	Praise for rhetorical skills (Manuel)	
Gemistos Plethon (PLP: 3630)	Philosopher	1390–1452		Preface to *Funeral Oration*, *Address (Memorandum) to Emperor Manuel II on the Situation in the Peloponnese*	
Helena Kantakouzene Palaiologina (PLP: 21365)	Empress	1396	Addressed by Manuel	*Dialogue*	Kydones
Isidore of Kiev (PLP: 8300)	Metropolitan of the Morea, later cardinal	1400–25	Letters addressed to Manuel	Panegyric, copyist	Guarino
Joasaph (PLP: 8923)	Monk and scribe			Introduction to *Funeral Oration*	Chortasmenos
John Chortasmenos (PLP: 30897)	Teacher, metropolitan, copyist	1390–1425	Addressed to Manuel	*Panegyric on the Emperor's Return from Thessalonike*	Bryennios, Balsamon, Chrysoloras, Pepagomenos
Manuel Holobolos (PLP: 21046)	*Grammatikos*	1390–1414		*Mazaris' Journey to Hades*	Bryennios

Appendix 2

The Contents and Structure of Manuel II's *Foundations*

Chapter	Topic
Theoretical-philosophical	
1.	On different kinds of life
2.	On the best kind of life
3.	On common human nature
4.	On the best time to choose a way of life
5.	On the happiness of the subjects which depends on the ruler's action
6.	On opportunities at the right time
Spiritual: God and church	
7.	On the service due to God
8.	On the service due to God
9.	On the service due to God
10.	On love for God
11.	On submission to the church
12.	On defending the church
13.	On support from God
Moral advice	
14.	On good versus evil
15.	On the necessity of displaying a pleasant behaviour
On individuals	
16.	On friendship
17.	On good counsellors

Chapter	Topic
18.	On the necessity of being surrounded by friends
19.	Individuals depend on communities
20.	Trusting the good, distrusting the knavish
21.	On real friendship
On actions	
22.	On truth and honesty
23.	On envy, treachery and dishonesty
24.	On the right measure and avoiding excess
25.	On the voluntariness of good and evil actions
26.	On evil actions
27.	On good actions
28.	On how to avoid perverted people
29.	Connection between the voluntariness of actions and human nature
30.	On responsibility for decisions and actions
31.	On choosing the right course of action
32.	On learning the right course of action from other people's experience
33.	On the ideal individual (ἄριστος ἀνήρ)
34.	On the rational differences between beneficial and damaging actions
35.	On reason and irrationality
36.	On reason
37.	On the natural human movement towards the good
On rulers' appropriate life and behaviour	
38.	On how to react to calumnies
39.	On maintaining contact with appropriate individuals
40.	Once one has knowledge of good and evil, one has to stay with the good
41.	Examination of daily activities
42.	On the ruler as imitator of God
43.	The metaphor of the state as body: the ruler as head of state
44.	On habit (ἕξις)
45.	On habit (ἕξις)
46.	On habit (ἕξις)

(Continued)

Chapter	Topic
47.	That the ruler is similar to all individuals
48.	On freedom and buying glory
49.	On pleasure
50.	On sins
51.	The emperor-legislator
52.	On the emperor's approach to different kinds of individuals
53.	On temperance in the use of force
54.	On fitting one's desire to realities
55.	On the misfortunes of life
56.	On peace and good relations with other Christian peoples
57.	On cautiousness in a ruler's action
58.	On cautiousness in a ruler's action
59.	On cautiousness in a ruler's action
60.	On the ruler's mildness
61.	On the ruler's politeness
62.	On the vanity of life
63.	On changes in life
64.	On the passing of time
65.	On the passing of time
66.	On fate and faith
67.	On actions beneficial to others
68.	On the deliberate course of action
69.	On the sufferings of Job
70.	That an individual must be judged according to his character (τρόποι) and not according to his fate (τύχη)
71.	On how to avoid wickedness
72.	That the emperor has to surround himself with good individuals
73.	On the four cardinal imperial virtues
74.	On indifference as a cause of evil
75.	On the importance of a ruler's education
76.	On the ruler's care for his subjects
77.	On how to avoid dissimulation (εἰρωνεία) and false pretensions (ἀλαζονεία)

Chapter	Topic
78.	On the use of rationality in making decisions
79.	On the necessity of keeping the mind focused
80.	On relaxation after periods of intense activity
81.	On honesty and hypocrisy
82.	On assuming a pleasant behaviour towards others
83.	On avoiding quarrels (ἔρις)
84.	On listening to the counsels of friends
85.	On the emperor as model for his subjects
86.	On the supreme good and the use of knowledge
87.	On the emperor's necessity of fighting in battle until the end
88.	On the emperor's military qualities and on his ancestors
89.	On military strategies
90.	On how to deal with enemies
91.	On using experience in order to predict future disasters
92.	On knowing the right moment to speak
93.	On thinking and speaking in an appropriate manner
Concluding remarks	
94.	On wisdom
95.	On foreseeing the future based on the present
96.	On the fact that acting appropriately is the act of a wise individual
97.	That the outcome of one's actions depends mostly on one's decisions
98.	On life as a gift from God
99.	That humans are both matter and spirit
100.	On relying on spiritual wisdom

Appendix 3

Translation of Gemistos Plethon's Preface to Manuel II's *Funeral Oration*

The exordium of the oration is deeply passionate and entirely appropriate and it has the features of a piece of funeral writing for the brother who passed away. After Manuel briefly evoked the fatherland and the family, our most divine emperor, who mentioned them, did not dwell at length on the section dedicated to these topics. He was eager to deal with the actions of the praised <brother>, which are many and need long descriptions; in order to provide a defence of these actions and since, because of the fact that <these actions> were obvious to everyone and known to everyone, it would not have been necessary to go through each of these aspects, he produced for him <his brother> a solemn text. Consequently, after he began his laudatory speech, first, he examined carefully his education from childhood and all aspects of his character, and what kind of man he was for everyone; then he proceeded to his brother's actions and deeds. First, he described his <Theodore's> activities which involved his father, himself <Manuel II> and other close members of the family at that time, and how he dealt with the different challenges of that time. After these, proceeding right away to the account of the situation on the Peloponnese, he mentioned the very first arrival in the province, because only by being expected <Theodore's arrival> did it bring profit <to the province>, and how he was welcomed by the happy inhabitants. Then he undertook the account of their uncle and nephew, taking care of the words in order not to say anything discordant or burdensome insofar as possible. Next, <he discussed> the Illyrians' transfer into the same province, because it was a difficult issue to decide whether one should accept them or not in the province, a situation which ultimately has been accepted, despite other people's opposition; yet he <Theodore> took the right decision since he used the Illyrians' settlement for a righteous purpose. And after this, he recalled the defeat of the neighbouring enemies and the seizing of the prince <Kantakouzenos>, thereby revealing himself as a stronger ruler. Then he returned to the deserters who came as barbarians, and first treated them with clemency, without imprisoning anyone ; then he also advanced against the barbarian himself, and thereby he attacked both, since he was drawn into war by those who came to him as deserters, while others were summoned from home. Then he described the arrival <in Serres> of Theodore and of himself which took place by necessity and happened contrary to the opinion of others; he also recounted the danger entailed by that arrival and other difficulties encountered there. Furthermore, <he narrated> that the emperor himself, due to the plans of the barbarian, saved himself in addition to rescuing again the great city (Constantinople) contrary to others' opinion, and this one now, even if he was considering that as an unavoidable situation, with great courage and skill fled from there <Serres> to the Peloponnese; and that, by his return, he managed to maintain not only all of his affairs in the Peloponnese, but also the endangered territories of those from beyond the Isthmus; and that, as the barbarian had left Greece and had sent a great and mighty army, he, by making use not of the magnitude of the opposing army but of a well-planned, appropriate strategy, prevented this <Ottoman> army from invading the country; and that because of this military achievement, he recovered and reasserted his authority over the territories that had once been under the barbarians as well as over the lands which we now possess. Then, after he proceeded to the common war with the barbarian, he also described that, because the Romans' situation was difficult to such an extent that he could not live well due to the misfortunes of many Christians and of many barbarians, he <the emperor> also mentioned his journey back <to Constantinople> and the departure to the West because of this situation. Then he offered a detailed account of the <despot's> deeds during those years: and first, he related that <Theodore> having handed Corinth over to the Knights Hospitaller because of the obvious danger, in fact saved it from the barbarians and that, in this situation, he secured great support. Then <he recounted> that since it seemed to him that it was better to leave the previous war with the barbarian to these ones <the Hospitallers> who had an entirely different rule, he set the country again in order, after he recovered it, without producing any injustice or causing any damage to the Knights Hospitaller. [. . .] Then he proceeds to the comparisons with the ancients, at which point in time as he recalls his brother's illness he again uses emotions; at the same time, he makes clear that there was no small sign of his courage in his deeds, despite his illness. Now, allowing the citizens present in the ceremony to speak, as it was fitting for them due to the many and great benefits they drew from Theodore, he repeats the *thrēnos*. He does so, and at the same time he asks for a moment of rest, holding in his voice because of great suffering, and also because he wished to hear other mourners speak, for the love of his brother and because of other reasons, as the emperor himself recounts in detail; for this reason that he began <the funeral oration> directly with an emotional *prooimion*, in order to avoid being totally drawn into accounts and praises, before the lament. In addition, when he moves to the consolation he stops, combining at every passage praises which were always beneficial and appropriate, so that he would neither exceed the plausible nor miss anything of what was necessary to be said.

Funeral Oration, 67–9

Appendix 4
Network of Ecclesiastics and Rhetoricians during Manuel II's Reign

Key

Author	Ecclesiastical author
Author	Court author
Author	Italian author

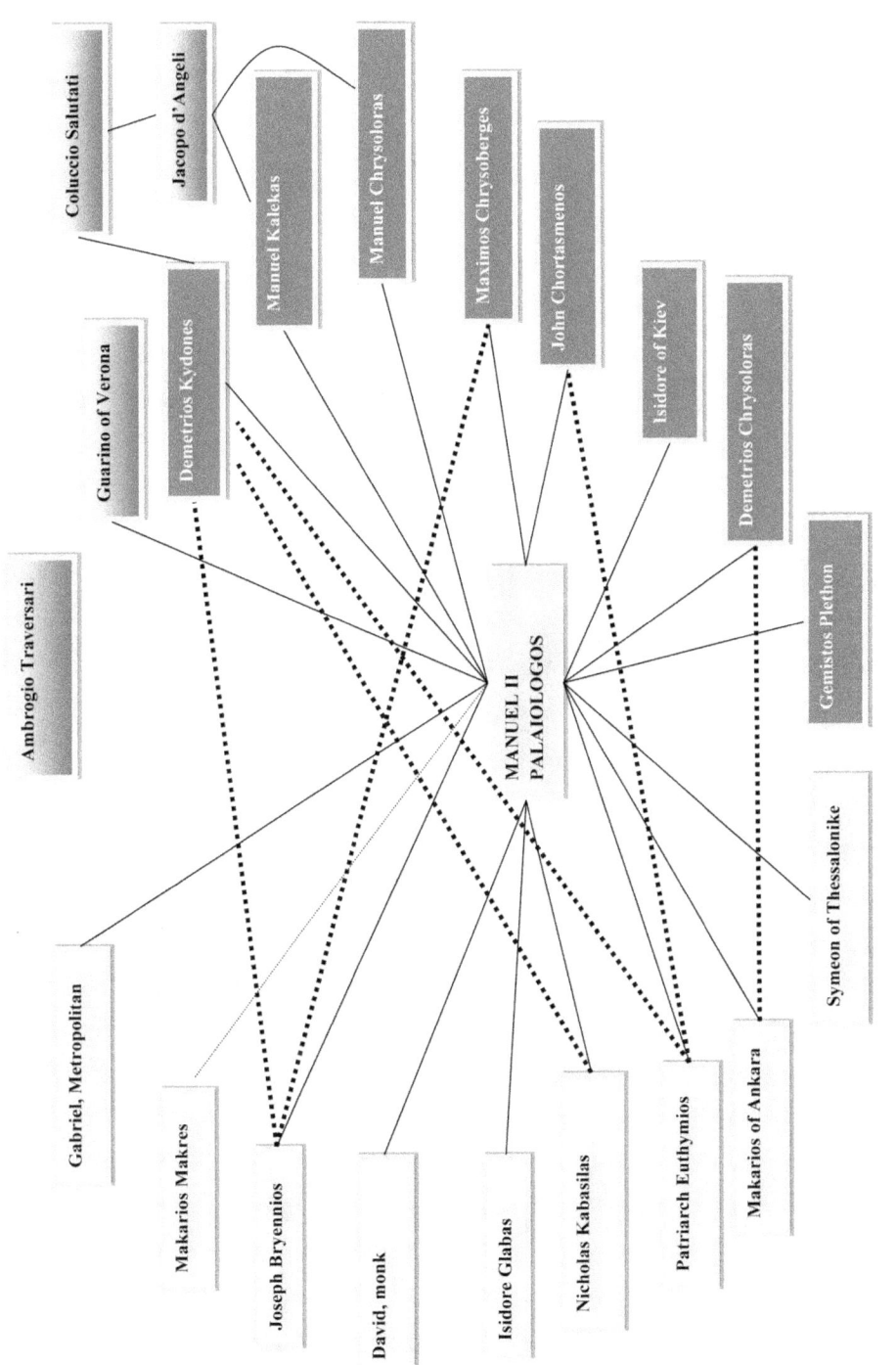

Bibliography

Manuscripts Consulted

Crypten. Z δ 1 (s. XV)
Vat. Barb. gr. 219 (s. XV)
Vat. gr. 1107 (s. XV)
Vat. gr. 1619 (s. XV)
Paris. gr. 1379 (s. XV)
Vindob. phil. gr. 42 (s. XV)
Vindob. phil. gr. 98 (s. XV)
Vindob. theol. gr. 235 (s. XV)

Primary Sources

The works of Manuel II Palaiologos

Admonitory Oration to the Thessalonians, ed. B. Laourdas, Makedonika 3 (1955), 290–307.
Confession Addressed to His Spiritual Fathers upon the Recovery from an Illness (unedited), in Crypten. Z δ 1, ff. 12r–65v.
Dialoge mit einem Muslim, ed. and trans. K. Förstel (Würzburg: Echter, 1995).
Dialoge mit einem Perser, ed. E. Trapp (Vienna: Böhlau, 1966).
Dialogue with the Empress-Mother on Marriage, ed. and trans. A. Angelou (Vienna: Verlag der Österreichischen Akademie der Wissenschaften, 1991).
Discourse on Drunkenness and Adultery, ed. J. Boissonade (Paris: Dumont, 1844), 274–307.
Foundations of an Imperial Education, PG 156, 313–84.
Funeral Oration on His Brother Theodore, Despot of Morea, ed. and trans. J. Chrysostomides (Thessalonike: Association for Byzantine Research, 1985).

Homily on the Dormition of the Theotokos, ed. M. Jugie, in *Patrologia Orientalis* 16 (Turnhout: Brepols, 1922), 543–66.
Homily on St John the Baptist, ed. C. Billò, *Medioevo Greco* 2 (2002), 49–63.
Homily on St Mary of Egypt (unedited), in Vat. gr. 1619, ff. 15r–29v; Vat. gr. 632, ff. 335r–50v.
Homily on the Nativity of Christ (unedited), in Vat. gr 1619, ff. 29v–46v; Marc. gr. 505, ff. 33r–54v.
Image of the Spring on a Royal Tapestry, ed. J. Davis, in C. Dendrinos (ed.), *Porphyrogenita: Essays on the History and Literature of Byzantium and the Latin East in Honour of Julian Chrysostomides* (Aldershot: Ashgate, 2003), 411–12.
Kanon paraklētikos, ed. E. Legrand (Paris: Maisonneuve, 1893), 94–102.
Letters, ed. and trans. G. Dennis (Washington, DC: Dumbarton Oaks, 1977).
Morning Prayers, PG 156, cols 564–74.
On the Procession of the Holy Spirit, ed. C. Dendrinos, in *An Annotated Critical Edition (Editio Princeps) of Emperor Manuel II Palaeologus' Treatise 'On the Procession of the Holy Spirit'* (PhD dissertation, University of London, 1996), 1–318.
Oration to His Subjects, PG 156, cols 561–2.
Panegyric on the Recovery of His Father from an Illness, ed. J. Boissonade (Paris: Dumont, 1844), 223–38.
Psalm on Bayezid, ed. E. Legrand (Paris: Maisonneuve, 1893), 104.
Seven Ethico-Political Orations, PG 156, 385–562.
Seven Ethico-Political Orations, ed. C. Kakkoura, in *An Annotated Critical Edition of Emperor Manuel II Palaeologus' 'Seven Ethico-Political Orations'* (PhD dissertation, University of London, 2013).
Several Words for Brevity and Peace in Deliberations, in Vat. Barb. gr. 219, f. 90v.
What Tamerlane Might Have Said to Bayezid, ed. E. Legrand (Paris: Maisonneuve, 1893), 103–4.

Other primary sources

Agapetos the Deacon, *Ekthesis*, ed. R. Riedinger (Athens: Hetaireia Philōn tou Laou, 1995).
Alexios, Makrembolites, *Dialogue between the Rich and the Poor*, ed. I. Ševčenko, in 'Alexios Makrembolites and his *Dialog between the Rich and the Poor*', ZRVI 6 (1960), 203–15.
Ambrogio Traversari, *Letters*, ed. P. Canneti and L. Mehus (Bologna: Forni, 1968).
Anonymous, *An Anonymous Greek Chronicle of the Sixteenth Century*, ed. M. Philippides (Brookline: Hellenic College Press, 1990).

Anonymous, *Funeral Oration on Manuel II*, ed. C. Dendrinos, in *Porphyrogenita: Essays on the History and Literature of Byzantium and the Latin East* (Aldershot: Ashgate, 2003), 423–51.
Anonymous, *Inscription of Parori*, ed. R.-J. Loenertz, *EEBΣ* 25 (1955), 206–10.
Anonymous, *Life of Arsenios*, ed. P. Nikolopoulos, *EEBΣ* 45 (1981–2), 406–61.
Anonymous, *Oration on the Siege of Constantinople (1402)*, ed. P. Gautier, *REB* 23 (1965), 102–17.
Anonymous, *Two Panegyrics Addressed to Manuel II*, ed. I. Polemes, *BZ* 103 (2010), 699–714.
Aphthonios, *Progymnasmata*, ed. H. Rabe (Leipzig: Teubner, 1926).
Bessarion, *On Substance: Against Plethon*, ed. L. Mohler, in *Aus Bessarions Gelehrtenkreis*, 3 (Padeborn: Ferdinand Schöningh, 1942), 149–50.
Clavijo Ruy González, *Embassy to Tamerlane, 1403–1406*, trans. G. Strange (London: Routledge, 2006).
Colluccio Salutati, *Letters*, ed. F. Novati (Rome: Forzani, 1905).
Demetrios Chomatenos, Πονήματα διάφορα, ed. G. Prinzing (Berlin: De Gruyter, 2002).
Demetrios Chrysoloras, *Comparison between the Emperor of Today and the Ancient Rulers*, ed. S. Lampros, in *PP* 3, 222–45 (Athens: Gregoriades, 1926).
Demetrios Chrysoloras, *Dialogue on Demetrios Kydones' Antirrhetic against Neilos Kabasilas*, ed. V. Pasiourtides (PhD dissertation, University of London, 2013).
Demetrios Chrysoloras, *One Hundred Letters Addressed to Emperor Manuel II*, ed. F. Conti Bizzaro (Naples: D'Auria, 1984).
Demetrios Chrysoloras, *Oration for the Theotokos*, ed. P. Gautier, *REB* 19 (1961), 340–57.
Demetrios Kydones, *De contemnenda morte*, ed. H. Deckelmann (Leipzig: Teubner, 1901).
Demetrios Kydones, *First Oration to John Kantakouzenos*, ed. R.-J. Loenertz in *Letters*, vol. 1 (Vatican: Biblioteca Apostolica Vaticana, 1956–60), 1–10.
Demetrios Kydones, *Letters*, ed. R.-J. Loenertz in *Démétrius Cydonès: Correspondance* (Vatican: Biblioteca Apostolica Vaticana, 1956–60).
Demetrios Kydones, *Oratio de non reddenda Gallipoli*, PG 154, 1009–36.
Demetrios Kydones, *Oratio pro subsidio Latinorum*, PG 154, 961–1008.
Demetrios Kydones, *Oration to John Palaiologos*, ed. R.-J. Loenertz, in *Letters*, vol. 1 (Vatican: Biblioteca Apostolica Vaticana, 1956–60), 10–23.
Demetrios Kydones, *Second Oration to John Kantakouzenos*, ed. G. Cammelli, *Byzantinisch-Neugriechische Jahrbücher* 4 (1923), 77–83.
Doukas, *History*, ed. V. Grecu (Bucharest: Editura Academiei Republicii Populare Romîne, 1958).

Gabriel, Metropolitan of Thessalonike, *Homilies*, ed. B. Laourdas, *Ἀθηνᾶ* 57 (1953), 142–73.

Gemistos Plethon, *Address (Memorandum) to Emperor Manuel II on the Situation in the Peloponnese*, ed. S. Lampros, in *PP* 3, 309–12 (Athens: Gregoriades, 1926).

Gemistos Plethon, *Admonitory Oration to Theodore Palaiologos*, ed. S. Lampros, in *PP* 3, 113–35 (Athens: Gregoriades, 1926).

Gemistos Plethon, *Against Scholarios in Favor of Aristotle's Objections*, ed. E. Maltese (Leipzig: Teubner, 1988), 1–46.

Gemistos Plethon, *On Virtues*, ed. B. Tambrun-Krasker (Athens: Akadēmia Athēnōn, 1987).

George Scholarios, *Dialogues on the Procession of the Holy Spirit*, ed. M. Jugie, L. Petit and X. A. Siderides, in *œuvres complètes de Georges Scholarios*, vol. 3 (Paris: Maison de la Bonne Presse, 1930), 1–49.

Gregory Palamas, *One Hundred and Fifty Chapters*, ed. R. Sinkewicz (Toronto: Pontifical Institute of Mediaeval Studies, 1988).

Guarino of Verona, *Letters*, ed. R. Sabbadini (Turin: Bottega d'Erasmo, 1959).

Hermogenes, *Rhetorical Texts*, ed. H. Rabe (Leipzig: Teubner, 1913).

Iamblichus, *Protrepticus*, ed. H. Pistelli (Leipzig: Teubner, 1888).

Isidore Glabas, *Homilies*, ed. V. Christophorides (Thessalonike: Aristotle University of Thessalonike, 1981).

Isidore Glabas, *Homilies for St Demetrius*, ed. B. Laourdas, *Ἑλληνικά* 5 (1954), 19–65.

Isidore Glabas, *Letters*, ed. S. Lampros, in ʽΙσιδώρου μητροπολίτου Θεσσαλονίκης ὀκτὼ ἐπιστολαί', *Νέος Ἑλληνομνήμων* 9 (1912), 353–91.

Isidore Glabas, *Two Unedited Homilies*, ed. K. Tsirpanlis, *Θεολογία* 42 (1971), 559–81.

Isidore of Kiev, *Encomium for John VIII*, ed. S. Lampros, in *PP* 3, 200–21 (Athens: Gregoriades, 1926).

Isidore of Kiev, *Letters*, ed. W. Regel, in *Analecta Byzantino-Russica* (St Petersburg: Eggers, 1891), 59–71.

Isidore of Kiev, *Panegyric Addressed to Emperor John VIII*, ed. S. Lampros, in *PP* 3, 132–99 (Athens: Gregoriades, 1926).

John Anagnostes, *Account of the Siege of Thessalonike*, ed. G. Tsaras (Thessalonike: Tsaras, 1958).

John Argyropoulos, *Ἀργυροπούλεια*, ed. S. Lampros (Athens: Sakellariou, 1910).

John Chortasmenos, *Briefe, Gedichte und kleine Schriften*, ed. H. Hunger (Vienna: Böhlau, 1969).

John Kananos, *The Siege of Constantinople*, ed. A. Cuomo (Berlin: De Gruyter, 2016).

John Kantakouzenos, *Histories*, ed. L. Schopen, 3 vols (Bonn: Weber, 1828–32).
Joseph Bryennios, *Conversation with an Ishmaelite*, ed. A. Argyriou, *EEBΣ* 35 (1966–7), 158–95.
Joseph Bryennios, *Τὰ εὑρεθέντα*, ed. E. Voulgares, 2 vols (Leipzig: Breitkopf, 1768).
Joseph Bryennios, *Forty-Nine Moral Chapters*, ed. L. Oeconomus, in *Mélanges Charles Diehl*, vol. 1 (Paris: Presses Universitaires de France, 1930), 225–33.
Joseph Bryennios, *Letters*, ed. N. Tomadakes, *EEBΣ* 46 (1983–6), 283–362.
Joseph Bryennios, *The Garden or the Anthology of Divine Cogitations or Thirty Theological Maxims and Two Hundred Ethical Maxims (Κῆπος ἢ ἀνθολογία τῶν θείων ἐννοιῶν ἢ γνῶμαι λ΄ θεολογικά καὶ σ΄ ἠθικά)* (unedited), in Vindob. theol. gr. 235, ff. 2–236.
Joseph Bryennios, *Oration on the Reconstruction of the Walls of Constantinople*, ed. N. Tomadakes, *EEBΣ* 36 (1968), 1–15.
Joseph Bryennios, *Τὰ παραλειπόμενα*, ed. E. Voulgares (Leipzig: Breitkopf, 1784).
Kalogeras, Nikephoros, *Μάρκος ὁ Εὐγενικὸς καὶ ὁ Βησσαρίων ὁ καρδινάλις: Εὐθύνας, ὡς πολιτικοὶ τοῦ ἑλληνικοῦ ἔθνους ἡγέται, τῇ ἱστορίᾳ διδόντες (οἷς προστίθεται καὶ πραγματεία περὶ τῆς ἐν βασιλείᾳ Συνόδου 1433–1437)* (Athens: Perris, 1893).
Laonikos Chalkokondyles, *Histories*, ed. J. Darkó (Budapest: Academia Litterarum Hungarica, 1922–7).
Leo VI, *Homilies*, ed. T. Antonopoulou (Turnhout: Brepols, 2008).
Leonardo Bruni, *Epistularum Libri*, 8 vols, ed. L. Mehus (Florence: Bernardi, 1741).
Libanius, *Opera*, ed. R. Förster (Leipzig: Teubner, 1909).
Makarios of Ankara, *Against the Latins*, ed. Dositheos, Patriarch of Jerusalem, in *Τόμος καταλλαγῆς* (Iaşi, 1692), 1–499.
Makarios Makres, *Life of St. Maximos Kausokalyves, Encomion of the Fathers of the Seven Ecumenical Councils, Consolation to a Sick Person, or Reflections for Endurance, Verses on the Emperor Manuel II Palaiologos, Letter to Hieromonk Symeon, A Supplication on Barren Olive Trees*, ed. S. Kapetanaki (PhD dissertation, University of London, 2001).
Makarios Makres, *Macaire Makrès et la polémique contre l'Islam*, ed. A. Argyriou (Vatican: Biblioteca Apostolica Vaticana, 1986).
Makarios Makres, *Μακαρίου τοῦ Μακρῆ συγγράμματα*, ed. A. Argyriou (Thessalonike: Center for Byzantine Research, 1996).
Manuel Chrysoloras, *Comparison of the Old and the New Rome*, ed. C. Billo, *Medioevo Greco* 0 (2000), 1–26.

Manuel Chrysoloras, *Epistolary Oration on Manuel Palaiologos' 'Funeral Oration'*, ed. Ch. Patrineles and D. Sophianos (Athens: Academy of Athens, 2001).

Manuel Kalekas, *Letters*, ed. R.-J. Loenertz (Vatican: Biblioteca Apostolica Vaticana, 1950).

Marinos Phalieros, Λόγοι διδακτικοί, ed. W. F. Bakker (Leiden: Brill, 1977).

Mazaris' Journey to Hades: Or, Interviews with Dead Men about Certain Officials of the Imperial Court, ed. and trans. J. N. Barry (Buffalo, NY: Department of Classics, State University of New York at Buffalo, 1975).

Menander of Athens, *Sententiae; Comparatio Menandri et Philistionis*, ed. S. Jäkel (Leipzig: Teubner, 1964).

Menander Rhetor, *Treatises*, ed. D. A. Russell and N. G. Wilson (Oxford: Clarendon Press, 1981).

Nikephoros Blemmydes, *Imperial Statue*, ed. H. Hunger and I. Ševčenko (Vienna: Verlag der Österreichischen Akademie der Wissenschaften, 1986).

Nikolaos Mesarites, *His Life and Works (in Translation)*, trans. M. Angold (Liverpool: Liverpool University Press, 2017).

Pero Tafur, *Travels and Adventures, 1435–1439*, ed. and trans. M. Letts (London: Routledge, 1926).

Photios, *Bibliotheca*, ed. R. Henry (Paris: Belles Lettres, 1959).

Pseudo-Kodinos, *Treatise on Offices*, ed. and trans. J. Verpeaux (Paris: Centre National de la Recherche Scientifique, 1966).

Sphrantzes, *Memoirs*, ed. V. Grecu (Bucharest: Editura Academiei Republicii Socialiste Romania, 1966).

Sylvester Syropoulos, *Memoirs*, ed. V. Laurent (Paris: Centre National de la Recherche Scientifique, 1971).

Symeon of Thessalonike, "Ἔργα θεολογικά', ed. D. Balfour, Ἀνάλεκτα Βλατάδων 34 (1981), 77–247.

Symeon of Thessalonike, *Liturgical Commentaries*, ed. S. Hawkes-Teeples (Toronto: Pontifical Institute of Mediaeval Studies, 2011).

Symeon of Thessalonike, *Liturgical Writings*, ed. I. Phountoules (Thessalonike: Hetaireia Makedonikon Spoudon, 1968).

Symeon of Thessalonike, *Politico-Historical Works*, ed. D. Balfour (Vienna: Verlag der Österreichischen Akademie der Wissenschaften, 1979).

Symeon the New Theologian, *Chapitres théologiques, gnostiques et pratiques*, ed. J. Darrouzès (Paris: Éditions du Cerf, 1980).

Themistius, *Orations*, ed. G. Downey and H. Schenkl (Leipzig: Teubner, 1965).

Theodore Metochites, Ἠθικὸς ἢ περὶ παιδείας, ed. and trans. I. Polemes (Athens: Kanaki, 2002).

Theoleptos of Philadelphia, *The Life and Letters of Theoleptos of Philadelphia*, ed. A. Constantinides Hero (Brookline, MA: Hellenic College Press, 1994).

Theophylakt of Ochrid, *Orations, Treatises, Letters*, ed. P. Gautier (Thessalonike: Association for Byzantine Research, 1980).

Collections of texts

Kock, Theodor (ed.), *Comicorum Atticorum Fragmenta*, 3 vols (Leipzig: Teubner, 1880–8).
Leutsch, Ernst (ed.), *Corpus Paroemiographorum Graecorum* (Hildsheim: Olms, 1965–91).
Rabe, Hugo (ed.), *Prolegomenon Sylloge* (Leipzig: Teubner, 1931).
Sharing Ancient Wisdoms, a library of gnomological material, <http://www.ancientwisdoms.ac.uk/library> (last accessed 5 April 2019).
Sideras, Alexander (ed.), *Die byzantinischen Grabreden: Prosopographie, Datierung, Überlieferung: 142 Epitaphien und Monodien aus dem byzantinischen Jahrtausend* (Vienna: Verlag der Österreichischen Akademie der Wissenschaften, 1994).
Sternbach, Leo (ed.), *Gnomologium Vaticanum* (Berlin: De Gruyter, 1963).
Walz, Christian, *Rhetores graeci*, 9 vols (Stuttgart: Cottae, 1832).

Collections of documents

Constantinides Hero, Angela (ed.), *Byzantine Monastic Foundation Documents: A Complete Translation of the Surviving Founder's Typika and Testaments* (Washington, DC: Dumbarton Oaks, 2000).
Darrouzès, Jean, *Recherches sur les offikia de l'église byzantine* (Paris: Institut Français d'Études Byzantines, 1970).
Darrouzès, Jean (ed.), *Les regestes des actes du Patriarcat de Constantinople. Les regestes de 1377 à 1410* (Paris: Institut Français d'Études Byzantines, 1989).
Dölger, Franz (ed.), *Regesten der Kaiserurkunden des Oströmischen Reiches von 565–1453* (Munich: Beck, 1960).
Majeska George (ed. and trans.), *Russian Travelers to Constantinople in the Fourteenth and Fifteenth Centuries* (Washington, DC: Dumbarton Oaks, 1984).
Miklosich, F. and Müller, W. (eds), *Acta et Diplomata Graeca Medii Aevii Sacra et Profana,* 6 vols (Vienna: Gerold, 1860–90).
Thiriet, Freddy (ed.), *Regestes des deliberations du Sénat de Venise concernant la Romanie* (Paris: Mouton, 1958).
Thomas, George (ed.), *Diplomatarium Veneto-Levantinum, sive Acta et diplomata res venetas graecas atque levantis illustrantia* (Venice, 1899; repr. Cambridge: Cambridge University Press, 2012).

Secondary Literature

Abbott, H. Porter, 'Story, plot, and narration', in D. Herman (ed.), *The Cambridge Companion to Narrative* (Cambridge: Cambridge University Press, 2007), 39–51.

Agapitos, Panagiotis, 'Mischung der Gattungen und Überschreitung der Gesetze: Die Grabrede des Eustathios von Thessalonike auf Nikolaos Hagiotheodorites', *JÖB* 48 (1998), 119–46.

Agapitos, Panagiotis, 'SO Debate: Genre, structure and poetics in the Byzantine vernacular romances of love', *Symbolae Osloenses* 79 (2004), 7–101.

Ahrweiler, Hélène, *L'idéologie politique de l'Empire byzantine* (Paris: Presses Universitaires de France, 1975).

Akışık, Aslihan, *Self and Other in the Renaissance: Laonikos Chalkokondyles and Late Byzantine Intellectuals* (PhD dissertation, Harvard University, 2013).

Alexandrescu-Dersca, Marie-Mathilde, *La campagne de Timur en Anatolie (1402)* (London: Variorum, 1977).

Allatius, Leo, *De ecclesiae occidentalis atque orientalis perpetua consensione* (Cologne: Kalcovium, 1648).

Altman, Rick, *A Theory of Narrative* (New York: Columbia University Press, 2008).

Anastos, Milton, 'Pletho's calendar and liturgy', *DOP* 4 (1948), 183–305.

Andreeva, Maria, 'Zur Reise Manuels II. Palaiologos nach Westeuropa', *BZ* 34 (1934), 37–47.

Angelov, Dimiter, 'Byzantine imperial panegyric as advice literature (1204–1350)', in E. Jeffreys (ed.), *Rhetoric in Byzantium* (Aldershot: Ashgate, 2003), 55–74.

Angelov, Dimiter (ed.), *Church and Society in Late Byzantium* (Kalamazoo, MI: Medieval Institute, 2009).

Angelov, Dimiter, 'The Donation of Constantine and the church in late Byzantium', in D. Angelov (ed.), *Church and Society in Late Byzantium* (Kalamazoo, MI: Medieval Institute, 2009), 91–157.

Angelov, Dimiter, 'Emperors and patriarchs as ideal children and adolescents: Literary conventions and cultural expectations', in A. Papaconstantinou (ed.), *Becoming Byzantine: Children and Childhood in Byzantium* (Washington, DC: Dumbarton Oaks, 2009), 85–125.

Angelov, Dimiter, *Imperial Ideology and Political Thought in Byzantium (1204–1330)* (Cambridge: Cambridge University Press, 2007).

Angelov, Dimiter, 'Three kinds of liberty as political ideals in Byzantium, twelfth to fifteenth centuries', in I. Iliev and A. Nikolov (eds), *Proceedings of the 22nd International Congress of Byzantine Studies*, vol. 1 (Sofia: Bulgarian Historical Heritage Foundation, 2011), 311–32.

Angold, Michael (ed.), *The Byzantine Aristocracy, IX to XIII Centuries* (Oxford: BAR, 1984).

Angold, Michael, *The Cambridge History of Christianity, vol. 5: Eastern Christianity* (Cambridge: Cambridge University Press, 2006).

Angold, Michael, *Church and Society in Byzantium under the Comneni, 1081–1261* (Cambridge: Cambridge University Press, 1995).

Angold, Michael, 'The decline of Byzantium seen through the eyes of Western travellers', in R. Macrides (ed.), *Travel in the Byzantine World: Papers from the Thirty-Fourth Spring Symposium of Byzantine Studies* (Aldershot: Ashgate, 2002), 213–32.

Bakker, Egbert, *A Companion to the Ancient Greek Language* (Oxford: Wiley-Blackwell, 2010).

Balard, Michel, *La Romanie génoise* (Rome: Società Ligure di Storia Patria, 1978).

Balfour, David, 'Saint Symeon of Thessalonike as historical personality', *Greek Orthodox Theological Review* 28 (1983), 55–72.

Balivet, Michel, 'Le personnage du "turcophile" dans les sources Byzantines anterieures au concile de Florence (1370–1430)', in Michel Balivet, *Byzantins et Ottomans* (Istanbul: Isis, 1999), 31–47.

Baloglou, Christos, 'The institutions of ancient Sparta in the works of Pletho', *Antike und Abendland* 51 (2008), 137–49.

Barber, Charles, and Jenkins, David, *Medieval Greek Commentaries on the Nicomachean Ethics* (Leiden: Brill, 2009).

Barker, Ernest, *Social and Political Thought in Byzantium: From Justinian I to the Last Palaeologus* (Oxford: Clarendon Press, 1957).

Barker, John, 'John VII in Genoa: A problem in late Byzantine source confusion', *OCP* 28 (1962), 213–38.

Barker, John, 'Late Byzantine Thessalonike: A second city's challenges and responses', *DOP* 57 (2003), 5–33.

Barker, John, *Manuel II Palaeologus (1391–1425): A Study in Late Byzantine Statesmanship* (New Brunswick, NJ: Rutgers University Press, 1969).

Barker, John, 'On the chronology of the activities of Manuel II Palaeologus in the Peloponnesus in 1415', *BZ* 55 (1962), 39–55.

Barker, John, 'The problem of appanages in Byzantium during the Palaiologan period', *Βυζαντινά* 3 (1971), 103–22.

Barker, John, 'The question of ethnic antagonisms among Balkan states of the fourteenth century', in T. S. Miller and J. Nesbitt (eds), *Peace and War in Byzantium: Essays in Honor of George T. Dennis* (Washington, DC: Catholic University of America Press, 1995), 165–77.

Bartusis, Mark, *Land and Privilege in Byzantium: The Institution of Pronoia* (Cambridge: Cambridge University Press, 2013).

Bartusis, Mark, *The Late Byzantine Army: Arms and Society, 1204–1453* (Philadelphia, PA: University of Pennsylvania Press, 1992).

Bazini, Helena, 'Une première édition des œuvres de Joseph Bryennios', *REB* 62 (2004), 83–132.

Beck, Hans-Georg, *Das byzantinische Jahrtausend* (Munich: Beck, 1994).

Beck, Hans-Georg, *Kirche und theologische Literatur im Byzantinischen Reich* (Munich: Beck, 1959).

Beck, Hans-Georg, 'Reichsidee und nationale Politik im spätbyzantinischen Staat', *BZ* 53 (1960), 86–93.

Bejczy, István Pieter, and Nederman, Cary J., *Princely Virtues in the Middle Ages, 1200–1500* (Turnhout: Brepols, 2007).

Bell, P. N., *Three Political Voices from the Age of Justinian: Agapetus, 'Advice to the Emperor': Dialogue on Political Science: Paul the Silentiary, 'Description of Hagia Sophia'* (Liverpool: Liverpool University Press, 2009).

Benakis, Linos, 'Aristotelian ethics in Byzantium', in C. Barber and D. Jenkins (eds), *Medieval Greek Commentaries on the Nicomachean Ethics* (Leiden: Brill, 2009), 63–9.

Berger de Xivrey, Jules, *Mémoire sur la vie et les ouvrages de l'empereur Manuel Paléologue* (Paris: Académie des Inscriptions et Belles-Lettres, 1853).

Berges, Wilhelm, *Die Fürstenspiegel des hohen und späten Mittelalters* (Leipzig: Hiersemann, 1938).

Bertelè, Giovanni, *Il libro dei conti di Giacomo Badoer: Costantinopoli 1436–1440: complemento e indici* (Padua: Esedra, 2002).

Blum, Wilhelm, *Byzantinische Fürstenspiegel: Agapetos, Theophylakt von Ochrid, Thomas Magister* (Stuttgart: Hiersemann, 1981).

Boojamra, John, *The Church and Social Reform: The Policies of the Patriarch Athanasios of Constantinople* (New York: Fordham University Press, 1993).

Boyle, Marjorie, *Rhetoric and Reform* (Cambridge, MA: Harvard University Press, 1983).

Bradley, Ritamary, 'Backgrounds of the title *Speculum* in medieval literature', *Speculum* 29 (1954), 100–15.

Briggs, Charles F., *Giles of Rome's De Regimine Principum: Reading and Writing Politics at Court and University, c. 1275–c.1525* (Cambridge: Cambridge University Press, 1999).

Brooks, Sarah T., *Byzantium: Faith and Power (1261–1557): Perspectives on Late Byzantine Art and Culture* (New Haven, CT: Yale University Press, 2006).

Brubaker, Rogers, *Ethnicity Without Groups* (Cambridge, MA: Harvard University Press, 2004).

Bryer, Anthony, and Lowry, Heath (eds), *Continuity and Change in Late Byzantine and Early Ottoman Society: Papers Given at a Symposium at Dumbarton Oaks in May 1982* (Birmingham: Centre for Byzantine Studies, 1986).

Burke, John, Betka, Ursula, Buckley, Penelope, Hay, Kathleen, Scott, Roger, and Stephenson, Andrew (eds), *Byzantine Narrative: Papers in Honour of Roger Scott* (Leiden: Brill, 2006).

Burns, J. H., *The Cambridge History of Medieval Political Thought c. 350–c. 1450* (Cambridge: Cambridge University Press, 1988).

Cameron, Averil, *Byzantine Matters* (Princeton: Princeton University Press, 2014).

Cameron, Averil, and Gaul, Niels (eds), *Dialogues and Debates from Late Antiquity to Late Byzantium* (New York: Routledge, 2017).

Cameron, Averil, and Hall, Stuart, *Eusebius: Life of Constantine* (Oxford: Clarendon Press, 1999).

Cammelli, Giuseppe, *I dotti bizantini e le origini dell'umanesimo, tome I: Manuele Crisolora* (Florence: Vallecchi, 1941).

Cavallo, Gugliermo, 'Sodalizi eruditi e pratiche di scrittura a Bisanzio', in J. Hamesse (ed.), *Bilan et perspectives des études medievales (1993–1998)* (Turnhout: Brepols, 2004), 645–65.

Çelik, Siren, *A Historical Biography of Manuel II Palaiologos (1350–1425)* (PhD dissertation, University of Birmingham, 2016).

Ceresa-Gastaldo, Aldo (ed.), *Massimo Confessore: Capitoli sulla carità* (Rome: Editrice Studium, 1963).

Charanis, Peter, 'Internal strife in Byzantium during the fourteenth century', *Byzantion* 15 (1941), 208–30.

Charanis, Peter, 'The monastic properties and the state in the Byzantine Empire', *DOP* 4 (1948), 53–118.

Charanis, Peter, 'The role of the people in the political life of the Byzantine Empire: The period of the Comneni and the Palaeologi', *Byzantine Studies* 5 (1978), 69–79.

Charanis, Peter, 'The strife among the Palaeologi and the Ottoman Turks, 1370–1402', *Byzantion* 16 (1942), 286–314.

Chivu, Mihai, *Ἡ ἕνωσις τῶν ἐκκλησιῶν κατὰ τὸν Ἰωσὴφ Βρυέννιον* (PhD dissertation, Aristotle University of Thessalonike, 1985).

Chrysostomides, Julian, 'Venetian commercial privileges under the Paleologi', *Studi Veneziani* 12 (1970), 267–356.

Clucas, Stephen, Forshaw, Peter, and Rees, Valery, *Laus Platonici Philosophi: Marsilio Ficino and His Influence* (Leiden: Brill, 2011).

Colenbrander, Herman, *The Limbourg Brothers, the 'Joyaux' of Constantine and Heraclius and the Visit of the Byzantine Emperor Manuel II Palaeologus* (Leuven: Peeters, 1995).

Congourdeau, Marie, 'Un procès d'avortement à Constantinople au 14e siècle', *REB* 40 (1982), 103–15.

Conti Bizzarro, Ferrucio, 'Demetrio Crisolora e Manuele II Paleologo', in F. Conti Bizzarro (ed.), *Demetrio Crisolora: Cento Epistole a Manuele II Paleologo* (Naples: D'Auria, 1984), 10–19.

Culler, Jonathan, 'Towards a theory of non-genre literature', in R. Federman (ed.), *Surfiction* (Chicago: Swallow, 1975), 255–62.

Cunningham, Mary, 'Dramatic device or didactic tool? The function of dialogue in Byzantine preaching', in E. Jeffreys (ed.), *Rhetoric in Byzantium* (Aldershot: Ashgate, 2003), 101–16.

Cunningham, Mary, and Allen, Pauline (eds), *Preacher and Audience: Studies in Early Christian and Byzantine Homiletics* (Leiden: Brill, 1998).

Dabrowska, Małgorzata, 'Ought one to marry? Manuel II Palaiologos' point of view', *BMGS* 31 (2007), 146–56.

Dagron, Gilbert, *Emperor and Priest: The Imperial Office in Byzantium* (Cambridge: Cambridge University Press, 2003).

Delaville Le Roulx, Antoine, *La France en Orient au XIVe siècle: Expéditions du Maréchal Boucicaut* (Paris: Ernest Thorin, 1886).

Dendrinos, Charalambos, *An Annotated Critical Edition (Editio Princeps) of Emperor Manuel II Palaeologus' Treatise 'On the Procession of the Holy Spirit'* (PhD dissertation, Royal Holloway, University of London, 1996).

Dendrinos, Charalambos, 'Co-operation and friendship among Byzantine scholars in the circle of Emperor Manuel II Palaeologus (1391–1425) as reflected in their autograph manuscripts', <https://pure.royalholloway.ac.uk/portal/files/1394250/Manuel_II_Palaeologus_and_his_circle_of_scholars.pdf> (last accessed 8 April 2019).

Dendrinos, Charalambos, 'Ἡ ἐπιστολὴ τοῦ αὐτοκράτορος Μανουὴλ Παλαιολόγου πρὸς τὸν Ἀλέξιο Ἰαγοὺπ καὶ οἱ ἀντιλήψεις του περὶ τῆς σπουδῆς τῆς θεολογίας', *Philosophias Analekta* 1.1–2, 58–74.

Dendrinos, Charalambos, 'Palaiologan scholars at work: Makarios Makres and Joseph Bryennios' autograph', in A. Giannouli and E. Schiffer (eds), *From Manuscripts to Books – Vom Codex zur Edition: Proceedings of the International Workshop on Textual Criticism and Editorial Practice for Byzantine Texts* (Vienna: Verlag der Österreichischen Akademie der Wissenschaften, 2011), 23–51.

Dendrinos, Charalambos (ed.), *Porphyrogenita: Essays on the History and Literature of Byzantium and the Latin East in Honour of Julian Chrysostomides* (Aldershot: Ashgate, 2003).

Dennis, George, 'The Byzantine–Turkish treaty of Gallipoli of 1403', *OCP* 33 (1967), 72–88.

Dennis, George, *Byzantium and the Franks: 1350–1420* (London: Variorum, 1982).
Dennis, George, 'The deposition and restoration of Patriarch Matthew I, 1402–1403', *BF* 2 (1967), 100–6.
Dennis, George, 'Four unknown letters of Emperor Manuel II Palaeologus', *Byzantion* 36 (1966), 63–6.
Dennis, George, 'John VII Palaiologos: "A holy and just man"', in Evangelos Chrysos and Angeliki Laiou (eds), *Βυζάντιο: Κράτος και Κοινωνία: Μνήμη Νίκου Οικονομίδη* (Athens: Institute of Byzantine Research, 2003).
Dennis, George, 'The late Byzantine metropolitans of Thessalonike', *DOP* 57 (2003), 255–64.
Dennis, George, 'Official documents of Manuel II Palaeologus', *Byzantion* 41 (1971), 45–58.
Dennis, George, *The Reign of Manuel II Paleologus in Thessalonica: 1382–1387* (Rome: Pontificium Institutum Orientalium Studiorum, 1960).
Dennis, George, 'The second Turkish capture of Thessalonica', *BZ* 57 (1964), 56–8.
Dennis, George, 'The short chronicle of Lesbos 1355–1428', *Lesbiaka* 5 (1966), 128–42.
Dennis, George, 'Two unknown documents of Manuel II Palaeologus', *TM* 3 (1968), 397–404.
Dennis, George, 'An unknown Byzantine emperor, Andronikos V Palaeologus', *JÖBG* 16 (1967), 175–87.
Dölger, Franz, 'Johannes VII., Kaiser der Rhomäer 1390–1408', *BZ* 31 (1937), 21–36.
Đurić, Ivan, *Le crépuscule de Byzance* (Paris: Maisonneuve, 1996).
Dvornik, Francis, *Early Christian and Byzantine Political Philosophy: Origins and Background* (Washington, DC: Dumbarton Oaks, 1966).
Eberhardt, Otto, *Via Regia: Die Fürstenspiegel Smaragds von St. Mihiel und seine literarische Gattung* (Munich: Fink, 1977).
Edwards, Mark, 'Oratory', in I. de Jong, R. Nünlist, and A. Bowie (eds), *Narrators, Narratees, and Narratives in Ancient Greek Literature* (Leiden: Brill, 2017), 315–53.
Eszer, Ambrosius Klaus, *Das abenteuerliche Leben des Johannes Laskaris Kalopheros* (Wiesbaden: Harrassowitz, 1969).
Ferluga, J., 'Archon', in Norbert Kamp and Joachim Wollasch (eds), *Tradition als historische Kraft: Interdisziplinäre Forschungen zur Geschichte des früheren Mittelalters* (Berlin: De Gruyter, 1982), 254–66.
Finley, Moses, *Politics in the Ancient World* (Cambridge: Cambridge University Press, 1983).

Frankopan, Peter, 'The literary, cultural and political context for the twelfth-century commentary on the *Nicomachean Ethics*', in C. Barber and D. Jenkins (eds), *Medieval Greek Commentaries on the Nicomachean Ethics* (Leiden: Brill, 2009), 45–62.

Frohne, Renate, *Agapetus Diaconus: Untersuchungen zu den Quellen und zur Wirkungsgeschichte des ersten byzantinischen Fürstenspiegels* (PhD dissertation, University of Tübingen, 1984).

Ganchou, Thierry, 'Autour de Jean VII: Luttes dynastiques, interventions étrangères et résistance orthodoxe à Byzance (1373–1409)', in M. Balard and A. Ducellier (eds), *Coloniser au Moyen Âge* (Paris: Armand Colin, 1995), 367–85.

Ganchou, Thierry, 'La famille Κουμούσης à Constantinople et Négropont, avant et apres 1453', in C. Maltezou and C. Papakosta (eds), *Βενετία-Εύβοια από τον Έγριπο στο Νεγροπόντε* (Venice: Institute of Byzantine and Post-Byzantine Studies, 2006), 45–107.

Ganchou, Thierry, 'Géorgios Scholarios, "secretaire" du patriarche unioniste Gregorios III Mammas? Le mystère résolu', in *Le patriarcat oecuménique de Constantinople aux XIVe–XVIe siècles: Rupture et continuité* (Paris: Centre d'Études Byzantines, Neo-Helleniques et Sud-Est Européennes, 2007), 117–94.

Ganchou, Thierry, 'Ilario Doria, le gambros génois de Manuel II Palaiologos: Beau-frère ou gendre?', *Études Byzantines* 66 (2008), 71–94.

Ganchou, Thierry, 'Le mesazon Démétrius Paléologue Cantacuzène, a-t-il figuré parmi les défenseurs du siège de Constantinople (29 mai 1453)?', *REB* 52 (1994), 245–72.

Garland, Lynda, '*Mazaris' Journey to Hades*: Further reflections and reappraisals', *DOP* 61 (2007), 190–200.

Gass, Wilhelm, *Die Mystik des Nikolaus Cabasilas vom Leben in Christo* (Leipzig: Lorentz, 1899).

Gaul, Niels, 'Performative reading in the late Byzantine *theatron*', in T. Shawcross and I. Toth (eds), *Reading in the Byzantine Empire and Beyond* (Cambridge: Cambridge University Press, 2018), 215–34.

Gaul, Niels, *Thomas Magistros und die spätbyzantinische Sophistik: Studien zum Humanismus urbaner Eliten der frühen Palaiologenzeit* (Wiesbaden: Harrassowitz, 2011).

Gaul, Niels, 'The twitching shroud: Collective construction of *paideia* in the circle of Thomas Magistros', *Segno e Testo* 5 (2007), 263–340.

Geanakopoulos, Deno, *Byzantine East and Latin West: Two Worlds of Christendom in the Middle Ages and Renaissance* (Oxford: Blackwell, 1976).

Geanakopoulos, Deno, 'Church and state in the Byzantine Empire: A reconsideration of the problem of Caesaropapism', *Church History* 34 (1965), 381–403.

Genette, Gerard, *The Narrative Discourse: An Essay in Method* (Ithaca: Cornell University Press, 1983).
Giannouli, Antonia, 'Paränese zwischen Enkomion und Psogos: Zur Gattungseinordnung byzantinischer Fürstenspiegel', in A. Rhoby and E. Schiffer (eds), *Imitatio – aemulatio – variatio: Akten des internationalen wissenschaftlichen Symposions zur byzantinischen Literatur* (Vienna: Verlag der Österreichischen Akademie der Wissenschaften, 2010), 119–26.
Gill, Joseph, *Byzantium and the Papacy, 1198–1400* (New Brunswick, NJ: Rutgers University Press, 1979).
Gill, Joseph, 'John V Palaeologus at the court of Louis I of Hungary (1366)', *Byzantinoslavica* 38 (1977), 31–8.
Gill, Joseph, 'John VIII Palaeologus: A Character Study', in *Silloge bizantina in onore di Silvio Giuseppe Mercati* (Rome: Associazione Nazionale per gli Studi Bizantini, 1957), 152–70.
Gill, Joseph, *Personalities of the Council of Florence, and Other Essays* (New York: Barnes and Noble, 1965).
Gouillard, Jean, 'Le synodicon de l'orthodoxie: Edition et commentaire', *TM* 2 (1967), 80–198.
Gounaridis, Paris, 'Επιλογές μιας κοινωνικής ομάδας', in C. Angelidi (ed.), *Το Βυζάντιο ώριμο για αλλαγές: Επιλογές, ευαισθησίες και τρόποι έκφρασης από τον ενδέκατο στον δέκατο πέμπτο αιώνα* (Athens: Byzantine Research Institute, 2004), 177–85.
Greimas, Algirdas, *Structural Semantics: An Attempt at a Method* (Lincoln, NE: University of Nebraska Press, 1983).
Grosdidier, Dominique de Matons, and Förstel, Christian, 'Quelques manuscrits grecs liés à Manuel II Paléologue', in B. Atsalos and N. Tsironis (eds), *Proceedings of the 6th International Symposium on Greek Palaeography*, vol. 1 (Athens: Hellenic Society for Bookbinding, 2008), 375–86.
Guran, Petre, 'Patriarche hésychaste et empereur latinophrone: L'accord de 1380 sur les droits impériaux en matière ecclésiastique', *RESEE* 39 (2001), 53–62.
Hackel, Sergei (ed.), *The Byzantine Saint* (Crestwood, NY: St Vladimir's Seminary Press, 2001).
Hadjopoulos, Dionysios, *Le premier siège de Constantinople par les Ottomans (1394–1402)* (PhD dissertation, University of Montreal, 1980).
Hadot, Pierre, 'Fürstenspiegel', in E. Dassman and F. Dölger (eds.), *Reallexikon für Antike und Christentum*, vol. 8 (Stuttgart: Hiersemann, 1972), 555–632.
Haldon, John F., *A Social History of Byzantium* (Oxford: Wiley-Blackwell, 2009).
Halecki, Oskar, *Un empereur de Byzance à Rome* (London: Variorum, 1972).

Harris, Jonathan, *The End of Byzantium* (New Haven, CT: Yale University Press, 2010).

Harvey, Elizabeth, *Ventriloquized Voices: Feminist Theory and English Renaissance Texts* (London: Routledge, 1995).

Heitsch, Dorothea, and Vallée, Jean-François, *Printed Voices: The Renaissance Culture of Dialogue* (Toronto: University of Toronto Press, 2004).

Henry III, Paul, 'A mirror for Justinian: The *Ekthesis* of Agapetos', *GRBS* 8 (1967), 281–308.

Herman, David, *The Cambridge Companion to Narrative* (Cambridge: Cambridge University Press, 2007).

Herrin, Judith, and Saint-Guillain, Guillaume, *Identities and Allegiances in the Eastern Mediterranean after 1204* (Aldershot: Ashgate, 2011).

Hersant, Yves, *Vie active et vie contemplative à la Renaissance* (Paris: Classiques Garnier, 2014).

Hilsdale, Cecily, *Byzantine Art and Diplomacy in an Age of Decline* (Cambridge: Cambridge University Press, 2014).

Hinterberger, Martin, and Schabel, Christopher D., *Greeks, Latins, and Intellectual History, 1204–1500* (Leuven: Peeters, 2011).

Hinterberger, Martin, and Hörandner, Wolfram (eds), *Byzantinische Sprachkunst: Studien zur byzantinischen Literatur gewidmet Wolfram Hörandner zum 65. Geburtstag* (Berlin: De Gruyter, 2007).

Hirsch, E. D., *Validity in Interpretation* (New Haven, CT: Yale University Press, 1967).

Holmes, Catherine, 'Political literacy', in P. Stephenson (ed.), *The Byzantine World* (New York: Routledge, 2010), 137–48.

Hunger, Herbert, *Die hochsprachliche profane Literatur der Byzantiner*, vol. 1 (Munich: Beck, 1978).

Hunger, Herbert, *Katalog der griechischen Handschriften der Österreichischen Nationalbibliothek. Teil 1: Codices historici, Codices philosophici et philologici* (Vienna: Prachner, 1961).

Hunger, Herbert, 'Philanthropia: Eine griechische Wortprägung auf ihrem Wege von Aischylos bis Theodoros Metochites', in *Byzantinische Grundlagenforschung. Gesammelte Aufsätze* (London: Variorum, 1973), 1–20.

Hunger, Herbert, *Prooimion: Elemente der byzantinischen Kaiseridee in den Arengen der Urkunden* (Vienna: Böhlau, 1964).

Hunger, Herbert, 'Eine spätbyzantinische Bildbeschreibung der Geburt Christi, mit einem Exkurs über das Charsianites-Kloster in Konstantinopel', *JÖBG* 7 (1958), 126–40.

Hunger, Herbert, 'Das Testament des Patriarchen Matthaios I', *BZ* 51 (1958), 288–309.

Hussey, J. M., *The Orthodox Church in the Byzantine Empire* (Oxford: Clarendon Press, 1986).
Irigoin, Jean, 'Une reliure de l'Athos au monogramme des Paléologues (Stavronikita 14)', *Paleoslavica* 10 (2002), 175–9.
Jacoby, David, 'Les archontes grecs et la féodalité en Morée franque', *TM* 2 (1967), 421–81.
Jacoby, David, 'Jean Lascaris Calophéros, Chypre et la Morée', *REB* 26 (1978), 190–3.
James, Liz, *A Companion to Byzantium* (Oxford: Wiley-Blackwell, 2010).
Jaworski, Adam, and Coupland, Nikolas, *The Discourse Reader* (London: Routledge, 1999).
Jauss, Hans Robert, *Toward an Aesthetic of Reception* (Minneapolis, MN: University of Minnesota Press, 1982).
Jeffreys, Elizabeth (ed.), *Rhetoric in Byzantium: Papers from the Thirty-Fifth Spring Symposium of Byzantine Studies* (Aldershot: Ashgate, 2003).
Jong, Irene de, Nünlist, René, and Bowie, Angus (eds), *Narrators, Narratees, and Narratives in Ancient Greek Literature* (Leiden: Brill, 2004).
Jugie, Martin, 'Le voyage de l'empereur Manuel Paléologue en Occident (1399–1403)', *REB* 95 (1912), 322–32.
Kakulide, Eleni, 'Η βιβλιοθήκη τῆς Μονῆς Προδρόμου-Πέτρας στὴν Κωνσταντινούπολη', *Hellenika* 21 (1968), 26–8.
Kaldellis, Anthony, *The Byzantine Republic: People and Power in New Rome* (Cambridge, MA: Harvard University Press, 2015).
Kaldellis, Anthony, and Siniossoglou, Niketas (eds), *The Cambridge Intellectual History of Byzantium* (Cambridge: Cambridge University Press, 2017).
Kaldellis, Anthony, *Hellenism in Byzantium: The Transformations of Greek Identity and the Reception of the Classical Tradition* (Cambridge: Cambridge University Press, 2011).
Kaltsogianni, Eleni, 'Zur Entstehung der Rede des Manuel II. Palaiologos auf die Heilige Maria von Ägypten [BHG 1044c]', *Parekbolai* 1 (2011), 37–59.
Kastritsis, Dimitris, *The Sons of Bayezid: Empire Building and Representation in the Ottoman Civil War of 1402–1413* (Leiden: Brill, 2007).
Katsone, Polymnia, *Ἀνδρόνικος Δ' Παλαιολόγος: βασιλεία και αλληλομαχία* (Thessalonike: Centre for Byzantine Research, 2008).
Kazhdan, Alexander, *A History of Byzantine Literature: 650–850* (Athens: Hellenic Research Foundation, 1999).
Kazhdan, Alexander, 'The Italian and late Byzantine city', *DOP* 49 (1995), 1–22.
Keller, A. G., 'A Byzantine admirer of Western progress: Cardinal Bessarion', *Cambridge Historical Journal* 11 (1955), 343–8.

Kennedy, George, *The Cambridge History of Literary Criticism* (Cambridge: Cambridge University Press, 1989).

Khoury, Théodore, *Manuel II Paléologue: Entretiens avec un Musulman* (Paris: Éditions du Cerf, 1966).

Kianka, Frances, 'The *Apology* of Demetrius Cydones: A fourteenth-century autobiographical source', *Byzantine Studies* 7 (1980), 57–71.

Kianka, Frances, 'Byzantine–Papal diplomacy: The role of Demetrius Cydones', *The International History Review* 7 (1985), 175–213.

Kianka, Frances, *Demetrius Cydones (c. 1324–c. 1397): Intellectual and Diplomatic Relations between Byzantium and the West in the Fourteenth Century* (PhD dissertation, Fordham University, 1981).

Kianka, Frances, 'Demetrios Kydones and Italy', *DOP* 49 (1995), 99–110.

Kianka, Frances, 'The letters of Demetrios Kydones to Empress Helena Kantakuzene Palaiologina', *DOP* 46 (1992), 155–64.

Kioussopoulou, Antonia, *Emperor or Manager: Power and Political Ideology in Byzantium before 1453*, trans. Paul Magdalino (Geneva: La Pomme d'Or, 2011).

Kioussopoulou Antonia, 'Les hommes d'affaires byzantins et leur rôle politique à la fin du Moyen Âge', *Historical Review* 7 (2010), 15–22.

Kioussopoulou, Antonia, 'La ville chez Manuel Chrysoloras: Σύγκρισις παλαιᾶς καὶ Νέας 'Ρώμης', *Byzantinoslavica* 59 (1998), 71–9.

Konidares, Ioannes, "Ἐπιτελεύτιος βούλησις καὶ διδασκαλία του οἰκουμενικοῦ πατριάρχου Ματθαίου (1397–1410)', *ΕΕΒΣ* 45 (1981–2), 472–510.

Kourouses, Sophia, 'Αἱ ἀντιλήψεις περὶ τῶν ἐσχάτων τοῦ κόσμου καὶ ἡ κατὰ τὸ ἔτος 1346 πτῶσις τοῦ τρούλλου τῆς Ἁγίας Σοφίας', *ΕΕΒΣ* 37 (1969–70), 235–40.

Krausmüller, Dirk, 'The rise of hesychasm', in M. Angold (ed.), *The Cambridge History of Christianity* (Cambridge: Cambridge University Press, 2006), 101–26.

Krynen, Jacques, *L'empire du roi: Idées et croyances politiques en France, XIIIe–XVe siècle* (Paris: Gallimard, 1993).

Kustas, George L., 'The function and evolution of Byzantine rhetoric', *Viator* 1 (1971), 55–74.

Kustas, George L., *Studies in Byzantine Rhetoric* (Thessalonike: Patriarchikon Hidryma Paterikōn, 1973).

Kyritses, Demetrios, *The Byzantine Aristocracy in the Thirteenth and Early Fourteenth Centuries* (PhD dissertation, Harvard University, 1997).

Kyritses, Demetrios, 'The "common chrysobulls" of cities and the notion of property in late Byzantium', *Βυζαντινά Σύμμεικτά* 13 (1999), 229–45.

Labowsky, Carlota, *Bessarion's Library and the Biblioteca Marciana* (Rome: Edizioni di storia e letteratura, 1979).

Laiou, Angeliki, 'Byzantine aristocracy: The story of an arrested development', *Viator* 4 (1973), 131–51.
Laiou, Angeliki, 'The Byzantine economy in the Mediterranean trade system: Thirteenth–fifteenth centuries', *DOP* 35 (1980), 177–224.
Laiou, Angeliki, 'Byzantium and the neighboring powers: Small-state policies and complexities', in Sarah T. Brooks (ed.), *Byzantium, Faith, and Power (1261–1557): Perspectives on Late Byzantine Art and Culture* (New Haven, CT: Yale University Press, 2006), 42–52.
Laiou, Angeliki, *Constantinople and the Latins: The Foreign Policy of Andronicus II, 1282–1328* (Cambridge, MA: Harvard University Press, 1972).
Laiou, Angeliki, and Bouras, Charalambos (eds), *The Economic History of Byzantium: From the Seventh through the Fifteenth Century* (Washington, DC: Dumbarton Oaks, 2002).
Laiou, Angeliki, and Morrisson, Cécile, *The Byzantine Economy* (Cambridge: Cambridge University Press, 2007).
Lauchert, Friedrich, *Die Kanones der wichtigsten altkirchlichen Concilien, nebst den Apostolischen Kanones* (Leipzig and Freiburg: Mohr, 1896).
Laurent, Vitalien, 'La date de la mort d'Hélène Cantacuzene, femme de Jean V Paléologue', *REB* 13 (1955), 135–8.
Laurent, Vitalien, 'Les droits de l'empereur en matière ecclésiastique: L'accord de 1380–1382', *REB* 13 (1955), 5–20.
Laurent, Vitalien, *Les grandes crises religieuses à Byzance: La fin du schisme arsénite* (Bucharest: Imprimeria Națională, 1945).
Laurent, Vitalien, 'Le rituel de l'investiture du patriarche byzantin au début du XVe siècle', *Bulletin de la Section Historique de l'Academie Roumaine* 28 (1947), 218–32.
Laurent, Vitalien, 'Le trisépiscopat du patriarche Matthieu Ier (1397–1410): Un grand procès canonique à Byzance au début du XVe siècle', *REB* 30 (1972), 5–166.
Lausberg, Heinrich, *Handbook of Literary Rhetoric: A Foundation for Literary Study* (Leiden: Brill, 1998).
Lauxtermann, Marc, *Byzantine Poetry from Pisides to Geometres: Texts and Contexts* (Vienna: Verlag der Österreichischen Akademie der Wissenschaften, 2003).
Lemerle, Paul, 'Le juge général des Grecs et la réforme judiciaire d'Andronic III', in *Mémorial Louis Petit: Mélanges d'Histoire et d'Archéologie Byzantines* (Bucharest: Institut d'Études Byzantines, 1948), 292–316.
Leonte, Florin, 'A brief "history of the Morea" as seen through the eyes of an emperor-rhetorician', in S. Gerstel (ed.), *Viewing the Morea: Land and People in the Late Medieval Peloponnese* (Washington, DC: Dumbarton Oaks, 2013), 397–417.

Leonte, Florin, 'Visions of empire: Gaze, space, and territory in Isidore's *Encomium for John VIII Palaiologos*', DOP 71 (2018), 249–72.

Leontiades, Ioannes, *Untersuchungen zum Staatsverständnis der Byzantiner aufgrund der Fürsten- bzw. Untertanenspiegel (13–15. Jahrhundert)*.

Likoudis, James, *Ending the Byzantine Greek Schism* (New Rochelle, NY: Catholics United, 1992).

Loenertz, Raymond-Joseph, 'Aux origines du despotat d'Épire et de la principauté d'Achaïe', *Byzantion* 43 (1973), 360–94.

Loenertz, Raymond-Joseph, *Byzantina et Franco-Graeca: Articles choisis parus de 1936 à 1969* (Rome: Edizioni di storia e letteratura, 1978).

Loenertz, Raymond-Joseph, 'Demetrius Cydonès, citoyen de Venise', *EO* 37 (1938), 125–6.

Loenertz, Raymond-Joseph, 'Écrits de Macaire Macres et de Manuel Paleologue dans les mss. Vat. 203 gr. 1107 et Crypten. 161', *OCP* 15 (1949), 185–92.

Loenertz, Raymond-Joseph, 'L'éxil de Manuel Paléologue à Lemnos 1387–1389', *OCP* 38 (1972), 116–40.

Loenertz, Raymond-Joseph, 'Isidore Glabas, métropolite de Thessalonique (1380–1396)', *REB* 6 (1948), 181–7.

Loenertz, Raymond-Joseph, 'Manuel Paléologue et Demetrius Cydones: Remarques sur leurs correspondances', *EO* 36 (1937), 271–87 and *EO* 37 (1938), 107–29.

Loenertz, Raymond-Joseph, 'Pour la chronologie des œuvres de Joseph Bryennios', *REB* 7 (1949), 12–32.

Loenertz, Raymond-Joseph, 'Pour l'histoire du Péloponnèse au XIVe siècle 1382–1404', in R.-J. Loenertz, *Byzantina et Franco-Graeca* (Rome: Edizioni di storia e letteratura, 1970), 227–65.

Loenertz, Raymond-Joseph, *Les recueils de lettres de Démétrius Cydonès* (Vatican: Biblioteca Apostolica Vaticana, 1947).

Loenertz, Raymond-Joseph, '*Res Gestae Theodori Ioann. F. Palaelogi*: Titulus metricus A. D. 1389', *ΕΕΒΣ* 25 (1955), 206–10.

Luttrell, Anthony, 'John V's daughters: A Palaiologan puzzle', *DOP* 40 (1986), 103–12.

Macrides, Ruth, 'Saints and sainthood in the early Palaiologan period', in S. Hackel (ed.), *The Byzantine Saint* (Crestwood, NY: St Vladimir's Seminary Press, 2001), 67–87.

Macrides, Ruth (ed.), *Travel in the Byzantine World: Papers from the Thirty-Fourth Spring Symposium of Byzantine Studies, Birmingham, April 2000* (Aldershot: Ashgate, 2002).

Macrides, Ruth, Munitiz, J. A., and Angelov, Dimiter, *Pseudo-Kodinos and the Constantinopolitan Court: Offices and Ceremonies* (Farnham: Ashgate, 2013).

Magdalino, Paul, 'Basileia: The idea of monarchy in Byzantium, 600–1200', in A. Kaldellis and N. Siniossoglou (eds), *The Cambridge Intellectual History of Byzantium* (Cambridge: Cambridge University Press, 2017), 575–98.

Magdalino, Paul, 'Byzantine churches of Selymbria', *DOP* 32 (1978), 309–18.

Magdalino, Paul, *The Empire of Manuel I Komnenos, 1143–1180* (Cambridge: Cambridge University Press, 1993).

Magdalino, Paul (ed.), *New Constantines: The Rhythm of Imperial Renewal in Byzantium, 4th–13th Centuries* (Aldershot: Variorum, 1994).

Maisano, Riccardo (ed.), *Manuele Crisolora e il ritorno del greco in Occidente: Atti del convegno internazionale* (Naples: [s.n.], 2002).

Majeska, George (ed. and trans.), *Russian Travelers to Constantinople in the Fourteenth and Fifteenth Centuries* (Washington, DC: Dumbarton Oaks, 1984).

Maksimović, Ljubomir, *The Byzantine Provincial Administration under the Palaiologoi* (Amsterdam: Hakkert, 1988).

Maksimović, Ljubomir, 'Charakter der sozialwirtschaftlichen Struktur der spätbyzantinischen Stadt (13.–15. Jh)', *JÖB* 31 (1981), 149–88.

Mamalakes, Ioannes P., *Georgios Gemistos Plethon* (Athens: Verlag der Byzantinisch Neugriechischen Jahrbücher, 1939).

Marinescu, Constantin, 'Manuel II Paléologue et les rois d'Aragon: Commentaire sur quatre lettres inédites en latin, expediées par la chancellerie byzantine', *Bulletin de la Section Historique de l'Academie Roumaine* 11 (1924), 193–206.

Masai, François, *Pléthon et le platonisme de Mistra* (Paris: Belles Lettres, 1956).

Matranga, Pietro, *Anecdota graeca e mss. bibliothecis Vaticana, Angelica, Barberiniana, Vallicelliana, Medicea, Vindobonensi deprompta* (Rome: Bertinelli, 1850).

Matschke, Klaus-Peter, 'Bemerkungen zu "Stadtbürgertum" und "stadtbürgerlichen Geist" in Byzanz', *Jahrbuch für Geschichte des Feudalismus* 8 (1984), 265–85.

Matschke, Klaus-Peter, *Die Schlacht bei Ankara und das Schicksal von Byzanz: Studien zur spätbyzantinischen Geschichte zwischen 1402 und 1422* (Weimar: Böhlau, 1981).

Matschke, Klaus-Peter, and Tinnefeld, Franz Hermann, *Die Gesellschaft im späten Byzanz: Gruppen, Strukturen und Lebensformen* (Cologne: Böhlau, 2001).

Mazal, Otto, *Byzanz und das Abendland* (Vienna: Österreichische Nationalbibliothek, 1981).

Mercati, Giovanni, *Notizie di Procoro e Demetrio Cidone, Manuele Caleca e Teodoro Meleteniota, ed altri appunti per la storia della teologia e della letteratura bizantina del secolo XIV* (Vatican: Biblioteca Apostolica Vaticana, 1931).

Mercati, Giovanni, *Scritti d'Isidoro, il cardinale ruteno, e codici a lui appartenuti che si conservano nella Biblioteca Apostolica Vaticana* (Rome: Biblioteca Apostolica Vaticana, 1926).

Mergiali, Sophia, 'A Byzantine ambassador to the West and his office during the fourteenth and fifteenth centuries: A profile', *BZ* 94 (2001), 588–604.

Mergiali, Sophia, *L'enseignement et les lettrés pendant l'époque des Paléologues (1261–1453)* (Athens: Centre for Byzantine Research, 1996).

Mešanović, Sanja, *Jovan VII Paleolog* (Belgrade: Vizantološki Institut Srpske Akademije Nauka i Umetnosti, 1996).

Meyendorff, John, *Byzantine Theology: Historical Trends and Doctrinal Themes* (New York: Fordham University Press, 1999).

Mitsiou, Ekaterini, Popović, Mihailo, Preise-Kapeller, Johannes, and Alexandru, Simon (eds), *Emperor Sigismund and the Orthodox World* (Vienna: Verlag der Österreichischen Akademie der Wissenschaften, 2010).

Mohler, Ludwig, *Aus Bessarions Gelehrtenkreis: Abhandlungen, Reden, Briefe von Bessarion, Theodoros Gazes, Michael Apostolios, Andronikos Kallistos, Georgios Trapezuntios, Niccolò Perotti, Niccolò Capranica* (Paderborn: Ferdinand Schöningh, 1942).

Morgan, Teresa, *Literate Education in the Hellenistic and Roman Worlds* (Cambridge: Cambridge University Press, 1998).

Mullett, Margaret, 'The madness of genre', *DOP* 46 (1992), 233–43.

Mullett, Margaret, and Smythe, Dion (eds), *Alexios I Komnenos* (Belfast: Belfast Byzantine Enterprises, 1996).

Nauck, August, *Lexicon Vindobonense* (Hildesheim: Olms, 1965).

Necipoğlu, Nevra, 'The aristocracy in late Byzantine Thessalonike: A case study of the city's archontes (late 14th and early 15th centuries)', *DOP* 57 (2003), 133–51.

Necipoğlu, Nevra, *Byzantium between the Ottomans and the Latins: Politics and Society in the Late Empire* (Cambridge: Cambridge University Press, 2009).

Nederman, Cary, 'Priests, kings, and tyrants: Spiritual and temporal power in John of Salisbury's *Policraticus*', *Speculum* 66 (1991), 572–90.

Nicol, Donald, 'A Byzantine Emperor in England: Manuel II's visit to London in 1400–1401', *University of Birmingham Historical Journal* 12.2 (1971), 204–25.

Nicol, Donald, 'Byzantine political thought', in J. H. Burns (ed.), *The Cambridge History of Medieval Political Thought* (Cambridge: Cambridge University Press, 1988), 51–82.

Nicol, Donald, *Byzantium and Venice: A Study in Diplomatic and Cultural Relations* (Cambridge: Cambridge University Press, 1988).

Nicol, Donald, *Church and Society in the Last Centuries of Byzantium: The Birkbeck Lectures, 1977* (Cambridge: Cambridge University Press, 1979).

Nicol, Donald, *The Immortal Emperor: The Life and Legend of Constantine Palaiologos, Last Emperor of the Romans* (Cambridge: Cambridge University Press, 1992).

Nicol, Donald, *The Last Centuries of Byzantium, 1261–1453* (Cambridge: Cambridge University Press, 1993).

Nikolaou, T. S., *Αἱ περὶ πολιτείας καὶ δικαίου ἰδέαι τοῦ Γ. Πλήθωνος* (Thessalonike: Center for Byzantine Research, 1989).

Nikolić, Maria, 'Georgios Sphrantzes or how to become an archon in Byzantium in the fifteenth century', ZRVI 47 (2010), 277–89.

Odorico, Paolo (ed.), *'L'éducation au gouvernement et à la vie': La tradition des 'règles de vie' de l'Antiquité au Moyen Âge* (Paris: Centre d'Études Byzantines, Néo-Helléniques et Sud-Est Européennes, 2009).

Odorico, Paolo, 'Les miroirs des princes à Byzance: Une lecture horizontale', in P. Odorico (ed.), *L'éducation au gouvernement et à la vie: La tradition des 'règles de vie' de l'antiquité au moyen-âge* (Paris: Centre d'Études Byzantines, Néo-Helléniques et Sud-Est Européennes, 2009), 223–46.

Odorico, Paolo, *Il prato e l'ape: Il sapere sentenzioso del Monaco Giovanni* (Vienna: Verlag der Österreichischen Akademie der Wissenschaften, 1986).

Oeconomos, Lysimachos, 'L'état intellectuel et moral des Byzantins vers le milieu du XIVe siècle d'après une page de Joseph Bryennios', in *Mélanges Charles Diehl*, vol. 1 (Paris: Presses Universitaires de France, 1930), 225–33.

Oikonomides, Nikos, 'La comédie de Katablattas: Invective byzantine du XVe siecle', *Diptycha* 3 (1982), 1–97.

Oikonomides, Nicolas, *Hommes d'affaires grecs et latins à Constantinople: XIIIe–XVe siècles* (Montréal: Institut d'Études Médiévales Albert-le-Grand, 1979).

Oikonomides, Nikos, 'John VII Palaiologos and the ivory pyxis at Dumbarton Oaks', *DOP* 31 (1977), 329–37.

Oikonomides, Nikos, 'Pour une typologie des villes "separées" sous les Paléologues', in W. Seibt (ed.), *Geschichte und Kultur der Palaiologenzeit: Referate des Internationalen Symposions zu Ehren von Herbert Hunger (Wien, 30. November bis 3. Dezember 1994)* (Vienna: Verlag der Österreichischen Akademie der Wissenschaften, 1996), 160–7.

Oikonomopoulou, Katerina, and Xenophontos, Sophia (eds), *Brill's Companion to the Reception of Plutarch* (Leiden: Brill, 2019).

Olmsted, Wendy, 'Topics (and deliberation): exemplifying deliberation', in W. Jost and W. Olmsted (eds), *A Companion to Rhetoric and Rhetorical Criticism* (Oxford: Blackwell, 2004), 173–89.

Oltramare, André, *Les origines de la diatribe Romaine* (Lausanne: Payot, 1926).

Ostrogorskij, Georges, *Pour l'histoire de la féodalité byzantine* (Brussels: Éditions de l'Institut de Philologie et d'Histoire Orientales et Slaves, 1954).

Ozbic, Maila, 'Ι ΚΕΦΑΛΑΙΑ di Andronico Paleologo', *BZ* 91 (1998), 406–22.

Page, Gill, *Being Byzantine: Greek Identity before the Ottomans* (Cambridge: Cambridge University Press, 2008).

Païdas, Konstantinos, *Τα βυζαντινά κάτοπτρα ηγεμόνος της ύστερης περιόδου (1254–1303): Εκφράσεις τοῦ Βυζαντινού βασιλικού ιδεώδου* (Athens: Grēgorē, 2006).

Papademetriou, Tom, 'The Turkish conquests and decline of the church reconsidered', in D. Angelov (ed.), *Church and Society in Late Byzantium* (Kalamazoo, MI: Medieval Institute, 2009), 186–200.

Papaioannou, Stratis, *Michael Psellos: Rhetoric and Authorship in Byzantium* (Cambridge: Cambridge University Press, 2013).

Patacsi, G., 'Joseph Bryennios et les discussions sur un concile d'union (1414–1431)', *Κληρονομία* 5 (1973), 73–96.

Peers, Glenn, 'Manuel II Paleologos's ekphrasis on a tapestry in the Louvre: Word over image', *REB* 61 (2003), 201–14.

Peritore, N. P., 'The political thought of George Gemistos Plethon', *Polity* 10 (1977), 168–91.

Pernot, Laurent, *La rhétorique de l'éloge dans le monde gréco-romain* (Paris: Institut d'Études Augustiniennes, 1993).

Pesce, Luciano, 'Cristoforo Garatone, Trevigiano nunzio di Eugenio IV', *Rivista di Storia della Chiesa* 28 (1974), 23–93.

Petit, Louis, Siderides, X. A., and Jugie, Martin (eds), *œuvres complètes de Georges Scholarios*, 8 vols (Paris: Maison de la Bonne Presse, 1928–36).

Phelan, James, and Rabinowitz, Peter J. (eds), *A Companion to Narrative Theory* (Oxford: Blackwell, 2008).

Philippidis-Braat, A., 'La captivité de Palamas chez les Turcs: Dossier et commentaire', *TM* 7 (1979), 109–222.

Phountoules, Ioannes (ed.), *Τὸ λειτουργικόν ἔργον του Συμεωὺν Θεσσαλονίκης* (Thessalonike: Hetaireia Makedonikon Spoudon, 1966).

Pizzone, Aglae, 'Introduction', in A. Pizzone (ed.), *The Author in Middle Byzantine Literature: Modes, Functions, and Identities* (Boston: De Gruyter, 2014), 3–20.

Polemes, Ioannes, 'Εισαγωγή', in *Θεόδωρος Μετοχίτης: Ηθικός ή περί παιδείας* (Athens: Kanaki, 1995).

Porter, Stanley, *Handbook of Classical Rhetoric in the Hellenistic Period* (Leiden: Brill, 1997).
Preiser-Kapeller, Johannes, 'Letters and network analysis', in A. Riehle (ed.), *A Companion to Byzantine Epistolography* (forthcoming).
Prinzing, Günter, 'Beobachtungen zu "integrierten" Fürstenspiegeln der Byzantiner', *JÖB* 38 (1988), 1–31.
Propp, Vladimir, *Morphology of the Folktale* (Austin, TX: University of Texas Press, 1984).
Rees, David, 'Joseph Bryennios and the text of Marcus Aurelius' *Meditations*', *Classical Quarterly* 50 (2000), 584–96.
Reinert, Stephen, 'Political dimensions of Manuel II Palaiologos' 1392 marriage and coronation', in C. Sode (ed.), *Novum Millennium: Studies on Byzantine History and Culture Dedicated to Paul Speck* (Aldershot: Ashgate, 2001), 291–302.
Reinert, Stephen, 'The Palaiologoi, Yildirim Bayezid and Constantinople: June 1389–March 1391', in J. S. Langdon, S. W. Reinert, J. S. Allen and C. P. Ioannides (eds), *Τὸ Ἑλληνικόν: Studies in Honor of Speros Vryonis, Jr.*, vol. 1 (New Rochelle, NY: Caratzeas, 1993), 289–365.
Reinert, Stephen, 'Political dimensions of Manuel II Palaiologos' 1392 marriage and coronation', in C. Sode (ed.), *Novum Millennium: Studies on Byzantine History and Culture Dedicated to Paul Speck* (Aldershot: Ashgate, 2001), 291–302.
Reinsch, D. R., 'Lieber den Turban als was?', in C. N. Constantinides, N. M. Panagiotakes, E. Jeffreys and A. D. Angelou (eds), *ΦΙΛΕΛΛΗΝ: Studies in Honour of Robert Browning* (Venice: Istituto Ellenico di Studi Bizantini e Postbizantini di Venezia, 1996), 377–89.
Rhalles, G., and Potles, M. (eds), *Σύνταγμα τῶν θείων καὶ ἱερῶν κανόνων*, 6 vols (Athens: 1852).
Rhoby, Andreas, 'Stadtlob und Stadtkritik in der byzantinischen Literatur', in M. Hinterberger and W. Hörandner (eds), *Byzantinische Sprachkunst: Studien zur byzantinischen Literatur gewidmet Wolfram Hörandner zum 65. Geburtstag* (Berlin: De Gruyter, 2007), 277–96.
Rigolot, François, 'Problematizing Renaissance exemplarity: The inward turn of dialog from Petrarch to Montaigne', in D. Heitsch and J.-F. Vallée (eds), *Printed Voices: The Renaissance Culture of Dialogue* (Toronto: University of Toronto Press, 2004), 3–23.
Roilos, Panagiotis, *Amphoteroglossia: A Poetics of the Twelfth-Century Medieval Greek Novel* (Washington, DC: Center for Hellenic Studies, 2005).
Rollo, A., 'A proposito del Vat. gr. 2239: Manuele II e Guarino', *Νέα Ῥώμη* 3 (2006), 375–8.

Runciman, Steven, *The Byzantine Theocracy* (Cambridge: Cambridge University Press, 1977).
Runciman, Steven, 'Manuel II and the see of Moldavia', in J. Chrysostomides (ed.), *Kathegetria: Essays Presented to Joan Hussey for her 80th Birthday* (Camberley: Porphyrogenitus, 1988), 515–20.
Ruys, Juanita Feros, *What Nature Does Not Teach: Didactic Literature in the Medieval and Early-Modern Periods* (Turnhout: Brepols, 2008).
Ryder, Judith, *The Career and Writings of Demetrius Kydones: A Study of Fourteenth-Century Byzantine Politics, Religion and Society* (Leiden: Brill, 2010).
Sansterre, Jean-Marie, *Mémoires et documents: Eusèbe de Césarée et la naissance de la théorie 'Césaropapiste'* (Brussels: Peeters, 1972).
Schenkeveld, A., 'Philosophical prose', in S. Porter (ed.), *Handbook on Classical Rhetoric in the Hellenistic Period* (Leiden: Brill, 1997), 199–210.
Schilbach, Erich, 'Die Hypotyposis der *Katholikoi Kritai Ton Romaion* vom Juni 1398', BZ 61 (1968), 44–70.
Schlumberger, Gustave, *Un empereur de Byzance [Manuel II] à Paris et à Londres* (Paris: Plon, 1916).
Schmitt, Oliver Jens, 'Kaiserrede und Zeitgeschichte im späten Byzanz: Ein Panegyrikos Isidors von Kiew aus dem Jahre 1429', JÖB 48 (1998), 209–42.
Schneider, Robert, 'Towards a cognitive theory of literary character', Style 35 (2001), 607–40.
Schreiner, Peter, *Chronica Byzantina Breviora: Die byzantinischen Kleinchroniken*, 3 vols (Vienna: Verlag der Österreichischen Akademie der Wissenschaften, 1975–9).
Schreiner, Peter, 'Hochzeit und Krönung Kaiser Manuels II. im Jahre 1392', BZ 60 (1967), 70–85.
Schreiner, Peter, 'Johannes Chortasmenos als Restaurator des Vat. gr. 2226', *Scrittura e Civiltá* 7 (1983), 193–9.
Schreiner, Peter, 'Literarische Interessen in der Palaiologenzeit anhand von Glehrtencodices: Das Beispiel des Vaticanus gr. 914', in W. Seibt (ed.), *Geschichte und Kultur der Palaiologenzeit: Referate des Internationalen Symposions zu Ehren von Herbert Hunger* (Vienna: Verlag der Österreichischen Akademie der Wissenschaften, 1996), 205–20.
Schreiner, Peter, 'Ein volkssprachlicher Text zur byzantinischen Kaiserkrönung aus der Zeit der Turkokratia', BYZANTIAKA 1 (1981), 51–8.
Seibt, Werner (ed.), *Geschichte und Kultur der Palaiologenzeit: Referate des Internationalen Symposions zu Ehren von Herbert Hunger* (Vienna: Verlag der Österreichischen Akademie der Wissenschaften, 1996).
Setton, Kenneth, *The Papacy and the Levant, 1204–1571* (Philadelphia, PA: American Philosophical Society, 1976).

Ševčenko, Ihor, 'Agapetos East and West: The fate of a Byzantine "Mirror of Princes"', *RESEE* 16 (1978), 3–45.

Ševčenko, Ihor, 'The decline of Byzantium seen through the eyes of its intellectuals', *DOP* 15 (1961), 169–86.

Ševčenko, Ihor, 'A neglected Byzantine source of Muscovite political ideology', *Harvard Slavic Studies* 2 (1954), 141–79.

Ševčenko, Ihor, *Society and Intellectual Life in Late Byzantium* (London: Variorum, 1981).

Shawcross, Teresa, 'A new Lycourgos for a new Sparta', in S. E. J. Gerstel (ed.),*Viewing the Morea* (Washington, DC: Dumbarton Oaks, 2013), 419–54.

Simon, Dieter, 'Balsamon zum Gewohnheitsrecht', in W. Aerts (ed.), *Scholia: Studia ad Criticam Interpretationemque Textuum Graecorum et ad Historiam Iuris Graeco-Romani Pertinentia Viro Doctissimo D. Holwerda* (Groningen: Forsten, 1985), 119–33.

Siniossoglou, Niketas, *Radical Platonism in Byzantium: Illumination and Utopia in Gemistos Plethon* (Cambridge: Cambridge University Press, 2011).

Siniossoglou, Niketas, 'Sect and utopia in shifting empires: Plethon, Elissaios, Beddredin', *BMGS* 36 (2012), 38–55.

Smyrlis, Kostis, 'The state, the land, and private property: Confiscating monastic and church properties in the Palaiologan period', in D. Angelov (ed.), *Church and Society in Late Byzantium* (Kalamazoo, MI: Medieval Institute, 2009), 59–79.

Stephenson, Paul, *The Byzantine World* (London: Routledge, 2010).

Stinger, Charles, *Humanism and the Church Fathers: Ambrogio Traversari [1386–1439] and the Italian Renaissance* (Albany, NY: State University of New York Press, 1977).

Stouraitis, Ioannis, 'Reinventing Roman ethnicity in high and late medieval Byzantium', *Medieval Worlds* 5 (2017), 70–94.

Stouraitis, Ioannis, 'Roman identity in Byzantium: A critical approach', *BZ* 107 (2014), 175–220.

Svoronos, Nikolaos, 'Societé et organisation interieure dans l'Empire byzantin au XIe siècle: Les principaux problèmes', in *Proceedings of the XIIIth International Congress of Byzantine Studies* (London: Oxford University Press, 1967), 1–17.

Tartaglia, L., 'L'opuscolo *De subiectorum in principem officiis* di Teodoro II Lascaris', *Δίπτυχα* 2 (1980), 187–90.

Temporini, Hildegard (ed.), *Aufstieg und Niedergang der römischen Welt: Geschichte und Kultur Roms im Spiegel der neueren Forschung. II, Sechster Band, Principat* (Berlin: De Gruyter, 1977).

Thomson, Ian, 'Manuel Chrysoloras and the early Italian Renaissance', *GRBS* 7 (1966), 63–82.

Thorn-Wickert, Lydia, *Manuel Chrysoloras (ca. 1350–1415): Eine Biographie des byzantinischen Intellektuellen vor dem Hintergrund der hellenistischen Studien in der italienischen Renaissance* (Frankfurt: Lang, 2006).

Tinnefeld, Franz, *Die Briefe des Demetrios Kydones: Themen und literarische Form* (Wiesbaden: Harrassowitz, 2010).

Tinnefeld, Franz, 'Intellectuals in late Byzantine Thessalonike', *DOP* 57 (2006), 153–72.

Tinnefeld, Franz, 'Vier Prooimien zu Kaiserurkunden, verfaßt von Demetrios Kydones', *Byzantinoslavica* 44 (1983), 13–30.

Thomadakes, N., "Ἐκ τῆς βυζαντινῆς ἐπιστολογραφίας: Ἰωσὴφ μοναχοῦ τοῦ Βρυεννίου Ἐπιστολαὶ Λ΄ καὶ πρὸς αὐτὸν Γ''", *ΕΕΒΣ* 46 (1983–6), 279–360.

Thomadakes, N., *Σύλλαβος Βυζαντινῶν μελετῶν* (Athens: Mina Myrtidi Press, 1972).

Toth, Ida, *Imperial Orations in Late Byzantium (1261–1453)* (PhD dissertation, University of Oxford, 2003).

Toth, Ida, 'Rhetorical *theatron* in late Byzantium: The example of Palaiologan imperial orations', in Michael Grünbart (ed.), *Theatron* (Berlin: De Gruyter, 2006), 429–48.

Toth, Ida, and Radić, Radivoj, 'Res gestae Theodori Ioanni filii Palaeologi en tant que source historique', *ZRVI* 34 (1995), 185–201.

Trapp, Erich (ed.), *Prosopographisches Lexikon der Palaiologenzeit*, 12 vols (Vienna: Verlag der Österreichischen Akademie der Wissenschaften, 1976–96)

Trapp, Erich, 'Quelques textes peu connus illustrant les relations entre le Christianisme et l'Islam', *BF* 29 (2007), 437–50.

Trapp, Erich, 'Der Sprachgebrauch Manuels II in den Dialogen mit einem Perser', *JÖBG* 16 (1967), 189–97.

Trapp, Erich, 'Τὰ τελευταία χρόνια του Θεοδώρου Β' Παλαιολόγου', *Βυζαντινά* 13 (1985), 959–64.

Trapp, Erich, 'Zur Identifizierung der Personen in der Hadesfahrt des Mazaris', *JÖB* 18 (1969), 95–9.

Treu, M., 'Demetrius Chrysoloras und seine hundert Briefe', *BZ* 20 (1911), 106–28.

Trojanos, Stephanos, 'Einige Bemerkungen über die finanziellen Grundlagen des Festungsbaues im byzantinischen Reich', *Byzantina* 1 (1969), 39–57.

Turner, C., 'Pages from late Byzantine philosophy of history', *BZ* 57 (2009), 346–73.

Ueding, Gert (ed.), *Historisches Wörterbuch der Rhetorik* (Tübingen: Niemeyer, 1994).

Vassis, Ioannis and Reinsch, Diether R. (eds), *Lesarten: Festschrift für Athanasios Kambylis zum 70. Geburtstag* (Berlin: De Gruyter, 1998).

Violante, T. M., *La Provincia Domenicana di Grecia* (Rome: Angelicum University Press, 1999).

Voordeckers, E., 'Les "Entretiens avec un Perse" de l'empereur Manuel II Paléologue', *Byzantion* 36 (1966), 311–17.

Vranoussi, Era, 'Deux documents byzantins inédits sur la présence des Albanais dans le Péloponnèse', in Ch. Gasparis (ed.), *The Medieval Albanians* (Athens: Centre for Byzantine Research, 1998), 293–305.

Vranoussi, Era, 'Notes sur quelques institutions du Péloponnèse', *Études Balkaniques* 6 (1978), 82–8.

Vryonis, Speros, 'Byzantine attitudes toward Islam during the late Middle Ages', *GRBS* 12 (1971), 263–86.

Vryonis, Speros, *The Decline of Medieval Hellenism in Asia Minor and the Process of Islamization from the Eleventh through the Fifteenth Century* (Berkeley, CA: University of California Press, 1971).

Vryonis, Spyros, 'Isidore Glabas and the Turkish *devshirme*', *Speculum* 3 (1956), 433–43.

Webb, Ruth, *Ekphrasis: Imagination and Persuasion in Ancient Rhetorical Theory and Practice* (Farnham: Ashgate, 2009).

Weiss, G., *Johannes Kantakuzenos – Aristokrat, Staatsmann, Kaiser und Mönch – in der Gesellschaftsentwicklung von Byzanz in 14. Jahrhundert* (Wiesbaden: Harrasowitz, 1969).

Wickham, Chris, *The Inheritance of Rome: A History of Europe from 400 to 1000* (New York: Viking, 2009).

Wilson, Nigel, *From Byzantium to Italy: Greek Studies in the Italian Renaissance* (Baltimore, MD: Johns Hopkins University Press, 1992).

Wirth, Paul, 'Die Haltung Kaiser Johannes' V. bei den Verhandlugen mit König Ludwig I. von Ungarn zu Buda im Jahre 1366', *BZ* 56 (1963), 271–2.

Wirth, Paul, 'Zum Geschichtsbild Kaiser Johannes' VII. Palaiologos', *Byzantion* 35 (1965), 592– 600.

Wodak, Ruth, and Meyer, Mark, *Methods of Critical Discourse Analysis* (London: Sage, 2001).

Woodhouse, C. M., *George Gemistos Plethon: The Last of the Hellenes* (Oxford: Clarendon Press, 1986).

Zachariadou, Elizabeth, 'Εφήμερες αποπειρές για αυτοδιοίκηση στις Ελληνικές πόλεις κατά τον 14ο και τον 15ο αιώνες', *Ariadne* 5 (1989), 345–51.

Zachariadou, Elizabeth, 'Süleyman Celebi in Rumili and the Ottoman chronicles', *Der Islam* 60 (1983), 268–96.

Zakythenos, Dionysios, and Maltezou, Chrysa, *Le despotat grec de Morée* (London: Variorum, 1975).

Zgoll, Christian, *Heiligkeit – Ehre – Macht: Ein Modell für den Wandel der Herrschaftskonzeption im Spätmittelalter am Beispiel der byzantinischen Kydonesbriefe* (Cologne: Böhlau, 2007).

Index

Acciaiuoli, Nerio, 3n
admonition, 76, 96, 112, 115, 121, 137–9, 146, 159–60, 173n, 178, 186, 189–94, 250, 274
advice
　literature, 137–40, 197
　moral and spiritual, 120, 121, 125, 128, 130n, 134, 192–6, 214, 248
　political, 33, 47, 90, 117, 129, 131–3, 135, 145, 150–9, 172–3, 260
　rhetorical strategies, 75
Aegean islands, 45
aesthetics, 107n, 276
Agallianos, Theodore, 50
Agapetos, 126n, 129–30, 135, 143–8, 158–60, 240, 266
Albanians, 207, 222n, 231, 235n, 242, 245, 268
Alexander the Great, 88, 121, 147n, 170, 226
Alexios I Komnenos, 148
Allatius, Leo, 14
alliances of the Byzantines
　with the Latins, 42, 84, 101, 216, 221, 242, 262, 270
　with the Ottomans, 19, 41, 57, 119, 208, 244
allusion, literary, 41n, 110n, 114, 118n, 123–4, 126, 136, 140, 170, 196, 212, 238, 253, 266
Ambrogio Traversari, 66, 157, 199
amplification, rhetorical, 149, 155–6
analogy, rhetorical, 125, 141n

Anagnostes, John, 81
Andronikos II Palaiologos, 47, 95, 163
Andronikos III Palaiologos, 51–3
Andronikos IV Palaiologos, 2, 5, 24, 47, 119, 210, 217, 226, 229, 272
Andronikos V Palaiologos, despot of Thessalonike, 127
Angelou, Athanasios, 113, 115n, 126
Angelov, Dimiter, 12, 22n, 50n, 263
Anna Komnene, 166n
Anna of Savoy, grandmother of Emperor Manuel Palaiologos, 119n
Anthony IV, patriarch, 20, 48, 57
antithesis, 141, 184, 154, 193, 232
apologetic literature, 23, 33, 109, 197
apophthegmata, 138, 145
Aquinas, Thomas, 78
archontes
　Constantinopolitan, 12, 31, 35, 37–8, 47, 52, 56, 109n
　Morean, 201, 207, 219, 221, 227, 243–50
Argos, 219–21
argumentation, rhetorical, 122, 130, 141, 147, 176, 180, 185, 187, 189, 195, 197, 210, 231
Argyropoulos, John, 157
aristocracy, 4, 7, 60, 65, 85, 269, 272
Aristotle
　general philosophy, 134, 166, 175n, 176
　Nicomachean Ethics, 166, 169, 170, 175, 177
army, 4, 128–9, 171, 222

Arsenios, patriarch, 49–50, 52, 56
Arsenite schism, 22, 24, 49, 55
Asanes, Constantine, 61, 66, 74, 242n, 256n
Asanes family, 58, 67, 77
Asanopoulos, Manuel, 63
Asia, 3, 39, 88, 227, 228
assonance, rhetorical, 154
Athanasios, Patriarch, 32, 47n, 50, 55
Athens, 171, 194, 203, 252
Athos, Mount, 19, 21–4, 49n, 55
Attica, 222
Aurispa, Giovanni, 67
audience
  general, 21, 38, 58, 60, 61, 64, 73, 114, 164, 171, 192, 208, 221, 227, 254, 269
  listeners, 61, 96, 153, 164, 184–5, 190, 209, 211, 223, 224, 268
  readers, 10, 107, 137, 153, 168, 195, 197, 223, 236, 268
  readership, 49, 190
autobiography, 95
autokrator, 265, 267
autonomy, 4, 57

Balsamon, Theodore, 75n, 248n, 254, 264
baptism, 156, 227
barbarians, 80, 110, 129, 171, 208–9, 222, 228, 258, 268, 289
battle
  of Ankara, 4, 13n, 78, 127, 162, 267n, 273
  of Maritsa river, 4
Barker, John, 13, 108, 126, 267
Barlaam of Calabria, 34n
basilisk, 39
Bayezid I, sultan, 3, 20, 112, 119, 214, 220–2, 227–30, 253
benevolence, imperial, 65, 179, 194, 243
Bessarion, cardinal, 67, 79, 80, 110n, 157, 176
Bible, 40, 148n, 166, 179
Bion of Borysthenes, 184
blame, public, 34, 81, 120, 197
blasphemy, 36
Blastares, Matthew, 50–3

Blemmydes, Nikephoros, 129, 135, 139n, 148, 159
Boucicaut Marshal, 3, 272
brevity, rhetorical, 32, 64, 139, 141, 156, 187, 189, 209, 261
Bruni, Leonardo, 65n, 66
Bryennios, Joseph, 20n, 21–2, 32, 35, 36, 42, 44, 101, 125, 142, 246, 271
  Forty-Nine Chapters, 35–6, 47, 142
  Garden, 54, 125, 142
  Letters, 23, 46
  Oration on the Reconstruction of the Walls of Constantinople, 32, 38
Buda, 2
Bulgarians, 84, 242, 268

canonists, 21, 29, 31, 46n, 53n
canons of the church, 27–30, 48, 53, 235, 254n
captivity, 37n, 213, 218
castigations, moral, 189–90, 192, 195
Catholic Church, 2, 33, 65, 68, 78, 114, 276
Çelik, Siren, 13, 110n, 128, 165n
centuria, 125, 130, 135–6, 141–9, 274
Chalkokondyles, Laonikos, 9, 94
chancellery, imperial, 9, 111
Charles VI, 3
Charsianites Monastery, 26n, 37n, 45
cheirotonia, 29
children, 41, 61, 98, 115, 118, 153, 205, 288
Chortasmenos, John
  Letters, 61, 67–8, 157
  Monody on Theodore Antiochites, 70n
  Moral Counsels, 89, 96, 98, 138, 152, 154
  Oration on the Miracles of the Theotokos, 78
  Panegyric Delivered upon the Return of the Emperor, 60, 76, 87, 92–3, 98
Christians, 35–6, 53, 129, 227, 228n, 230, 289
Christological symbolism, 53
chronicle, genre, 106, 234
Chrysoberges, Andreas, 50n
Chrysoberges, Maximos, 66, 69, 271
Chrysokephalos, Manuel, 72n, 136

INDEX

Chrysokephalos, Matthew, 202
Chrysoloras, Demetrios, 61, 67, 68, 75, 82, 85, 254
  Comparison, 63, 78, 90–1, 97–8, 161, 163
  Dialogue on Demetrios Kydones' Antirrhetic, 78n
  One Hundred Letters, 77, 138, 209n, 138, 251
Chrysoloras, John, 72, 126
Chrysoloras, Manuel, 65, 66, 68–70, 72–3, 76, 79, 80, 109, 111, 140, 199
  Epistolary Oration, 84, 87–9, 206, 210–12, 233
Chrysostomides, Julian, 14, 200, 236
civil wars, 4, 29, 253n
clarity (σαφήνεια), 32, 76, 188
classes, social, 4, 82, 240, 275
classical models, 32, 130, 170–2, 184–5, 187, 195, 203, 260
clergy, 25–9, 31, 36, 47, 53, 74, 93
Colchidians, 44
commemoration, 25, 200, 203, 223, 253
comparison, literary form, 63, 260; *see also synkrisis*
compilation, 162–3
conciseness, rhetorical, 77, 139, 141, 156, 181
confession, of faith, 22n, 51, 53, 109, 227n
conquest, 41, 146n, 222
consecration, 53–5
consensus, 132, 223
consolation, rhetorical genre, 205, 290
Constantine VII Porphyrogennetos, 109n, 254, 264
Constantine XI Palaiologos, 43, 47, 51n, 52, 64n, 80, 95
Constantine the Great, 50–1, 206, 254
Constantinople
  fall of, 9, 37, 45, 56
  fortifications, 3, 38, 41
  population, 83, 268, 272
  rhetorical representations, 85–8, 206
  sieges and blockades, 3, 39, 63, 79, 112, 113, 217, 228, 237, 243
consumerism, 38, 83
contemplation, of God, 20, 143

conversion
  to Catholicism, 2, 65, 109, 157n, 276
  to Islam, 40
copyist, 70, 74
Corinth, 220, 222, 225, 229, 289
coronation, 47, 49, 50–3, 94, 246
corrections, textual, 10, 72, 212, 161n
correspondence, epistolary, 60, 66, 69n, 70, 73n, 190
corruption, 35–6
Council of Basel, 25n
Council of Ferrara-Florence, 31, 42, 157
counsel *see* advice
court
  ceremonies, 3, 50–1, 53, 60, 62, 94, 122, 209, 246–7
  officials, 26, 50, 52, 58, 64, 89, 111, 221, 252, 273, 275
  titles, 2, 46, 265
courtiers, 6, 9, 66, 90, 100, 120, 127, 132, 181, 243
Crete, 33–5, 46, 142
crisis, political, 55, 266
criticism, 36, 42, 57, 61, 79, 119, 123, 161, 181, 189, 193, 235, 243, 260
Croesus, 171, 174, 185
Culler, Jonathan, 106
Cyclop, 118, 228
Cyprus, 45
Cyrus, 121, 170

da Monte Croce, Ricaldo, 40
Dagron, Gilbert, 46, 94n, 254n, 263
Damian, hieromonk, 21, 23n
David, hieromonk, 21, 23, 55, 74
David, king, 171, 226, 255
Decembrio, Uberto, 66
decline, political-economic, 34–5, 41, 43, 54, 57, 80, 83, 238
deliberative rhetoric, 8, 58, 80, 109–10, 113, 117, 120, 122, 129, 184–5, 249, 267, 274
Democritus, 100
demonstrative rhetoric, 113, 117, 119, 122, 140, 204
dēmos, 202, 264

Demosthenes, 108, 110, 188n, 191, 195, 211n, 264
Dendrinos, Charalambos, 14, 108n
Dennis, George, 71, 108n
dephensor of the church, 22n, 51
deposition of patriarch, 25, 26n, 27–8, 48
depoutatos, 51, 53
Despotate of Morea, 210, 217–21, 226, 229
diatribe, 183–5, 190, 249, 266, 273–4
didacticism, 124, 149–51, 154, 156, 159, 187, 191
didaskalos see teacher
Dionysius the Areopagite, 3
diplomacy, 13, 65, 219, 267
disciple, 21, 65–6, 69, 70, 79, 127, 173, 181, 184, 190, 193
discourse analysis, 7–10
disobedience, 36, 85, 110
dispositio, rhetorical, 107, 116, 167, 188, 196, 208, 209
Dokeianos, John, 93
Dominican, 40, 66, 271
Donation of Constantine, 50
Doukas, Constantine, historian, 9, 157
Dragaš, Helena, 3
dramatisation, literary technique, 116, 156
drunkenness, 34, 36, 81, 119n, 137, 170

ecclesiology, 34
economy of Byzantium, 22n, 25, 34, 39, 65, 79, 122, 238, 266
ekphrasis, 23, 85
election, of patriarch, 26, 29, 30n, 49, 50
emotion, 117, 118, 166, 177–80, 184–5, 206, 208, 224, 234, 289
encomium, 50, 71, 87, 92, 144, 157, 200, 202, 204, 206, 209, 227, 232, 234
England, 3, 144n
enslavement, 82
epic poetry, 136
Epictetus, 184
Epicurus, 34n, 173n
epideictic rhetoric, 58, 77, 209, 211, 213
epigram, 85
Epiphany, 64–5
epistemonarches, 46–7
epistolography, 10, 23, 47, 77

epitaphios logos, genre, 75, 76n, 204–5, 210–11, 218, 233
ethics, 33, 35, 80, 118, 142, 159–60, 162, 182, 184, 195, 196, 251, 262, 265
ethos, 176, 185, 193, 234–5, 258, 269, 274, 276
Eugenikos, John, 21, 31n, 42, 47, 51, 52n, 53, 139n
Eugenikos, Mark, 20n, 21, 43, 56, 57, 67, 79, 142, 275
eulogy, 86, 203, 206, 212, 215
Europe, 3, 26–7, 39n, 68, 88, 91, 153, 199
Euthymios II, patriarch, 20–1, 23, 28, 30, 47, 240, 271

factions, 19, 44, 273
families, aristocratic, 37, 58, 64, 65, 75, 273
fatherhood, 89, 93, 157
fatherland, 76n, 86, 92, 112, 205–6, 245–6
feedback, literary, 10, 60, 71n, 72, 212
Ferdinand I of Aragon, 73n
Florence, 79, 85, 273
florilegium, 133, 142–3
fortress, 85, 220
fragmentariness, 77n, 127, 138, 145
friendship, 21, 24, 66n, 68, 109, 151, 153n, 196, 230, 259
France, 3, 144
funeral oration *see epitaphios logos*
funerary texts, 204–5, 209
Fürstenspiegel, 144–5, 148; *see also* mirror of princes

Gabriel, Metropolitan of Thessalonike, 21, 33, 34n, 35, 72, 162, 254
Gallipoli, 84, 99, 109, 245, 268
Garatone, Cristoforo, 273
Gattilusio family, 100, 272
Gazes, Theodore, 202
Gemistos Plethon, 90–101, 175–6, 241, 275
  Address on the Situation in the Peloponnese, 9, 23, 82, 83n, 86
  On virtues, 162–3, 175, 241n
  Preface to the Funeral Oration, 72, 85, 202, 212, 232

generosity, imperial, 65, 111, 139, 190, 194, 218
genos, 88
genre, theoretical aspects, 1, 9, 11, 76, 91, 106–8, 110, 113, 116, 120, 135–8, 172–4, 179, 200, 204, 209, 233, 238, 249, 265, 272
Genoese, 218, 245
gifts, 13, 26, 36, 47, 53, 71, 81, 114, 153, 171
Glabas, Isidore, 21, 33, 34, 36–8, 41, 46, 183, 190
gnomes, 136–8, 140–1, 146, 154, 156, 160, 188
gnomologium, 125, 135, 137, 138, 140, 142, 145, 188
Graeco-Roman culture, 88, 196
Guarino of Verona, 66, 73, 126, 199–200, 202, 236, 273
Gyges, 171, 174

Hades, 228
Hagia Sophia, 50n, 51, 247
hagiography, 32, 211, 267
handbook, rhetorical, 48, 76, 91n, 116, 127, 135, 184, 189, 272
Hellenism, 35, 69, 86, 101, 244, 272
Hellenistic period, 7, 136, 144, 148, 184, 196, 262n
Henry IV, king of England, 3
Heresies, 28, 33, 34n, 48
Hermogenes, 76, 110, 136, 184
Herodotus, 174n, 191, 192n, 195
heroism, rhetorical *topos*, 92, 203, 205, 208, 217, 225, 234, 236, 252–3
Hesiod, 97, 136
hesychasm, 20–2, 24n, 33, 55, 115, 142
Hexamilion wall, 4, 63, 85, 244
hierarchy, court, 132, 168, 194, 206
hierocratic claims, 47, 48–56
highbrow literacy, 6, 20, 32, 111, 122–3
holiness, 46, 53, 175
Holobolos, John, megas chartophylax, 26
Homer, 123n, 135, 157, 208, 245n
homilists, 32, 254

homily, genre, 9, 20–1, 43, 55, 63, 67, 71, 75, 78, 109, 162, 163, 173, 183, 190, 194, 197, 208, 243, 249, 253–5, 261
homodiegetic narrative, 215
hortatory rhetoric *see* deliberative rhetoric
Hospitallers of Rhodes, Knights, 3n, 207, 209–10, 214, 216–17, 219–22, 229–31, 235, 242, 289
humanists, 66–7, 69–70, 73, 85, 88, 116, 126, 199, 231
humility, 181, 194, 196, 251
Hungary, 2
Hunger, Herbert, 126, 129, 134n
hunting, 121, 151, 153n, 162
hymns, 38, 97, 242n
hypopsephios, 26
hypothekai, rhetorical genre, 135–6, 142–3, 147, 153, 274

Iagoup, Alexios, 119, 267
Iamblichos, 183, 306
identity, 7, 53, 55, 65, 67, 78, 88–9, 96, 98, 111, 131, 167, 169, 208, 255, 285
  Hellenic, 10, 43, 79, 86–7, 101
  Roman, 10, 32, 43, 50, 80, 86–8, 147, 243, 245, 249, 254, 262, 272
ideology, imperial, 47–50, 52, 56, 91–3, 100, 130, 225, 246–9, 252, 254–5, 263–4, 270
Ignatios, pilgrim, 257
illness, 14, 19, 120, 188, 218, 239, 265
Illyrians, 167, 231, 252, 255
imagery, literary, 11, 97, 125, 155, 197
inauguration, ceremony, 52–3
innovation
  rhetorical, 277, 77, 149, 238, 160, 211
  theological, 28, 33, 42n
insignia of power, 237
isapostolos, emperor, 29
Isidore, cardinal of Kiev, 3n, 23, 70, 110, 138
  Letters, 201–2, 212
  Panegyric, 76, 78, 83n, 85–9, 91, 92–4, 96, 98, 99, 137, 168, 206, 211
Islam, 33, 40, 41, 55, 57, 243
Isocrates, 135–6, 139, 143, 146, 148, 205, 211, 244–5

Italy, 65–8, 72–4, 79, 80, 85, 100, 153, 157, 199
Italian city-states, 11, 85, 246

Jacopo d' Angeli, 66, 79, 88
Jauss, Robert, 107
John V Palaiologos, 2–5, 65, 70, 73, 75, 90, 92–3, 114, 193, 214, 216, 229, 238, 276
  and the church, 23–4, 30–1
  and the Latins, 29, 65, 90, 101, 119
  and the Ottomans, 3, 110, 119
John VI Kantakouzenos, 3, 22, 40, 63, 65, 70, 93, 95, 114, 119, 169, 261, 264
John VII Palaiologos, 2, 3, 5, 24, 47, 65, 67, 70, 85, 93, 109, 118, 166, 219, 251, 254, 255, 262, 265, 270, 272
  and the dynastic succession, 20, 27, 118, 119, 127, 249, 261, 267
  and the Ottomans, 119–20, 220, 237–8, 244
John VIII Palaiologos, 8, 71, 78, 86, 93, 94–5, 111, 113, 126, 146–9, 154, 157, 159, 161, 164, 197, 211, 244, 250, 252, 256, 266–9, 274
John of Salisbury, 144
Joseph II, patriarch, 41, 56
journey, 3, 26, 64, 66, 91, 96, 112, 116, 126
judges, 30, 36, 37, 47, 56, 94, 99, 121, 165–6, 178, 234, 256, 260
judicial activity, 37, 99, 231, 234
jurisdiction, 4, 45, 56
Justinian, 145–6, 148

Kabasilas, Nicholas, 21, 45, 68, 71, 74, 133
kairos, rhetorical, 218
Kalekas, Manuel, 22, 25, 65, 66, 68–71, 76, 78, 79, 83, 88, 163, 201, 207, 271
Kalopheros, John Laskaris, 65, 66, 271
kalyptra, 39
Kananos, John, 219
Kantakouzenos, Matthew, 5
Kantakouzenos, Theodore, 85
Kantakouzenos family, 5, 58, 64–5
Kekaumenos, 129, 145
kephalaia, literary genre, 124–5, 128, 135, 136, 138, 141–4, 154, 160, 249, 250
Kerameus, Neilos, 20, 29

kidnapping, of children by Ottomans, 41
kingship, 7, 58, 99, 126, 145, 147, 166, 170, 171, 185, 196, 197
kinship, 58, 153, 154, 180, 182, 190
knights, 207, 209, 235, 242
knowledge, scientific and practical, 46, 59, 67, 80, 89, 100, 131, 140
Kokkinos, Philotheos, 20, 29, 114, 142, 183
kommerkion, 111
Komnenos dynasty, 46, 60, 64, 77, 95, 148, 166, 254, 264
Kydones, Demetrios, 23, 24n, 50, 60, 74, 190, 238, 246
  Apologiae, 84, 173
  Letters, 62, 80–1, 175n, 90, 98, 99, 108, 110, 114, 119, 144, 169, 193, 207
  mentorship, 65–9, 71
  Orations, 62, 93, 210

lamentation, speech, 77, 97, 205, 208, 210, 223
landowners, 4, 85, 92, 230, 234, 244
language differences, 11, 44, 80, 107, 141, 183, 195, 247
Laonikos Chalkokondyles, 9, 94
Laskarids, 22
Laskaris, Theodore II, 49, 95, 147n, 261, 264
Latin
  language and translations, 40, 199
  spirituality, 2, 7, 20, 33, 50, 65, 242
  West, 4, 22, 39, 45, 72, 73n, 80, 84–5, 271
Latinophiles, Byzantine, 66–7, 238, 268
Latins, 4, 13, 19, 20, 22, 38, 39, 41–6, 57, 80, 84, 86–8, 101, 201, 208, 213, 217, 225, 228, 230, 234, 235, 242, 268, 270, 272
law, 21, 29, 40, 57, 89, 111, 129, 137, 144, 145, 147, 182, 247, 254
learning, 81, 89, 106, 150, 157–8, 169, 170, 257–8, 262
leavened bread, 42, 44
lectures, 33, 125, 164, 174, 183–4, 186, 192, 274
legend, 86, 170, 239, 244, 260

legislators, 40, 86, 91, 132, 163, 174, 239, 244, 247
legitimacy, political, 22, 53, 111, 116–17, 122, 244
Leo V, 254
Leo VI, emperor, 254, 261, 264
Lesbos, 90, 97, 100, 247
letter, literary form, 61, 77, 86, 106, 119, 124, 182
letter collection, 9, 59, 69, 75, 240
Leunclavius, Johannes, 161
Libanius, 60, 97
liberator, 84, 91, 267
liberty, political, 4, 47, 57, 109, 241, 249
Libya, 81
lineage, dynastic, 272, 275
literacy, 6–7, 122, 123, 196, 262
literary court, 1, 10, 68–70, 202
literary theory, 11, 271, 105–8
literature, late Byzantine, 108–10, 138
liturgy, 9, 25, 37, 42, 66, 242, 271
lobby, 85
Loenertz, R.-J., 62n, 65n, 66, 69
Louis I, king of Hungary, 2
loyalty, political, 2, 216, 225, 227, 245
Lucian, 116, 209
Lycourgos, 86, 101
Lydian, 174, 239
Lysias, 211

Macedonia, 2, 3, 30, 221
Macrides, Ruth, 49, 50
Magistros, Demetrios, 202
Magistros, Thomas, 60n, 73, 81, 83, 99n, 100, 129, 135, 145n, 263n
Makarios of Ankara, 21, 28, 30, 33, 46, 52–3, 275, 48
makarismos, 205
Makrembolites, Alexios, 81, 116
Makres, Makarios, 9, 21–4, 33, 40, 41, 43, 45–6, 55, 63, 72, 74, 91, 110, 183, 200, 204, 209, 243, 254, 271, 273
Manuel I Komnenos, 64n, 95n, 254
Manuel II Palaiologos
 and the Church, 22–31
 and the scholars, 59–60, 71–5
 self-image, 218
 self-promotion, 191, 267

self-representation, 9, 246, 233, 267
Admonitory Oration to the Thessalonians, 9, 109, 241, 249
Anacreontic verses, 261
Confession Addressed to His Spiritual Fathers, 109
Dialogue with the Empress-Mother on Marriage, 8, 113–23, 238, 246, 265, 271
Dialogues with a Muslim, 9, 14, 108n, 109, 244, 255
Epistolary epilogue, 123–5, 161, 171, 182, 185, 188, 190, 194–6, 204, 208, 224, 240, 247, 253, 261
Foundations of Imperial Education, 8, 39, 77, 105, 113, 124–62, 166, 169, 170, 176, 180, 187–8, 191–2, 195–7, 237, 239, 240–1, 247–67, 271, 273–4
Funeral Oration, 6, 8, 14, 70, 71n, 72, 85, 140–1, 199–236, 242–50, 252–3, 256–7, 260, 262, 264–7, 269–71, 273–4
Homilies, 71–2, 109, 178, 254–5
Letters, 59–61, 64–5, 69–77, 114, 133, 162, 199, 219, 238, 240–3, 246, 256
Panegyric on the Recovery of His Father from an Illness, 9, 110, 178, 255
Prefatory letter, 124, 126, 127, 147, 149–53, 158–9, 182, 232, 241, 258, 259
Psalm on Bayezid, 112, 243
Seven Ethico-Political Oration, 8, 11n, 14, 124–5, 161–98, 244, 252, 255, 271, 274
Words on Brevity and Peace, 139, 261
manuscript evidence and transmission, 67, 70, 72, 74, 146, 271
manuscripts
 Crypten, Z δ 1, 71
 Vat. gr. 1619, 72
 Vat. gr. 1107, 23
 Vat. gr. 632, 212
 Vat. gr. 914, 96
 Vat. Barb. gr. 219, 139
 Vindob. phil. gr. 98, 2, 111–13, 201
 Vindob. phil. gr. 42, 111
 Vindob. gr. 235, 54, 125

Maritsa, battle of, 4
Martin V, Pope, 20, 41
martyrs, 33, 226
Matthew, metropolitan of Ephesus, 40
Matthew I, patriarch, 20, 23n, 25–6, 27n, 28–9, 30n, 45, 48, 54, 65, 79
Maximos the Confessor, 142n, 143
Maximos Planoudes, 263n
maxims, 136–8, 142, 148n, 154, 188n
Mazaris' Journey to Hades, 64, 66, 96, 116
Mediterranean, 4, 13, 67, 230, 270
Mehmed I, sultan, 63
Menander Rhetor, 77, 91, 204, 206–8
mentorship, 23, 61, 64–6, 69, 72–4, 79, 108, 114, 149, 190, 238, 258
merchants, 111, 239, 276
Mesarites, Nicholas, 78
mesazōn, 65, 70, 71, 193
metanarrative comments, 215, 234
metaphor, 11, 118, 134, 141, 155
Metochites, Theodore, 99–101, 126, 163, 173
Michael VIII Palaiologos, 24, 31, 46, 50
Michael Apostolios, 64, 74n, 136, 163, 172
Michael of Ephesus, 166
miracles, 78, 92, 110
mirror of princes, 118, 125, 128, 134n, 135, 143–6, 148, 160, 169, 267
mixed voluntary actions, 170, 251
moderation, 130, 137, 167, 168, 171, 175, 180, 207, 251, 252, 270
Moldavia, 30, 47
monasteries, 4, 22, 24, 26–8, 37, 45, 247
monasticism, 19, 22–4, 37, 45, 49, 56
Monemvasia, 219, 221
monody, literary genre, 76n, 77, 97, 204, 208–10, 233
monologue, 174
moralisation, 32–5, 37, 126, 142, 174, 191–3
morality, 36, 115
Morea, 4, 5, 8, 63, 67, 70, 85, 92, 199–201, 203–5, 210–12, 217–21, 224–5, 227, 229, 230, 231, 233–6, 243, 249, 253, 257, 265, 271, 274
Moreotes, 85, 92, 219–22, 235–6, 240

Moses, 182, 248, 261
müderris, 243
Mullett, Margaret, 106, 148
Muslims, 9, 14, 39–41, 82, 108, 109, 228, 243, 244, 255
Mustafa, 266
myrrh, 52n, 53
mysteries, 98, 254
Mystras, 5, 71, 74, 76, 79, 100, 201, 236, 265
myths, 11, 86, 118, 194, 170, 174, 195, 228, 260

narratees, 211, 223, 224, 234
narrative, 78, 197, 199, 200, 203, 205, 209–21, 223, 225–7, 229, 231–6, 253, 257, 262, 264–5, 267
narrativisation, 78, 234
narratology, 216
narrator, 209–11, 213, 215–20, 223, 227, 231, 233–6
narratorial voice, 214, 215, 221
nation, ideas of, 43, 86, 88, 112, 129, 233, 238, 246, 254, 269
nature, concept of, 124, 129–31, 134, 156, 166, 169, 175, 180
Necipoğlu, Nevra, 12, 26n, 37n, 39, 201
negotiations, 13, 20, 25, 41, 42, 44, 57, 72, 74, 116, 208, 219, 222, 226, 243
neo-Pythagorean, 147
Nestor, 170, 239
network, social, 10, 60, 65, 68, 69, 71, 75, 105, 273
New Testament, 188, 248
Nicol, Donald, 3, 4, 13, 20, 144, 147
noblemen, 227, 267
non-voluntary actions, 176, 187
Notaras, Lukas, 39
novelty, 205, 207, 232, 251

oath, 51, 53, 231
obedience, 3, 49, 54, 134, 230, 242
obligation, 32, 64, 93, 154, 155, 166
Odysseus, 226, 239
oikeioi, 28–9, 58, 264
oikoumenē, 86–7
Old Testament, 112, 182n, 255

opposition, 57–8, 78, 84, 85, 90, 101, 107, 122, 156, 176, 249, 269
  anti-hesychast, 114
  anti-imperial, 22–4, 31, 41, 43, 266
  anti-Latin, 20, 39
  anti-Ottoman, 39
  anti-unionist, 56, 60
oracle, 171
orality, 10, 105, 116, 122, 123, 249, 273
oratory, 8, 64, 77, 90, 92, 120, 136–7, 210–11, 231, 234, 250, 253, 263–4, 273
ornamentation, 140, 137, 169
ornatus, rhetorical, 140, 199
Orthodoxy, 20, 22, 41, 44, 45, 47, 55, 57, 68, 78, 109
Ottomans
  alliances with Byzantine rulers, 2, 19, 57, 63, 119, 222, 243
  attacks on Byzantium, 4, 20, 21, 38, 40–1, 75, 100, 109–10, 43
  Byzantine representations, 84, 110, 208–9, 227
  conquest of Thessalonike, 33, 41
  customs, 225
  invasion of the Peloponnese, 243
  occupation of Argos, 219
  territorial possessions in Morea, 222

Pachymeres, George, 166
Paeonians, 44
paideia, 80, 172
palace, imperial, 27, 51, 61–3, 74, 98, 255
Palaiologina, Helena, 70, 114
Palaiologos, family, 58, 64, 65, 89, 264
Palamas, Gregory, 37, 114, 142
Palamism, 33
Pammakaristos Monastery, 4
pamphlets, 27, 28, 54
panegyric, rhetorical genre, 6, 63–4, 86, 90–1, 94, 144, 182, 203–5, 214, 275
Pantokrator Monastery, 24
papacy, 119
parainesis, 124, 138, 144, 173, 197
parallelism, rhetorical, 146, 154, 184, 223
parallels, rhetorical, 87, 112, 116, 139, 143, 194, 240, 247

parents, 93, 205, 206, 216, 225, 229
paroemiographic literature, 136, 163
Pasiourtides, Vasos, 68, 78
patristic literature, 135, 179, 192
patronage, literary, 33, 58, 59, 60, 64, 71, 74, 101, 114, 273
peace, 63, 110, 139, 171, 211, 217–19, 220–4, 231, 253, 261, 266
Peleus, 157
Peloponnese, 4, 5, 9, 30, 63, 67–9, 75–6, 82, 83, 86, 90–2, 98, 105, 126, 153, 200, 207, 212–14, 216–17, 219–22, 225, 230–1, 237, 240–5, 267, 274
Pepagomenos, Demetrios, 74–5
performance of texts, 6, 8, 10, 11, 59, 60, 62–4, 73, 90, 114, 164, 201, 204, 211, 255, 271
Pericles, 203
Persian, 97, 228, 243, 244
persuasion, rhetorical, 32, 106, 115, 117, 150, 172, 185, 219, 249, 256, 275
Phalieros, Marinos, 148, 159
Pharisees, 248, 261
philanthropy, 165, 178, 247
Philo, 136, 145
philosophy, 67, 91, 95, 96, 137, 194, 195, 268
  philosopher-king, 95, 96, 101, 147, 261, 262, 264, 268, 275
Photios, 135–7, 144, 148
physicians, 58, 226
Plato, 67, 82, 96, 123, 166, 174, 175, 177, 179, 185, 187, 195, 226
Platonic notions, 34, 67, 96, 116, 145
Platonism, 86, 101
pleasure, 81, 108, 133, 137, 164, 165–9, 174–7, 178, 184–6, 189, 192, 226, 239, 256
plot, narrative, 218, 221, 231, 234
poem-ekphrasis, 85
poetry, 85, 136, 148, 197, 266
polemics, 40, 42, 108, 142, 183, 228
Poliaina, 30
politeia, 55, 100, 246
polyphony, literary, 197
population, 4, 5, 37, 81, 109, 207, 226, 231, 245, 272

Potamios, Theodore, 271
potentates, Byzantine, 31, 52
Poulologos, 116
poverty, 184, 230, 242, 268
praise, 33, 45, 54, 58, 61–3, 75, 87, 91,
    95, 115, 119, 123, 138–40, 167, 190,
    193, 200, 203, 205–8, 212, 232–6,
    250, 263, 273–4, 276
  poetics, of praise, 212, 234
prayers, 32, 37–40, 53, 54, 109, 229, 247,
    253, 254, 266, 272
preaching at court, 19, 22, 83, 183, 275
precepts, moral, 96, 139, 141, 152, 158,
    180, 182, 192, 205
presbyter, 142–3
prestige, 4, 56, 62, 224, 266
priesthood, 46, 52–4
prison, 214, 218, 229
pro-Catholic views, 68–9
progymnasmata, 116, 136, 137
pro-Latin views, 39, 41, 68, 74, 78
prolepses, 215, 231
pronoia, 25
propaganda, 10, 90, 92, 94, 111, 240, 241,
    245–7, 249, 251, 267, 269
prophet, 40–1, 171, 243
prosphonemation, 64, 76, 93, 163
prostagma, 25, 29, 111
prostitution, 26, 36
protreptic speeches, 112, 153, 165, 172–5,
    184, 191, 194, 195, 197
proverbs, 154, 172, 188
psalm, 112, 243
pseudo-Basil, 145, 146
pseudo-Isocrates, 136, 143
pseudo-Kodinos, 22, 50, 51, 56, 247
psogos, rhetorical, 75, 112, 119, 177, 227,
    243, 244
pupils, 67, 127

Quintilian, 262
quotations, 135, 139, 141, 179, 188, 244
Qu'ran, 40

race, 36, 43, 88, 227
radicalism, 79, 82, 86, 101, 260, 269, 275
ranks, 49, 51–3, 181, 227

reader-response theory, 107–8
realism, political, 160, 238, 241, 245
realpolitik, 62
rebellion, 119, 190, 210, 214, 217, 218,
    221, 227, 229
reconciliation, 27, 28, 238, 251
relics, 13, 267
Renaissance, 133
renewal, 169, 246, 249, 253
repentance, 165, 178, 181
repetitions, 134, 148, 154, 197
reputation, political, 21, 61, 138,
    199, 260
revision, textual, 9, 23, 71, 110–11,
    113, 115, 162, 165
revival, 62, 69, 73, 203
revolts, 91
Rhakendytes, Joseph, 137
rhetorician-king, 275
rites, 48, 242
ritual, 36, 40, 48–9, 50, 52, 60, 202
rivalry, 27, 36, 48
Romanness, 43, 86–8, 245, 268, 275
Romans, 43, 44, 80, 87–8, 90, 94–5,
    227, 245
Rome, 20, 24, 29, 42, 50, 70, 84–7,
    101, 144
Romhellenes, 88
rubrics of speeches, 92, 204–9, 223, 247
rulership, 8, 93, 126, 161, 171, 174, 179,
    197, 238, 262, 267
Russia, 57
Russians, 24, 44, 246
Ryder, Judith, 2, 62, 84, 109

sacerdote, 28, 47, 53, 254
sacrality, 93, 101
sacraments, 33
sacrilege, 36, 40
sainthood, 49
saints, 32, 33, 42, 49, 255
Salutati, Coluccio, 65, 66
salvation, 56, 263, 276
satire, 64, 116
schism, 22, 24, 41, 46, 55
Scholarios, George, 20, 21, 56, 63, 72, 267
scholasticism, 78

school, 79, 137, 148, 151, 157, 164, 184, 190
sciences, 89, 142, 168
scribes, 58, 67
Scriptures, 175, 190
Scythians, 243, 249
Secular literature, 28, 48, 51, 52, 159, 249
Selymbria, 5, 50
senate, 109, 111, 202
sentences, 138, 141, 154, 159; *see also* maxims and gnomes
sententiousness, 160
Serbs, 3, 84, 222, 242, 245, 268
sermons *see* homily
Serres, 3, 210, 213, 214, 219–21, 235
Ševčenko, Ihor, 54, 59, 65, 68, 73, 80, 81, 89, 126, 135, 145, 146, 160
shipwrecks, 152, 259
sin, 34, 35, 72, 165, 166, 168, 178
Skaranos, Demetrios, 66, 73, 271
slanders, 41, 224
slavery, 37, 54, 84, 137
Slavs, 144–5
social change and reform, 1, 4, 6, 12, 33, 55
social divide, 34, 37–8, 79, 81, 116
Solomon, 95, 133, 170, 255
Solon, 163, 167, 171, 174, 194, 239, 244, 259
sophists, 136
Spaneas, 148
speculum, 144, 145; *see also* mirror of princes
Sphrantzes, George, 4, 9, 12, 23, 133, 266
Stobaios, 148
stoicism, 35, 163
story, narratological concept, 210, 213–18, 220–1, 225, 227, 234–5, 244
Stoudios Monastery, 27, 28
Strategikon, 129, 145
strongholds, 207, 210, 214, 217, 219, 222, 235, 242
Strozzi, Pala, 66
succession, imperial, 2, 8, 42, 93, 94, 105, 111, 113, 120, 127, 149, 153, 193, 252, 261, 265, 268, 269, 275
syllogisms, 78, 142, 181

Symeon of Thessalonike, 21, 31, 33, 34, 37–40, 42, 46–54, 78, 130, 142–3, 246, 249, 275
synkrisis, rhetorical, 260
synod, 20, 22, 26–30, 48, 50–1, 57, 65
Syropoulos, Sylvester, 20, 30–1, 43, 54, 56, 275

Tafur, Pero, 74
Tamerlane, 4, 112
Tatars, 4, 39
taxes, 45, 82, 83, 267
teacher, 21, 28, 65–9, 79, 85, 95–6, 98, 99, 101, 149, 150–3, 157–9, 172, 190–1, 194, 200, 226, 233, 243, 248, 254, 259, 265, 269, 273–5
teacher–student relation, 21, 68, 69
teachings, 65, 80, 99, 107, 140, 147, 150, 151, 158, 183, 189–92, 194, 260–1, 268
teenage, 146, 149, 150, 154
Teiresias, 171
Terpandros, 97
textbooks, rhetorical, 157
Thassos, 93
theatra, 58–64, 71, 73, 105, 164, 256, 265, 271, 273
theios, title, 66
Themistius, 173
Theoleptos, 47
theology, 23, 24, 33, 48, 56, 77, 78, 89, 98, 142
Theon, 137
Theophylakt of Ochrid, 135, 145, 148, 152, 158
Theotokos, 71, 78, 81, 83, 109, 178, 253–5
Thessalonians, 9, 33n, 38, 46, 57, 81, 109, 245, 249
Thessalonike, 2–5, 9, 21, 23, 31, 33–42, 46, 47, 49–54, 60–1, 63, 67, 69, 72, 74, 76, 109–10, 162, 190, 218, 227–9, 237, 240, 241, 246, 254, 265, 268, 272, 275
Thessaly, 2, 3, 91–2, 221
Thrēnos, 77
Thucydides, 203

Tiberius, 254
topoi, literary, 12, 118, 203–5, 209, 211
Toth, Ida, 12, 58–60, 64, 77, 78, 92, 110
translation, 14, 24, 27, 40, 61, 66, 72, 115, 199, 202, 205, 212, 243, 271
treaty, 110, 129, 219, 222, 245, 268
Triballians, 44
Triboles, 60, 74
trisépiscopat, 25–8, 30, 48
triumphs, 60, 91, 147, 194
Turks, 33, 35, 39, 40, 171, 213, 222, 243
typikon, monastic, 22
tyrannicide, 144–5
tyranny, 85, 145, 239
tyrants, 27, 144, 228, 243, 247

Unction, ceremony, 46, 48, 52, 53
union of churches, 20, 24, 31, 41–4, 57, 60, 67, 76, 94, 114, 227, 263
unionism, 32, 46
universalist claims, 48, 89, 101
unleavened bread, 44
urban, 3, 86
Urban VI, Pope, 3
usurpation, 118, 214
utopia, 82, 86, 101, 241, 275

variatio, rhetorical, 77, 197
vassal, 4, 119, 238
Venetians, 39, 57, 66, 111
Venice, 72, 111, 271

Vergerio, Paolo, 66
vernacular literature, 49, 116
virtues
   cardinal, 91, 131, 145n, 193, 198, 211
   imperial, 91, 99, 101, 121, 165, 167, 168, 172n, 176, 192, 196–7, 247n, 250, 260, 274–5
   intellectual, 45, 90, 195, 212
   moral, 98, 143, 166, 175, 218
   physical, 128, 130, 151, 154, 155, 205, 207, 218, 252, 260
   system of virtues, 91, 98, 166, 168–9, 186, 192, 256
vituperations, 117, 177
voice, literary concept, 8, 105–7, 124, 125, 135, 149–51, 157–9, 161, 188–90, 193, 195, 198–200, 214–16, 233–5, 238, 254
voluntariness, concept, 166, 169, 187, 239, 260

war, 4, 13, 92, 211, 222, 232, 242
warriors, 40, 231
wealth, 37, 38, 81, 82, 101, 150–2, 171, 184, 189, 194, 230, 240, 258, 259, 274

Xanthopoulos, Kallistos, patriarch, 20, 172
Xerxes, 171, 174, 258

EU representative:
Easy Access System Europe
Mustamäe tee 50, 10621 Tallinn, Estonia
Gpsr.requests@easproject.com

www.ingramcontent.com/pod-product-compliance
Lightning Source LLC
Chambersburg PA
CBHW071827230426
43672CB00013B/2778